MANAGEMENT OF SOCIAL AND NATURAL RESOURCE CONFLICT IN NEPAL
Realities and Alternatives

MANAGEMENT OF SOCIAL AND NATURAL RESOURCE CONFLICT IN NEPAL
Realities and Alternatives

BISHNU RAJ UPRETI

(PhD Conflict Management,
MSc Management of Agricultural Knowledge Systems,
MA Sociology, BSc Agricultural Economics)

Reserch Associate
School of Soial Sciences and Public Policy
King's College London, Strand
University of London
United kingdom

ADROIT PUBLISHERS
DELHI-110 053

Published by
ADROIT PUBLISHERS
C-8/2, Yamuna Vihar, Delhi-110 053
Phones : 3266030, 3242552

Branch Office
AKHIL BOOK DISTRIBUTORS
4675/21, Ganpati Bhawan, Ansari Road,
Darya Ganj, New Delhi-110 002
Phones : 3266030, 3242552
e-mail: akhilbooks@yahoo.com

ISBN : 81-87392-32-0

Layout by
Sudhir Kumar Vatsa

Laser Typeset by
Nidhi Laser Point
e-mail: nidhi_vatsa@hotmail.com

Printed in India on behalf of M/s Adroit Publishers by
Arpit Printographer, B-7, Saraswati Complex,
Subhash Chowk, Laxmi Nagar, Delhi-110 092

Dedicated to my father
Late Durga Prasad Upreti
who taught me
the
purpose of life

Foreword

Nepal's social and political processes have been characterised by conflict and disputes that have inflicted social tensions and seriously disturbed social relationships. When such conflict turns into violence it poses a major threat to peace and security, fuels criminality and engenders instability. In the recent decades we are ignoring indigenous methods of conflict resolution taking legal arrangement for granted, instead of integrating formal legal and indigenous conflict management practices to resolve overwhelming social and natural resources related conflicts for the interest of social transformation and agrarian change. Management of conflict does not limit only to top-down policy and legal arrangements. It is a dynamic process of seeking a fair resolution active involvement of conflicting parties in a bottom-up and interactive way. Developing faiths and gaining trusts are important aspects in dealing with social conflict. Desired national objective can only be achieved in an environment of peace, security and stability. Peace, security and stability can be achieved through granting human rights to individual that promotes humanism, a desired 'ism' for peace and prosperity.

To address growing social and natural resource related conflict the fundamental causes have to be identified, right strategies have to be devised and they have to be effectively and sincerely implemented. Mediation is one of such strategies where eroding indigenous conflict management practices need to be reinvented, reinvigorated, rebuild and revised to restore social relationships, to maintain social fabric, to root-out enmity, to achieve win-win outcomes and to establish 'grass-root justice'. The book *Management of social and natural resource conflict in Nepal: realities and alternatives'* written by Dr. Bishnu Raj Upreti examines the imperatives of grass-root justice and gives alternative perspective and pragmatic methodology in conflict management. The author gives voice to the poor and marginalised people to promote grass-root justice. The interactive conflict management methodology proposed in the book integrates legal and indigenous conflict resolution practices to overcome the weaknesses of existing conflict management systems. Conflict management related provisions made in Local Self-Governance Act 1999 gives legal and regulatory framework to the interactive conflict management.

The book suggests to disentangle politicisation of overgrowing social conflicts to maintain fair and speedy resolution. This is a unique move to effectively execute legal administration at all level. The author has given an alternative approach in managing social conflict and contributed to the national debate on the need for peace building. The authors' initiative is not only timely, it also shows the ways for creative actions to resolve social conflict, sensitise and mobilise civil society, political organisations, legal and regulatory institutions, indigenous knowledge and skills to initiate all necessary complementary measures that would enhance grass root justice and positive social change.

I would like to thank Dr Upreti for writing this book in the time of escalation of social conflict. I believe that people engaged in conflict and conflict management will greatly benefit from it.

Thank you

Laxman prasad Aryal

2nd January, 2002

Laxman Prasad Aryal
Hon. Justice, Supreme Court
Kathmandu

Preface

In the 20th century conflict around the world reveals a harsh reality. Failure to properly manage ethnic, political, social, and economic conflict turned into violence and even escalated into bloody war in several parts of the world. Most of these Violence and wars are observed in poor and developing countries. Failure to meet social, political, and economic needs due to scarcity of resources, corruption, bad governance, changing economic conditions, increased religious and ethnic strife and international vested interests have provided fertile ground to escalate conflict into violence and civil war. Arm conflicts are significantly increasing through out the world. For example, in 1999 there were 40 armed conflicts being fought on the territories of 36 countries, up from 36-armed conflicts in 31 countries in 1998, 37 in 32 countries in 1997. Most of these arm conflicts were developed from the social tension, feeling of injustice and discrimination. When conflict escalates into violence and civil wars, pervasive despair of sorrow and grief are the unwanted realities and irrepressible damage to society is unavoidable. Building peace in such a situation become far more costly and difficult than to address root causes of social conflict before it escalates into such violence.

To address root causes of social conflict requires devising appropriate alternatives that prevent escalation of conflict into violence. Proper attention is needed to define requirements to address structural causes of conflict, to refine and reforms the existing conflict resolution mechanisms based on their critical review and promote alternative methodology to empower general public. If we address the fundamental causes of conflict by giving primary attention to the conditions such as unemployment, marginalisation of particular ethnic groups or regions, the failure to establish democratic ideals in governance systems, equitable distribution of resources and so on, conflict can be transform into process of desirable social change.

In the context of Nepal a thorough analysis of fundamental structural causes of conflict, proper assessment of performance of existing conflict resolution apparatus of government and timely corrective measures are desperately essential. This book attempts to analyse these structural causes and performances of state conflict resolution systems. Responding constructively to social and natural resource conflicts requires more ingenuity, creativity, commitment and alternative methodology. This book provides alternative methodology to address over growing social and natural resource conflict in community. Transformation of conflict into positive non-coercive social change needs perspective of promoting social justice, focus on structure, process, and strategies for empowering people and building strong communities and civil society. This book gives some thoughts in this direction.

This book has demonstrated that existing legally engineered conflict resolution systems of government organisations are expensive, pro-elite, and inaccessible to the poor and are heavily influenced by power and position. Therefore, they are not able to properly address social conflict in community. I do not expect all readers to agree with my arguments and no doubt some will vehemently disagree with some of the issues raised in this book. However, I hope it will provoke useful debate and discussion to promote effective management of social conflict for the desirable social change and agrarian reform. This book challenges the dominant thinking and prevalent belief that social conflict is pathological, dysfunctional and should be suppressed through legal engineering to harmonise and homogenise the heterogeneous society. I share the merits of this book with all those who helped me in developing it, but I alone bear any responsibility for its shortcomings.

Bishnu Raj Upreti
Centre for Environmental Strategy
University of Surrey,
Guildford, UK

Acknowledgement

This book is the product of collective efforts of several people in terms of contributions through support, comments, criticisms, collaboration, information and insights. I would like to express my sincere gratitude to all of them. I am indebted to all respondents in the field for their valuable time and information to bring this work to its present state. I am also particularly indebted to key informants for sharing valuable and secret information during the research period.

I am grateful to Laxman Prasad Aryal, Honourable Justice of Supreme Court for his time to read the manuscript and writing the foreword, Adroit Publishers, New Delhi and D. K. Sharma for taking responsibility to publish this book and Bidur Dangol (Mandala Book Point) for his help to make contact with Adroit publishers.

I would like to express my sincere gratitude to Professor Dr Niels G. Röling, Professor Dr. Paul Richards, Professor Dr. A. W. Van den Ban and Dr. Otto Hospes (Wageningen University-the Netherlands), Professor Dr Franz von Benda-Beckmann (Max Plank Institute of Social Anthropology-Germany), Professor Dr. Joanna Pfaff Czarnecka (University of Bielefeld, Germany) and Dr. Stephen Biggs (University of East Anglia) for their valuable comments on the earlier version of the book.

I owe special thanks to Subodh Pyakurel (INSEC), Bishnu Prasad Ghimire (Reading University), Andreas Kläey and Susanne (Wymann Centre for Development and Environment of University of Bern) for their valuable comments on the manuscript for their valuable comments in the manuscript,

Pashupati Chaulagain (Members of Parliaments-Dolakha) for his encouragement, NEPAN and Chet Nath Kandel for organising special session of talk programme to share the contents of the manuscript and Kiran Pokharel (Radio Sagarmatha) and NEPAN for broadcasting the issues raised by this book into public. I thank Dr Philip Scott Jones and Dr. Michael Warner (UK) for sending me reference materials and Günther Baechler (Head of the Conflict Prevention and Transformation Division) of SDC for sharing his experiences on conflict issues. I am highly indebted to Jurg and Susanne von Dach for arranging me to visit Jungfrau Mountain area of the Swiss Apls to study resource conflict. I thank to Dinesh Prasain and Chandra Laksamba (University of Surrey) for their help during writing this book. I would like to thank Binod Timilsena, Ava Subedi and Devendra Shrestha from Action Aid Nepal for their help in editing the book.

I must express my deep sense of gratitude to my father-in-law Kabi Ghale for his enormous continuous support, my brothers Shankar and Saroj Upreti, sister Gauri Upreti-Chudal and Sharmila Shivakoti for their help in various stages of writing this book.

Last but not least, I am grateful to my parents, my wife and our two children. My parents late Durga Prasad and Mrs Shata Kumari Upreti who nurtured in me the spirit of education. My wife Yamuna, my great friend, a wonderful mother to our children and a great woman, who tremendously enriches my life, surrounding me with extraordinary love and affection, support and encouragement and managing all the emotional and practical aspects of our family life, together with her extremely busy professional responsibilities. Her continuous encouragement, constructive comments and inspiration have been invaluable to write this book on time. Our daughter Asmita (9), who had to sacrifice the presence of her father, her share of affection and guidance with her study, especially at the time of her mother's visits abroad for meetings and seminars and our son Ayush (2) for his sacrifice when I was away from home. I would like to express my heartfelt gratitude to all of them.

Few Words

Land, water and forest are the items of natural resources which nature has given to Nepal in abundance. The potential that these resources have, if harnessed in a planned and proper manner, economic prosperity of Nepalese people is guaranteed.

In the exploitation of these natural resources the interests of various user groups and stakeholders have been encountered. These encounters are rightly observed by Bishnu Raj Upreti, the author of this book, in the form of conflict. The various diverse interests which is common phenomenon in Nepalese society, if given a smooth sailing become motive force for development.

The attempt of the author of this book to develop an alternative approach to conflict management in his own words "... on the basis of understanding the existing causes of natural resource related conflicts and their resolution practices" is highly commendable.

6th January, 2002

Sindhu Nath Pyakurel
Senior Advocate

President
Nepal Bar Association
Kathmandu

Abbreviations

AAN	ActionAid Nepal
ADB	Asian Development Bank
ADB-N	Agricultural Development bank-Nepal
ADR	Alternate Dispute Resolution
AFMIS	Andherikhola Farmers Managed Irrigation System
AIT	Asian Institute of Technology
AM	Adaptive Management
APP	Agriculture Perspective Plan
APROSC	Agricultural Project Service Centre
CBD	Convention of Biological Diversity
CBO	Community Based Organisation
CBS	Central Bureau of Statistics
CDO	Chief District Officer
CF	Community Forestry
CFP	Community Forestry Programme
CIAT	International Centre for Tropical Agriculture
CIFOR	Centre for International Forestry Research
CM	Conflict Management
CMNR	Conflict Management in Natural Resources
CPNML	Communist Party Nepal Marxist-Leninist
CPNUML	Communist Party Nepal United Marxist Leninist
CPR	Common Property Resources
CR	Conflict Resolution
DAC	District Appraisal Committee
DADO	District Agricultural Development Office

DAO	District Administration Office
DDC	District Development Committee
DDDC	Dolakha District Development Committee
DFO	District Forest Office
DGIS	The Netherlands Directorate General for International Co-operation
DIO	District Irrigation Office
DLDO	District Livestock Development Office
DLRO	District Land Reform Office
DoF	Department of Forest
DoI	Department of Irrigation
DSCO	District Soil and Water Conservation Office
DWRC	District Water Resources Committee
DWSO	District Water Supply Office
ENAP	Environment and Population Awareness Programme
EPC	Environment Protection Council
FAO	Food and Agricultural Organisation of the United Nations
FECOFUN	Federation of Community Forest Users Nepal
FMIS	Farmers Managed Irrigation Systems
FUG	Forest Users Groups
GDP	Gross Domestic product
GO	Governmental Organisation
Ha	Hectare
HAS	Human Activity Systems
HIMWANTI	Himalayan Grassroots Women's Natural Resource Management Association
HMG/N	His Majesty's Government of Nepal
ICM	Interactive Conflict Management
ICIMOD	International Centre for Integrated Mountain Development
IFAD	International Fund for Agricultural Development
IHDP	Integrated Hill Development Project
IM	Irrigation Management
IMC	Irrigation Management Centre

IMF	International Monitory Fund
IIMI	International Irrigation Management Institute
INGO	International Non Governmental Organisation
IPM	Integrated Pest Management
IRDP	Integrated Rural Development Project
ISSP	Irrigation Sector Support Project
IUCN	International Union of Nature Conservation
JHPIP	Johns Hopkins Population Information Programme
JMA	John Miller Associates
JMIS	Jointly Managed Irrigation System
LDO	Local Development Officer
LPRC	Landless Problem Resolution Committee
LSGA	Local Self Governance Act
MAKS	Management of Agricultural Knowledge Systems
MG	Mediation Group
MoF	Ministry of Finance
MPFS	Master Plan for the Forestry Sector
MOWR	Ministry of Water Resources
MOIC	Ministry of Information and Communication
MRMG	Mountain Resource Management Group
MSc	Master in Science
Mw	Megha-watt
NC	Nepali Congress
NCS	National Conservation Strategy
NFN	NGO Forum Nepal
NFYP	Ninth Five Year Plan
NGO	Non Governmental Organisation
NORAD	Norwegian Agency for Development Co-operation
NPC	National Planning Commission
NR	Natural Resources
NRA	National Research Associates
NRM	Natural Resource Management
NSCFP	Nepal Swiss Community Forestry Project
NTFP	Non-Timber Forest Products
NWO	Netherlands Organisation for Scientific Research

OP	Operational Plan
PACT	Private Agencies Collaborating Together
PF	Panchayat Forest
PPF	Panchayat Protected Forest
PPP	Park and People Project
PR	Property Rights
PWA	Protected Watershed Area
RAAC	Regional Appraisal and Approval Committee
RPP	Rastrya Prajatantra Party
RRN	Rural Reconstruction Nepal
SDC-N	Swiss Development Co-operation/Nepal
SL	Social Learning
SMNR	Sustainable Management of Natural Resources
SNV	Netherlands Development Organisation
Sq km	Square Kilometre
SIAST	Saskatchewan Institute of Applied Science and Technology
TRIPs	Trade Related Aspects of Intellectual Property Rights
UAIS	Upper Andherikhola Irrigation System
UK	United Kingdom
UN	United Nations
UNDP	United Nations Development Programme
UNEP	United Nations Environment Programme
UNIDO	United Nations Industrial Development Organisation
USA	United States of America
VDC	Village Development Committee
WB	World Bank
WC	Ward Chairman
WEP	Women's Empowerment Project
WRA	Water Resources Act
WRM	Water Resource Management
WTO	World Trade Organisation
WUA	Water Users Association
WUC	Water Users Committee

Contents

CHAPTER 1

Understanding Social and Natural Resource Conflict—The context

1.1. Introduction

Conflict is a state of clashing or opposing interests and it occurs with positional differences over values and belief systems, self-determination and access to and distribution of power. In the Webster's Dictionary conflict is described as 'a battle, contest of opposing forces, discord, antagonism existing between primitive desires and instincts and moral, religious, or ethical ideals'. Conflict occurs when two or more people oppose one another because of difference in their needs, wants, goals or, values. Conflict is almost always accompanied by feelings of anger, frustration, hurt, anxiety, or fear. Ability of people to manage conflict can influence the outcome of a conflict. The conflict has to be of some duration and magnitude of at least two parties that are determined to pursue their interests and win their case. Conflict in this book covers observable differences in opinion, misunderstandings, clashes of interest, disagreements, complaints in public, protests by argument and physical assault, antipathy, filing cases with the district administration[1], police and courts. When the latitude of tolerance crosses the bottom line then conflict occurs. Feelings of unfairness, suspicion,

---

1. In Nepal District Administration Office is responsible for the functioning of law and order district in co-ordination with the District Police Office. Generally, most of conflict cases go to the DAO first and if they are not solved there then they go to court.

injustice, mistrust, etc. ultimately lead to conflict.

Conflict management (CM) is a process of making progress. As a part of improving the conflict situation, progress may be develop in mutual gains, learning, achieving agreements, laying foundations for further negotiation or fully resolving conflict. Progress is a way of thinking about a conflict situation that recognises that conflict are inevitable and ongoing part of social process and management of these conflict comes from continual improvement in areas of substance and relationships (Daniels and Walker, 1997: 35). In the context of natural resources the perceived inconsistencies between people about acquired rights, incurred obligations, or contradictions of two or more jurisdictions lead to conflict. In the legal sense CM is the application of the laws and regulations to ensure rights and provide remedies that reconcile the inconsistencies and decide which systems are to govern particular cases (Oli, 1998).

Natural resources (NR) in this book refer especially to land, water and forest/pasture. Similarly natural resource management (NRM) means appropriation, distribution, utilisation and conservation of natural resources and the legitimate way of controlling them. In addition to general conflict the book has analysed five inter-connected social conflicts cases related to natural resources. In these cases, conflict between villagers and local elite erupted due to misuse of externally obtained financial resources, inappropriate decision and priority to alter the existing resources use patterns, about access and control of locally available natural resources, ownership, tenancy rights and property relations.

This book is not in itself about the normal concerns of natural resources such as resource development and maintenance, functioning of user committees, people's participation, resource-use efficiency, use of technology, application of rules, sharing of benefits, etc. Nor is it about the financial analysis of NRM, or about the assessment of co-ordination and administration of the NRM sector. It is about what all these issues create: conflicts. Conflict study involves investigating almost all aspects of human activity and interactivity ranging from the behaviour of individuals to group characteristics. I have shifted the focus away from the dominant pattern of treating 'conflict' as a particular pathological event in a particular point of time that needs to be resolved by using legal and regulatory interventions. Rather, I have focused on conflict as an inevitable process in society that can be used as a constructive and non-coercive means for social transformation and agrarian change. It is important that quality and consequences of resolution - how fair the resolution is and what are the implications of the conflict resolutions society at large - are more important than the actual resolution of the conflict itself. I prefer to use the tern 'conflict management' instead of Conflict Resolution (CR) because it is not always possible to resolve all conflicts but it is possible to manage them. Conflict resolution implies that conflict is totally resolved whereas CM may or may not totally resolve the conflict. Actions may be taken, which although they may not be able to resolve the conflict completely, keep the situation working and minimise tension and antagonism. Nourishing these actions enhances the favourable situation for the total resolution of a conflict. Conflict management is the practice of identifying and handling conflict in a sensible, fair, and efficient manner. Conflict can be managed by developing and using skills such as effectively communicating, problem solving, and negotiating with a focus on interests instead of positions.

In natural resources, resource-use negotiation is a deliberate process of submission and consideration of offers to share resources until the parties involved accept an offer. It can not be assumed that all conflict can instantly be resolved. Conflict management in this book basically focuses on negotiations about the issues in dispute at a community level. I focused on conflict as a source of learning to create opportunities for social change in society. Learning is a complex activity, which manifests itself in a change in people's behaviour. It is rooted in the human capacity to improve their understanding and skills on the basis of day-to-day experiences (Engel and Salomon, 1997), external knowledge and surrounding environment. Therefore, when there is conflict it gives people opportunities to think, understand the causes of the problems and look for solutions. They learn from conflict. Social and natural resource conflict in this book is seen in the wider context of historical, political, cultural, economic, institutional, organisational and technological dimensions that provide the basis for the creation, escalation, stalemate or settlement of conflicts. Therefore, the description and analysis of social conflicts, their interconnections with other socio-political issues and their implications to society are the central concerns of this book. An attempt has been made to look at the inter-linkages of natural resource related conflicts with other broader social conflicts in the process of agrarian change. I have mainly used two analytical perspectives to explain conflict and to design an interactive conflict management (ICM) approach. The first is a legal anthropological perspective, giving special attention to legal pluralism, which focuses on the plurality of state, religious or local customary legal rules that provide substantive criteria for evaluating conflicts, as well as providing procedures to manage/settle them. The second is social learning, a strong perspective to improve the conflict situation through collective learning, concerted action and negotiation.

The importance of CM and its linkages with other social issues are directly connected with the conceptualisation of conflict by communities and their response to it. This in turn shapes the ideological basis for the conduct, practices and behaviour of people in daily life. The fast changing socio-political situation and the pace of modernisation in Nepal have given new direction to the management of social conflict (Adhikari et al., 2000). An alternative approach to CM has been proposed on the basis of understanding the existing causes of social conflicts and their resolution practices. The contribution of the alternative approach will be to promote collaboration, among actors involved in managing conflict in society.

1.2. Social Dimensions of Natural Resource Conflict

In this section I briefly discuss the social dimension of conflicts. Social dimension refers to human related aspects of negotiations, such as knowledge, technology institutions and forums (platforms) (Röling, 2000). In the study of conflict it is important to understand the role of the human dimension (Röling, 1997). Land, forest and water are the most important natural resources for the economic development of Nepal (Pandey, 1999). Conflict is common in the use and management of these natural resources. Therefore, management of conflict is crucial to improve the performance of NRM and to achieve sustainable development. In the contemporary development discourse natural resources are usually perceived as hard objectively fixed bio-physical facts (e.g., soil, crops, livestock, disease and pests, water, yields, erosion, caring capacity, bio-diversity, physical properties, etc.) and such factors as human goals, organisation and technological aspects (Röling and Maarleveld, 1999) are usually ignored. Röling, (1997) illustrates the notion of soft and hard science in NRM in his commonly used term "Soft Side of Land Perspective'. It is important to look beyond the common categorisation of social science as soft science and technical science (biophysical) as hard science. It implies that positivist and consctructivist thinking exists within both sciences. For example, even within social sciences there are both positivist thinking such as the resolution of conflict by enforcing acts and regulations and use of the courts and police and constructivist thinking such as the resolution of conflict through learning, negotiation and collaboration. Basically, conflict over natural resources is the outcome of societal arrangement, human intention and behaviour (Röling, 1997) framed within those biophysical properties. Therefore, both the hard and soft dimensions of natural resources are essential for a better management of conflicts. Resource management decisions and activities of resource users, performance of bureaucracy, functioning of user groups and associations, access to and control over resources, customary practices and state laws/regulations, livelihood requirements and the welfare of people are therefore important issues to be addressed in conflict management.

In Nepal, most national planners, policy makers, bureaucrats and professionals still treat 'technology as a black box' and give little attention to human intentions and behaviour in managing natural resources. Responsive institutions, collective learning, negotiation and concerted action in my opinion are vital components to be considered for sustainable management of natural resources. Several researchers and academicians (for example, Röling, 1997; Benda-Beckmann, 1999; Mollinga, 1998; Vincent, 1996; Uphoff, 1986, Chambers, 1988) have the view that NRM is not only a technical domain, but it is more importantly a social discourse, shaped and influenced by social processes and intentional human activities. A plural legal situation can create several conflicts because of its uncertain and manipulative nature. Most of the legal reforms have yet to be translated into real practices. If and when they are practised they are manipulated by power brokers and the weaker section of society still feels uncertain and insecure. Therefore, these processes and related human activities have to be considered carefully.

During my twenty one years of professional experience in rural development and NRM sectors as a development sociologist and agriculturist, I have increasingly realised that a government's policies and donor's strategies are more focused on management and control of natural resources through prescriptive technical solutions rather than a meaningful participation of people. This leads to conflict and disturbances in self-regulated ecological systems services. We are now entering the twenty-first century, where conflict between economic objectives and sustainable ecological services of natural resources is accelerating. Obviously the increasing problems such as the lack of pure drinking water, loss of bio-diversity, climate change, environment pollution and other ecological-challenges are the combined result of population growth and economic motives. These problems are not only disrupting self-sustaining natural resources systems but also creating severe conflicts in society. Therefore, an economically guided focus for these problems is in itself a source of further conflict.

1.3. Scarcity of Natural Resources as a Sources of Social Conflict

A report of the Johns Hopkins Population Information Programme (JHPIP) states that nearly half a billion people world-wide are currently facing water shortages (JHPIP, 1998). By 2025, one in every three people will live in countries short of water. At present, thirty-one countries are facing water stress or water scarcity and by 2025 the number will explode fivefold. The World Water Forum (2000) also stresses that more than one billion people in the world have no access to water of sufficient quantity and quality to meet even a minimum level of health, income, safety and freedom from drudgery. The World's projected total of 8 billion people in 2025 will enormously increase pressure on natural resources and may cause a catastrophe. The competition between industrial, urban, and agricultural use for natural resources is mounting and the per capita consumption of natural resources is increasing (JHPIP, 1998). Regional conflicts over natural resources are brewing and could turn violent as shortages grow. In all continents and countries, people are already bickering over access to natural resources and competition for their use can be fiercer in the future. For example, serious conflicts are developing concerning large dams such as the Lesotho Highlands Water Project in the Malibamatso and Little Orange Rivers in South Africa and the Arun Hydropower Project in the Arun River in Nepal funded by the World Bank. For such projects the World Bank is not only facing an onslaught of criticism over its support for big dams, but also for creating severe conflict in the host countries. As world water scarcity bites deeper into economies dependent on cheap water supplies, there is conflict over river catchments and lakes. Dams such as the Three Gorges Dam in China have become symbols of official tyranny, with whole cities being flooded and engineers being given free reign to resettle populations who are inconveniently living in river valleys (Ohlsson, 1995). Due to the competition for available natural resources by an over-growing population, the vital ecosystems on which humans and other species depend are severely threatened (JHPIP, 1998; World Water Forum, 2000). The earth has lost 15 percent of its topsoil over the last 20 years due to inappropriate agricultural practices. Water logging, salination and alkalisation affect another 1.5 million hectares of mostly irrigated agricultural land. Desertification and drought are severely limiting the production potential of the global agricultural system and posing several ecological challenges[2] (Jiggins and Röling, 2000). All these processes are creating conflict between different interest groups.

Figure 1.1   Demographic Change, Developmental Pressures and Resource Degradation as Source of Conflict

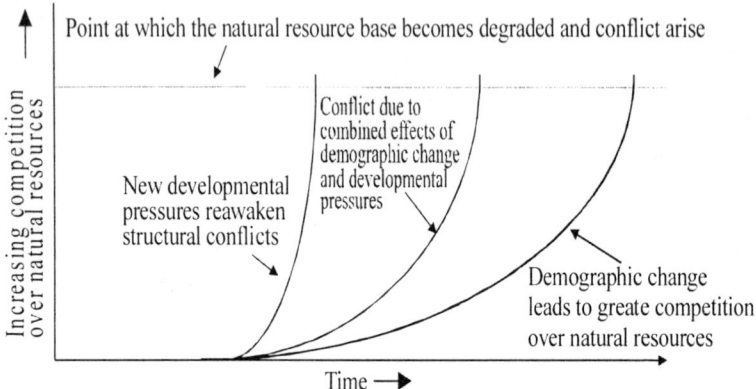

Source: Adapted from Warner, 2001

Political and economic motives drive conflict in natural resources. Either international water conflicts such as the dispute between Egypt, Ethiopia and Sudan about the Nile

---

2 See Beak *et al.*, (1994) for details about future risks, problems and challenges to modern societies. Also see Lubchenco (1998) for challenges to science to achieve sustainable future environmental management.

with respect to flooding and water flow/diversion, the dispute between Belgium and the Netherlands about the Maas and the Schelde with respect to salination and industrial pollution, the conflict between France, the Netherlands, Germany and Switzerland about the Rhine with respect to industrial pollution, the conflict between India and Bangladesh about the Brahmaputra and the Ganges with respect to siltation, flooding and water flow diversion, the conflict between Mexico and USA about the Rio Grande and Colorado rivers with respect to salination, water flow and agrochemical pollution (Ohlsson, 1995) or the conflicts such as in the Amazonian, Borneo and Sumatran forests, the Massai forest conflict, the Yellowstone National Parks conflict or land disputes such as between Israel and Palestine, the Kashmir land disputes, grazing land dispute between the Tibetan autonomous region of China and Nepal or the Kalapani land dispute between Nepal and India, land conflict between ethnic people and the white minority in Zimbabwe, they all are derived from political, economic or environmental motives. Internationally and domestically, the political wrangling and strife over natural resource is predicted as one of the fundamental issues of the new millennium.

Globalisation is increasingly posing new challenges and creating new conflicts (Adhikari *et al.*, 2000). For example, the conflict between Article 27.3b of the Trade Related Aspects of Intellectual Property Rights (TRIPs) of the World Trade Organisation (WTO) and the Convention on Biological Diversity (CBD), increasing bio-piracy, uncertainties and threats caused by genetically modified organisms and terminator technology in the agricultural sector, etc. are all creating conflict in society.

From the foregoing discussion, it is clear that the new millennium will face severe problems due to scarcity of natural resources. If there is scarcity of resources, there is competition, so natural resources will be a continuous source of future conflict. In this context few sentences of the speech delivered by Fidel Castro on the occasion of the 50th anniversary of the World Health Organisation is worth mentioning. *"...The weather is changing, the seas and the atmosphere are heating up, the air and the water are polluted, the soil is eroding, the deserts are growing, the forest is disappearing, water is getting scarce. Who will save our species? The blind and uncontrollable laws of the market? Neo-liberal globalisation? ...."* (Idris, 1998:5).

Population pressure, poverty and scarcity of resources are the root causes of social and natural resource conflicts in Nepal. Land and forest resources are over-exploited because of heavy dependence of the ever-growing population (both human and animals) in the natural resource base. Water and mineral resources however are under-utilised owing to a lack of financial resources and infrastructure (NPC, 1998; Pandey, 1999). Increasing natural resources degradation and its negative impacts on the environment and society is creating several conflicts. Due to a governmental and donor focus on economic development objectives there has been little attempt to effectively integrate poor people's concerns and conservation objectives in these economic objectives (Blaikie *et al.*, 1983). These problems are therefore directly linked with governance, accountability and transparency (Shrestha, 1999; Pandey, 2001) as well as a historical power-skewed socio-cultural legacy.

Water is one of the most important natural resources of Nepal. Nepal is theoretically the second richest country in the world with regard to water and possesses about 2.27 percent of the water resources of the world. It is estimated that there are a total of 6000 rivers (CBS, 1995). Principal forms of water use in Nepal are for drinking water, irrigation, hydropower and other industrial use. Nepal is drained by three major river systems. The country has a theoretical hydropower potential of 83,000 MW. Both surface and groundwater is used for drinking purposes. The physiographic and economic condition of the country, political conflicts and vested interests limit the proper utilisation of water in Nepal (Upreti, 2000d). Even considering the vast amount of water available, drinking water is scarce in many parts of the country. Industrial use of water in urban centres has created competition and conflict in inter and intra sectoral water use. Irrigation in mountain and hill regions, which contain 83 percent of the Nepal's total area, is difficult because of steep slopes and the fragile geography, which causes recurring landslides and soil erosion. Out of 26,41,000 ha cultivated land only 39 percent (10,55,617 ha) is irrigated. Of that irrigated area only 37 percent of the land has all round irrigation facilities available (NPC, 1998: 485). The growing population requires more food and growing more food requires more water. Physiographic characteristics and climatic factors affect such consumptive use of water but it varies spatially and seasonally. This leads to an unequal distribution. Nepalese water resource management (WRM) is therefore characterised by an unjust and insufficient use of water, contradiction and conflicts. The social dimensions of WRM are still getting little attention both in policy making and in practice. Water scarcity, competition and conflict are common characteristics framed under social, economic, political and legal issues in Nepal (Upreti, 1998a).

The growing population, factories and farms in Nepal all need more water and other natural resources. Therefore competition between domestic consumption, industries, and farms is increasing and turning into disputes. Water pollution is another strategic issue of conflict. We can see examples in Kathmandu Valley where the river systems are almost collapsing because the river-water is no longer useable. Conflict between the needs of populations living upstream of river basins and those dwelling downstream is mounting. Natural resources in Nepal are now becoming a highly sensitive political issue and source of conflict. The Melamchi Megha Drinking Water Project is a prime example of such a conflict.

Irrigation, a principal sector of water use in Nepal, intended to minimise the water scarcity in the field of agriculture, is creating its own conflicts and competition (Benda-Beckmann *et al.*, 1997). In total, farmer-managed small scale irrigation systems serve more than half of all irrigated land in Nepal (Pradhan and Pradhan 1996). However, they are facing various problems such as poor maintenance, conflict caused by state intervention, siltation and canal damage, etc. Achievement compared to the investment made in the irrigation sector in consecutive five year plans is not satisfactory (NPC, 1998). The Nepal Agricultural Sector Review (1989) and Irrigation Master Plan (1990) reports indicate that irrigation-project performances in Nepal are not satisfactory and require urgent attention (Gautam *et al.*, 1992). The land tenure system in Nepal has its roots in irrigation (e. g., high tax imposed on irrigated land), regulated by a feudal elite and landlords (Benda-Beckmann *et al.*, 1997). The history of irrigation in Nepal shows that most of the past irrigation systems were built at the initiatives of religious leaders and landlords. Even today, the descendants of the former feudal landlords have considerable influence on irrigation management. Irrigation issues nowadays are also linked to hydropower and more attention is given to down-stream benefits from hydropower development (MoWR, 1993).

Forests are another important natural resource for economic and social development. Forest resources are one of the major resources directly contributing to the survival of rural people in Nepal (Upreti, 2001b; Malla, 1997; Gilmour and Fisher, 1991). Forest resources directly fulfil forest-related subsistence needs of women, poor and backward people as well as commercial needs of well-off people. They are providing inputs for agriculture, livestock, and supply medicinal herbs, timber and non-timber forest products. Forests also support irrigation, conserve watersheds, improve the condition of the soil, provide recreation for tourists through forest-based eco-tourism and national parks and wildlife reserves, provide a habitat for flora and fauna and provide raw materials for the forest-based industries (Upreti, 1999a). Much of the agricultural production systems of the country are directly and/or indirectly based on forest resources (NPC, 1998). However, the Nepalese forests are severely threatened by political and commercial interests. In

1964 forests covered more than 45 percent of the total area of the country, this being reduced to 29 percent by 1998 (NPC: 1998:290). It is reported that the forest area of Terai is being destroyed at the rate of 1.3 percent per year (ibid.). Smuggling of forest products is posing another serious challenge. The productivity of the forest sector is decreasing due to uncontrolled migration and encroachment, smuggling, illegal hunting, grazing, forest fire, and lack of scientific forest management, poor political commitments and bureaucratic performance. Deforestation is resulting in an increasingly loss of habitats for birds, wild animals and reptiles. IUCN reported that 24 species of mammals, 9 species of reptiles, 27 species of birds, 2 species of insects and 13 species of plants have become endangered in Nepal (NPC: 1998: 219).

The decline of the forest resources at present has an adverse effect on water resources, productivity of agriculture and livestock. The Master Plan for the Forestry Sector (MPFS) 1989 planned to meet people's basic needs for fuel-wood, timber, fodder and other forest products on a sustained basis, and to promote people's participation in forestry resources' development, management and utilisation (HMG/N, 1989). However, the progress in this direction is very disappointing, with the exception of community forestry in the hill region. Nevertheless, recently, conflict is mounting between the government (bureaucrats in the forestry sector) and the Federation of Community Forestry Users-Nepal (FECOFUN) to take control of community forestry. Encroachment of forest and pasture areas by illegal settlers is another severe problem in the forestry sector.

The land use systems in Nepal are rapidly changing, together with a changing social transformation process, due to the information revolution, technological advancement, and market intervention and globalisation processes. As a consequence, changes in land-use are promoting out-migration, over exploitation of natural resources and escalating several conflicts. The lack of a conducive land-use policy and planning, weak institutional arrangements and a rapid population growth are exerting enormous pressures on land resources. Well-planned land use is one of the most important aspects for economic and social development. If land is managed and used properly, according to its quality, type, capacity, physiographic characteristics, not only the agricultural productivity can be increased but also other social and economic benefits can be derived (Upreti, 2000e).

Land is not only a crucial resource for Nepalese people who have their livelihood based in agriculture but also a basis of wealth and power. Major land use categories in Nepal include forestry, agriculture, grasslands and pastures and settlements. Land varies considerably in terms of its potential for different uses due to a wide variation in topography, soil composition, and climate. Due to the increasing human population and increasing numbers of unproductive livestock extreme pressure is being exerted on land resource (NPC, 1998). Soil erosion, fertility decline, sedimentation and floods have degraded and continue to degrade the land. Causative factors of soil loss are steep slope cultivation, use of marginal land, overgrazing, forest fires, and population pressure. Land is not only the main property of Nepalese people but also the important contributing factor to the creation of conflict.

Internal migration is rapidly increasing the population in urban centres and putting additional pressure on fertile land in the urban areas (NPC, 1992). More than 90 percent of urban centres are located in the fertile agricultural areas. Huge quantities of land are used annually in building construction by government, semi-government, non-government and the private sectors (NPC, 1998). The increasing pace of rural to urban migration is deteriorating the productivity of the land in both rural and urban areas (HMG/N, 1992). The government is not able to develop mutual links between rural and urban areas and unable to provide equal opportunities in the rural areas. Far and Mid-Western regions of Nepal are almost neglected in development priority and infrastructure development. The regional imbalance, lack of infrastructure and employment opportunities and the unavailability of basic service facilities are the triggering factors for migration from rural to urban areas (MoF, 1998) that lead to social conflict and tension. Land encroachment and unplanned settlements are the result of such migration whereby an imbalanced situation develops between men and land resources.

Land distribution is very skewed. Gross disparities in land ownership are one of the major causes of poverty, injustice and social discrimination (Shrestha, 1997). Due to such disparity, a large number of people have no access to productive land resources. More than 70 percent of farmers have less than one hectare (ha) of land (NPC, 1998). Substantial regional variations in the distribution of agricultural lands exist in Nepal. The Terai region occupies 17 percent of the total land area comprising 49 percent of the total agricultural land whereas Hill covers 63 percent of total land and accounts for 40 percent of agricultural land. Mountain occupies 20 percent of total land with 11 percent of agricultural land. The Human Development Report-Nepal 1998 shows that the bottom 40 percent of agricultural households use only 9 percent of the total agricultural land owning less than 0.5 ha while the top 6 percent occupies more than 33 percent of the total. These inequalities are manifested in the higher incidence of poverty. Owner-tiller is the dominant type of land entitlement in Nepal as 85 percent is owner operated and the remaining 15 percent are rented. The same report also highlights that the Nepalese land resource is besieged by multifarious problems such as duel ownership in land tenure, fragmentation, unequal distribution, institutional obstacles and unfocused government policies. Duel ownership is severely limiting productivity as neither owner nor tenants invest in the land. Rural Credit Survey of Nepal Rastra Bank (1994) has indicated that investment in land improvement in Nepal is less than 3 percent of the household income. The incidence of "landlessness" is increasing rapidly. Small holders are marginalised and transformed into landless people (Shrestha, 1997). This means that a few landlords control a huge fraction of the country's land. Tenant farmers have no motivation to maximise the production potential of tenanted land due to dual ownership and insecurity.

Fertile lands are increasingly used for non-agricultural purposes (i.e., urban settlement, industry and infrastructure). Land fragmentation is being increased due to cultural and legal provision to divide parental land between sons. This has severe negative consequences for productivity. Legal measures to protect land fragmentation and promote land consolidation are ineffective (Ghimire, 1992; New Era, 1988). Land in the Terai is facing extreme pressure due to migration of people from the hills and mountains. Because of a lack of effective land-use planning, the agricultural sector is not able to reach its potential by using specialisation and diversification. Erosion, landslides and floods in the Hill areas have seriously affected the river banks, lower slopes of the Hills and the fertile land of the Terai region and have had a negative impact on agriculture, irrigation, hydro-electricity, forest and bio-diversity, the environment, road systems, transport and tourism. Development of land according to the land-use plan, based on geographical features, diversity, structures, capacity and quality and its effective utilisation is still a widely ignored issue in Nepal. People are still not sensitive to the importance of land-use planning (agriculture, pasture, residence, urbanisation, and industrialisation) nor is the government sufficiently responsive to these issues.

Land management practices in Nepal are still insensitive to the negative effects on the wider environment, and become a source of conflict. For example, cultivation on the steep-slope land in the foothills of the Himalayas in Nepal is contributing to floods in the delta areas of Bangladesh (Tear Fund, 1999). Highly fertile lands of Terai regions and urban centres are rapidly being covered by buildings as city centres expand (Upreti, 2000e). Land-use planning based on land efficiency classification is very weak (NPC, 1998). Proper information and mapping of the land is lacking. On one hand the available land resource in the country is inadequate to supply the facilities and social services for the ever-increasing population, on the other hand available land resources are not utilised in an effective and productive manner and are becoming a continuous source of conflict. Although the 1964 Land Act was amended in 1997 to eliminate widely prevailing dual ownership (owner-tenant arrangement), the act is not being effectively enforced. The same act has made provision for a ceiling on land holding. However, this is only limited, either in document or implemented to those who have no power to manipulate it. Land administration is not able to serve its purpose due to corruption[3] and miss handling. The astonishing example is the misuse and abuse of land under land trust (*Guthi* land). The Absence of a national land-use policy and programme, and a narrow sectoral approach, have led to land use problems and conflicts.

The land under *Guthi* (land trust)[4] is still extremely controversial and conflict between tenants and *Guthi* Sansthan (*Guthi* Corporation Office) is long standing. The elimination of dual-land ownership is merely a slogan of the government and political parties. The number of landless farmers and Kamaiya[5] are increasing (Ghimire, 1992), as is the encroachment of public land and forest. Due to all these land-related problems, agriculture in Nepal is still far from being

---

3. Corruption is defined as behaviour which deviates from the formal duties of a public role because of private (personal, close family, private clique) pecuniary or status gains; or violates rules against the exercise of certain types of behaviour regarding influence.
4. The literal meaning of *Guthi*-land is 'land trust'. *Guthi*-land in Nepal is a religious land ownership arrangement. Such lands are either allocated by the state or by individuals, for a religious or philanthropic purpose. There is a special act and legal provision to manage *Guthi*-land in Nepal.
5. Kamaiya is an inhumane bonded labour system existing in western Nepal (Banke, Bardiya, Kailali, Kanchanpur) where more than 15000 people were working as quasi slaves with landlords. The government has now freed them. See K.C. 2001 for details. However, their settlement problem is causing another level of conflict and feeling of injustice as the govt is unable to properly settle them.

commercially successful. Keshav Badal, a noted politician and activist involved in the land-related movement in Nepal concludes that the fundamental cause of land problems is the feudalistic social system nurtured by the cultural and political system (Badal, 1999). Similar observations were made by other noted personalities involved in land reform movement in Nepal such as Jaga Nath Acharya and Narayan Man Bijuchhe Rohit (ActionAid Nepal, 2001).

The land reform campaign, although initiated in 1951, has so far been merely a political slogan rather than significantly contributing to its reform. The Sukumbasi Samasya Samadhan Ayog (Land-less Problem Resolution Commission-LPRC) is a political platform of ruling parties to reward their workers rather than solve the problems of landless people. All major political parties have been incorporating the reform of land, agriculture, water and forest in addition to other many issues into their election manifestos, but none of them are fulfilling their commitments.

Despite the fact that much more effort, time and money are being invested by the government, donors and local communities in NRM and despite the fact that several natural resources related offices have been established in all districts[6], conflicts and disputes are still increasing (Upreti, 2000d). Several research findings show that conflicts are increasing due to the intervention of external development organisations without a proper understanding of local systems, lack of users participation in NRM and defective policies (IIMI, 1987; 1990; Ansari and Pradhan, 1991). For example, the policy of His Majesty's Government of Nepal (HMG/N) in its eighth (1991-1997) and ninth (1997-2002) five

---

6. The District Irrigation Office (DIO), District Water Supply Office (DWSO), District Forest Office (DFO), District Land Reform Office (DLRO), District Soil and Water Conservation Office (DSCO), Land Survey and measurement Office, Electricity Office, District Land Revenue Office are instituted in each district. In addition to them, District Development Committee (DDC) and Village Development Committees (VDCs) are also actively involved in NRM.

year plans gave a high priority to an integrated NRM approach. However, translation of these policies into practice has been weak due to political differences and conflict of interests among the actors.

The current debate among politicians, policy makers, bureaucrats, diplomats, water energy experts, engineers, social scientists, academicians, foresters, land-use planners, private entrepreneurs and farmers on the priority of macro v/s micro projects, multiple use of water, geographical preferences, community-led forest management, land use change, etc. is contributing to a re-think of the dominant NRM approach in Nepal. The dominant NRM approach means the approach adopted by the government in its policies and practices. Within the government policy framework the majority of donors and technical experts are promoting such NRM approach. Many donors in NRM (bilateral, multilateral and international non-governmental organisations (INGO), charity organisations etc.) have been supporting HMG/N departments, development banks, NGOs and the private sector in Nepal for more than four decades. Despite the efforts of the government on NRM in its eight successive five-year plans and donors' financial and technical support conflicts are mounting and interventions are not able to achieve the desired objectives. The recent research findings of the Citizen's Poverty Watch Forum on 'Impacts of Foreign Aids in Nepal' conclude that foreign aids *"tends to increase dependency and disparity in society. The lack of long term commitment on the part of implementers, and their failure to understand societal structure as well as specific requirements for social change means that foreign aid has failed to generate sustained development path so far. Further achievements have not been commensurate to resources imputed. Faulty implementation methods and inappropriate fund flows are also to blame. Infrastructure built with aid has, as a whole, not benefited the poorest section of the population..."* (Citizen's Watch Poverty Forum, 2001:47).

It is important to note that all social natural resource conflicts are created in differentiated and specialised local environments across the country. The specific natural resources related conflicts of the Terai are different from those of steep hills and mountains. Hill and mountain natural resources are facing different conflicts created by problems such as landslides, shifting rivers/streams, high soil losses, deforestation, etc. whereas NRM projects in Terai are facing problems of siltation and river shifting, land and forest encroachment, illegal harvesting of natural resources, deforestation, etc. However, more common problems of both areas are resource degradation, conflict about access, rights and obligations, fair distribution, maintenance and benefit sharing (Ostrom and Benjamin, 1993). Various endogenous and exogenous factors such as population growth, globalisation of market, environmental and technological changes are imposing new conflicts. Many large and small NRM projects implemented by different agencies are introducing new conflicts as well as having various negative impacts on society. For example, ignorance of the importance of indigenous knowledge in planning and designing new systems, extortion, alteration of local rights and regulations, replacement of old institutions by new ones, imposition of technocratic solutions, are some of the immediate implications of new interventions (Basnyat, 1995; Benjamin *et al., 1994*). These interventions have their own firmly fixed and uniform policy and a rigid procedure based on reductionist-positivist orientation. They are technocratic in nature and generally do not acknowledge local diversities. This is becoming one of the major causes of social conflict in society.

There are several factors causing conflict in society. Conflict can arise if the new NRM policy of the government contradicts with local cultural practice. The economic motive of people to acquire more from the existing natural resources on a competitive basis also leads to conflict. Conflict is also growing due to the contradiction between environmental and economic interests. Changes in historical use patterns in natural resources can bring conflict into a community. Similarly, contradictions of legal arrangements and customary practices have promoted several conflicts.

Conflicts produce both positive and negative consequences and alter existing social relations. They induce change in resource management and utilisation, policy process, livelihood strategies, land and agriculture, gender relations, power structure, and individual and collective behaviour. In most cases the combined effect of some or many of such factors can escalate or resolve a conflict. Moreover, the intensity and effect of these factors differs between communities and within a community depending on when the effects are felt.

Natural resource management has been the subject of recurring discussions throughout the Nepal's post-Rana regime's history. Both before and after the restoration of democracy in 1990 issues have been raised and answers sought with regards to sustainable NRM. This apparent interest in natural resources, however, does not focus on conflict, one of the major issues in NRM. Several efforts have been made to utilise available natural resources to increase the economic growth of the country. As a part of this national policy, attempts have also been made to reform the land use pattern, the agricultural system, and forest management and to develop new irrigation systems while improving existing ones by increasing their productivity. During this process several conflicts have erupted at different levels and intensities in several parts of the country. Nevertheless, such conflicts are still not receiving proper attention at the level of researchers, policy makers and implementers. Physical and technical issues, lacking social dimensions, dominate research agendas of Nepalese NRM. This has tremendous implications for the sustainability of natural resources. Surprisingly, very few studies focus on the roles and impacts of social conflicts in Nepalese NRM (Sukla *et al.*, 1997; Pradhan *et al.*, 1997; Upreti, 1998a, Khanal, 1998, Shrestha, 1996a, 1996b; Khanal, 1996). Even these studies are not in-depth or comprehensive enough to understand the dynamics of conflict: causes and consequences, mechanisms and strategies of resolution and/or management, use of power and position, implications of conflict to NRM, environment and society, etc. What is available from both professional and academic research is an acknowledgement of the existence of natural resource conflict and a general prescription for its resolution, rather than a focus on how conflicts actually occur, how they are managed and what ought to be the future strategy for handling conflict. There are some studies on land conflicts mainly carried out by (legal) anthropologists but they do not suggest much on how these conflicts could be managed. Many research studies have indicated that conflict is prevalent in natural resources. However, there is little information on how and why conflicts escalate, in what context conflict occurs, what factors are generic causes to create or resolve any natural resources related conflict, and how these conflicts can be managed or resolved. There are not many studies on conflict related to development interventions and their policy implications. Looking to the current status of the natural resources conflict study it became clear that there has been no systematic and in-depth study on community level natural resources related conflicts, their impact on NRM and their contribution to agrarian social change in general and clear suggestion of methodologies for the improvement. This was the reason I began to explore these issues and dynamics of social conflict in natural resources and their management practices in Nepal. Obviously, any single work can not solve societal problems but it can hopefully improve the situation.

1.4. Purpose of the Book and Methodological Issues

This book is mainly based on the research I did to complete my PhD. The purposes to write this book are threefold. Firstly, to understand and analyse the dynamics of social conflicts and their management practices. Secondly, based on the outcome of the first objective, to develop an alternative approach for community-level CM, if appropriate. Thirdly, to initiate a debate on conflict as a source of learning and contribute to agrarian change. My intention is not to misrepresent existing CM approaches. Rather, based on the study of existing practices, to develop an alternative approach to deal with social conflict that will contribute to sustainable NRM. In doing so, I have focused on both regulatory and legislative resolution measures as well as local indigenous resolution practices applied in social conflicts. I have not only considered the causes of social conflicts and their resolution but also took into account the implications of conflict resolution for natural resources and society as a whole. This book is the result of my academic and professional background. This book has explored the causes and inter-linkages of conflict with local power and politics, external intervention and customary practices. It also examines the transformation of these conflicts in society. To analyse the conflict three broad sets of questions were formulated. The first set of questions focuses on understanding of the genesis, causes, transfer, and management of conflict. The second set particularly focuses on understanding the implications of conflict in society. The third set of questions attempts to develop an alternate CM approach, for future improvement, based on the findings of the first two. However, the three sets of questions are not mutually exclusive, but are closely associated with and complementary to each other. They were: 1) What are the common social conflicts in natural resources and their management practices in a community and why do they occur? 2) What are the implications of these conflicts in resources and society? And 3) How can these conflicts be effectively managed at local level?

In this section, I briefly describe how I did study to write this book, and my motives and choices concerning the research methods used to answer the above questions. To investigate the dynamics of social conflict a methodology is required which facilitates analysis of behavioural patterns, perceptions, causes, interrelations and interactions among the actors. Hence, my methodological approach is a sociological interpretative study based on the fundamental connection between context and practice over time. Therefore, the most basic guiding factors in selecting methods of study were the practices of everyday social life of the actors and their strategies, manoeuvres, discourses, and struggles. In order to explore the dynamics of conflicts in society, methods and techniques of qualitative research were used to collect the required information. Qualitative research is a field of inquiry which crosscuts disciplines, fields and subject matters and it is surrounded by complex and interconnected terms, concepts and assumptions (Denzin and Lincoln, 1998:2). Denzin and Lincoln (1998) argue that qualitative research is a set of interpretative practices that entails semiotics, narratives, content discourse, archival, phonemic analysis, discourse analysis, ethnographies, interview, psychoanalysis, cultural studies, survey research, participant observation and even statistics. Qualitative research places the emphasis on process and meaning and does not focuses much on rigorous examination and 'measurements (if measured at all) of the casual relationship in terms of quantity, intensity, amount and frequency. Rather it stresses the socially constructed nature of reality, the relationship between the content, context and spatial and temporal factors and seeks answers to how social experiences are created and given meanings (Ibid.: 8). Qualitative research is a process because it interconnects sets of theory, methods and analysis. In this research process researchers approach with a set of ideas and frameworks (theory, ontology) that specify a set of questions (epistemology) that are examined (methodology, analysis) (ibid.: 23). In general four major interpretative paradigms structure qualitative research: positivist and post positivist, constructivist-interpretative, critical (Marxist, emancipatory) and feminist-post structural (ibid.: 26).

The theoretical perspectives and the research problem itself influenced the choice of the strategy of the study. The strategy focused on 'what information most appropriately answers specific research questions and which strategies are most effective for obtaining it (Denzin and Lincoln, 1998). To understand how social conflicts evolve in natural resources and how they are resolved, it is necessary to appreciate the intricacy of the social systems within which they are happening. Hence ethnographic, exploratory case studies were conducted to collect such information. A case study is a method of sociological analysis of socio-cultural phenomena to draw inferences and to formulate propositions (Mitchell, 1983). A case study allows an investigation into an on-going phenomenon with a real life context, in which the investigator has no control over behavioural events. It also better explains the decision process, why and how decisions are taken and implemented. Hence, an extended case study was the most preferred method used in this research to explore the dynamics of natural resource conflicts. A case study was my preferred strategy in examining contemporary conflict events. The strength of a case study is its ability to deal with the full variety of evidence: documents, interviews, observations, etc. (Yin, 1984). It provides sound ways of understanding the dynamics of social conflicts in natural resources. Natural resource-related conflicts involve different actors embedded in social processes. These actors create discourses through interpretation of the conflict situation. It is therefore important for the researcher to integrate different social interpretations of conflict into the inquiry process. The integration of a local perspective, empirical knowledge and different theoretical perspectives into a research process is complicated. Furthermore, studying conflict management in natural resources from both the legal-anthropological and social-learning perspectives is more complicated because of their different aims and focuses. Therefore a flexible set of guidelines is used as a strategy for collecting and analysing empirical materials. This strategy led me to specific sites, persons, groups and institutions having relevant interpretative material. The meaning of human behaviour, motivation, interaction and action are expressed in daily practices of actors. A qualitative interpretative approach of conflict study is more appropriate to explore such behaviour, which can not be captured by quantitative methods (Alasuutari, 1998; Silverman, 1993; Seale, 1998). From the field study I realised that a case study is most suitable when a how or why question is being asked about a contemporary set of events, over which the investigator has little or no control (Silverman, 1993). The strength of a case study is that it has no pre-packaged research design. Rather, different information collection techniques, sampling and analysis techniques can be used throughout the research process (Yin, 1984). This method is useful in understanding the local dynamics of access and control of resources, knowledge and power (Seale, 1998).

The Dolakha district was selected as a case study district based on the availability of multiple social and natural resource conflict and my previous professional association. The specific case studies were carried out in the Pawoti and Sailungeshwor Village Development Committees (VDCs)[7] of Dolakha district of central Nepal. The criteria used to select the study site were:

1. Presence of different social conflict cases, in a cluster,
2. Involvement of multiple layers of actors in social conflicts related to natural resources,
3. Presence of relatively old and new conflicts to examine the transformation patterns,
4. Involvement of more than one VDC in the conflict (transboundry conflict),
5. Manageable geographical coverage to conduct the research,

These criteria were interrelated. The first and the second

---

7. VDC is the lowest political and administrative unit. Before 1990 this unit was called Village Panchayat. Panchayat was an autocratic party-less political system that existed in Nepal before 1990 when all political parties were banned and democratic values were suppressed. The crown was the source of power and was above the constitution. In this system there was a provision of Village Panchayat (smallest political unit), District Panchayat (district level government) and Rastrya Panchayat (central parliament). Chairperson, Vice-Chairperson and nine members represented district Panchayat from the nine regions within the district. District Panchayat was replaced by District Development Committee and House of Parliament replaced Rastrya Panchayat after the restoration of democracy in 1990.

criteria, presence of different conflicts and involvement of multiple actors, are fundamental in any conflict study. The third criterion, old and new conflicts, was important to assess the effect of the temporal factor in escalation or stalemate of conflict. The fourth criterion, transboundary conflict, was useful to comparatively examine the role of local governments in the management of larger conflicts. The fifth criterion was more pragmatic in order to carry out the study within a specified time frame. The starting point of this study was the inventory of all conflicts that occurred in the study area. In 1997, I conducted six months MSc fieldwork in the same area to study negotiation on natural resource related conflicts. I wanted to use the well-established rapport with the local community to carry out further study and use the information gathered earlier. In addition to the information collected in 1997, with the help of two research assistants I documented all the different types of conflict in the study area by using key informant interviews, focus group discussion, and observation. A total of 54 focus group discussion meetings and 230 key informant interviews were conducted to document the conflict. I also conducted semi-structured interviews using check lists with politicians, bureaucrats, and conflict case winners from formal organisations and the general public involved in conflict to record some quantitative information. During the exploratory research period villagers informed about conflict in their villages on the basis of their memory and some historical documents. That not only gave a broad overview of the conflicts and a larger list for selection of the specific cases for the detail study but also caused difficulties in deciding which cases to study. With the help of local leaders, staff of GOs and NGOs working in that area, VDC officials, teachers, social workers and a review of available literature (mainly project reports) the following 5 social conflict cases were selected for the in-depth study:

1. Conflict in a farmer-managed irrigation system,
2. Conflict on a forest/grazing land,
3. Conflict on a spring source for drinking water,

4. Conflict in a donor funded and government developed irrigation system, and
5. Conflict on a religious agricultural land.

When the specific cases were identified respondents were selected purposefully: those who were someway involved in these five cases, in order to explore specific information related to conflict. So all people involved in the five conflict cases were primary respondents of the study. The detailed narrative of these cases is presented in the fifth, sixth and seventh chapters.

While the specific case studies were conducted in the two VDCs of the Dolakha district, the general study of the social conflict was made in 11 reference groups of six districts involved in NRM activities. These are the groups organised in a village by community members to accomplish functions such as management of forests, irrigation, pasture land, trials and bridges, seed production, etc. About 10-30 households are organised into each group. NGO, donor-funded projects and government agencies support many such groups. The purpose of using reference groups was twofold. Firstly to compare the characteristics of social conflict in natural resources and secondly, to document the specific social conflicts in these areas. Of these 11 groups 2 were from Kanchanpur district (Mahendranagar Municipality and Jhalari VDC), 2 from Banke district (Kohalpur and Bageshwori VDCs), 2 from Chitwan district (Bhandara and Piple VDCs), 2 from Kaski district (Arbavijaya and Bharatpokhari VDCs), 1 from Ramechhap district (Ramechhap VDC) and 2 from Dolakha district (Bhimeshwor Municipality and Kavre VDCs). The criteria used to select reference groups were involvement of those groups in dealing with social conflict in their activities supported by some organisations. To find the appropriate groups, I got a list of groups involved in conflicts from the organisations supporting them and made a selection considering geographical representation, caste, ethnicity, and economic status and gender aspects (some women groups were deliberately selected).

Selection of the cases for the study was guided by the objective of improving the understanding of social conflict in natural resources at a local level. This obviously had implications on the selection of methods and techniques. Focus group discussions, life histories, informal observation/ discussion, informal/semi-structured and key informant interviews, transacts, archival study, participation in national seminars and workshops were the main techniques used to collect information via the ethnographic study (Spradly, 1979). Ethnographic study refers to a social scientific analysis of social forms, which gives attention to culture and issues of social identity (Pecock, 1986) and therefore, is also called descriptive anthropology (Vidich and Lyman, 1998). Some quantitative data were gathered from contacting people especially involved in conflict issues and from secondary sources. Checklists were used to guide the research process. Secondary data were collected from different documents and reports and reviewed extensively. However, community level CM practices in Nepal are extremely poorly documented. Due to that single reason there is very little evidence available for the study and analysis of social conflict in natural resources. Information related to social conflicts has been collected at three levels. The first level was the case study VDCs and reference sites where more in-depth information was collected. The second level was the district and the third level was the national level where more general information on social conflict was gathered. At the district level the main sources of information were people coming from different VDCs to district headquarters to settle conflict cases in CDO, court, the police station, DFO, land related offices, water related offices, political

Figure 1.2 Collection of information through focus group discussion

leaders, lawyers, staff of different offices, human right activists, police personnel, workers of NGOs and trade unions. At the national level the sources of information were documents/ reports from researchers, central natural resource related departments, INGO staff, national politicians, senior bureaucrats, social workers users federations, District Development Committees, District Irrigation Offices, District Forest Office, District Water Supply Offices, District Police Offices, District Administration Offices (DAO), District Court, District Agriculture Offices, District Land Reform Offices, Survey and Trigonometric Offices, and other relevant organisations. The general characteristics of social and natural resource related conflicts observed in the case study sites were compared with the eleven reference groups of three Hill and three Teari districts. The findings of the case study sites were used as checklists (or comparison indicators) to compare the similarities and differences of the characteristics of social conflicts in other parts of Nepal. Several meetings in each group were made with representatives of the groups and also visited disputed geographical areas (forest, land and water bodies) together with the group members to get an insight of social conflict.

All case studies were primarily geared to explore, describe and analyse conflict phenomena at a local level. This was the corner stone of the research process. Well-established relationships of mutual trust between researcher and villagers became fundamental in obtaining sensitive information related to the conflicts in the case study sites. I have attended several conflict resolution meetings and the ongoing negotiation process in the village organised by villagers themselves, by NGOs and VDCs. I also observed the conflict resolution process accomplished in the district headquarters by different governmental organisations. On the spot observation gave me fresh ideas on how different actors in general and powerful elite in particular, play a role in conflict management. Observations also served as a good source of material to discuss in interviews and meetings. In this way issues were explored in greater depth and new insights gained about information collected by other methods. In the midst of the research process some elderly people, who were actively involved in the conflict, were selected to recall their life histories. The information obtained from the life histories was used as reference material to discuss in meetings and group discussions.

Observation was also made on the confrontation, emotional expression, public-private behaviour of actors during the research period. Institutional interviews with representatives of various organisations were also collected. Close attention to specific events was particularly enlightening. The analysis is based on constructivist, descriptive and interpretative[8] methods with illustrative quotes (Lamers, 1994). In terms of analysis constructivist paradigm assumes a relativist ontology (there are multiple realities), a subjectivist epistemology (knower and subject create understanding) and different set of methodological procedures. It focuses on credibility, transferability, dependability and confirmability instead of positivist criteria of internal and external validity, reliability and objectivity (Denzin and Lincoln, 1998:27). The analysis focused on searching out the common characteristics, causes and relationships of social conflict and resolution process. There was a continuous interaction between the collection and analysis of information, seen as an interaction process in the field. Analysis and interpretation of the information by people themselves was one of the important aspects of data collection. During the process of analysis I have visited overseas Development Institute, London, Department of Human geography, University of Zurich, SDC-Bern and Centre for Development and Environment, University of Bern to discuss the theoretical issues related to management of social conflict in natural resources. These discussions became extremely useful to develop the Interactive Conflict Management method.

To better understand the context of social conflict it is essential to know about the general characteristics of the area

---

8. Schwandt (1998: 221-259) vividly explains about these methods in the chapter called "Constructivist Interpretivist Approach to Human Inquiry".

where they are occurred. In this section I am briefly presenting the general characteristics of the study district and the case study sites where conflict issues were observed ands analysed. The study area is the Dolakha District which is situated in the central mountain-region of Nepal, from 27°28" to 28°0" latitude North and 85°50" to 86°32" longitude East, 133 km North East from Kathmandu, the capital city of Nepal. The total area of the Dolakha district is 2191 sq. km with the district headquarters in Charikot. Forests and meadow densely cover the district and it is very rich in flora and fauna. The altitude range of the district is from 763 to 7137 meters. Of the total land area 35% is high Himal, 40% high hill and 25% is mid hills (Dolakha District Development Committee-DDDC, 1999). The climate in the lower parts of the district is sub-tropical to temperate with the temperature range from 8° to 17° Celsius. The average annual rainfall is 2043.5 mm. The land use pattern of the district is 14% cultivated, 7% fallow, 16% grazing, 44% forest and 19% other lands out of the total 214278 ha in the district. This district is the frontier area between central Nepal and the Tibetan Autonomous Region of China.

Total population of the district is 191073 (in 1998) with 39554 households. The population density is 87.2 persons per square km (National Research Associate-NRA, 1999). However, the population is not uniformly distributed over the district. The southern parts are much more densely populated than the northern belts. The population growth rate is 1.4% per year and family size is 4.8 per household (DDDC, 1999). The literacy rate is 41 % (NRA, 1999). The percentage of children below 10 years is 29.2%. The percentage of landless and marginal farmers is 48.22. The population composition of the district is heterogeneous and made up of Chhetri, Brahmin, Damai, Kami, Sarki caste groups and Tamang, Sherpa, Jirel, Surel, Newar ethnic groups. The majority of the population is Chhetri (34.2%) followed by Tamang (16%), Brahmin (11.4%) and others (38.4%). Hindu (76.76%) and Buddhist (23.13%) are the most common religions in this district. Only 0.11% of the people

Table 1.1. Relative Indicators of Development
in Dolakha District-1997

S.n.	Indicators	Rank*	Remarks
1.	Overall composite index of development	24	Worst[1]
2.	Poverty and deprivation index	23	Worst[1]
3.	Women's empowerment index	29	Intermediate[2]
4.	Natural resource endowment index	43	Intermediate[2]
5.	Socio-economic infrastructure development index	18	Worst[1]
6.	Gender imbalance ratio in literacy status	54	Worst[3]
7.	Educationally disadvantaged population	42	Intermediate[2]
8.	Percentage of landless and marginal farm households	61	Worst[3]
9.	Per capita food production	72	Worst[3]
10.	Overall literacy rate	43	Intermediate[2]
11.	Infant mortality rate	10	Best[3]
12.	Drinking water coverage (in %)	36	Intermediate[2]
13.	Percentage irrigated area	47	Intermediate[2]
14.	Road density (in %)	35	Intermediate[2]
15.	Bank coverage	62	Worst[1]
16.	Co-operatives	17	Best[3]
17.	Health institution	49	Intermediate[2]
18.	Per capita regular budget allocation	31	Intermediate[2]
19.	Per capita development budget allocation	34	Intermediate[2]
20.	Percentage of area with slopes above 30 degrees	53	Worst[3]
21.	Per capita forest area (ha)	30	Intermediate[2]
22.	Percent cultivated area	56	Worst[3]
23.	Gross rural-population density	21	Best[1]
24.	Gender discrimination index	24	Worst[1]
25.	Health and development index	49	Intermediate[1]
26.	Infrastructure development index	27	Intermediate[1]
27.	Post office	53	Worst[3]

Source: National Research Associates, 1999 (Adapted).
*Rank among the 75 districts of Nepal
  1= The highest rank starts with the 75th position of the district (75-51 best, 50-26 intermediate and 25-1 worst)
  2= Between 26th to 50th and 50th to 26th position of the district
  3= The highest starts with first position of the district (1-25 best, 26-50 intermediate and 51-75 worst)

follow other religions. The drinking water coverage in the district is 57.87 % whereas percentage of irrigated area is 8.62. The percentage of the are with slope above 30 degree is 69.65. The per capita forest area is 0.43 ha. The percentage of cultivated area is 11.2 (NRA, 1999).

The district is politically divided into 51 VDCs, one Municipality and two electoral constituencies for parliamentary election. The major political parties found in the district are The Communist Party of Nepal-United Marxist-Leninist (CPN-UML), Nepali Congress (NC), The Rastrya Prajatantra Party (RPP) Nepal Communist Party (Maoist) and The Communist Party of Nepal-Marxist Leninist (CPN-ML). The CPN-UML dominates the elected political representatives (more than 95%). The economy of the district is based on agriculture on which 91.9 % of the population depends (DDDC, 1999). The remaining 8.1% of the population are engaged in services, business, labouring, etc. Rice, wheat, maize, finger millet, potatoes, legumes, fruits and vegetables are the major agricultural products and cows, buffalo, sheep, goats and pigs are the main animals reared in the district. The productivity of the major cereal crop is less than 2 tons per ha. Food deficiency is a major problem. Rural roads and telecommunication are gradually improving in the district (DDDC, 1999). Tamakoshi, Khimti, Charnawati, Rolwaling, Dolti, Gumu, Ghyang, Andheri are major rivers. Kharidhunga Orient Magnesite and Khimti Hydro Power are the two main projects operated in the district. The main development programme activities currently implemented in the district by various GOs and NGOs using governmental funds and or with the support of donor communities are:

- Rural Self Help and Electoral Constituency Development programmes,
- Marginal, Backward and Dalit Community Promotion programme,
- Suspension Bridge and Drought Mitigation Support programmes,
- Social security, irrigation, drinking water, rural road development, special area development, livestock service, education, women's development programmes

- Cottage and small scale industry development, community and leasehold forestry, soil conservation programmes,
- Agriculture loan service, family planning, public health and sanitation and rural energy.

Watershed and water-source conservation, erosion and landslide control and riverbank and cultivated area protection are major water-related activities implemented in the district. Rehabilitation of damaged and degraded lands, community afforestation and natural regeneration of forests, solar and biogas promotion and water-turbine promotion are other major development activities. Drinking water and irrigation construction and rehabilitation, cadastral survey and land mapping, pasture development and private plantation are some of the major MRM related ongoing activities in the study area. Main donors supporting different development activities in the study area are:

- Swiss Agency for Development and Co-operation (SDC) in integrated rural development, forest, health, road and trade school programmes,
- UNDP for local governance and rural energy programmes,
- NORAD for the electricity sector,
- Dutch-DGIS for bio-gas and Chhyorolpa river control,
- Asian Development Bank for irrigation and the leasehold forest programme,
- International Fund for Agriculture Development (IFAD) for agricultural loans and leasehold forest,
- World Bank for drinking water programmes.
- German Development Cooperation for rural road development programme

Pawoti and Sailungeshwor VDCs of the Dolakha district were the case study sites. Before 1982, Pawoti and Sailungeshwor both were under one village panchayat. Because of political reasons it was divided into two in 1982. Demographic settings and socio-cultural characteristics of both VDCs are similar and therefore only one description is given to cover both. The research VDCs are located in the southern part of the district and therefore, relatively densely populated.

Table 1.2. Population Composition of Case Study Sites

S.n.	Population Characters	Pawoti	Sailungeshwor	Total
1	Total population	4786	4039	8825
1.1	Male	2295	2034	4329
1.2	Female	2491	2005	4496
2	Total households	925	813	1738
3	Household size	5.03	4.97	-

Source: NRA, 1998 (Pp. 267-278)

The case study area is relatively densely populated with 1738 households and a population of 8825. These villages are situated in the south of the district, 5 hours walking distance from the district headquarters. The socio-political history of this area goes back about 300 years. One Brahmin family came and settled there from the Kumaon area of India via western Nepal, which is expanded now to 400 families. Gradually this family enlarged and expanded to a larger area. Later, at the time of the Rana regime, one member of this family got a chance to work directly with Rana as a Subba. He received many favours from the Rana regime and managed to recruit his family members in their service. Later he emerged, as a local functionary of Ranas to rule the village and his extended family became very powerful. The sons and grandsons continued to serve Rana in the same way until the end of the Rana regime in 1951. Even after 1951 there was still a strong hold of these families in the village because they were Mukhiya, Jimuwal and feudal landlords. Local people who were in the village before that family settled there were suppressed. Another feudal landlord emerged in the Sailungeshowr area when the severe conflict escalated between the brothers of the Subba family. At the same time, another Bramin Koirala family from Dumja came and settled there and expanded their influence in one of the villages in the Pawoti VDC, which is now expanded to 50 families. The Koirala family became powerful when the head of the family became Mukhiya of that area. These families developed as strong powerful centres in the study area. In short, until 1990, the study sites were dominated and exploited by a few powerful people. Since 1980 economic opportunities have increased, due to governmental-development interventions in rural development, made possible by the financial and technical support of The Swiss government. A number of poor people got better-paid, wage-earning work in The Lamosanju Jiri Road project and The Integrated Hill Development Project. They then became less dependent on local landlords. This led to the local landlords suffering from a shortage of labour during the peak agricultural season. With this economic empowerment the bargaining power of villagers was increased and they started to ask for a better wage. The situation completely changed when the political system altered. The powerful elite of the study area were not only suffering from a decline in their power and authority by being marginalised by the new political system, but also by the aggressive behaviour of the local people who had previously been suppressed and exploited. For example, some Damai families violently attacked one of the most powerful elite families, killed one son, and severely wounded five other family members. The people who had been oppressed could not cope with the pace of change. Several conflicts, confrontations and acts of revenge and counter-revenge increased in the villages. A strong sense of hostility developed between two groups of people. With the emergence and functioning of political parties the intensity of the conflicts and confrontations decreased. The earlier respect and obedience had entirely disappeared and completely changing the social organisation of the village. With the collapse of the traditional power structure together with a change in the political system there was a drastic shift from a rigid feudal social organisation to a more fluid and political ideology-based power relationship (Upreti, 1998b)

Major caste and ethnic groups in the study sites are Brahmin, Chhetri, Tamang, Damai, Kami, Sarki and Newar. Although the Brahmin caste is not the major part of the population, they dominate almost all social and development activities in the study sites. This is especially true for the descendants of the three feudal families mentioned above.

They are relatively rich landlords, who have access to power centres and are educated and resourceful compared to other caste and ethnic groups. They have accumulated a large proportion of the land and control most of the available natural resources. The Chhetri is the second-most powerful caste group in the study area. Damai and Kami, so-called untouchables, are extremely exploited by the local elite. Women are still in a subordinate position in all caste and ethnic groups in the study area.

The size of land holdings, wealth and education are major factors explaining social variation in the study area. Land is the single most important resource for survival and a symbol of social prestige. The land-holding system in the study area is quite distorted. In both VDCs less than 10% of people own more than 60 % of the cultivated land. About 40% of "middle-level" people own 30% of land and the remaining 50% of the population own less than 10% of the total land. The social disparity is greater in the Sailungeshwor VDC. However, the number of landlords has drastically been reduced over the past three decades because landlords have sold their land in order to invest in cities, deposit money in banks, and maintain their social status.

The wide gap between rich and poor started to reduce from the early 1980s when the Swiss funded Integrated Hill Development Project and the Lamosangu-Jiri Road Project came into being. The former project helped to reduce social differences by supporting non-formal education, primary and secondary school education, giving scholarships to support higher education and assisting in school building. They also supported drinking water and irrigation-infrastructure projects, income generation, livestock development and the development of small-scale cottage industries. Though there was criticism of the huge inappropriate infrastructure (mainly office buildings) and expenditure of this project, it is the first project in the study area to reduce social differences. The Road project gave direct employment opportunities to poor people and reduced economic variation. This 110-Km road was mainly constructed by using physical labour. Large numbers of poor people got employment opportunity. The daily-wage rate of the project was 3-5 times more than what they were getting in the village. The project also gave them weekly rations so that they also had food security. Later other infrastructure projects such as the Busti Khimti Road project and the Khimti Hydro power Project also gave more employment opportunities. All these helped to reduce the social differences and economic gap between the rich and poor people in the village and altered the patron-client type of feudalistic social relationship.

The literacy rate in the study sites is only 23% (DDDC, 1999). Of the total population almost 90% of the people are Hindu and the remaining are Buddhist. The majorities of the inhabitants survive on subsistence agriculture and are hardly able to fulfil their annual food requirement. Many of them go to the nearby market centres and cities to earn a wage. There is tension between powerful people and tenants about land rights so proper utilisation of the land is lacking and the production potential of the agricultural land is limited. Farmers rear local breeds of livestock mainly cows, buffalo, sheep, goats, pigs and poultry. Potatoes are the main staple food for the people of the upper belt of the case-study sites. There are few primary schools, only one secondary school, a sub-health post and a post office. However, these organisations are not able to provide proper services due to political interference and lack of resources. As seen in the district politics, the CPN-UML, NCP, RPP, CPN (Maoist) and CPN-ML are the major political parties active in the study sites. In both VDCs the ruling party is the CPN-UML. A few powerful district level politicians are also from this area and they have greatly influenced several natural resource related activities. The persistent tension and conflict between two powerful political parties, the CPN-UML and the NCP is a common characteristic of the study sites. Irrigation and drinking-water projects, a local governance programme, community forestry, rural road construction and water turbines are major development activities implemented in the study sites with the financial support of foreign donors and government agencies.

1.5. Structure of the Book

This book is divided into nine chapters. The first chapter discusses the problem context and methodological issues. The Second chapter develops the theoretical grounding of social conflict. This chapter provides the conceptual basis to analyse social conflict and highlights the idea of treating conflict as an inevitable part of the social process. In this chapter an attempt has been made to elaborate anthropological and social learning theories. Concepts such as mediation, negotiation, arbitration, adjudication, litigation, legal pluralism, property rights, forum shopping, constructivist perspectives, soft system thinking, cognitive systems, communicative rationality, platforms for negotiation and adaptive management are discussed.

The third chapter basically introduces Nepal, presenting a brief socio-economic, cultural, political, and historical overview. This is followed by a discussion on the political economy of natural resources. A brief review of Nepalese NRM policies, laws and regulations is presented. Chapter four documents general natural resources related conflicts and their characteristics observed in the study area. It then presents social conflicts related to natural resources in the study area. Then it discusses the most common formal and informal conflict management practices used to resolve conflicts.

Chapter five presents three cases involving land, water and forest conflicts. The first case involves an old farmer's managed irrigation system, which has led to severe conflicts between old and new users. The second case highlights the conflict between a powerful elite group and general villagers to control a part of forest-pasture land. The third case deals with the conflict between two groups of people to access and control a spring source for drinking water. The major factors affecting forest and water conflicts are discussed. Power relationships, ownership issues, the role of external organisations and local institutions, the effects of temporal and spatial forces, the role of gender and social relationships are analysed. Finally some lessons are drawn from the conflict.

Chapter six presents a case of the Asian Development Bank funded irrigation project where severe conflicts erupted in the process of its planning and construction. This chapter shows that formal intervention, if implemented improperly, not only fails to develop the canal irrigation system but also implants severe conflicts in the community. Participation, decision making, transparency issues, functioning and performance of a water users committee, the role of technology, issues of corruption and the roles of communication and information were analysed as contributors to conflict

The seventh chapter describes the conflict about religious agricultural land where landowners and tenants struggled to control ownership rights. The role of socio-political change, practical applications of rules and laws in reality, time and effects of context, people's initiatives, the importance of social relationships are analysed in relation to the escalation, transformation and the resolution of any conflict.

In chapter eight overall analyses of all five cases are made based on broader theoretical references. Dynamics of natural resource conflicts are discussed and common conflict management options and procedures used in the study area are presented. Different factors such as property rights and ownership issues, the role of formal and informal laws, caste, ethnicity and social relationships, power and politics, corruption, communication, information and networks, emergence of local organisations, leadership and gender issues are scrutinised. Finally implications of conflict are presented.

Chapter nine presents an alternative method called interactive conflict management (ICM). Based on the findings of preceding chapters, this chapter attempts to overcome the weaknesses of existing CM practices by proposing a learning-based, people-centred and action-oriented method of conflict management. This chapter analyses opportunities and challenges of ICM, its institutionalisation aspect and provides a general procedure to accomplish conflict resolution. Then it presents the opportunities and challenges of ICM.

CHAPTER 2

Theoretical Basis to Analyse Social and Natural Resource Conflict

2.1. Introduction

In the preceding chapter I described the societal problems and, the interrelationships between conflict. This chapter provides theoretical ground and conceptual basis to analyse social conflicts. Perspective shapes our understanding to examine conflict dynamics. In this chapter an integrative framework is developed to analyse conflict. In doing so various concepts related to conflicts, legal anthropology and social learning are discussed. More precisely, concepts such as conflict, legal pluralism, temporal, spatial and contextual dimensions of conflict, negotiation, mediation, arbitration, adjudication, litigation, forum shopping are discussed. Similarly, conceptual elements of social learning such as constructivism, soft-systems thinking, cognition, communicative rationality and platforms for negotiation are presented. The concepts used in this chapter may generate a lot of debate about their epistemology, ontology, and methodology. However, these concepts have practical significance in understanding problems and enabling possible solutions on social conflicts to be put forward.

An analytical framework helps in thinking about phenomena, to order data and to reveal patterns (Rapoport, 1985). Therefore, an analytical framework is a heuristic device designed to identify and analyse the relevant characteristics of a social conflict. The analytical framework used in the book is derived from my work experiences, theoretical background and field research. Two contemporary complementary theoretical perspectives have been used to analyse natural resource related conflicts. A legal-anthropological perspective gives conceptual tools to explore the diversity of laws (plurality of state, religious and local customary rules) and provides substantive criteria to evaluate conflicts and their interrelationships as well as procedures to manage them. A social learning perspective provides conceptual roadmaps to look for improvement of the existing conflict.

While analysing conflict I am looking at a wide range of issues, from misunderstanding, disagreement, hostility, verbal exchange, public complaint, filing cases, physical assault, personal and social dislocations, injurious social relations, to violence and civil unrest at different levels (between individuals, between individuals and group and between groups). To understand conflict per se it is essential to answer the questions: what is conflict? Why and how do conflicts arise and what are the issues involved? What are the common conflict management (CM) practices? Who are the actors? What strategies, approaches, and forums are used to resolve and/or manage conflict? What factors govern conflict? What are the implications of conflict to natural resources and society as a whole? In any conflict, the issues involved, its cause, the role of temporal and spatial factors, strategies and the process of CM are some of the important components to be examined to explore the possibility for improvement.

2.2. Understanding basics of conflict

Conflict is a fluid and ambiguous word. Different people in different contexts interpret it differently. Conflict can refer to a debate or contest; a disagreement, argument, dispute, quarrel; a struggle, battle or confrontation; or a state of unrest, turmoil, chaos violence (Warner, 2001). Community members use these words to characterise situations in different social settings, from emotional or psychological process of the individual to relationships within or between different social groups. Conflict is an active stage of disagreement between people with opposing opinions, principles and practices manifested in different forms (grievance, conflict and dispute) (Walker and Daniels, 1997). Grievance is an initial stage of conflict in which individuals or a group are perceived to be unjust, and provides grounds for resentment or complaints. This condition potentially erupts into conflict. When this stage turns into conflict antagonism is caused by a clash of cultural, political, social or economic interests between individuals and groups. At the final stage of conflict, people make the matter public and opting for confrontation (Buckles, 1999; Bush, 1995; Caplan, 1995; Walker and Daniels, 1997; Warner, 2000). Felstiner et al. (1981) coined the phrase 'injurious experiences' to describe the process of transformation patterns of conflict. According to the stages of transformation of conflict are: a) *Naming* (when unperceived injurious feelings are transformed into perceived injurious experiences). b) *Blaming* (when it transforms into a grievance). c) *Claiming* (when people charge the responsibility to the opposite party and demand a remedy from them). d) *Dispute* (when the demanded remedy is wholly or partly rejected).

Generally the term 'conflict' has interpreted as the opposite of peace. Many people interpret conflict as undesirable and destructive to society and that has to be avoided, contained or eliminated. However, this is a narrow and one-dimensional interpretation of conflict. Such interpretation does not allow to distinguish between different levels and forms of conflict (Warner, 2001) and their possible contribution to positive social change. Conflicts occur in all society. It is manifested within an individual, between individuals, within a family, between extended families, among community members and social groups, between community groups and external organisations, between different caste and ethnic groups, between political parties, between countries, etc. Conflict is an indicator of a changing society. Rapid changes due to new technologies, commercialisation of common property resources, privatisation of public services, growing consumerism, and government policies for managing natural resources – all are contributing to emerge conflict (Warner, 2001). Therefore, it is merely impossible to stop these changes and associated conflict. The only way is to acknowledge, manage and transform conflict into a force for positive social change.

Conflict occurs in any society and it may or may not be managed or resolved. It transforms over time and leads to different outcomes with a multitude of short term and long term effects (these may be positive or negative to society) (Yordan, 2000; Rafia, 1991; Scimecca, 1993). Conflict has two stages i.e., latent conflict (a relatively permanent condition between conflicting parties with divergent and competing interests) or active (actual interplay of the disputants over a specific problem). Conflict can be categorised into four groups based on its solvability. They are: i) a terminal conflict that seems unsolvable by agreement and results in a win-lose situation; ii) a paradoxical conflict, which looks obscure and of questionable solvability having a lose-lose outcome, iii) a litigious conflict, which seems solvable and produces a win-win or a consensus result (Martinelli and Almeida, 1998) and iv) Illusory conflict where disputants want the same thing but fail to realise it.

Two main schools of thoughts exist concerning conflict (Rubin *et al.*, 1994; Rubestein, 1993, Sanddelin, 1997). One school of thought views conflict as 'pathological and dysfunctional'. In this perspective, conflict generally carries negative connotations and is interpreted as something irrational that needs to be suppressed because it is opposite to co-operation and peace (Warners and Jones, 1998). This view is mechanistic in its interpretation of conflict (Martinelli and Almeida, 1998). Another school of thought considers that conflict can also be a functional means for social change and acknowledges its prevalence. In this book I am distancing my arguments from the interpretation of conflict as 'always' pathological and dysfunctional. I accept the view that conflict could also be a constructive social process to establish group boundaries, strengthen group consensus, develop a sense of self-identity, and contribute towards social integration, community building and progressive economic and social change (Doughorty and Pfaltzgraff, 1990; Warners and Jones, 1998; Buckles, 1999). According to this perspective conflict is a continuous social process and has great influence in shaping and reshaping social relations and the power structure of society (Martinelli and Almeida, 1998). Unlike the mechanistic view, Warner and Jones (1998) argue that conflicts encompass adaptation by a society to a new political, economic and physical environment. New innovations, policies and procedures, laws and regulations, local power relationships and privatisation and globalisation processes determine the causes and intensity of a conflict. Whether conflicts serve a useful social function for non-coercive social transformation is therefore should be a central concern.

Summary of Potential Causes of Conflict:

- Opposing interests (or what we think are opposing interests)
- Competition over scarce resources, time
- Ambiguity over responsibility and authority
- Differences in perceptions, work styles, attitudes, communication problems, individual differences
- Increasing interdependence as boundaries between individuals and groups become increasingly blurred
- Reward systems: community members work in situations with complex and often contradictory incentive systems
- Differentiation: division of labour which is the basis for any organisation causes people and groups to see situations differently and have different goals
- Equity vs. equality: continuous tension exists between equity (the belief that we should be rewarded relative to our relative contributions) and equality (belief that everyone should receive the same or similar outcomes).
- Divergent philosophies: when strongly held beliefs were in opposition
- Lack of basic understanding of relationship between different components of social processes: when the social impacts of their activities on society are poorly understood by the involved actors

- Unwillingness to respond to social, political, cultural, technological, economic and any other changes
- Poor communication: failure to exchange the information between actors.

Conflict in society is also influenced by the social context such as organisation and structure of society, patterns of interaction such as escalation or de-escalation, mode of manifestation such as violence, disagreement, time (specific period of time), belief of conflicting parties and the degree of incompatibility of their goals and power structures. Conflict has many dimensions. It occurs at different levels (e.g., from interpersonal, family and community to international). It also varies in nature (e.g., from use of resources to personal identity). It follows different patterns under different conditions (e.g., from disagreement to physical confrontation, violence to bloody battles) (Jandt *et al.*, 1996). Implications of conflict can be different to different people with different backgrounds and perspectives (Sidaway, 1996). Anger, emotion and mistrust, can play a great role in escalation of conflict in society (Grey, 1989). Perception of reality by different people rather than the reality itself greatly influences conflict, because people behave according to their perception and interpretation.

There are several methods to analyse social conflicts. The interpretative method (Bell *et al.*, 1989) is used in this book because of its practical merits. The interpretative method helps to examine conflict by analysing structures, processes, functions and their relationships as well as the pattern of interaction among people. It focuses on questions such as; what are conflicts, why do conflicts arise and how are they resolved or managed? Opting for the interpretative method of analysing conflict has also implications for the methodology, as it relies on an ethnographic study. Ethnography is a process of close observation and interpretation of behaviour and function of people and organisations through intimate participation in a community (Denzin and Lincoln, 1998). An ethnographic study focuses on understanding how conflicts arise (actual occurrence) and how they are subsequently handled, considering power relationships and the social context (Caplan, 1995). This means that both the personal, psychological and collective social dimensions of the parties in the conflict have to be analysed. The behavioural analysis of individuals considers anger, emotions and the response of individual actors in conflict and draws inferences based on them. In the analysis of the social behaviour of the disputants towards natural resource related conflict the conflict needs to be examined at the level of groups, social classes, political movements, religious and ethnic entities, coalitions and cultural systems. This analysis basically focuses on the collective behaviour of the disputants. In a natural resource related conflict both individual and collective behaviour is important. The following three methods of analysis are useful in studying conflict (Bell *et al.,* 1989):

1. Interpretative analysis is empirical in nature and describes how people behave: how they perceive uncertainties, accumulate evidence, and update perceptions; how they learn and adapt their behaviour; why they think the way they do. Interpretative analysis is mainly used by social scientists to analyse conflict without influencing the behaviour of people.

2. Abstractive analysis deals with how an idealised, rational persons act. This analysis is more common in behavioural analysis of individuals involved in conflict.

3. Prescriptive analysis is more advisory in nature and focuses on what people should do to make better choices, what thoughts, decision aids, conceptual schemes and methodology are useful, not for idealised, mythical people, but for normal people (Bell *et al.,* 1989; Kremenyuk, 1991). It is evaluated by its pragmatic value (i.e. ability to help people to make better decision).

In the context of addressing social conflict, two seemingly opposite views are common. The first more dominant view held by policy makers and planners assumes that there is a uniform single rational system to address social and natural resource conflict. It is predominated by assumptions of experts' authority such as governmental departments and the imposition of their conceptions, rules and procedures (Upreti, 2001a; Pandey, 1999) to resolve conflict. That can be observed in Nepalese policy and legal documents. Another view, which I agree with, despite it not being as widely accepted, assumes that all values related to natural resources are situational, contextual and socially constructed, and therefore, a uniform single unitary approach in NRM can not function properly. This second view recognises that there is no single absolute technical solutions (technocratic absolutism) (Anderson, *et al.*, 1997). Technocratic absolutism is dominant in Nepal. However, this book adheres to the second view in analysing social and natural resource conflicts.

Conflict, wantedly or unwantedly, is a part of social process and function of social development and change. How to use conflicts to serve a useful social function is to be a central concern. The functionality perspective of conflict contradicts with the theory of functionalism. In functionalism Durkheim argues that society is held together by the values that people in that society share, hence society is normally in a state of equilibrium based on moral consensus. Functionalists rule out disequilibirum or conflict. Talcot Parson's structural functionalism also considers conflict as dysfunctional and abnormal condition of society. An alternate perspective was put-forward by Karl Marx citing a vivid case of conflict between two basic economic classes of people. He emphasises that there is always constant conflict between the bourgeois's who own the means of production and the proletariats who sell their labour. Dahrendorf further elaborates that social organisations typically contains two groups (those who rule and those who are ruled) with opposing interests, thus conflict is not only limited to class struggle over economic resources but also can be a power struggle between interest groups. Scimecca (1993) criticises Marxian analysis of conflict in the ground that he emphasises on an economically determined system of social relationship and conflict than co-operation. Max Weber in his Social Action Theory suggests that societies vary between conditions of equilibrium and conflict. In this perspective conflict is endemic in social process but tends to operate in favour of powerful people of the society. Weber gives the explanations that how power legitimatise and stabilised in a society. Weber's social action theory has four major components: role of power, emphasis on organised system; legitimacy and self-interests.

Essential Elements of Weber's Conflict Theory:

- Conflict are endemic in social life
- Power is differentially distributed among groups and individuals in society,
- Social order is achieved in any society through rules and commands issued by more powerful persons to less powerful people and enforced through sanctions,
- Both the social structure and normative system of a society are more extensively influenced by powerful persons and come to represent the interests of these powerful people.
- Social changes are often disruptive to powerful people than ordinary people. Hence powerful people oppose change.
- Changes in a society occur as a result of action by person who stands to benefit from these changes.

Source: Adapted from Sidaway 1996:40.

Two main interpretations are more common in conflict discourses. They are:

- Legal anthropological interpretation (Gulliver, 1979; Moore, 1995; Starr and Collier, 1989; Benda-Beckmann *et al.*, 1998) which treats legal orders (both customary and state), codes, discourses and languages through which people deals with various conflicts or conflicting interests, and
- Communicative interpretation which deals on communication (Habermas, 1989) and collective learning for negotiation (Röling, 1996; Lee, 1993). Interpretative approach explains the questions what are conflicts, why they are conflicts and how they are resolved or manages as well as what ought to be the best alternate CM approach. These two perspectives compliment each other to give holistic view in analysing conflict.

Summary of characteristics of conflict:

- Conflict requires at least two parties,
- Conflict arise from position scarcity and resources scarcity
- Conflict behaviours are those design to destroy, injure, thwart, or otherwise control another party or other parties,
- Conflict requires interaction among parties in which actions and counteractions are mutually opposed,
- Conflict relation always involve attempts to gain control of scarce resources and positions or to influence behaviour in certain directions; a conflict relationship always involves the attempt to acquire or exercise power or the actual acquisition or exercise of power,
- Conflict relations constitute a fundamental social-interaction process having important consequences,
- A conflict process or relation represents a temporary tendency towards disjunction in the interaction flow between the parties,
- Conflict relations do not represent a breakdown in regulated conduct but rather a shift in the governing norms and expectation.

Source: Adapted from Sidaway, 1996

Analytically, conflict can be broadly categorised into psychological and sociological approaches of analysis. In general, psychologists, biologists, game theorists, and decision-making theorists take the behaviour of individuals as a point of departure to analyse conflict. They analyse conflicts from the knowledge of individual to draw inferences. This approach is commonly called a psychological approach. Sociologists, anthropologists, geographers, organisation and communication theorists, political scientists, international relation analysts and system theorists on the other hand examine conflict at the level of groups, collectivities, social institutions, social classes, political movements, religious and ethnic entities, coalitions and cultural systems, etc. This analysis focuses on knowledge of collective behaviour from social structures and institutions (Dougherty and Pfaltzgraff, 1990:189).

In managing conflict an interpretative social reality model

(Littlejohn *et. al.*, 1994) is common. This model presents moral, conflict and justice interpretations of social realities to manage conflict.

1. *The Moral Realities*—consist of assumption about proper conduct. They are deep philosophical principles that define what is means to be a person to live a life and include one's most basic moral assumptions.
2. *Conflict Reality*—consist of participant's meanings for conflict itself. The Table 2.1 shows the specific categories of conflict reality.

Table 2.2. Conflict Reality in Sociological Approach of Conflict Management

Outsider Reliance Model	Conflict Management Model	Avoidance and Prevention Model
Based on adjudication (to be settled by officials, court trials) and authority/ influence (settle by priests, police, local village heads, etc.) Third party intervention is the precondition of this model. Parties in dispute are less assertive in resolution of dispute themselves Win-lose results are more common in this strategy	• Conflict maintenance: sees conflict as healthy, function and manageable • Economic bargaining: promote exchange to resolve conflict by negotiation and compro-mise • Power: sees conflict as a struggle for the resources in which the strongest side prevails e.g., war, fighting • Coalition: sees differences of opinion and interests that is settle by weight and alignment (as in election) • Consensus: sees difference of opinion on alternative solutions, which can settle by discussion and creative problem solving	Libertarian: sees conflict as a difference arising from freedom of thought and action of individual. Conflict avoidance: conflict as a personally disruptive and harmful so needs to be avoided In this model the sole strategy is to either to suppress or to prevent the conflict. But in this case the result of suppression of conflict is more harmful than the result of prevention.

Source: Adapted from Littlejohn et. al., 1994

3. *Justice Reality*—It consists of principles used to establish the proper outcome or consequences of CM. Elements of Justice reality are retribution, competition and distribution. In retribution punishment is the criterion of justice. It aims to punish wrongdoers and use of force is more common. Fear and threatening are psychological instruments to respect the resolution. The assumption is that rules and regulations should govern the behaviour of people. In competition model winning is what determines justice. It tends to minimise loss and maximise gains. Every party in dispute use tactics and tricks to win. Cost of winning of one party is to bear by other party. There is always lack of mutual understanding and trust between the parties in dispute. Most theories of justice are distributive because justice is most often defined as a fair distribution of resources. This model contains four kinds of justice.

- Entitlement: justice- distributes resources according to prior qualifications e.g., ownership, rank, role
- Equality justice- divides resources equally without considering other factors
- Equity justice- those who contribute more get more "to each according to work'.
- Social welfare justice-distribute resources according to larger systems benefit

Theorists like Bottomore (1969) suggest that 'theory of conflict' should enumerate its divers forms, its incidence and extent, as well as investigate the causes and effects of conflict. Theory of social conflict serve two specific purposes i.e. those of understanding the dynamics of conflict in social change and those which focus on management of conflicts in society (e.g., negotiation, mediation and communication theories) (Sidaway, 1996). Basically conflicts are based on five fundamental issues: control over resources, preferences and nuisances, values (over what should be), beliefs (about what is), and the nature of the relationship between the actors. People are constantly negotiating and resolving conflict in their life. Given that societies are becoming less hierarchical, less based on positional authority, less based on clear boundaries of responsibility and authority, it is likely that conflict will be an even greater in future.

Potential Positive and Negative Outcomes of Conflict:
Positive: conflict can

- Motivate people to try harder-to win
- Increase commitment, enhance group loyalty
- Increase clarity about the problem
- Lead to innovative breakthroughs and new approaches
- Clarify underlying problems and facilitate change
- Focus attention on basic issues and lead to solutions
- Increase energy level; making visible key values
- Sharpen approaches to bargaining, influencing, competing by involving in conflict
- Finally contribute to agrarian reform and social change

Negative: conflict can

- Lead to anger, avoidance, sniping, shouting, frustration, fear of failure, sense of personal inadequacy
- Withhold critical information
- Lower productivity from wasteful conflict
- Sidetrack careers; relationships ruined
- Disrupted patterns of work
- Consume money and time which loss productivity
- Escalate to violence and disintegrate social harmony and collapse society

2.3. Legal Anthropology, Legal Pluralism and Conflict

It is very important to identify the key actors involved in the conflict and the reasons why they are involved. These questions directly lead to the study of behaviour and actions of these actors. A legal anthropological perspective leads researchers to see the key factors governing behaviour such as norms and ideology, power structure, etc. This perspective helps to clarify discrepancies between rules and behaviour, their interpretation, and enables social relations in actions and interaction to be seen clearly (Caplan, 1995). In recent days, legal anthropology focuses more on understanding the social practices in the frame of multiplicity of legal institutional arrangements and normative repertoires in society (Spiertz, 2000). The contribution of a legal anthropological perspective in conflict study is illustrated by Benda-Beckmann *et al.*, (1997:222) as: *"Adopting a legal anthropological perspective means giving primary attention to description and analysis of the current legal situation and trying to understand the significance of that legal situation for the actual forms and practice [..]. It means asking about the interrelation between law and social practice, rather than engaging in conventional doctrinal legal science "*. Caplan (1995) adds that a historical perspective is an appropriate anthropological framework to study conflicts in natural resources. This diversity logically brings one to the notion of legal pluralism.

Legal pluralism covers different types of laws such as state law, folk law, customary law, indigenous law, religious law, etc. (Benda-Beckmann *et al.*, 1997). Therefore, it is an umbrella concept that helps in understanding the diversity in the role of cultural, social and normative practices in communities because it shows the condition in which more than one legal system or institution co-exist to deal with the same set of activities (Benda-Beckmann, 1999). It helps in understanding the legal order of society, as it is based on a pluralistic conception of the law (Griffiths, 1983).

Society does not operate in a vacuum. Human behaviour determines the activities or conflict in society and its all aspects depend on human decisions and activities. Hence, contradictions, confusions and conflicts are common in society due to the diversity and inconsistency in application of customary practices and formal legal procedures, different perceptions of ownership and rights and management differences. The actions and behaviour of people towards natural resources is not shaped and guided by a single comprehensive law. They are guided by several local norms, practices and beliefs, folk and legal regulations, which Benda-Beckmann calls 'Jungle of legal pluralism'. They are commonly different and even contradictory (Benda-Beckmann, 1999) and serve as a source of conflict. Even normatively defined government laws are reshaped by actors and translated into practice differently according to local situations. Spiertz (2000) argues that legal pluralism means that in many life situations different people can make use of more than one normative repertoire to rationalise and legitimise their actions. Governments or customs determine the rights over natural resources, but practices may be different than these prescriptions. People are faced daily with different legal and customary practices and normative rules embedded in the multiplicity of native and legal systems (Benda-Beckmann *et al.*, 1997).

Complexity and interwoveness of the legal environment is the source of both conflict and its resolution in society. Access to and control over natural resources may be defined differently by different legal systems. These different legal constructions provide an additional potential source for conflicts. In reality, the existence of plural legal systems in a community is in itself a source of conflict in natural resources. State laws seek to regulate natural resources according to their framework whereas local and customary norms may or may not follow this framework. Many times the state laws are modified or changed in practice, by the actors themselves, to fit the local situation. This type of variation becomes a source of conflict in practice. Practically, natural resources users have different and even sometimes conflicting perspectives, values, objectives and knowledge systems. These differences are reflected in their behaviour. Their course of action is shaped by various normative and customary rules. In the context of NRM, the concept of legal pluralism leads to the conclusion that conflict is the inevitable product of plural legal situations (plural values, norms, and multiple interpretations).

Laws and regulations administered by government are only one of the many forces to change human behaviour and action. There are other guiding factors such as customary practices, religious rules, local norms, economic opportunities and technological advancement, which considerably influence human behaviour in relation to control, use and management of natural resources. People adopt customary practices locally to address the changing circumstances, which Benda Beckmann, *et al.*, (1997) call 'local laws' that greatly influence NRM in society. Enforcing new laws by government may not necessarily resolve conflicts related to utilisation and management of natural resources. In this regard it is noteworthy to state that the Nepalese courts are only involved in settling a small number of the numerous conflicts over natural resources (Benda-Beckmann *et al.,* 1997). Other different, local forums and processes rather than courts may manage to settle the majority of such conflicts. Hence, legal pluralism is an element of the context in which conflict management of natural resources takes place.

Basically conflicts over natural resources are about access and control and profit from their use. Access and control are greatly influenced by property relations. Property rights (PR) are therefore a central issue in natural resource conflict. Property can be considered as the rights and obligations of individuals or groups to use the resource base. Property rights are complex because resource tenure often involves bundles of rights, including users rights, rights to exclude others, rights to manage and the rights to sell (Schlager and Ostrom, 1992). Theoretically people can acquire rights over natural resources either using their historical association or citing riparian rights or interpreting legislated laws in their favour (Bromley, 1992).

Benda-Beckmann (1999:2) points out that *"Natural resource property rights serve to legitimate control over the means of production, whether production is for market or for subsistence. They can be an important material basis for the social continuity of groups. They usually have political functions for states and non-state social organisation, and tend to be a source of individual power and prestige. Natural resource property often also has considerable cultural religious meaning [..]. Given this political, economic and ideological importance, legal property regulations and rights therefore constitute crucial social resources in people's strategies, negotiations and struggle over natural resources"*. Hence, it is important to analyse the context (e.g., the presence or absence of rules about the uses of natural resources, market forces, political dimensions, power dynamics, alternatives to exploitation of common resources, ways of monitoring and controlling the behaviour of others) to understand the conflicts in natural resources.

To understand conflict associated with property rights it is essential to look at the social nature of property and property institutions. As McCay and Acheson (1987) explained property rights deal with sanctioned behavioural relationships between people that arise from the existence of things and pertain to their use. Property rights are closely embedded in the historical social context and their meaning can vary from community to community and the cultural context (Benda-Beckmann, 1999). To answer the question 'how do property rights claims affect natural resources related conflicts, one needs to explore the use-pattern and the relationship between power and access to and control over natural resources.

Natural resources such as forests or land, traditionally used for one particular purpose (for example religious forest or grazing) are now allocated to other purposes (such as the construction of a particular project). Therefore the rights over natural resources are also changing to address these needs and changes either by state induced forces (for example, Water Resources Act 1992, Forest Act 1993; Land Act 1964; Local Self Governance Act 1999) or by local practices. These changes are affecting or altering the existing access and control patterns as well as ownership rights and can ultimately induce conflict. A concrete example is the government-induced land measurement and registration programme, which gave rise to several conflicts in the community.

Natural resources are often interchangeably used with common property resources (CPR) and common property is often confused with open access (*res nullius*). Common property resources may not necessarily be all natural resources and vice versa. But community members may treat many natural resources as common property resources because of their mode of appropriation and management. This misnomer originated from the human ecologist Garrett Hardin's "tragedy of the commons". The thesis 'The Tragedy of the Commons' (Hardin, 1968) emphasises that 'when CPR are used by an increasing number of people, often for different purposes, and agreement governing resource use are absent, collective use may lead to over exploitation, degradation and eventual ruin of the resource, which is attributed to the users' incentive to maximise their own utility,'(Steins, 1999:3) This served as a basis for policy formulations that prioritise private or state control over resources and leads to contradictions and conflicts between resource users and the state (controllers). Hardin (1968) argues that the source of problems is common property, which poses an irreconcilable contradiction between individual and common interests. The notion "common" created confusion because Hardin fails to distinguish between common property management and open access (Steins, 1999; McCay and Acheson 1987; Benda-Beckmann, 1999; Richards, 1997). Critics argue that Hardin's generalisation is too vague, because all natural resources used by villagers do not have open access, but are used under special arrangement. Common property is controlled and managed by groups of resource users, with correlated duties, rights, rules and obligations that help to collectively regulate individual use (Schlager and Ostrom, 1992). This occurs in a variety of cultural, institutional and ecological settings, and with different kinds of resources. In most cases these resources have been defined by different interest groups in different ways according to geographical, physical and cultural criteria (Steins, 1999) and this leads to unavoidable conflict. Before the emergence of contemporary nation states, people lived with the availability of plenty of natural resources and therefore there was no competition and conflict. At that time, all decisions related to access, distribution, control and management were framed within cultural, social and institutional mechanisms (Bhatya, 1997). The legacy of such a specific interface between natural resources and people still exists. However, over time, governments and several other interest groups have directly intervened to regulate these natural resources. People who were using these local natural resources want to continue these arrangements, but there are mounting economic pressures. All these contradictions lead to conflict.

2.4. Contextual, spatial and temporal dimensions of conflict

The Origin, escalation and resolution of a conflict is highly influenced by its context, time and location. What are the conditions that determine or modify social conflict? Historical, cultural, political, economic, institutional and social context, power relationships, norms, values, practices, and property rights and ownership issues play crucial roles in conflict. What are the issues of conflict and why? How does a conflict evolve? What are the sources of conflict? What are the outward and inward linkages of conflict? These are the important considerations in any conflict. The degree and intensity of the same conflict can change over time. The chronological background of a conflict and any effect of time on its escalation or resolution are important aspects in conflict study. All these issues need to be properly examined to fully understand a conflict.

2.5. Conflict-management Options and Forums

What strategies and processes are used to resolve conflict? Why do people prefer particular strategies (e.g., communication, pattern of interaction, learning, psychological forcing, adjustment, reactive, consensual, problem solving, contending, empowerment, inaction, avoidance, with-holding, etc.)? What forms and means are used to resolve or manage conflict? Answers for these questions are discussed in detail in chapters four to eight in this book and some basic concepts related to CM practices, forums and outcomes are discussed in the following section.

Generally, both right-based (legal) and interest-based (alternate) approaches are observed in contemporary CM practices. Right-based approaches focus on litigation and adjudication procedures through the courts and police. In contrast, interest-based approaches look for mediation, negotiation and other collaborative methods to resolve conflict. However, right-based claims may also pursue particular interests and may be settled without reference to rights and interest-based conflict can also be settled according to rights. Therefore, right-based and interest-based approaches are not mutually exclusive in dealing with conflict. The redirection of behaviour and reallocation of resources are common strategies in conflict resolution. Other

Table 2.2. Context Specific Structural Causes of Social Conflict in Society

Causes	Key characteristics	Examples
Social	• Unequal, unjust or unrepresentative social structures • Social exclusion • Vertical social stratification	• Difference in education, wealth and income, information, • Lack of legal awareness • Insecure social system, vulnerability and deprivation • Inaccessible to social benefits e
Legal	• Legal systems with bias towards certain group	• Legal arrangements providing privilege to powerful, e.g., Land Act discriminative to unregistered tenants or bounded labour
Economic	• Economic arrangement and power biased towards certain group of people	• Economic power and influence of commercial companies over indigenous practices • Government policies and provisions favouring to extractive industries ignoring local interests and customary ownership
Political	• Party and ideological biases and discrimination	• Misuse of power and administrative resources by the ruling political party members and government to create problems to the supporters of opposition and minority parties
Cultural	• Ethnic minorit groups hold deep-seated values that define their identify • Cultural discrimination by state/government	• Indigenous people and minority hold different values for their identity • Elites and politicians exploit racial, religious, tribal, ethnic or linguistic differences and prejudices • Groups dislike each other

Source: Adapted from Warner 2001

strategic factors may be reframing perspectives and realigning structural forces to be used in the resolution or escalation of a conflict (Fisher, 1997). In managing social conflict, education and the appeal for appliance to rules are more pragmatic options than coercion and threats. Options such as force, withdrawal, collaboration, accommodation, compromise, consensus, passive acceptance, cheating, lying, requesting, entreating, manoeuvring, pressuring, threatening, demanding, monitoring, arguing by rules, staying neutral, exploiting are various strategies used in CM. In all these strategies disputants use some sort of forum to bring about a favourable outcome. The preference for a particular CM procedure depends upon the context and time. However, the following are common CM methods observed in contemporary CM study:

2.5.1. Negotiation

Negotiation is a voluntary process that deals with a conflict situation between the negotiating parties. Negotiation includes any instance in which two or more people meet, face to face and communicate with each other for the purpose of influencing each other's decision, to reach a mutually acceptable solution of the conflict issue. Negotiation takes place between parties (may be individuals, groups or organisations) to resolve incompatible goals. Hence, negotiation deals with diverse interests in conflicts (Pruitt and Carnevale, 1993). Negotiation clarifies conflict situations. People have different and often conflicting interests and objectives. Therefore, negotiation is part of the problem solving processes (Gulliver, 1979). Leeuwis (2000) argues that the role of negotiation is increasingly widening and is not only limited to CM but it is also becoming a wider methodological principle and basis of organising broader participatory development efforts. The purpose of negotiation is to discover mutually acceptable outcomes in disputes through the means of persuasion or inducement. Gulliver (1979) explains that patterns of interactive behaviour in negotiation are essential despite marked differences in interests, ideas, values, rules and assumptions among negotiators of different societies. He argues that a fuller understanding of the negotiation process will be achieved when it is considered in its full socio-cultural context. Therefore, he focuses his attention on the process of negotiation, recognising that a conflict and its negotiation occur in broad cultural contexts and in social institutions. He compares joint decision making (negotiation) by seeking common patterns that characterise interactive behaviour with adjudication or unilateral decision making (using third party judges to adjudicate disputes).

Negotiation can be categorised into two distinct forms i.e. distributive and integrative. Characteristics of distributive negotiation are to focus more on resource distribution (win-lose). The attitude of negotiating parties is firm with attention given to their own interests and a far-reaching consequence may be a lose-lose situation. Characteristics of integrative negotiation are to create resources (win-win situation) where negotiating parties are open to alternatives and also give attention to the interests of others, through participatory problem solving. It leads to a collective decision and commitments by the negotiating parties to achieve an optimally collective solution (Moscovici and Doise, 1994). This type of negotiation is more important in the context of NRM. Integrative negotiation is a voluntary process in which conflicting parties meet face to face to reach a mutually acceptable solution.

Negotiations generally focus on the best alternative for a negotiated agreement, interest (issue, position and criteria), and process (they create a condition for effective problem solving). Existing power relationships play an important role in the negotiation process. Actor specific characteristics such as position, function and personality determine power relations in negotiation. The actual use of the power depends on the context.

Pruitt and Carnevale (1993) distinguished five broad strategies useful in negotiation. They are: concession making (reducing goals/demands), contending (trying to persuade the other party to concede or trying to resist similar efforts by the other party), problem solving (trying to develop other alternatives), inaction (doing as little as possible by putting off meetings and talking around the issues) and withdrawal (dropping out of the negotiation).

2.5.2. Mediation in conflict

Mediation is the intervention in a conflict situation, of an acceptable, impartial and neutral third party who has no decision making authority, but who will assist contending parties to negotiate an acceptable settlement of issues in the dispute. The mediator's neutral role as facilitator involves assisting parties, privately or collectively, to identify the issues in dispute and develop proposals to resolve them. Mediators may meet privately and hold confidential and separate discussions with the parties to a dispute. In some cases mediation may be compulsory under the terms of laws or court rules. In other cases it may be voluntary, by agreement of the parties. Some jurisdictions have rules requiring mediation of disputes at some point in the litigation process. Mediation helps parties seek to resolve their disputes in a manner, which avoids hostility and preserves an ongoing relationship.

Mediation holds an important place in CM because it is a problem solving approach and creates opportunities for mutually benefiting resolution. According to Bush and Folger (1994a), mediation has the potential to change the people themselves who are in the very midst of conflict, giving them both a greater sense of their own efficacy and greater openness to others. Mediation has transformative potential for recognition and empowerment (Bush and Folger, 1994b). It makes agreement possible, which the disputants find satisfactory and improves their relationships. Mediation focuses on reframing the process of changing how a person or party to a conflict conceptualises his, hers or anothers' attitude, behaviour, issues and interests and how a situation is defined (ibid.). In the procedural context, mediation involves a third party who makes it possible for conflicting parties to reach an agreement. The role of mediators is important in discerning interests from positions, reframing issues, and questions, giving fair consideration to different opinions, assisting in finding mutual gain and solutions and writing up an agreement in a contractual language for its effective implementation (Pendzich *et al.*, 1994).

Historically, mediation is one of the most common indigenous methods of conflict resolution. Laxman Prasad Aryal, senior Judge of the Supreme Court says, *"mediation is the best way to resolve conflict at local level. Mediation goes back to pre-historic time. God Krishna extensively used mediation to settle social and political conflicts. Mediation is also a symbol of grass-root justice where both parties win. However, mediation practices are disappearing from communities and replaced by arbitration and other form of legal arrangements. But to make conflict resolution cheap, accessible and to achieve win-win outcomes mediation should be reinvented, reinvigorated, rebuild, revised and practised intensively that maintains social fabric, root-outs enmity and establish grass-root justice"* (interviewed on 2nd January 2002).

2.5.3. *Arbitration in Conflict*

In arbitration both conflicting parties consent to the intervention of a third party whose judgement they agree to accept in advance. Disputing parties agree to perform an ordeal or a divination and accept the outcome as a decision (Nader and Todd, 1978). It is an informal process by which all parties agree, in writing, to submit their disputes to one or more impartial persons authorised to resolve the controversy by rendering a final and binding award. So, arbitration is a self enforcing conflict resolution strategy. The effectiveness of the resolution depends upon the quality and impartiality of the third party. Does it make sense to use arbitration in NRM conflict? This is contextual; arbitration can assure that a person who is familiar with the context decides why the dispute arose. Use of arbitration depends upon circumstances.

Arbitration can be grouped into binding and non-binding (advisory). In binding arbitration disputing parties agree in advance about the decision (award) of arbitrator(s). Arbitrator(s) decide after hearing each party's presentation of evidence and argument. The decision of the arbitrator is final. Commonly disputing parties do not appeal against the arbitrator's award. Nevertheless, they may seek judicial treatment from binding arbitration if they feel that the arbitrator (s) exceeds the authority conferred under the parties' agreement to arbitrate, or if the arbitrators deny a fair hearing, or demonstrates bias or prejudice towards one of the disputing parties. Another type of arbitration is called advisory or non-binding. This operates similarly, except that the award of the arbitrator is not intended to be final or binding. Instead, the award is intended to provide guidance to the parties so that they can consider the persuasive influence of their positions, as reflected by the advisory arbitrator's award. Alternatively, arbitration may be mandatory under the terms of rules or agreements to which the parties have agreed in advance of any dispute (Denzalay and Garth, 1996). In other cases, arbitration may also be voluntary, which means disputing parties voluntarily submit disputes to an arbitrator by agreement in order to minimise any expense and delay. In voluntary arbitration, parties consensually enter into an agreement to arbitrate. Parties may also agree to arbitrate a dispute at the time a dispute arises, or at any time before a final judgement is entered in a court proceeding (Sangraula and Gurung, n.d.; Pruitt and Carnevale; 1993).

In what sense does arbitration differ from litigation? Arbitration entirely avoids all the technical pleading requirements of litigation. Arbitration can be conducted in private, and its records can be kept private. Litigation is open to the public and documents, unless sealed by the court, become public documents (Denzalay and Garth, 1996). In court, judges deal with matters of conflict. In arbitration the arbitrator(s) decides on the case to hear. In arbitration agreements, the parties may determine the extent to which the arbitrator will attempt to mediate the dispute. Courts typically use formal rules of evidence and require certain formalities in the presentation of evidence. In most cases, witnesses will be required to come to the hearing. In litigation, post-hearing briefs and post-trial briefs are required (Sangraula and Gurnung, n.d.; Denzalay and Garth, 1996). In arbitration, the parties can agree (either in the arbitration agreement or at the time of the hearing) as to whether they wish to file post-hearing briefs. In litigation, the decision is apt to take the form of a general verdict, which simply indicates the party who prevailed and the amount owed. In contrary, in arbitration, the parties may specify that the arbitrator provides a written decision explaining its rationale. In litigation, parties may obtain provisional remedies whereas such remedies are generally not available in arbitration (Denzalay and Garth, 1996).

2.5.4. Adjudication in Conflict

In adjudication a third party who has the authority to intervene in a dispute whether or not the disputing parties wish it, intervenes and renders a decision with the means he or she has at his or her disposal, and furthermore enforces compliance with that decision (Nader and Todd, 1978). However, even if the third party exerts his or her authority to resolve the conflict, there are several other factors and actors play roles to enforce the decision on the conflicting parties. Adjudication is ideologically based on law. When other soft strategies and methods do not work this strategy is the best option to resolve conflict related to natural resources.

In adjudication, cases are brought to court by mobilisation of other agents of the state (e.g., the police, public prosecutor) or sometimes individuals. Characteristics of such cases are highly legally formalised procedures, reference to (some) law as the relevant criteria for decision-making, and the power to give and enforce judgement even against the wishes of the parties involved. In well-developed plural systems, there may be different processes of adjudication using different courts and different legal systems (personal communication with Franz von Benda-Beckmann).

2.5.5. *Litigation in Conflict*

Litigation is a formal process, which looks for legal solutions when one of the conflicting parties files a case in court. It is also a conflict management strategy applicable to all legal conflict management methods. A litigation perspective helps to analyse the behaviour and interactions of conflicting parties (Griffiths, 1983). This perspective focuses on social relationships, feelings, perceptions, attitudes, ideas, and interpretation of conflicting parties in a specific situation. Hence the object of litigation theory is a social phenomenon and normative claims, which looks on how social facts are involved in the litigation process.

To properly understand conflict in the community, litigation structure, process and system behaviour and their interrelationships need to be analysed. How does litigation behaviour take place within the existing norms and institutions? How litigation processes proceed within such structures and how litigation proceeds as a system behaviour are important questions in the study of conflict because conflict itself is a function of system relationships (ibid.). To approach litigation from the perspective of legal pluralism opens the way to the analysis of litigation in relationship to pluralistic social structures and relationships, instead of to the monolithic court structure in natural resource related conflicts. There are normative structures, which deal with the litigation of conflict. Understanding the process of litigation requires an understanding of society. Analyses of conflict from a litigation perspective focus mainly on three aspects: litigation structures, the litigation process and output of the litigation system (ibid.). The litigation process is generally a single flow system leading to an ultimate entry into a litigation institution: court. Some scholars say that prevention of conflict must be regarded as an alternative to litigation.

2.5.6. *Forums Shopping and Shopping Forums*

In which forum people prefer to resolve conflict and why they do so is an important issue in conflict study. Benda-Beckmann (1984) calls this phenomenon "forum shopping".

She states that "disputants have a choice between different institutions and they base their choice on what they hope the outcome of the dispute will be". (Benda-Beckmann (1984:37). In the discourse of conflict, not only disputants engage in forum shopping but also different institutions may look for possibilities to engage in CM. This is called 'shopping forums'. Not only do parties shop, but the forums involved use disputes for their own, mainly local political ends. These institutions and their individual functionaries usually have interests different from those of the parties, and they use the processing of disputes to pursue their interests. That means that as well as disputants "forum shopping", there are also "shopping forums" engaged in trying to acquire and manipulate disputes from which they expect to gain political advantage, or to fend off disputes which they fear will threaten their interests. They shop for disputes just as disputants shop for forums (Benda-Beckmann, 1984:37-39).

Various forms of social networks, shopping forums and platforms exist locally to manage or resolve conflict. Social variables such as trust, norms, customary behaviour and networks can improve the efficiency of the society to resolve conflict by facilitating co-ordinated actions. Working together is easier in a community blessed with a substantial stock of togetherness and social integrity, which facilitate co-ordination and co-operation for mutual benefit. Where there is lack of trust and no-reciprocity in the behaviour of resource users, local efforts to resolve conflict are constrained. Hence, existing social organisations, based on norms of reciprocity within interconnected and overlapping associations in community need to be analysed in the light of forum shopping and shopping forums to resolve conflict. Factors such as access to forums, relationships with particular groups of people, local context, power relations, etc. influence the choice of forums. The shopping procedure may be mediation, negotiation or a lawsuit in court.

2.6. Social Learning: Alternative Paradigm in Managing Social Conflict

Outcomes and consequences of conflict need to be critically examined to seek an improvement in a conflict situation. Often the outcome of conflict resolution may be an increase in the gap between powerful and powerless. This means that the quality of the outcome and its social implications are more important than the resolution itself. What are the achievements and why are they achievements in natural resources and society as a whole? What are the weaknesses and strengths of existing CM approaches and how can they be improved? The answers to these questions will greatly help in devising a proposal for the improvement of an effective CM. There are generally three types of outcome viz.: lose-lose (negative), win-win (positive) and win-lose (one party gains). All three types of outcome depend upon the severity, complexity and managerial approach of the conflict. It is not always possible to bring about a win-win outcome, although a well-planned facilitation may increase its chances. Time is another important factor to determine the quality of any outcome. Here outcome means the result of the conflict resolution, who gains and who loses at different levels, from an individual to society as a whole.

The foregoing discussion has presented ideas on what and how to look at the causes and complexity of conflicts and CM practices adapted by actors. While understanding the dynamics of conflict and the existing status of CM methods and their outcomes, it is logical to discuss some theoretical concepts to explore the possibility of improvement of the CM situation in natural resources. The social-learning perspective discussed in the following section gives an idea on how to manage social and natural resource conflict in society. I am using the concepts discussed in this section to design an alternative ICM approach.

Social learning (SL) is an alternate, action-oriented perspective, which deals with the complex social problems by using participatory processes. Social learning encompasses a positive belief in a potential social transformation based on critical self-reflection and effective communication (Röling and Wagemakers, 1998). Social learning basically emphasises multiple perspectives. Social processes such as the creation of a common platform (forum) for collective action, interactive goal setting, accommodation, shared learning, vision building from multiple realities, leadership development, resources mobilisation and concerted action are important elements of SL.

Social learning emphasises collective learning (Röling and Jiggins, 2001) for the improvement of the situation. It comprises a collection of phenomena which include: learning through observation and interaction with their social context, learning by social aggregates, learning pertaining to social issues, and learning that results in recognisable social entities such as collective decisions, concerted action, etc. (Maarleveld and Dangbegnon, 1999). Social learning focuses on the procedures and incentives that promote dialogue among planners, policy makers, researchers, politicians, managers and resource-users to minimise the conflict and to sustain the ecological capacities of natural resources. It, therefore, structures learning to produce human behaviour that will achieve desirable societal outcomes. Hence it is emerging as an alternative paradigm to improve a situation. Paradigm encompasses three elements: epistemology, ontology and methodology. Epistemology asks, how do we know the world? What is the relationship between the inquirer and the known? Ontology raises basic questions about the nature of reality and methodology focuses on how we gain knowledge about the world (Denzin and Lincoln, 1998:185)

Social learning thus helps to promote alternate CM since it makes a difference to the behaviour of people in a conflict situation. Hence, it aims to find the potential of people within themselves and their relationships within and outside their community that will enable them to resolve conflicts by negotiation (Goldstein, 1981). Conflict management in the context of social learning is experiential learning (Kolb, 1984).

Rather than focusing on an individual agency or structural incentives as determinants of human behaviour it emphasises on how people collectively learn and gain insights. It predicts and controls the way their actions help to manage conflict to sustain natural resources. A constructivist perspective, soft-system thinking, a cognitive system and communicative rationality are the guiding principles of social learning (Maarleveld and Dangbegnon, 1999; Röling and Jiggins, in press). Social learning helps CM in two ways: firstly, it enables people to modify their accustomed behaviour, and secondly, it helps them to develop new forms of adaptive behaviour. It focuses on the personal, symbolic and social construction of reality (Maarleveld, *et al.*, 1997).

The goal of social learning in the context of CM is to bring people together for collective decisions and actions to resolve natural resource related conflicts. It views learning as a heuristic processes and does not only limit itself to scientific-academic knowledge. It exists among the people concerned and adapts to constantly changing circumstances. It is a combination of 'finding out' and 'taking action' to resolve or manage natural resource related conflicts collectively. The process involves feelings, attitudes and values that markedly affect the disposition of the actors. It is a process of adjusting to circumstances for negotiation. It helps to resolve conflict through new experiences both by adapting oneself to change and by using new understanding in the situation people are experiencing (Lee, 1993). It is a dynamic process of adaptation and action to resolve conflict. People learn by action and adaptation, in relation to changes in their environment. They change their environment by their acts and thereby produce knowledge for themselves. Therefore, the basis for managing conflict is experience, observation and the experiences of others. Over time, learning becomes a process through which experience is transformed into knowledge of how to tackle the conflicts (Wilson and Morren, 1990) in a society.

2.6.1. Constructivist Perspective in Conflict Management

A constructivist perspective adopts an epistemological position where multiple realities emerge from interaction (Jiggins and Röling, 2000). These constructs are based socially and experientially. Constructivism assumes multiple and conflicting social realities as the product of human intellect and adaptation (Guba and Lincoln, 1994). Berger and Luckmann (1967) vividly explain the social construction of reality. There are, however, limitations to such a social construction of reality. What people take to be objective knowledge and truth is the outcome of the perspective they developed (Schwandt, 1998). Röling (1996) explains the constructivist perspective as: *"over time, groups of people, through discourse, develop an inter-subjective system of concepts, beliefs, theory and practices that they consider to be reality. Based on their intention and experience, people construct reality creatively with their language, labour and technology. The same people change their reality during the course of time in order to adjust to changing circumstances."* In NRM multiple actors are involved and therefore they construct multiple realities. Hence, this perspective helps to look at things on the basis of potential multiple realities constructed by people through negotiations and agreements. The differences between legal provisions and actions and behaviour of people discussed in section 2.2.2 are based on multiple realities.

As noted earlier conflict is the outcome of human activity due to differences in interests, objectives and world views (Chandhoke, 1995; Rau, 1991), which therefore need to be analysed through the systems' thinking (Checkland, 1981). A constructivist perspective emphasises looking for improvement of NRM through effective CM. To tackle conflicting goals of the actors, especially when the conflicts are on ecological services and environmental issues related to natural resources, people need to agree to interact and act according to the negotiated and shared goals (Röling, 1997). To achieve this joint learning and concerted action, adaptation to change by local initiatives using various platforms for negotiation (Röling and Jiggins, 1998) is essential.

2.6.2. Soft-systems Thinking in Conflict Management

Soft-systems thinking was developed as an alternative way of thinking in response to the failure of the hard systems approach to deal with societal problems (Holling, 1978; Checkland, 1981; Gunderson, *et al.*, 1995; Röling and Wagemakers, 1998). Hard-system thinking is based on reductionist and positivist assumptions. In contrast, soft systems are constructs with arbitrary boundaries (Checkland, 1981). According to soft-system thinking the world around us is structured as whole entities i.e. systems, with each system having properties different from the sum of its own parts, as well as from other systems around it (Bawden, 1995). Soft-system thinking gives perspective in understanding the dynamics of conflict and in seeking solutions within the existing social system, due to its holistic focus on a broader social and natural-resource system. According to Röling (1997) soft systems are constructs with arbitrary boundaries, which emerge as a result of collective learning and action. So natural resource related conflict needs to be considered bearing this in mind. In the context of NRM, many conflicts emerge due to lack of proper attention to soft-system aspects and too strong a focus on hard systems (such as carrying capacity or technical aspects) alone.

Social learning has a pragmatic importance in improving a conflict situation because of its focus on the knowledge network, and creation of a platform mechanism for concerted action to enable rural people to manage conflict themselves in a collaborative way. This process is called soft-system methodology. Human activity analysis is the centre of soft-system methodology, which explores messy, complex problematic situations with fuzzy goals and ill-structured problems to achieve purposeful action for improvement (Checkland and Scholes, 1990). It brings people together for collective learning, joint decisions and concerted action (Röling, 1997) when they face similar problems. People develop common understanding when they accommodate different objectives. In the First Chapter we saw that the relationship between humans and natural systems and their interplay are characterised by conflict and uncertainties. Therefore, social learning mobilises the human agency for collective action, through shared, self-reflective under-standing, to manage natural resources.

2.6.3. Cognitive Dimension in Conflict Management

Cognition is the process of perception, emotion and action (fig. 2.2) (Capra, 1996, Maturana and Varela, 1992, Röling, 1999). The notion of cognition thus helps to examine the potential for creating a collective agency for ecological rationality (Röling and Jiggins, 2001), a collaborative management of conflict in this context.

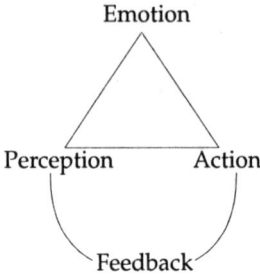

Figure 2.1 The Cognitive System as domain of existence (Adapted from Röling, 2000)

The interrelation of cognition (process of perception, emotion and action) is a basis for organisation of human action. The concept of cognition provides opportunities for purposeful collective redesigning of human interaction and behavioural modification in pursuit of the effective management of natural resource conflicts.

As cognition is being emotional, perceptive and reflective, when people perceive injustice or conflict in their society, they assess it with emotions and act and or react accordingly. Consequently, such reaction or action forces change in any conflict situation (either resolves or escalates). When they obtain feedback they again receive information for further adaptation and action. Therefore, it is a cyclic process of learning and action to manage conflict. The only resolution of conflict arises from purposeful cognitive human interaction.

The four components viz. values (effective management of conflict), context (people create conflict, which poses challenges that need to be managed), action (management of conflict through collective action) and theory (by using social learning) are important in conflict management. From the social learning perspective of CM contemporary conflict should be used as a valuable source of learning for non-coercive social change and effective management of conflict to achieve sustainability of limited natural resources. What is important in this issue is the role of people in conflict. To achieve sustainability of natural resources through effective CM, collective action is needed which has to be informed by soft-system thinking. This is the heuristic conceptual framework for seeking an improvement in the conflict.

2.6.4. *Communicative Rationality in Conflict Management*

Communicative rationality[1] applies when people realise shared goals on the basis of convergence of their multiple realities towards arguments about concerted actions (Jiggins and Röling, 2000). Communicative rationality (Habermas, 1989) is a deliberate strategy for interaction through dialogue to identify the root causes of conflict and explore solutions. Collective decision-making and concerted actions are the next subsequent steps based upon shared understanding and commitment of people. Habermas (1989) says that in communicative action, participants are not primarily oriented to their own individual goals so they can harmonise their plan of action on the basis of common situation definitions. Communicative rationality emphasis peoples' ability to solve problems on the basis of agreement for concerted action. This perspective helps in realising collective action in CM.

---

1. Habermas (1989) explains instrumental, strategic and communicative rationality.

Communication is one of the crucial factors in conflict (Jandt, 1973; Likert and Likert, 1976). Communicative rationality highlights the role of communication in concerted action (Jiggins and Röling, 2000). Communication in this context is defined as 'transmission and reception of ideas, facts, opinions, attitudes and feelings through one of more information media that produces a response' (Hellriegel *et al.*, 1999).

2.6.5. *Platforms for Negotiation and Adaptive Management in Conflict Management*

A platform can appear in various forms. It may already exist in a community as social capital or be newly created to negotiate resource-use conflicts. Social capital is vaguely used and interpreted in the contemporary development discourse. However, social capital in the context of CM is used as defined by Uphoff (2000:1): *'an accumulation of various types of social, psychological, cultural, cognitive, institutional and related assets that increase the amount (or probability) of mutually beneficial co-operative behaviour'* to resolve conflicts, that yield benefits from natural resources being more productive, more efficient, more innovative and more sustainable. All cultural and religious customs and values are not social capital, if they do not promote mutually beneficial collective behaviour to deal with NRM-related problems and conflicts. The aim of a platform is to create favourable circumstances to negotiate collective decisions and concerted actions (Maarleveld and Dangbegnon 1999; Röling 1996). It is demonstrated by: Integrated Pest Management (IPM) in Indonesia, Landcare Movement in Australia, Chipko Movement in India, Integrated Arable Farming in the Netherlands, Community Forestry and Ecotourism in Nepal that creating appropriate platforms to manage natural resources is possible (Campbell, 1992; Leeuwis, 1999; van der Fliert, 1993; Upreti, 1999a; Gilmour and Fisher, 1991). Creation of a platform is an interactive process and arises from multiple perspectives and goals and communicative action (Ramirez, 1997). A platform helps to bring different actors involved in conflict together to understand the social dynamics of conflict, actors' networks and ability. It concentrates on different strategies of the actors in the areas of struggle, focuses on negotiation between conflicting interests and accommodates differences. Natural resource management encompasses both hard ecosystems (i.e., natural laws defining outcomes) and soft system (social processes that govern the outcome). The interface (Long, 1989) between hard and soft systems helps to create platforms for interaction, action and negotiation.

Platforms can demonstrate the impact of humans on natural resources, social interdependence of resource users and encourage collective decisions, facilitate a joint learning process and promote concerted actions on NRM. When natural-resource users feel negative consequences of conflict they search for solutions: create new concepts and ideas and negotiate a course of collective action. The interfaces between natural resources and users who have different interests, incompatible goals, differential access to power and information are important in the platform creation process. Social interdependence (due to the increased use of limited natural resources) leads to conflict and struggle that needs to be negotiated through appropriate platforms.

Adaptive management is emerging as a guiding principle for sustainable NRM. It focuses on designing an interface between society and natural resources (Röling, 2000). It shifts from a dominant linear-economic-goal seeking management strategy to social learning about complex systems. Holling (1995:30) says *"the release of human opportunities requires flexible, diverse and redundant regulation, monitoring that leads to corrective action, and experiential probing of the continually changing reality of the external world"*. He further argues that *"the essential point is that evolving systems require policies and actions that not only satisfy social objectives but also achieve continually modified understanding of the evolving conditions and provide flexibility for adapting to surprise (Holling, 1995:14)"*. To show the importance of learning in adaptive management, Lee (1993:9) emphasis that *"adaptive management is an approach to natural resource policy that embodies a simple imperative: policies are experiment, learn from them"*. The interactive process associated with adaptive management requires good facilitation and negotiation skills, institutionalised interests (of organisations), and flexibility to seek for new ways and innovative strategies. To translate adaptive management principles into concrete form of multidisciplinary action (e.g., conflict resolution or management) is essential.

CHAPTER 3

Glimpse of Nepal

3.1. Introduction

The objective of this chapter is to briefly introduce Nepal and the study area to provide a background to the empirical analysis in subsequent chapters. In this chapter a brief account of historical profile, cultural profile, socio-economic profile political profiles are given. Then natural resource dynamics of Nepal is discussed with political economy of Nepalese natural resources, policies, practices and achievements in NRM and overview of the laws related to water, forest and land including an overview of other general laws related to natural resources.

Nepal, four times the size of the Netherlands, is a country of almost bewildering topographical, ethnic and linguistic diversity. This country has a history of more than three thousand years during which it has existed both as a single united state, then as a collection of independent but interrelated petty kingdoms and finally, since the 1770s as a united kingdom under the present Shah dynasty (New Era 1988:2). Nepal is a landlocked mountainous country surrounded in the East, West and South by India and the North by the Tibetan autonomous region of China. It is situated in South Asia, between a longitude of 80°4-88°12 East and a latitude of 26°22-30°27 North (CBS, 2000). The total area of the country is 147181 Sq. Km which covers 0.09 % of the global land surface. Topographically, Nepal is divided into Mountain, Hill and Terai regions running across the country from East to West. Physiographically 83 % of its land lies in hills and mountain ranges and the remaining 17 % belongs to Terai (CBS, 2000). The altitudinal (elevation) variation ranges from 60 meters in the south-east to the 8848 meter Mount Everest, the highest peak in the world, in the north. Nepal, situated in the Central Himalayas, is a country having large and unique variations in terms of physiography and agro-ecology (CBS, 1996). The country's economy depends largely on the use of its natural resource base.

Among the least developed countries of the world, Nepal's economic growth has been hampered by the lack of commitment, economic opportunities and infrastructure (NPC, 1998). Nepal stands as the poorest country in the world with a per capita income of around US $ 200 (Acharya, 1998). Growing poverty and environmental deterioration has further exacerbated the problems. Environmental problems in the country emanate from excessive dependence on the use of natural resources (EPC, 1993). Despite a magnitude of foreign aid (both grants and loans) to enhance economic development of the country the wellbeing of Nepalese people has not increased. Instead the gap between the rich and the poor has increased (Acharya, 1998). A persistence of poverty is the outcome of inappropriate use of foreign aid and misallocation and abuse of national resources by the government.

3.2. Historical Profile

Originally, the Kathmandu Valley was called Nepal. Before unification, there were several small states headed by local kings and functionaries. Sharecropping and tenancy systems were developed by that time to collect revenues to run the states. The historical context of Nepal is concisely presented in the SNV-Nepal's Evaluation Report 1985-1995 (p. 14-17). This report states that three times in the history of Nepal a single principality grew into a sizeable state and promised to provide some degree of unity. In the 10th century, the Malla kings in the far West started their expansion, which led to a period of growth in a considerable part of present Nepal. The Mallas achieved their golden age in the middle of the 14th century, but by the end of that century the prosperous kingdom was broken into 30 petty states. The Sen dynasty then took power from the Mallas and ruled in Nepal. It soon also disintegrated and the Malla dynasty returned. By that time Rajput warriors from India started to play a vital role in the politics of Nepal and later came to rule the Gorkha region of central Nepal. Prithvi Narayan Shah was one of these Rajput kings ruling Gorkha, who had expanded his power and conquered the Kathmandu Valley in 1769. With his continuous and rigorous efforts over 30 years he laid the foundation of modern Nepal.

After 70 years of growth and expansion, Nepal faced the Anglo-Nepal war in 1814-16. Consequently, Nepal lost considerable parts of her lands as a result of the Sugauli Treaty with the British and became confined to its present borders. With the support of the British, the Rana dynasty ruled the country in the name of the king, from 1846 to 1951, usurping all power and appointing themselves as hereditary Prime ministers. The people and the king became unhappy with the performance of the Ranas and the Rana regime was ultimately overthrown in 1951 with a tripartite agreement between Rana, the Nepali Congress Party (NCP) and the Indian Government. Nevertheless, even after the Rana regime, democratic institutions did not develop well. The first general election took place in 1959 and the NCP gained a majority in parliament. However the democratically elected government did not perform well. Furthermore the interpersonal conflict between former King Mahendra and the then Prime minister B.P. Koirala escalated and virtually ended with the dismissal of parliament in 1960, imprisonment of the prime minister and a ban on political parties. A new constitution was promulgated in 1962 with the introduction of a new Party-less Panchayat Political System[1]. The King was

---

1. Government distributed several thousand radios to all members of the Village Panchayat in order to explain the philosophy of this political system and government policies and programmes.

above the constitution with enormous power. This political system also failed to fulfil the aspirations of the people. Popular uprisings brought the collapse of the Panchayat system in 1990. Since then different political parties (mainly NCP) are governing the country with an extremely poor performance in terms of economic growth, poverty reduction, human rights, social security and development.

Since the beginning, the relationship with India was conditioned by security and economic concerns. In this respect Nepal is persistently struggling to establish her own independent national identity. India wants to maintain free entry and employment of Indian nationals in Nepal, intervention in internal affairs of Nepal, economic exploitation of Nepalese natural resources for the benefit of India and virtual control of the Nepalese economy. However, Nepal wants to be free from Indian dominance. Such conflict between two countries has great policy implications. The 500 miles of open boarder between India and Nepal also complicate the problems.

3.3. Cultural Profile

Nepalese culture is characterised by Tibetan cultural tradition in the high hills and mountain areas and a strong influence of Indo-Gangetic civilisation in the southern part of the country. The mid-hill regions have an admixture of the two (NFN, 1999). The intrusion of a Hindu caste society into a Tibeto-Burman society has led to a whole range of ethnic groups and castes in Nepal. The caste structure is based on the Hindu *Varna* System which divides people into four categories according to their occupational activities viz.: Brahmin (learned people, priests), Chhetri (warriors), Vaishya (traders, agriculturists), and Sudras (engaged in menial services). Originally it merely meant the type of work one does but gradually it became hereditary (SNV, 1998). This hereditary transformation of *Varna* (from parents to offspring irrespective of their work speciality) distorted into the present complex and rigid caste system in Nepal. Though, untouchability and discrimination on the basis of caste was formally outlawed by the 1963 National Code and the Constitution of the Kingdom of Nepal, it still prevails widely in Nepalese society. Nepalese society is characterised by the vertically stratified Hindu caste systems and different Tibeto-Burman ethnic groups (Hoftun, 1999; Bista, 1991; Stiller, 1976). Although there are still a number of geographical regions and villages of homogenous ethnic affiliation, generally most settlements in Nepal are ethnically mixed and shared by Brahmin, Chhetri, Newar, Tibeto-Burman ethnic groups[2] and the traditionally untouchable occupational[3] caste groups. Racially Nepalese people can be grouped into two: Mongolians and Aryans. The Mongolians came originally from Tibet with their Tibeto-Burnam language and cultural tradition and scattered in mountain regions before Aryans entered from the South. State polity and inter-ethnic relations, then and now, are dominated by a feudalistic mode of socio-cultural structure (Bista, 1991; Stiller and Yadav, 1979; Gellner *et al.,* 1997). A hierarchical structure of the caste system and ethnic groups exists in Nepal with high Hindu caste groups at its apex. The Brahmin and Chhetri caste groups and the Newar ethnic group[4] are socio-economically and politically dominating in the country. Such stratification is reflected in the political structures (parliament, government bureaucracy) as well as the highly uneven distribution of the agricultural land and other

---

2. There are 53 ethnic groups recognised by the government in Nepal. Some major ones are Tamang, Sherpa, Gurung, Magar, Rai, Limbu, Thakali, Jirel, Bhote.

3. The untouchable occupational caste group includes Damai, Kami, Sharki, Chamar, Pode, Satar, etc. People from other castes and ethnic groups do not eat food and water touched by them. In the recent days they are called 'Dalit'. 'Dalit' is a more respected word used to recognise the untouchable groups in Nepal.

4. Some people argue that Newer does not belong to ethnic group. But the state has included Newar in the category of Janajati (ethnic group).

economic resources of the country. It is estimated that the top 5% of the population control 40% of agricultural land and the bottom 60% control only 20%. About 50% of the households own less than 0.5 hectare of agricultural land (NFN, 1999).

Family structure is mainly compound and patrilineal with an extended family (Bista, 1991). Women suffer from unequal power relations due to their subordinate position created by the prevailing culture. They suffer more than men from a low literacy rate, lack of property rights and asset ownership, limited decision making roles, low access to political and bureaucratic positions, etc. Women bear the major burden of domestic and agricultural work, working more hours than men, suffer from social harassment and get less food and less attention during illness (Upreti, 1995). Women and children from economically poor households suffer the most. *Karma*, a fatalistic belief that 'the control of personal life circumstances of an individual is determined by divine force, not by ownself is still influential in Nepal. This belief undermines personal responsibilities and displaces it to a supernatural force. This is one of the major factors hindering the progress of women (SNV, 1998; Bennet, 1983).

3.4. Socio-economic Profile

Nepal's current population is 22.9 million (CBS, 2000). Out of that 90% of the population resides in villages (NPC, 1998). Rising population pressure on natural resources and a sectoral-development approach have led to the deterioration of the environment (EPC, 1993). The major part of income in Nepal is spent on food and other essential goods. Nepal has· yet to create a foundation for sustained economic growth and development. It has experienced a high rate of Hill-Terai migration since the 1950s, due to the declining productivity in the Hill regions and better economic opportunities in the Terai (Seddon, 1987). Urban-growth rate is currently 7.6% of which 40% is through migration. Over 80% of Nepal's total population depend on agriculture for their livelihood and the contribution of the agricultural sector to the Gross Domestic Product (GDP) is 40% (Ministry of Finance, 1998:5) without any substantial support of the government (Karki, 1998). Agriculture and related activities account for 82.2% of the rural and 34.4% of the urban employment (NPC, 1995). This phenomenon has created pressure on the natural resource base and has resulted in further fragmentation of agricultural land. Of the total population, 49% is estimated to be below the poverty line (NPC, 1998). Nepal has a land to man ratio of 0.2 hectare/capita and has predominantly a subsistence agricultural economy. The Nepalese farming system is characterised by strong crop-livestock-forest integration. The Mountain-farming system is dominated by livestock production whereas in the Hills and Terai crop production dominates the farming system.

Poverty incidences increase with the remoteness of the country. People living in inaccessible areas are more entrenched in poverty and fall into the deprivation trap. Urban poverty is mainly the by-product of increased rural deprivation. The vicious circle of rural poverty is created by the cumulative effects of small and fragmented land holdings, low and stagnating agricultural productivity, little or no savings, lack of employment opportunity off the farms, a feudalistic vertical social stratification and a lack of governmental commitment (Dahal *et al.*, 1999; Hoftun, 1999; Pandey, 1999). This is further aggravated by the large size of families, natural calamity, and culturally determined social obligations such as marriage, birth and death ceremonies which force the poor to make extravagant expenditures (NGO Forum Nepal-NFN, 1999).

Despite the country's planned development efforts since 1950s, the basic indicators of life and the economy have in most cases deteriorated or remained almost unchanged (NFN, 1999; Khadka, 1994; Pandey'1999; Shrestha; 1999). The literacy rate is low (40 %), access to modern health services remains very limited, especially in rural and remote areas. Major social indicators show that the average life expectancy is limited to 57.52 years (CBS, 1998), the infant mortality rate is 74.4 per 1000 live births, the child mortality rate 118 per 1000, the crude death rate is 10.7 per 1000, the crude birth rate is 34.54 per 1000 and the total fertility rate is 4.43 (CBS, 1998). Malnutrition, diarrhoea, pneumonia and respiratory infections remain the major causes of death in children. The majority of the people suffer from food deficiency, which ultimately forces them into out migration. The Human Development Index ranks Nepal 144th out of 174 countries.

3.5. Political Profile

The popular movement of 1990 had overthrown the party-less Panchayat political system, which ruled the country for three decades. Since the restoration of democracy in 1990 a Westminster style of parliamentary system is governing the country with a constitutional monarchy where three components viz.: Legislature, Executive and Judiciary exist independently. The country's administrative system is composed of 21 ministries under a politically appointed minister from among the elected or nominated parliamentarians. A secretary from the civil service heads the bureaucracy of a ministry under the leadership of the minister. The country is administratively divided into five regions, seventy-five districts and 3913 VDCs and 58 municipalities (CBS, 2000). Districts are the substantive unit of governance, most of the ministries are represented at this level. Some ministries are extended even up to VDC levels. The District Development Committee (DDC) is the locally elected body that governs districts. The VDCs in rural areas and municipalities in urban areas are the lowest administrative unit in every district. They are directly elected, based on the adult suffrage. The village political structure is basically a reflection of socio-cultural stratification and guided mainly by the social status and economic power of local elite. Socially and economically powerful elites are at the top of the political decision making (NFN, 1999). Therefore, allegiance to such power centres is an inescapable compulsion to poor people. Given this extremely skewed power relationship, exercising an independent political judgement is still far from possible (Pandey, 1999).

Despite the facts that a democratic political system is operating in the country, democratically elected political parties are ruling the country and a progressive constitution exist in Nepal, the governing practices are still undemocratic (NFN, 1999). Most voters are poor, ill informed and illiterate and therefore, money and muscle powers are the determining force for winning elections. Consequently, bureaucracy is becoming highly politicised, deprofessionalised, non-responsive and increasingly corrupt (NFN, 1999; Pandey, 1999; Shrestha, 1999; Propublic, 2000). As a result, most of the government -implemented development programmes have failed (Propublic, 2000; Pandey, 1999). Nepotism and favouritism are the glaring characteristics of Nepalese politics. The manifestation of bare patronage called *Chakari* (institutionalised flattery) and having one's own people (who are trustworthy, loyal and to be helped) from an inner circle of associates who can be approached whenever need arises. Strengths and weaknesses of anyone in Nepal are measured in terms of quality and quantity of circles of *Afnomanche* of which he or she is part (Bista, 1991:98). An *Afnomanche* circle is developed by family connections, loyalty to particular persons, affiliation to political parties, bribery and commission and increasingly establishing informal sexual relations (Karuna Management Technology 4, quoted in SNV, 1998). The phrase source-force is also interchangeably used to denote *Afnomanche*.

After 1990, political feuds and fractions have severely divided people (SNV, 1998; Upreti, 1998b). Consequently, an increased sense of ethnic isolation to establish their own identity has emerged with a defensive reaction against the domination of the Brahmin and Chhetri (Bista, 1991:56). The public schooling system in Nepal is fully politicised, as teachers are active members of trade unions and or different powerful political parties. Commercialisation of the education system is deliberately isolating poor people, those who are not able to meet the financial requirement to educate their children in private school (NFN, 1999). This situation is creating an immense social divide and severe conflict in the society.

Despite excellent constitutional provisions there has been a great deal of frustration about the performance of the government and political parties. They are seen to have failed to deliver the services envisioned by the constitution and the raised expectation of the people during the popular movement to overthrow the party-less Panchayat political system (Dahal *et al.*, 1999). The general public is disillusioned with the functioning of the multiparty political system as it has failed to ensure political stability (AAN, 1997). The past decade has witnessed a failure of government to ensure democratic values. This situation is clearly outlined in the report of Electronic conference (25th January to 1st February, 2001) organised by the Harvard programme on Humanitarian Policy and Conflict Research. The report entitled 'Conflict Prevention Initiative: Setting Priorities for Preventive Action in Nepal, Final Report of the Web Conference' describes the contributing factors to instability in Nepal as: frustrated democratic expectations, inequitable political representation, corruption and loss of credibility of government, inability of government to address the human insecurity, social inequalities, lack of confidence in financial institutions and outsiders interference (PHPCR/HSPH, 2001:2). Governments led by different political parties have spent considerable time and resources on prolonging their own regime rather than grounding and shaping democratic principles and processes (Baral, 1998). Though freedom of expression is ensured, political dishonesty and moral turpitude is seen as rife (Badal, 1999). During the 11 year period of functioning democracy the major political parties [Nepal Congress, Communist Party of Nepal (united Marxist-Leninist), Rastrya Prajatantra Party, Nepal Sadbhawana Party, Communist Party of Nepal (Marxist-Leninist)] have captured power and ruled the country by heading the government, either in coalition, or in a majority/minority status. Nevertheless, intra and inter party wrangles are an inherent characteristic of all the parties. Fabulous promises by all parties in their election manifestos and public speeches, to miraculously transform the country's economy, to uplift the socio-economic condition of the destitute millions of people, to develop basic infrastructures in rural areas and to eliminate monstrous corruption have remained only promises for a decade (Pandey, 1999; Khanal, 1999).

The problem is further complicated by the Maoist People's War in Nepal. Maoist People's War is a political movement initiated by the Nepal Communist Party (Maoist) since February 12, 1996 to change the present political system in Nepal and to establish the people's democratic republic. Earlier it was only in few districts, but within four years it has spread all over the country. The web conference report states that *"Maoists have found considerable support among those dissatisfied with the corruption and lack of development under parliamentary democracy"* (PHPCR/HSPH, 2001:3). Since 1997 major political parties, who support the Constitution of the Kingdom of Nepal 1990, promised to bring the Maoist movement under control. The government and the ruling party should have had a paramount role in this process. However, they are not able to achieve it so far. Instead the government has to impose 'state of emergency' and mobilisation of army to control situation after deadly attacks to army camps and district headquarters by the Maoist guerrillas.

A common practice in Nepal is the use of political gimmicks by political parties such as "BP among the Poor", "Ganeshman Peace Campaign", "Afno Goan Afai Banaun (Build our village ourselves)", "Gramin Swablamban (rural self-help)", "Nau Sako Karyakram (Nine point programme)", etc. In reality, the poor are finding it more difficult to maintain a bare subsistence level (Khanal, 1999). Owing to various experiments in economic policy, which are essentially detached from the harsh realities confronting people, economic hardships have increased. Beneficiaries of all these economic reforms are not the downtrodden masses, but a few people without whose blessing no government or political parties can survive in the country (NFN, 1999). In the past 10 years, the country has witnessed a despair in democracy due to the extremely poor performance of the government and the political parties (Baral, 1998). Prices of essential commodities are greatly exceeding affordable limits of the general public. Law and order is worsening and outstanding issues with neighbouring countries have been shelved. Moral laxity among leaders holding public responsibility is on the rise, the magnitude of corruption among public figures is alarming. The objective of the political leaders is to cling to the corridors of power at any cost. Normless politics and habitual dishonesty are the major characteristics of political leaders (Khanal, 1999). Apparently, the indomitable opposition seems to have fallen a hapless victim to political megalomania. The amount of corruption cited by various media reports and the expression of dissatisfaction with politicians practically dwarfs those cited as taking place during the party-less regime (Propublic, 2000; Pandey, 1999; NFN, 1999). Those who are at the helm of power seem to have already realised that their degenerate political milieu has rendered them incompetent to deliver anything substantial. They are desperately looking for easy scapegoats to whom they can attribute their dismal failures (NFN, 1999). This is clearly reflected in their public statements as symptoms of political psychosis. It is overwhelmingly realised that the colossal promises on economic development, to uplift the poor and to restore law and order given by the government and leaders of political parties are simply dreams the Nepalese people have to live with. Nepalese politicians all have their moral standards custom-made (Khanal, 1999). It is often discussed and debated that a substitute for democracy is hard to find, but it is questionable whether the Westminster system will serve as an effective model to tackle the economic depravity and insurmountable social problems (NFN, 1999).

In Nepal, even professional politicians holding high public office have irresolute moral principles that change depending on the circumstances (Khanal, 1999). Political ripples created by alleged moral laxity on the part of responsible members of national political parties are still being felt. Whether or not the conduct of political leaders of this country befits the norms of democracy, the way they are exonerated is definitely deplorable (ibid.). It is true that in a Nepalese feudalistic society, to a certain degree, moral turpitude is an accepted phenomenon and a tragic reality. However, when politicians have gained a popular mandate from the people on issues such as the eradication of corruption, economic reform, etc. it is not easy to condone. In a real democracy, such degenerate morals would have been extinguished from active politics. Moral decadence and wanton extravagance are common phenomenon amongst political leaders (ibid.). What is alarming today is the proportion and style of unethical conduct amongst the leaders of political parties and public figures (Badal, 1999). Leaders of the democratic political parties and the elected representatives are responsible for nurturing social decency and democratic culture in the country. If their own moral standards are deteriorating, the characteristics of society are likely to be the same. It is doubtful how many politicians have followed the proper code of conduct and not been involved in corruption and political manoeuvring. How are politicians accumulating enormous wealth within such short periods of time? The answers to these questions all indicate the moral standard of Nepalese politicians and ultimately the state of democracy in Nepal. If the present trend in moral laxity continues unabated the social situation will deteriorate. The present pseudo-democratic rhetoric in Nepal (Khanal, 1999) will lead to social disintegration. Statements of Nepalese politicians also reflect how democracy is functioning in Nepal. The ex-Prime Minister and the Chairperson of the Nepali Congress Party Girija Prasad Koirala while addressing a central-level seminar on Reforming the Electoral Procedure said *"democracy is yet to establish firmly in Nepal"* (The Kathmandu Post, 12 July, 2000). General Secretary of CPNUML and the Leader of the Main Opposition Party Madav Nepal said *"there is a gap between the democratic system envisaged by the constitution and the one currently in vogue. The democracy in practice is just an elite democracy even though elites not satisfied with the achievement during the past ten years. In order to become inclusive, the polity must orient towards the poor and its fruits to the grassroots. The system cannot be deemed democratic unless it maintains peace, enhances public good and promotes equality"*. The Speaker of the Parliament Tara Nath Ranabhat said *"The State has been unable to deliver the expected level as political parties failed to forge a national consensus on matters of public interests. The result is that people at the grassroots level have been deprived of the fruits they deserved. The state on the one hand has been unable to make laws promised by the constitution while many of the laws have been superfluous on the other."* National Assembly Chairman Mohammed Mohasin said *"It is time to review if the system is moving ahead as desired by the people and correct it if it is on the wrong track."* (The Telegraph, 28 June 2000). Lawmaker Suresh Malla says, *"The government has become the prisoner of non performance. The tale of curbing corruption is like making castle in the air. Any clean parliamentarian becomes corrupt no sooner he holds the portfolio of Ministry of Works and Transport. This has become the tradition of Nepal"* (Propublic, 200:15). *"I have had no works done yet without bribing,"* says Rajendra Khetan, a renowned industrialist. *"Those sitting on top of bureaucracy, the secretaries, department chiefs and politicians are the root of corruption in Nepal,"* says Krishna Ballav Sharma Kafle, the Commissioner of the Commission of Investigation of Abuse of Authority (Propublic, 2000:2). I am not arguing that all politicians and bureaucrats are corrupt. Some bureaucrats and politicians are proficient, ethical, hard working, scrupulous and sincere. But they have not much influence in the existing political and bureaucratic culture. This situation clearly calls for attention to be given to political and bureaucratic restructuring in Nepal. In this context it is noteworthy to state the assessment of the United Nations Development programme (UNDP) on the performance of political process in Nepal. The UNDP (1998) highlights that 'it is not only the government that is found wanting by popular judgement, the political process itself as a mechanism for articulating and aggregating interests and resolving conflicts is now under increasing threat. The growing sense of insecurity and wide spread public apathy against government, politics, the elite and even the professions is indicative of the nature and extent of afflictions in the polity' (Chapter 12-Human Development Report).

3.6. Natural Resource Dynamics in Nepal

3.6.1. Political Economy of Natural Resources in Nepal

Political economy refers to the public power or decision-making over access to and control over resources. The basic questions are who gains, who loses, who has control and how? While discussing the political economy of natural resources it is important to discuss how politics function in a particular social setting. In agrarian societies such as Nepal, though people use the land, the true owner is the state and a feudalistic mode of production exists. Society is not a mere sum of individual acts, but rather a complex totality of interacting individuals tied up with specific social and economic relationships and interdependent structures. Individuals in society are embedded to particular class-relationships and class interests. Political life is an expression of dependency and state domination. The elite, particularly formal power holders, have an interest in maintaining such a dependent structure so as to get the most benefit from the system (Bista, 1991). This is truly reflected in Nepalese rural societies where there are hierarchies of chains of relationships, which have an exploitative structure. There is a formal power structure that is represented by the elite at different levels, i.e., at the political level, top civil servants, businessmen, religious leaders, etc. At the local level these elite fulfil their interest through power. They share certain common ideologies and political positions, values and perspectives (Rana and Dhungel, 1997) and act accordingly to maintain the existing mode of resources management and utilisation. Investment of resources in the development is organised accordingly.

History of the Nepalese political economy of natural resources shows that prior to 1734, when present Nepal was a fragmented groups of petty states, people were deliberately encouraged to cultivate as much forest and pasture land as possible. This ensured them a good living and increased the productivity of land. They then paid a certain portion of their return to the state (Malla, 1997; Regmi, 1978a). Until 1950 it was common for the state to grant tax-free land to officials, religious organisations and individual favourites of the kings or rulers (Regmi, 1978b). Traditionally land was considered as the property of the state [state landlordism] and this land is called *Raikar* (Regmi, 1976).

There were mainly two types of land tenure system in Nepal, i.e., Raikar and Kipat. All other tenured forms of land were derived from Raikar (Regmi, 1976; 1978a; 1978b). The meaning of Raikar land has changed since 1951, from crown-land to land owned by individuals. *Raikar*-land ownership denotes an ultimate state ownership over those lands, which were actually cultivated by individuals as direct tenants of the state. The tenancy of *Rraikar* land has two categories, i.e., the actual tenant-cultivators and the tenant owner. The later category of tenants are those who paid rent to the state, but who could sell or bequeath their *Raikar* land where as the former category (the tenant cultivators) had no right to sell sublet or otherwise alienate the land which had been allotted to them. The usufructory assignment of *Raikar* land to individuals and institutions as a deliberate means of rewarding and insuring their loyalty, paying them for services rendered and promoting social and religious activities. The *Raikar* land grant was practised in several forms viz.: *Birta, Jagir* and *Guthi, Rakam, Rajya, and Sera*. Only the state had the right to alienate land through sale, mortgage or bequest (Ibid.). Using this right of alienation the state granted cultivated or uncultivated state-owned *Raikar* lands to individuals in the form of *Jagir, Birta, Rakam, Sera and Rajya* and charitable or religious organisations in the form of Guthi (Regmi, 1963; 1976).

A Birta grant was given to a noble as a reward for a service rendered to the state. It had no time limits and it could be rented out or, inherited until confiscated or recalled by the state. *Birta* owners usually had full rights to possess, occupy, sell, lease, subdivide and bequeath their lands. Most *Birta* lands were not taxable. It has become the foundation of the modern, private-land-property arrangement. *Jagir* land holding was more conditional and subtle and often granted to government servants rather than to members of the ruling elite. A *Jagir* assessment was usually an assignment of the income from *Raikar* lands in lieu of a salary and it could not be assigned or sold. *Jagir* rights lapsed together with the cease of employment, or at the discretion of the government. The *Birta* and *Jagir* forms were abolished in 1959. with the enacting of the *Birta* Abolition Act and converted to *Raikar* land (New Era, 1988; 28-31). *Sera* was a form of land tenure explicitly used by the royal palace to meet the food-grain and other land-related requirements. *Rakam* is another form of land tenure where cultivators have to compulsorily provide unpaid labourers to the government as carpenters, masons, and postmen. *Rajya* was another modified form of land tenure granted as the princely state award for members and relatives of Royal families. This land-granting practice was common, up until the Rana regime. Rulers granted large portion of lands to soldiers as Jagir to keep them under their control. Rana rulers confined the land-grant practices to their relatives and key officials.

The Guthi land-tenure system also included the endowment of private lands (obtained from the state) by individual landlords for religious purposes. Kipat was an ancient type of communal land tenure where ethnic community was granted land by their king in recognition of traditional communal traditional tenure. Headmen had the authority to grant individuals the right to cultivate certain areas and collect forest products from other areas (Regmi, 1978a). In the kipat land-tenure system individuals derive kipat-land rights, from their association with particular ethnic groups, located in a particular area (Regmi, 1963). Regmi (1972:27) states that *"individuals who cultivated land in their capacity as a member of a Kipat-owing ethnic group owed allegiance primarily to the community, not to the state"*.

Almost one third of agricultural and forest land of the nation was granted to private individuals by 1950 and the remaining belongs to Rana themselves (Regmi, 1978a: Malla, 1997). Local functionaries, all favourites of Rana, implemented the land-grant policy in the village and were able to assure most benefit for themselves. They obtained a great deal of land from the state through *Jagir* and *Birta* grants and rented these lands to peasant farmers under tenancy arrangements. In this way local functionaries turned into landlords. Peasant farmers had to pay half of their crop yield as rent to the local landlords. Gradually, to ensure their rent, landlords introduced the *kut* (contract) system where only those tenants who were able to pay high rents could get a contract. Irrespective of the performance of their crops, even if the crops failed, farmers had to pay rent as *Kut*. Eventually these peasant farmers effectively turned into slave labourers of the *Jagir* and *Birta* holders (Regmi, 1978a; Stiller, 1976). After 1951, the government nationalised all the forest in Nepal to release land from *Birta* holders, especially from Rana families (Regmi, 1978b). However, this did not function well in practice. Historically land resources in Nepal played a crucial role in socio-economic and political change and were used by principalities and national governments for their political goals (Regmi, 1978b).

Large portions of all these forms of land tenure were cultivated under tenancy arrangement, in the form of share cropping. Some landlords were entrusted by the government as *Mukhiya (Talukdar* and *Jimuwal)* in the Hill regions and Chaudhari and Jimidar in Terai regions (pradhan, 2000) to work on land administration. They had the authority to establish settlement in new areas, to collect tax and pay part of it to government (Regmi, 1976). Mukhiya is a traditional institution, recognised by the government of that time to collect land revenue. Mukhiya is a general term to represent a Taluk (responsible for upland-revenue collection) and a Jimuwal (responsible for low-land revenue collection). If they take responsibility for both types of land then they are called a Mukiya. The literal meaning of Mukhiya is the main person of the village. Up until mid seventies the Mukhya was very powerful in rural Nepal. Gradually this position is becoming weaker and weaker and recently the government also removed their legal authority to collect land revenue.

The emergence of a unified nation was the outcome of the consolidation of small kingdoms, fiefdoms and principalities. The state began to regulate the available natural resources to generate revenue to run the country. This led to the establishment of control mechanisms: different departments and regional offices, policies, acts, rules and regulations to systematically control the available natural resources. It can be seen from the above brief history of land tenure systems in Nepal that the rulers used land as a means of maintaining functionaries for the consolidation of power and maintaining good relations with family members, close allies, members of the nobility, military personnel, civil employees, royal courtiers and potential foes (Acharya, 1993). The mode of production in and distribution of natural resources was very much feudalistic in nature. The landless people and bonded labourers are not able to acquire land (Karki, 1999). A large segment of Nepalese society is still promoting an unjust socio-cultural system (Dahal et al., 1999). Therefore, conflict is not only ubiquitous between landlords and landless but also between state v/s poor and state v/s landlords (Ghimire, 1992; Zaman, 19973; Upreti, 1988). Because of theses reasons the existing regulatory measures do not justify their existence.

In the history of Nepalese development (especially between 1951 and 2000), development intervention as a means of agrarian change had three complementary objectives: i) to raise production and productivity ii) to raise livelihood and iii) to sustain the existing natural resource base. The emphasis given in national policies and planning [for example, The Ninth Five Year Plan (NFYP), Nepal Agriculture Perspective Plan (APP)] was to increase production, achieve a trade balance and increase employment opportunities in natural resource sector and enhance national economic growth by effectively utilising the available natural resources. However, the performance level of such interventions through NRM in alleviating poverty in Nepal has not yet reached expectations. There is evidence that productivity-oriented achievements are not fully able to address problems, such as the widening gap between rich and poor, unemployment and degradation of the natural resource base. These problems are not only creating inequality but also creating fundamental conflict between the rich and the poor. The growing Maoist movement in Nepal is an example of such conflict. The implications of such conflicts are long term and are dividing society, disrupting social harmony and cohesion. In this context Chambers (1988:7) explains that *"the problem of poverty in South Asia at least is not now a problem of production, or of food availability: it is a problem of who produces the food and of who has power to obtain it"*. In contrast to seeing production and productivity as an end, a livelihood perspective sees production as a means of enhancing the well being of rural people. According to Chambers (1988:7), livelihood thinking *"is assessed in terms of the adequate and secured livelihoods it generates and sustains, putting antipoverty efforts, and people, before production per se"*. Raising productivity still dominates thinking in Nepal. For example, Both the Ninth Five Year Plan and Agriculture Perspective Plan fully focused on economic growth of the agricultural sector. Natural resources have strong and diverse impacts on different categories of people (land-less farmers, wage labourers, tenant farmers, women, landlords, powerful elite, etc.) depending on time and other changing circumstances. The sustainable contribution of NRM in reducing the vulnerability of impoverished people, sustaining ecological services from natural resources, stabilising social mobility and improving the quality of life of the rural poor is yet to materialise. It can only take place through a strong political commitment, clear vision, fair and responsive administration, protection from malpractice such as rent-seeking (Wade, 1982), expansion of institutional understanding (Ostorm, 1990), and embracing collective learning and concerted action (Röling and Wagemakers,

1998). The economic transformation of more than 49 %of Nepalese people, who are below the poverty line, is still more wishful thinking than a reality. In contemporary Nepal ethics and responsibility (providing livelihood to the burgeoning population) do not drive NRM objectives, rather they are driven by the accumulation of wealth and power.

3.6.2. Policies, Practices and Achievements

Since the mid-1970s, emphasis has been given to land use based on regional and ecological potentials such as livestock development in the Mountain regions, promotion of horticulture in the Hill regions, and cereals and cash-crop promotion in the Terai (NPC, 1998). Explicit concerns were expressed about environmental degradation and a number of policy measures for sustainable management of natural resources were stipulated (Chapagain *et. al.*, 1999). These concerns were reiterated in the successive five-year plans. Community participation in NRM was emphasised in the Sixth Five-Year Plan (1981-85). The Seventh (1986-1990) and Eighth (1991-1995) Five-Year Plans also emphasised NRM by users (for example, the community forestry programme (CFP) hands-over government forests to local communities). The Ninth Five-Year Plan (1997-2002) has also focused on appropriate management and utilisation of natural resources by maintaining the balance between environment and development. Land-use planning is supported by irrigation, technology and other inputs to maximise the production level. In this plan His Majesty's Government of Nepal (HMG/N) has focused on holistic water resource development and its tie with the Twenty Year Agriculture Perspective Plan (1995-2015) (NPC, 1998: 483). Government policy gives priority to 'holistic river basin approaches and the link between irrigation development and the APP. Promotion of the role of NGO's and users' associations, the hand over of NRM to users, natural resource related training for farmers, monitoring of technical, social, environmental and economic impacts of natural resources and people's participation are just a continuation of past rhetoric. The

MPFS 1989, APP, Irrigation Policy, Nepal Environmental Policy and Action Plan, all are rhetorically focusing on community-led resource management (NPC, 1998). Critics say that the current NRM policy is supply driven and guided by hidden economic and political interests. To-date in Nepal the effects have not been considered of making and executing policies on complex social dynamics and of breaking the isolated sectoral focus on NRM (Upreti, 1999a & 2000a; Pandey, 1999; Khadka, 1994).

National Planning Commission (NPC) in its Eight Five Year Plan's Review states that the low economic growth rate of Nepal is due to political instability (NPC, 1998:3). In public finance, regular expenditure is increasing by 44.21 %. The budget deficit over the eight five-year plans has increased. In development expenditure, large portion is obtained by foreign aid. The share of foreign loans in the total foreign aid is 68.5 %. The share of foreign assistance in development expenditure in Nepal is high, i.e., 90, 80, 55, 46, 48, 51, 71, 66 and 59 % in first to ninth plans, respectively (Thapa, 2000). The annual, average percentage change in the consumer price index is 8.3. In foreign trade the annual average percentage-growth rate of exports is 10.4 compared to a 26.6 percent growth in imports (NPC, 1998:51), which is leading to a big trade imbalance. The statement of the NPC, government's central planning and monitoring body, *"despite the planned development efforts of more than four decades, high economic growth rate has not been achieved, and plans have been unable to make expected impact on the living standard of general people"* illustrates the situation. The latest critical assessment of planned development of Nepal has been made by the noted development planner and economist Devendra Raj Panday in his book "Nepal's Failed Development: Reflections on the Mission and the Maladies" (1999) that gives a comprehensive idea about the Nepalese development policies and programmes.

Effective devolution of power still remains a mirage despite the provision made for it in the constitution. Acts and regulations further limit this delegation of power.

Centralised planning has persisted as the basis for national resource allocation. It is inherently incapable of responding to the specificity of local needs and priorities, especially of people below the poverty line (NFN, 1999; Acharya, 1998). Spending large amounts of scarce national resources has failed to make a significant contribution to the reduction of poverty and an improvement in the well being of Nepalese people. This is mainly because of misuse of resources and political and bureaucratic corruption (Shrestha, 1999; NFN, 1999). Despite the re-establishment of a democratic political system in the country a decade ago the legacy of the autocratic Panchayat regime is not over. Nepalese society, especially political parties are not operating according to the ideals of democracy (SNV, 1998). Despite the availability of the progressive constitution to exercise democratic ideals, it is witnessed embracing opportunism and corruption in public life. Corruption continues to be rampant at all levels and is becoming part of the culture of the Nepali political system. The Maoist's insurgency and counter actions by the government mean that atrocities against ordinary citizens are becoming more common. Several foreign and Nepalese political scientists, thinkers and analysts say that the eruption of the Maoist movement is the result of successive failure of the government to govern the country according to the ideals of the constitution (PhPCR/HSPH, 2001:1-18).

Several development programmes were implemented since 1951 with no positive impacts on poverty and livelihood. For Example the Integrated Rural Development Projects (IRDP), a dominant development programme of the late seventies, eighties and early nineties, has a history of grand failure in Nepal (Pandey, 1999; Upreti, 1995). However, there are some successful programmes such as the Community Forestry, farmers self-help groups, Farmers-Managed irrigation Systems, community resource management. The major reason for these successes is not because of government support but mainly because of local initiatives. However, these local-initiated successful progra-mmes are not getting sufficient attention and are facing continuing problems. The current attempts by the Forestry Department to control community-forestry are an example of such problems. The majority of them have been donor-driven or donor-initiated. Interference and influence by donors in economic policies and financial regulations is clear as the Word Bank, the Asian Development Bank, the International Monetary Fund (IMF), UNDP and other bilateral and multilateral donors dictate governmental macro-economic policies and development programmes. For example, in 1999 and 2000 they forced the government to increase the price of basic needs such as electricity, petroleum, water, chemical fertiliser and to remove food depots from remote rural food-deficit areas. The donor community has often warned the Nepalese government about its failure to check misuse of resources and rampant corruption (Propublic, 2000). The promotion of energy production, rural infrastructure development and industrial development is weak. The effect of globalisation and economic liberalisation, is to sharply widen the gap between the rich and poor, making basic facilities inaccessible to poor people. The national economy and financial policies are completely guided by the giant Indian economy and interests of bilateral and multilateral donors.

The mushrooming of NGOs (about 40,000 is estimated) in Nepal is also trapping and misusing huge resources in the name of poor people, while trying to operate in parallel with the government. The Role of NGOs in Nepal is very ambiguous. The majority of politicians, senior bureaucrats, present or former members of the NPC or their family members and relatives have registered NGOs and collect money using their position, influence and linkage. The vast majorities of these NGOs are indirectly affiliated with one of the powerful political parties and are mobilised as a mean of winning elections or expanding party politics. Some of them are working for the religious interests of international missionaries.

Conservationists and activists have consistently expressed their bitter opposition to big natural resources related projects, especially hydropower projects in Nepal. These projects are seen as a source of illicit revenue for politicians to gain votes. Critics say that these political projects largely serve the economic interests of international companies, political leaders and senior bureaucrats and remain a continuous source of conflict. Environmental lobbyists and NGOs argue that the social dislocation and environmental damage caused by such large projects is high. Some disgruntled planners and politicians are also pointing out the confusion and ambiguity in the long term NRM-strategy of the government. They blame the water authorities, who for political reasons, are merely selecting a few large projects such as the Karnali-Chisapani, Arun, and Kaligandaki projects, which cause conflicts later. The Arun and Tanakpur hydropower projects are evidence that Nepal has entered into the era of water politics and water conflicts (Himal, 1995).

To effectively resolve conflicts to advance the outcomes from NRM, a deeper understanding and appreciation of local dynamics and power relationships that characterise community-based NRM activities are needed. There needs to be an appreciation of economic and social status, local knowledge systems, values and understandings and objectives of the users (Anderson *et al.*, 1997). Coping with the strategies and actions of these users determines the success or failure of CM in NRM. Successful NRM is that which promotes equity, increases the standard of living of users, provides ecological services and uses conflicts as a source of learning. How conflicts are managed in a collaborative way to attain these goals, depends on collective learning and adaptive action based on negotiated agreement at group, community, regional and national levels. Indigenous NRM is, in most cases, successful in Nepal. Nevertheless, hands-on NRM policies and programmes the state bureaucracy is viewed as the only suitable approach in Nepal.

Together with emerging landlordism and exploitation of peasant farmers, the struggle for land rights by landless peasants has increased. As a result, the government initiated land-reform measures such as land consolidation, resettlement, land reform (Karki, 1999). Evidence shows that rural landlords, senior civil servants, political leaders and ruling elites, got maximum benefit by exploiting such governmental initiatives and very few real landless people benefited. Bribery in land transactions is a common characteristic in these initiatives (ibid.). Rhetorically, the Landless Problem Resettlement Committee, started in 1976, was expected to be a landmark in securing land for landless people. In practice the land-settlement and reform processes in Nepal, then and now, is highly politicised and works to safeguard the economic and political interests of politicians and senior bureaucrats.

The increasing concern for sustainable development in recent years has raised the issues of economic, social and cultural development through effective land-use planning. This orientation has added a critical dimension to the rapid pace of urbanisation in Nepal and has effected land-use practices. Indigenous knowledge-based specific land use and management patterns, agro-ecological practices and conservation and management of land resource have been overlooked. Fast changing land-use patterns are not adequately valuing local land-management systems and agricultural practices. A painful example of the adverse effect of urbanisation on land resource degradation can be seen in the Kathmandu valley and other major cities, where large areas of very fertile land have quickly been covered by buildings and other infrastructures. Due to weak governmental policy people are purchasing pieces of these fertile lands and keeping them fallow to sell for housing. This is severely reducing the productivity of the land. Squatters and landless people are encroaching onto the land for residential purposes. A serious threat to the fertile land in urban centres is the brick industry, which is using the topsoil of thousands of hectares of fertile land and riverbeds to meet the ever-growing demand for brick for construction. The construction industry is also responsible for damaging thousands of hectares of fertile land to supply sand. The political distribution of land, based on vested political interests, through the politically motivated organisation, the Landless Problem Resettlement Committee is creating much conflict.

Nepal has a highly unequal society in terms of land distribution mainly due to its feudalistic socio-political structure, a weak institutional framework and policies, a lack of commitment by and determination of the politicians and poor performance by the bureaucracy (Ghimire, 1992). Nepal's present socio-economic structures show that land is the main property and source of income for Nepalese people. Due to the vertical social structure and highly stratified economic condition, large portions of land have been accumulated by local elite (Karki, 1999). The present land-tenure arrangement in Nepal is still unfavourable to vulnerable groups of people. The execution of stable-land rights granted by the Land Act is weak and customary land rights are heavily slanted in favour of the elite and restricted to maintain patron-client relationships between landlords and tenants. Control of the land by women is minimal and they even have no rights to parental land. Landlords and the village elite class have largely controlled the new land-property regime. They are close to political power centres, well informed about any legal provisions on the land and able to influence bureaucracy, either in an open fashion or in more indirect and subtle ways. Private appropriation and sale of lands by powerful politicians and privileged local landlords, which were traditionally under communal control, are negatively affecting land management. Land fragmentation is further increased by the cultural and legal provision of dividing land between the sons of a family. No effective legal measures have yet been taken to protect land fragmentation and promote land consolidation. Land-use planning based on land-efficiency classification is weak (NPC, 1998). There is little land-related information and the states lack agro-biodiversity documentation and land-use maps. The available land resource in the country is inadequate to supply the facilities and social services for the ever-increasing population. Migration is rapidly changing the land-use patterns and cropping systems of the Terai (alluvial plains) and this is being further complicated by landless and land poor migrants (popularly known as Sukumbasi) (Ghimire, 1992). Several uncultivated areas (especially forests) which are potentially suitable for agriculture are being encroached, devegetated and cultivated. Expansion of cultivation to forest, marginal land and grazing land has several direct effects on land use.

The policies and programmes of both government and donors have not been successful in reducing poverty in Nepal. The government is spending only 2.5 %of its national income on the social sector while the donors share is only 6.5 %, which is much less than the recommended minimum (AAN, 1997). The bulk of the resources (both natural and financial) go to the rich and powerful, while the poor suffer from the problem of daily survival. Nepal's food productivity index has not increased in the last 20 years and food insecurity is increasing over time. *"The food insecurity situation is further enhanced due to the removal of half of the total food depots from remote rural areas under the pressure of Asian Development bank (ADB)"* says Co-ordinator of the National Alliance for Food Security-Nepal. The existing acts and regulations have many loopholes and weaknesses, which are not able to ensure the interests of the poor. Most NRM programmes and projects did not specifically address poverty alleviation and hence failed to meet the needs of the poor. The structural adjustment programme, which started in 1985 in Nepal with the objective of industrial and trade liberalisation, domestic resource mobilisation, financial sector reform and poverty alleviation did not bring any significant positive impact on the Nepalese economy. The annual economic growth rate remained stagnant, below 4 %, but an enormous rise in outstanding debt led to a rapid increase in prices and double-digit inflation. The liberalisation policy enhanced the privatisation of some of the social services such as health, education and transport. These tend to be marginalised and sidelined to the poor due to their inability to access these expensive services. The Agriculture Perspective Plan (APP) highlights that per capita food grain production is decreasing (376 kg in 1974/75 to 277 kg in 1991/92) and there is an increasing trend in poverty incidence (40 percent in 1976/77 to 49 percent in 1991/92). There is also an increasing trend in the ratio of agricultural import to agricultural export (one-half during the period of 1975-79 to two-and-a-half during the period of 1990-93) (APROSC and JMA, 1995). This poor performance of the agricultural sector is directly affecting the poor and marginalising farmers. The fragmentation of villagers along party political lines has drastically increased with a multiparty democracy and is seriously causing conflict in communities. Civil organisations, which have become politically split, have been totally occupied with matters within their own constituency without any broader involvement in social development. The rapid changes in the NRM sector indicate that conflicting interests will continue to cause problems and the need for strengthening our ability to manage such conflicts is evident.

3.6.3. Legal Dimension-review of Acts and Regulations Related to Natural Resources

In this section I briefly present major state laws and regulations related to land, water and forests. The origin of many of these laws and regulation lie in the historical dynasties of Shah, Malla, Lichvi and Kirat (Khadka, 1997). The first codified law is the Muluki Ain of 1854 that was revised as New Muluki Ain in 1963. This codified law is still influential in Nepal. The Constitution of the Kingdom of Nepal 1990 foresees people as the source of power. Article 26 (3) of the constitution requires the State to pursue the policy of mobilising the nation's natural resources. Similarly, Article 26 (4) stipulates special arrangements for the protection of rare wildlife, forests and vegetation. The constitution ensures access to water and any other public utilities as a natural right of Nepalese citizens without any discrimination. Article 17 of the constitution explains that all citizens have the right to property and private property can not be confiscated without paying due compensation. Water resource situated on private land, according to the constitution, can be considered as the private property of owners so far as its use is mingled with the use of the land (Khadka, 1997). Article 126 of the constitution states that ratification by parliament is necessary for accession to, acceptance or approval of a treaty or any agreement about natural resources and its distribution to users. Any agreement or treaty related to natural resources, which extensively or seriously affects the nation in the long term, should have ratification and approval by a two-thirds majority of the members present at a joint sitting of both houses of parliament. This article created great controversy in Tanakpur Barrage case when the government claimed that the Tanakpur deal with the Indian government is only an understanding between India and Nepal, but not a formal agreement. However, The Supreme Court, finally decided it was an agreement and so needed the approval of a two-thirds majority of the parliament. Many of these acts contradict each other and do not encompass the spirit of the constitution. For example, the LSGA 1998 is contradicted by 51 other acts of Nepal (Saptahik Bimarsha Weekly, 16 June 2000). The following table shows the major laws.

WATER-RELATED LAWS

The Water Resource Act (WRA), 1992 specified water utilisation issues and states that water in the kingdom are state owned. However, the right to use water is granted to the public with certain provisions. Water rights relate not only to consumption, but also to discharge, destruction, pollution and related conservation work (Oli, 1998; Khadka, 1997). The WRA is intended for the judicious and effective use of water. The emphasis has been placed on harnessing the country's immense hydro-energy resource. The WRA does not recognise the existence of individual or community ownership of the water resource of Nepal, irrespective of its origin, place, mode of use, or the nature of its management (Khadka, 1997). According to this act any water source

Table 3.1. Overview of Major Laws Related
to Land, Water and Forests

General Laws related to Natural Resources	Land-related Laws	Forest-related Laws	Water-related Laws
Constitution of the Kingdom of Nepal, 1990	Public Roads Act 1974	Forest Acts 1993	Water Resources Act 1992
Muluki Ain (National Code) 1963	Land Acquisition Act 1977	Forest Regulations 1995	Water Resources Rules 1993
Local Administration Act 1971	Nepal Mines Act 1966	Environment Protection Act 1996	Fixation of Electricity Tariffs Rules 1993
Public Offence and Punishment Act 1970	Soil Conservation and Water Management Act 1982	Environment Protection Regulations 1997	Vehicle and Transportation Management Act 1992
Local Self Governance Act 1998	Land Act 1964	Buffer Zone Management Regulation 1996	Aquatic-Animal Protection Act
Solid Waste Management and Resources Mobilisation Act 1987	Birta Abolition Act 1959	National Parks and Wild-life Conservation Act 1973	Trekking and River Rafting Regulation 1984
King Mahendra Trust for Nature Conservation Act 1982	Trust Corporation (Guthi) Act 1976	Private Forest Nationalisation Act 1956	
Arbitration Act 1981	Tenancy Right Acquisition Act 1963	Environment Protection Act 1996	
	Land Survey and Measurement Act 1963		
	Land Tax Act 1961		
	Mines and Minerals Act 1985		
	Pasture Land Nationalisation Act 1973		
	Land Revenue Act 1977		

Source: Upreti, 2001a

located on private land is the property of the state and negates the constitutionally awarded property right to use it by the Nepalese people.

According to the WRA, individuals are entitled, without obtaining a license, to utilise water for their own drinking and domestic use, to irrigate their own land, to run local water turbines, for personal transport by boat, etc. without causing damage to others. However, they are not able to use water freely for any reason. According to section 3 and 4 of the WRA, no person is entitled to use the water resource, except for the purposes listed above without obtaining a license. Rule 8 of the water-resources regulation made provision for a District Water Resource Committee (DWRC) under the chairpersonship of the CDO in each district. This committee has representatives from the DADO, DFO, DWSO, DIO, District Electricity Office/project, Local Development Officer and the DDC, all bureaucrats except the DDC representative. Persons willing to use water for the collective benefit should be able to obtain a license from the DWRC. The WUC registered by the DWRC, then it becomes an autonomous corporate body. The license obtained under the act, can be sold or transferred to others. The licensee is liable under the WRA to pay a charge/annual fee to HMG/N to utilise the water resource. HMG/N may prescribe the necessary quality standard or tolerance limit of the water resource and may totally prohibit water pollution. The license can be cancelled when the licensee acts contrary to the WRA and its regulations or does not comply with an order given by the responsible officer (Khadka, 1997). Priority for obtaining a licence under the WRA is given in this order drinking water and domestic use, irrigation, agricultural/ animal husbandry enterprises, hydro-electricity, cottage industries/industrial enterprises/ mining, navigation, recreational use and other uses.

FOREST-RELATED LAWS

Forests are classified into private and national, based on the ownership of the land on which the forest biomass stands.

Forest grown on private land is private but although ownership of the land in the case of national forest lies with the state, management responsibility may be assigned to different institutions, for example community forestry. The Private Forest Nationalisation Act, 1957 was enacted by HMG/N to eliminate private *Birta* ownership[5] and to control the destruction of national forests. This act unintentionally miss-interpreted the problems (Belbase and Regmi, 1998). Forests managed by indigenous systems were appropriated and their traditional rights were curtailed. This nationalisation of the forests led to people purposefully deforesting private forestlands to protect them from nationalisation. Communal forest management responsibilities became dysfunctional and open access to forest resources resulted in serious destruction of them, that the government was not able to control. The Forest Act of 1961 defined forest categories, listed forest offences, prescribed penalties and defined the roles and responsibilities of the Department of Forest (DoF). In this way, the Act restored governmental control over forest resources. The poor performance of nationalised forests led to this act being amended in 1978. Provision was made to hand-over degraded forest to Panchayat unit in the form of the Panchayat Forest and the Panchayat Protected Forest. The Panchayat Forest and Panchayat Protected Forest were collectively termed community forests. In this transition process, forest policies, laws, regulations and operational guidelines were revised, user's participation was encouraged, and donors changed their funding priorities. Users, NGOs, and Community Based Organisations (CBOs) became involved in forest management.

The Forest Act 1993 was enacted to meet the sprit of the Constitution. Revised Forestry Regulations came into existence and emphasised the hand-over of government forests to particular user groups. The Forest Act, 1993 and

---

5. Approximately one-third of the valuable land/forest of the nation given to individuals by the feudal Rana regime as reward for military service

The Forest Regulation 1995 recognises Forest Users Groups (FUG) as a legal entity and emphasises the importance of their institutionalisation. A FUG registered according to Section 41 of the Act is an autonomous and corporate body with perpetual succession. According to rule 29 (1) of the Forest Regulations a user's group must submit an application to the DFO fulfilling the conditions prescribed by HMG/N to take over community forests. The DFO grants legal certificates to FUG of community forests. Section 25 (1) entitles users to develop, conserve, use and manage CFs, to sell and distribute the forest products and fix their prices according to the Operational Plan. The operational plan of any FUG has to be approved by the DFO. According to rule 26 (2) a FUG can even develop, manage and utilise forests on public lands after getting approval from the owners and acceptance from the DFO. The boundaries of villages, towns and districts have no effect on handing over a forest area as community forest. The FUG is authorised to impose penalties to any of its members who breach the rules or the operational plan. However, it is not clear who has authority to pose penalties on the offender other than other FUG members. The Forest Act (first amendment 1999) authorises the DFO to penalise the officers of a FUG if they are working contrary to the Forest Act, Regulation and operational plan. The Act and regulation also gives authority for having a separate fund for the FUG, obtained from grants, donations, assistance from individuals/institutions and sale of forest products. At least 25 % of the FUG fund must be spent on forest management activities. Activities prohibited in community forests by Rule 31 are: functions restricted by the operational plan, to destroy forest or transfer land ownership of community forests, to clear forest areas for agricultural purposes (cultivation of annual crops is not allowed), to build huts and houses, to take any action which may cause soil erosion, to capture or kill wildlife in violation of prevailing laws and to extract or transport rocks, soil, boulders, sand, pebbles, charcoal, lime and herbs protected by prevailing laws. According to Section 27(1) of the Act, the DFO has the authority to cancel the registration of a FUG if it is considered to be not respecting its operational plan or not fulfilling the conditions of the Act and Regulations. According to the Forest Act a FUG does not have direct ownership rights to the community forestland. Users entertain only usufruct rights of management of the forests. There are several inherent contradictions between the Forest and Local Self-Governance Act about the control of natural resources. For example, according to LSGA, the authority to control forests held by the VDC, remains with VDC. However, according to the Forest Act, FUGs are authorised to decide matters effecting community forests irrespective of the authority of VDC. The VDC has the authority to hear complaints about pasture, grass and fuel wood in a VDC area, but the Forest Act does not recognise such authority. The Local Self-Governance Act places DFOs under the control of the DDC, but DFOs are reluctant to acknowledge this arrangement. However, the forest act says little about the forest, which has been managed by the community for a long time without being taken over from the government as community forest. Several contradictions and ambiguities have arisen relating to demarcation of forest boundaries, usufruct rights etc. (Chapagain *et al.*, 1999).

LAND-RELATED LAWS

The Tenancy Right Acquisition Act was introduced in 1952. However, the Land Act 1957 was the first regulation giving tenants security against eviction in Nepal. As part of the land reform process the *Jagir, Birta, Rajya and Rakam* tenure systems were abolished in 1952, 1959, 1961 and 1963 respectively (Acharya, 1993). The Land Act 1964 and Land Rules 1964 introduced a ceiling on land holdings and land consolidation measures. Consequently landlords transferred any land above the amount allowed to fictious persons or put them in the name of agricultural industries, in order to keep ownership (Zaman, 1973). The Land Survey Act, 1963 classifies agricultural land into different categories according to cropping practices. The Land Administration Act, 1967 states that only those lands registered with the government are considered cultivated land. The Pasture Land Nationalisation Act, 1973 empowers the government to nationalise alpine, pasture-land under traditional ownership with provision for delegating the use and management of such land to local village boards. The Soil and Water Conservation Act, 1982 gives the government a wide range of powers to regulate land use practices for conservation of natural resources and the environment. The Birta Abolition Act, 1959, Agriculture Development Act, 1966, Land Acquisition Act, 1977 and Land Revenue Act, 1977 were enacted to reform land resources in Nepal. Currently, based on property ownership land can be grouped into government lands (*Sarkari jagga*), public land (*Sarbajanik jagga*) and private land (*Niji jagga*) (Pradhan 2000). However, the state has the right to acquire private and public lands for the benefit of the public by paying compensation (ibid.). Most of the cultivated and residential lands are private. Private land is the land owned by individuals or groups by paying tax to the government and can be sold, leased or bequeathed. Forests, mountains, grasslands, wetlands, areas covered by roads and water bodies are either government or public lands (Pradhan, 2000).

The Civil Code, 1962 made several provisions related to the land. Chapters on land cultivation (*Jagga Aawad Garneko Mahal*), encroachment of land (*Jagga Michneko Mahal*), building houses (*Ghar abnauneko Mahal*), partition (*Ansa Bandako Mahal*) and succession (*Aputaliko Mahal*) deal with land-related conflicts. The Birta Abolition Act, 1959 was intended to abolish the feudal system of utilising land without paying any revenue to the state (Oli, 1998:35). The Nepal Mine Act, 1966 stipulates that any minerals located in the land of any individuals within the kingdom of Nepal shall be the property of the government. Any person or organisation must obtain certification of eligibility to mine those minerals (ibid.:40). The Guthi Corporation Act, 1976 and the chapter on Guthi of the 1963 National Code deal with guthi lands. Section 2(C) of the act defines guthi as: 'endowment made by any philanthropist through relinquishment of his/her title to movable or immovable property or any income-yielding fund, for the construction, operation or maintenance of any temples, rest-houses, road-side shelter, inn, well, tank, bridge, school, houses, or institutions in order to run a monastery or celebrate a religious occasion, ceremony or festival or any religious and philanthropic purpose' (ibid.: 41). Section 3 of the same act establishes a Guthi Corporation to manage *guthi* property. Sections 55, 56 and 57 deal with the punishment of anyone who registers the *guthi* land as *raikar*, who misappropriate ornaments or subverts the norms of traditional religion. Section 59 (1) empowers the Guthi Corporation to take action against those who commit the actions specified in sections 55 to 58. Section 60 gives judicial power to the Corporation to record statements, summon witnesses, and produce evidence. The *guthi* property has to be used for the purpose for which it was originally established. According to the decision of Supreme Court of the Kingdom of Nepal 'the right of *guthi* holders of *guthi* property handed down from ancestors is only to own and utilise it in accordance with the terms and conditions, by continuing the worship and religious festivals. No individuals shall have the sole right to it and no one can destroy or misappropriate the same (ibid.: 41-42).

The Land Act, 1964 was intended to divert inactive capital and pressures of the growing population from the land to other sectors of the economy. This act defines tenancy conditions, ownership rights and the ceiling for holding land. The revised act makes it possible for tenants to have 50 % legal ownership of tenanted land without making any investments. According to the act any land held by a person in access of the ceiling set forth in section 7 devolves to the government and any individual's rights to it terminate. However, this still has not properly been translated into practice. It is reported that more than 35 % of the NRM related-conflict cases in Nepalese courts are related to land disputes (Oli, 1998:44).

The Arbitration Act, 1981 makes legal provision for

arbitration in disputes. Section 3 of the act states that any dispute under bilateral or multi-lateral agreement may be settled through arbitration. This means that it is not possible to have arbitration in those conflicts, which are not covered by contract or agreement. This act is mainly for commerce, trade and industry-related conflicts, not for social and natural resource conflicts.

LEGAL PLURALISM AND CONFLICT IN NATURAL RESOURCES

Formal laws and regulations are not the only set of rules and legal principles that govern the actions and behaviour of people engaged in social conflicts. In reality people are confronted with a wide range of co-existing, multi-layered formal and informal legal phenomena. In practice the legal system is extremely complex due to it's multiple structure and local adjustments. In practice, not only state laws but also religious, customary, and local laws influence NRM and related conflict. To understand management of conflict it is crucial to understand the role of legal pluralism, which does not limit the solution of all social and natural resource conflicts to the interpretation of statutory laws and governmental regulations. The interpretation of natural-resource rights, the social and economic functions of natural resources and their management practices are different in these plural legal systems in society (Pradhan *et al*, 1997). Mere origin of laws and regulations from the state does not necessarily ensure the anticipated results in society. All the actors (those who develop and execute laws and those who follow the laws) have to respect these laws and modify their behaviour accordingly. This is a huge challenge for contemporary Nepal. People use legal rules and laws to legitimise their claims and counter claims in social and natural resource conflict. During this process local people interpret these rules differently generating new informal, unofficial rules. In this respect all laws (generated from the source of state power and authority, custom or religion) become intermingled in practice and state law alone can not govern society.

Different local innovations, in the form of customary practices, may exist in a community to sustain the resource base and resolve conflict. Handing these down to successive generations and people is strictly adhered to. For example, Oli (1998) in his study in the Lamjung district found that primary users of grazing and forest lands have customary rights to appropriate, manage and control them. However, they allow secondary and tertiary users to collect or harvest resources, as defined by them, in return for nominal payment. Such practices are also found in the high hills of the study district. The aim of regulating resources in this way was to maintain a balance between socio-economic and ecological benefits through local management systems. However, such traditional rights and resource management systems are increasingly weakened by the government through the introduction of new systems of users' rights. This has not only led to enormous conflicts between new and old users but also to the disappearance of indigenous community led NRM practices (Malla, 1997; Oli, 1998; Upreti, 1998b).

According to both formal and customary laws, many of the community-based natural resources are interpreted as common property resources of the state (*res publica*) but used by community as communal property (*res communis*). None of the resources in village are interpreted as no-one's property (*res nullis*). According to the respondents of both research sites and reference sites, access to natural resources was not open to all in their community, rather they were shared, managed and developed according to their local customs. It is interesting to note that people have been adopting and adjusting these local management practices to external changes by gradually modifying their customs which have developed since ancient time.

High-hill and mountain farmers in the study area, especially from the northern part of the district still mainly practice a transhumant system (migratory practices) of animal rearing. In this system farmers adopt the indigenous practice of shifting animals to the high altitude up-side grazing area (locally called *Unbauli*) by March and returning them to the down side grazing area (locally called as *Undauli*) in early October. They even have defined harvesting limits of some of the most commonly used plant species such as *Arundrinaria spp.*, herbal plants, wild oilseeds and the Nepali paper-making plant[6] (*Daphne bholua*) to prevent them from over use. The rotational grazing rules are strictly followed by herders to prevent deterioration of grazing lands from overgrazing, and enable regeneration in trampled areas. Those who disobey these rules are punished. These rules do not allow herders from other areas to graze in their common area or harvest forest products. These rules, protection practices and management systems were working properly before the intervention of the government. The provision of licensing for hunting and NTFP harvesting, the development of transportation (road) and telecommunication facilities are affecting these indigenous management systems. The issues discussed above have shown that legal centralism is not the solution for natural-resource conflict and the importance of legal diversity needs to be acknowledged.

---

6. This is a special plant called "Lokta" which has been used by local people since time immemorial to make indigenous Nepali paper. This was a regular source of income for rural people in earlier times. Later, after the imposition of government rules the indigenous paper making industry became ruin by commercial traders.

CHAPTER 4

Conflict as an Inevitable Part of Society— An Overview of Social Conflicts and their Management in Nepal

4.1. Introduction

In the previous chapter I explained the historical, cultural, socio-economic and political contexts and legal framework that affect social and natural resource conflicts in Nepal. This chapter highlights major social conflicts and gives account of their characteristics, their management practices and different constellations of conflicting parties i.e., individual v/s individual, individual v/s group, group v/s group and individual/group v/s agencies of the state. The observed conflicts ranged from simply perceived injurious experiences to transformation of them into disputes and violence. Internal, external and contextual causes, specific ways of dealing with the conflicts, legal aspects, performance of state instituted conflict resolution mechanisms and the role of spatial and temporal forces in conflict are discussed.

4.2. General Conflict in Society

Several social conflicts observed in the study area. These conflicts were related to borrowing and transactions, caste and ethnicity, external development interventions, family matters, party politics, character defamation, prostitution and sexual abuse, religious clashes, etc. However, all these conflicts were interwoven and linked with natural-resource conflicts, making it impossible to draw a clear demarcation between social and natural resource conflicts in practice. Major social conflicts observed in the study area are as follow.

4.2.1. Transaction-related Conflict

Common transaction-related conflicts reported in the study area were lending and borrowing, repayment, fake documents and forgery, receipt of loans, extending credit, wage payment (between wage labour and landlords), share of livestock and results of the sale of animals and grain. The failure to repay a debt in time was the most common cause of conflict in lending and borrowing. Village moneylenders charge up to 60% interest rate (5% per month). If borrowers fail to pay the principal amount and or interest within the agreed time then they take the property (land, gold, animals and other valuable materials) from the house of the borrowers. That creates severe conflict. In the study area there is still a practice of lending cereal grain measured with smaller utensils (*pathi*) and receiving payment measured with a bigger one. The lender adding a zero to the amount lent in the signed written document is still prevalent. One respondent anonymously, explained that several years ago he received 500 rupees from his neighbour *Mukhiya* and paid the interest every year in terms of kind (paddy grain). But after 7 years the Mukhiya asked him to pay 5000 rupees as a principal amount. When he refused to do so, saying that he had only borrowed 500 rupees then he was shown the agreement document with 5000, which had his fingerprint. The 'zero' had simply been added to the 500 in the document. Conflict also arose due to changes in an original document or the preparation of fake documents. Delayed or lack of payment for animals sold on credit was another common transaction-related conflict. In most such cases, the conflicts were managed locally, usually in favour of well-off people, without escalating into serious disputes. In a close society people, especially the weak ones, do not want to ruin the established relations. They adjust their dissatisfaction. However, since the early 1990s such a pattern of tolerance has become socially redefined. These conflicts are therefore becoming a means of adjusting the existing pattern of relationships to changing conditions.

4.2.2. Caste and Ethnicity-related Conflicts

Ethnic identity and the superiority felt by higher caste groups were major causes of ethnic/caste-related conflicts. People from the Tibeto-Burman ethnic group, who are also called *Matuwalis* (as they traditionally prepare liquor and drink regularly in their home), are prone to taking part in open conflict and are also quick in resolving them. This trend is also observed in drunken Brahmin, Chhetri and Newar people. In general, Brahmin, Chhetri and Newar try to hide conflict and keep it in a latent stage until they think they will benefit from it. Main forums creating conflicts and their negotiations among *Matwalis* were fairs, religious occasions, festivals and marriage ceremonies where conflicts about molesting girls, borrowing and lending or for drinking excessively without reason are common. Over the last few decades Brahmin and Chhetri have also become increasingly involved in such activities. Recently, some people, mainly untouchables, are protesting against the caste-bias injustices such as untouchability, prohibition to enter temples and other religious and public places, which lead to conflict between orthodox Hindu religious groups and activists. It is observed that conflicts within a caste, clan or family are, as much as possible, settled internally. Making liquor and selling it in the community is increasing conflicts in the study area. Even some Brahmin families[1] are involved in the liquor business, which gives rise to a lot of conflict within the Brahmin caste people and between the villagers. Love marriage from cross caste groups has caused several conflicts in the village. For example, there was severe conflict when the daughter of the most powerful Brahmin elite, *Luplon* was taken by an untouchable *Matwali-Kalesarkiko chhoro*. A similar situation was

---

1. According to the Hindu custom Brahmin families are not allowed to make and drink liquor.

observed when a higher caste Brahmin married the daughter of the powerful Mukhiya. The Mukhiya banned all religious functions in the village performed by the close relatives and family members of the bridegroom. He also threatened to attack and socially reject them, if they did not obey his authority. In both cases the children of their daughters became instrumental in bringing the families into negotiation, resulting in a normal relationship.

4.2.3. Family Related Conflict

Conflicts between a wife and husband due to: polygamy, carelessness to wives, child marriage, inter-caste marriage, fraudulent marriage, separation, alimony and divorce were common. Similarly, pregnancy and abortion, paternity, conflict between parents and sons and/or between brothers for parental property partition were also observed. In polygamous families feuds often took place between wives especially for recognition, respect, property holding and alimony. People generally do not report cases related to rape and molestation due to shame and the severe negative consequences on the remaining life of the women.

Children can be a source of conflict as well as an effective means of its resolution and a means of developing relations. Children are normally responsible for grazing cattle in the study area. If the grazing animals damage crops in the surrounding fields while the children play, then crop owners often catch the animals and punish the children. This has led to conflict between parents and crop owners. Fights between children also lead to conflict between their families. However, some sever conflicts between families were eased and brought to the negotiation stage by the children. By the children going to each other's homes, eating together, playing together and sharing their parent's regret for disputes, interaction is initiated between the elders for negotiation.

4.2.4. Development Intervention-related Conflicts

Development interventions have introduced several conflicts

into the study area. Work of some NGOs and activists have created conflicts as their support focused on a particular group, mainly disadvantaged people, leaving the local elite feeling ignored and humiliated. Conflicts created by development interventions are not only causing obstruction to successful implementation of such projects but also creating social misunderstanding and tension in society. The consequences of such conflict result in the loss of faith, loss of property, physical fight, migration, etc. Several conflicts erupted simply because of technocratic, positivist top-down development interventions. Most of them were designed to fulfil the vested interests of the vicious circle of technocrats-bureaucrats and politicians. The most common conflicts related to development interventions were misuse of externally obtained financial sources (cash and kind) and abuse of authority. It was pointed out that conflict due to nepotism in the allocation of development funds to party supporters, elite, relatives, and influential people is a well-established reality in villages. Some time this was arranged differently, by dividing the total amount of such a fund among different political parties by mutual consensus to minimise the conflict between them.

For example, in 1999, a wider conflict arose in the Pawoti VDC due to the initiation of seasonal road construction. Initially, the VDC who decided to construct a seasonal road to its headquarters from external financial support as well as by its own resources, obtained no objections from landowners for the alignment of the road. Later two groups of people within the VDC confronted to bring the road to go to their village in the opposite direction. Then the landowners who had previously agreed to provide land refused. This conflict was linked with forest (which route causes more damage to forests), water (destruction of canals, drinking water ponds/sources) and land (landslide and loss of fertile land). Development interventions from external agencies such as the World Bank (WB), UNDP, ADB are creating serious conflicts, mainly due to their ignorance of local dynamics and top-down decisions based on normative legal and policy frameworks. For example, Kaplan (1995), citing the land measurement and registration programme of the government, argues that when outsider organisations enter the village setting, the number of conflicts enormously increases. In the sixth chapter, I will discuss in detail how external-development intervention creates conflict. It is interesting to note that the same irrigation and drinking water schemes are being financed/supported by different development programmes (e.g., DDC programme, Agricultural development Bank-Nepal (ADB-N) loan, DIO, DWSO, VDC) for maintenance and repair. Even more interesting is that technicians force users to demand high cost structures in their rehabilitation systems while farmers prefer simple structures.

4.2.5. *Party Politics Related Conflict*

Political arguments are one of the major causes of conflict in the study area. The Nepal Mediation Study Report (Kaplan, 1995) shows that allegiance to political parties is intruding enormously and overriding other traditional forms of allegiances. This is more common in high caste groups, people close to city centres and educated ones. After the restoration of democracy, society divided into rightist and leftist political camps. They are interpreting issues according to their ideology and political interests. Leftist communist groups are further divided into leftist and ultra leftist. The Communist Party-Maoist represent the ultra-leftist group and they have been struggling for 7 years to establish socialism through class struggle and a people's revolution. The term class struggle is used mainly in Marxist conflict theory for an inevitable struggle between social classes, which result from their conflicting interests. It implies that the process of social stratification endangers potential or actual attempts on the part of whole social classes, or segments of them, to maintain or redistribute existing arrangements of power, wealth and prestige. Other leftist and rightist political parties are working under the framework of multiparty democracy in Nepal. This ideological conflict between the Maoist and other political parties is becoming a major threat to peace and security in the country.

4.2.6. *Other Conflicts*

There are several other conflicts observed during the study period, which do not belong to any of the above groups. These are: theft, looting, physical fights and damage of property, character defamation, drug and girl trafficking, prostitution, sexual abuse (harassment, rape and molestation), blame of religious (between Hindu and Christian) and cultural (between Brahmin/Chhetri and other ethnic groups) invasions and caste biased injustice and witch hunts.

4.3. Common Natural-resource Related Conflicts

Since the Rana regime, conflicting interests between demands of the state revenue, commercial exploitation of natural resources, local community's need, and conservation objectives are the centre of conflict in NRM (Malla, 1997; Regmi, 1972; Oli, 1998; Upreti, 2000e). Changes in legislation, policies, and strategies together with the changes in the political system have provided fertile ground for emerging conflicts. Many conflicts have arisen as a response to conflicting NRM agendas; policy clashes, competition over access to natural resources, jurisdictional overlap among the government agencies, political and commercial interests and pace of exploitation of these resources (Shivakoti *et al.*, 1996; Oli, 1998; Malla, 1997). The Nepal Mediation Study Report (Kaplan, 1995) indicates that land, water and forest-related conflicts are the most frequent in Nepal.

Most of natural resource related conflict cases reported were related to the appropriation, use, and control of land, forest and water, which is hardly surprising in a country where more than 80% of the population is based in the agricultural sector. Both the national statistics and field data confirm that land issues dominate the majorities of non-criminal disputes. The earlier research finding of New Era (1988) also indicated that 27% of the total number of conflict cases were related to land.

Numerous land and forest-related conflicts were created mainly due to the unsystematic and incomplete land-registration and record-keeping process (Chapagain, *et al.,* 1999) and contradictions in the respective acts. (Thapa and Weber, 1994; Upreti, 1999a; Oli, 1998; Khadka, 1997). It was already mentioned in section 3.5 that several policies and regulations related to land, agriculture, forests and water contradict each other. For example conflict exists between the Forest Act, 1993, Water Resources Act, 1992 and Local Self-Governance Act, 1998 on control of forest and water resources. In a key informant interview one of the law experts says: ' *natural resource related laws and regulations are not only creating numerous conflicts but also virtually failing to govern the natural resources sector. A lack of a sincere commitment to execute laws and manipulation of them for individual benefit are omnipotent characteristics of the Nepalese legal sector'.* Conflict between: national parks/reserves and local people, industries and civil society, larger natural resource projects such as the Kaligandaki Hydropower Project or the Melamchi Drinking Water project and local people, government agencies and NGOs and those between forest bureaucrats and FECOFUN are just a few examples among the thousands of natural resource related conflicts observed in Nepal. The legacy of the long existence of the top-down approach is still strong and devolution of power is easier said than done. In any natural resource projects and programmes' interventions, bureaucrats from central, regional and district levels, as well as DDC and VDC first seek their authority and power within such interventions. They try to manoeuvre these projects and programmes in their favour, entangling them in a power struggle rather than giving support to local communities. Major conflict related to land, forest and water is presented in the following section:

4.3.1 Land-related Conflicts

Several land-related conflicts were observed in the study area. Conflicts over boundary and demarcation between different individual landowners and between government and individuals were common. The issue of ownership and land rights was another important area of conflict. The legality and legitimacy of the right and ownership is often questioned and challenged by people in different land-ownership arrangements. Tenancy rights and tenant eviction were other major conflict issues in the study area. The Land Act of 1964 (and its various amendments) has made provision for tenancy rights and the abolition of dual ownership. This is also highlighted in different land-related policies and legislation. Tenants, especially after the restoration of democracy in 1990, wanted to establish their right to the tenanted land. Landlords were very fearful about the potential decision of the government to transfer ownership rights to tenants and therefore, wanted to evict their tenants. That raised several tenancy-related conflicts. For example, after the overthrow of the autocratic Panchayat political system, people, mainly poor and tenants, were enthusiastic to establish their ownership rights in the tenanted lands and to see a fair deal against land related exploitation by powerful people. The expectation of poor people and tenants was further accelerated by the election manifestos and slogans of the major political parties, especially those of the communist parties (e.g., the Communist Party of UML promised in the 1991 election that their government would give land to the landless and homes to the homeless). Gradually all the optimism and hopes were shattered as there was no change in the land-based exploitation.

Alignment of new canals, roads, trials and drinking water systems over land of particular individuals were other issues in land conflict. Obstruction of existing paths and public land (pastures, forests, wastelands, etc.) encroachment was another common land-conflict issue. Conflict over mortgaged land, with the failure of payment resulting in the land being seized was also common in the study area. Control of the *Guthi* land and its revenues, classification of land quality and share/contract amounts were other area of conflicts. Legally, land is classified by government into *Abal* (best), *Dwoyam* (relatively good), *Sim* (normal) and *Char* (worst) on the basis of land quality (fertility status, availability of irrigation and texture and structure of soil) and economic valuation. Looting of crops, crop damage, redemption, land registration and cancellation, fraudulent sales, reclamation, partition and order of succession and gifts were still more serious areas of conflict in land-resource in the study area. In the land-conflicts major actors were landlords and tenants struggling to protect their ownership and rights, to establish new rights, to prevent and to execute the legal arrangements favouring tenants and poor people. Other actors involved were staff of various land-related offices of the government, local politicians, and the general public.

Several land-related conflicts simply erupted due to the weaknesses of the present land-related acts and further weakneses in their implementation in Nepal, as they were unable to ensure the rights and interests of tenants and poor farmers. Execution of stable land rights granted by the Land Act was weak and manipulated by powerful people. Conflicts were also enhanced by customary land rights because of their exploitative nature in maintaining the patron-client relationship between landlords and tenants. Control over the land (be it *Guthi* or any tenural forms) by women is minimum and even when they have access, they still have no right to parental land. The patrilineal transformation of land and the exclusive inheritance rights of males is keeping women away from having land rights. This women's land-right issue is now one of the main areas of conflict. Parental lands have to be shared by the sons, not by the daughters. If parents give some land to their daughters and their brothers oppose it, this will lead to conflict. However, there is now a strong debate in Nepal, on the 'right of women' to parental property'. If the landowner is socially weak, absent from village or unaware of the details of his parental land and if the tenant is powerful, then the case for *de facto* land ownership is strong. For example, villagers explained that one villager, had been out of the village for 40 years when his father died. His 0.25 ha land was cultivated by a powerful member of the elite of the village. When he came from India and requested that his land be given back to him to cultivate, the elite member claimed tenancy rights. The District Land Reform Office granted him the tenancy right and this land was legally divided. This was the first and the last case in this village to grant tenancy right to the tenant since the execution of the Land Act in 1964. It was allowed to happen because the tenant was a powerful elite member. It was not possible for the landowner to survive, as the remaining half of the land (0.25 ha) was not viable, and he returned to India. The same person then also bought the rest of his land.

As a part of the land-reform programme, the government carried out the land-measurement programme (*Napi*) for better land-use planning. This single project created more than 5000 conflicts in the study district. The then Chairman of the Dolakha Bar Association, Mr Saroj Upreti explained that more than 200 conflict cases in each VDC were observed during the period of land measurement. However many were settled locally in the village. Some were resolved by VDCs, some by semi-judicial organisations and only a very small portion of the total conflict cases came to court. Common conflicts created by the *Napi* are related to boundaries, land of one people/household (generally weak, illiterate) being recorded under the name of another person (generally resourceful), public lands recorded in an individual's name and not recording an individual's land, etc. In this paragraph I describe how land survey and measurement (*Napi*) creates conflict in the community. To begin a land survey in the district, the Survey Office requests the relevant documents from the DLRO (*Malpot Adda*). The LRO provides the documents as well as instructs the *Mukhiyas* to make their records available to the surveyors. The land measurement starts with the establishment of a benchmark in the field for which the landowner is meant to receive compensation although this generally failed to happen. This is the beginning of manipulations and conflict. Notice of the impending survey has to be given to the VDC concerned and it also has to be posted in public in designated conspicuous places to inform all concerned people. This ensures that land owners and tenants who claim ownership or some rights to lands such as communal grazing, irrigation or religious places have a chance to make their claim known to the surveyors within the given period stated in the notice. Such a notice and the presentation of claims are extremely important as the survey regulation states that if claims are not presented within the given time (some weeks), unclaimed land will be recognised as *ailani jagga* (land owned by the government). It was reported in the study area that those people who were clever and aware of these rules made claims on public lands, lands of people whose household heads were away or had died. They were able to record these lands in their name by offering bribes to the surveyors. Some people were not aware of the notice and were not able to make their claim in time. Parts of some people's lands were deliberately omitted by the surveyors to use to bargain for bribe. The role of the elite (both neo-elite who emerged after restoration of democracy and the older elite of the panchayat regime) was crucial in manipulating the land measurement. Even when people noticed that their land was omitted, or recorded under someone else's name a simple objection and counter claim was not sufficient. Claimants have to present evidence such as testimony of neighbours, tax payment receipts obtained from *Mukhiyas* and the traditional record kept by *Mukhiyas* in support of their claims. Here again manipulation can occur as party politics may influence neighbours' testimony and Mukhiya can manipulate/falsify records and receipts. The survey team, who was suppose to investigate the validity of various claims and conflicts, were also involved in bribery. The surveyors, authorised to grant land ownership rights to people on the behalf of the government, enforce their authority over the disputed lands to meet personal interests. Though, there is a provision to go to court within 35 days if one of the parties is not satisfied with the decision of surveyors. However, the decision of the court is based on the legal evidence, which are mainly the available documents, prepared by DLRO, Mukhiyas and surveyors and obviously favouring the surveyors. After completion of the survey, the Survey Office distributes ownership certificates popularly known as *lalpurja* (red seals, which were used as sign of their legitimacy). The *lalpurja* contains information on the identity and the residence of the owner, the plot number, location, size and identity of its tenants, if any (New Era, 1988). Tenants are also supposed to be awarded a certificate attesting to their testimony. However, the respondents are often informed that they have to pay a bribe to receive *lalpurja* and tenancy certificates. Otherwise, it may take weeks and months to receive these certificates, and paying a bribe is cheaper for the villagers than staying in the expensive district headquarters. Another provision made by the law is that tenants have to have written receipts of the payment of their share from the landowners to qualify for the tenancy claim. All the tenants contacted during the research period said they had received no such receipt from the landowners. They said: *"how do we get the receipts If the talsing (land owners) do not give us them?"*

4.3.2. Forest-related Conflicts

The most common conflicts related to forests were: owner-ship issues between individuals and the local community and/or government, identification of users and access to forest products. Other frequent conflicts were royalty payments, illegal exploitation and export of NTFPs, hunting and poaching of wild animals and animal products from the forests. Forest encroachment, collection of firewood for funerals[2], use of trees from the forest to build wooden bridges over rivers and streams, leadership of forest users groups (FUG) and implementation of and deviation from the

---

2. Mourners collect firewood from (national) forest without permission of DFO (practically it is not possible to obtain permission) for cremation of dead body but foresters arrest them charging them with unauthorised collection of wood from forests. Similar problems are also observed in building wooden bridges over the rivers and streams.

operational plan, were also frequently reported in the study area. These conflicts are between FUG, between individuals and FUG and between FUG and the DFO. Conflict is common when the forest is spread over more than one administrative unit and geographical and political boundaries. It is also related to how the forest products are used, the purpose of their use (subsistence v/s commercial interests), degree of participation and contribution (who does how much), confusion on policies and the intervention of different organisations in the same area. Due to the growing poverty in rural areas, many poor people are involved in illegal harvesting of forest resources for their survival. Powerful people may use this illegal action as an opportunity to force them to work on their farms (Khadka, 1997) and junior forest professionals use it as a source of income. The main forest related conflicts are described below:

CONFLICT IN IDENTIFICATION OF USERS

Community forestry[3] is currently dominating the forestry debate in Nepal. Many conflict cases related to national forests in general and community forests in particular, were observed. In case of community forestry, poor and especially low caste people were not included when forming community FUG. Neither the governmental forest staff nor other members of the community informed them about formation of the FUG. Likewise people living far from the forest, perhaps not using it regularly, who are called secondary users (Shrestha, 1996b), such as charcoal makers, were often excluded from the FUG list. Later they were not allowed their occasional use of forest products and this served as a source of conflict.

---

3. 74 Community forest refers to a part of a national forest, which is handed over by the government to a forest users group for its development, conservation and utilisation for the collective benefit of users. The ultimate ownership of such forest rests with government.

CONFLICT IN SHARING BENEFIT

This is the major cause of conflict in community forests. Based on the size of their family members and how many animals they own, powerful and rich people take more forest products, irrespective of the equal contribution of all members of the users groups in forest management. These issues give rise to conflict amongst the users. Provisions made in the operational plans and the constitution of FUG did not work in these situations. Conflicts were also observed in sharing forest products such as grass, fodder, timber and other edible products from government forests. The frequent conflicts in several communities were observed when licensed traders from outside the community collected medicinal plants from higher altitude forests managed and used by villagers. When the boundary of the VDC is changed and the existing forest-use by villagers falls under the jurisdiction of another VDC, then conflict is inevitable. Existing users make their claims on the basis of their traditional use of the forest and new villagers claim on the basis of forest belonging to their VDC (Shrestha, 1996a, 1996b; Khanal, 1998). Frequent conflicts are occurring in community forests due to the ignorance of VDC boundaries in dealing with community forest issues (hand-over of the forest to the community for example) according to the new forest rules which are contradictory to the Local Self-Governance Act. If a piece of national forest lies in more than one VDC when people from both VDCs request its change into a community forest, then conflict on boundary demarcation for the better part is inevitable.

CONFLICT IN PARTICIPATION AND CONTRIBUTION

If the same people use more than one forest it can cause problems in its management and protection, which invite conflict between users. All FUG members studied were not equally active in participating in meetings, contributing voluntary labour for surveillance and other forest management functions often because of their physical absence (job outside the village, head of the family away for some reasons, etc.). Active members in such cases did not allow equal benefits to be given to less active ones. Lack of participation and contribution was more prominent amongst widows and marginalised, poor families who had to earn a daily wage for their survival and were not able to actively participate. Those members who lived close to the forest were more vigilantly involved in forest protection, since they can see potential forest offences being committed by outsiders even if they are not on duty. Such unassigned surveillance duties make them claim more resources from the forest although this had not been agreed by the community (Shrestha, 1996b). It is interesting to note that users from higher social-status and caste groups did not often physically participate in the surveillance of the forest, despite there being a provision that all members should do this on a rotational basis, including during unsociable hours. Despite this, they receive equal or even greater benefits from the forests. Due to their social status, other users did not openly complain, which led to resentment, injustice and the development of negative feelings towards forest management.

CONFLICT IN LEADERSHIP

One of the frequent sources of conflict in community forests is the leadership. The position of Chairperson of a community forest is prestigious in a village and is sought by many people. It is further exacerbated by the political interest of various parties (Shrestha, 1996b; Khanal, 1996). People, who are interested in active politics, use this position as a stepping ladder. This creates a lot of conflict in the community, which then turns to political conflict. More detail about leadership conflict is presented in the chapter five.

FOREST USERS GROUPS' WRITTEN ARRANGEMENT V/S PRACTICE

The operational plan and constitution are the core of a community forest. All activities to be carried out by FUG have to be clearly defined in the operational plan and be according to the frame of the constitution. However, deviations have often been found due to lapses or laxity of the forest staff or the zealous pursuit of group members to get more income from the forests, which have led to several conflicts (Shrestha, 1996a). The operational plan defines the numbers of trees to be removed or specifies the amount of forest products to be appropriated. However, users do not always follow the plans. In some cases, forest staff are guided by hidden interests suggest to deviate from the operation plan (Shrestha, 1996b). This is more common on valuable forests where high value wood is abstracted. The DFO then seize the timber which has been illegally harvested leading to continuos conflicts, unless they are solved by bribes or settled through the exercise of power or legal measures.

The majority of the FUG members are unaware of forest-related legal provisions. Only a few people, mainly local teachers and political workers, are aware of the rules and regulations. They are able to manipulate the rules, in collaboration with foresters, to obtain more personal benefits from the forest resources.

Recently, the severe conflict between FECOFUN and the governmental forest department escalated when the government altered the existing community forestry provision and restricted the authority of users in community forests given by the forest act. FECOFUN wants forests to be managed by the communities themselves but bureaucrats are reluctant to transfer forest management to local communities, especially where high value forests are concerned, because of the conflict of interests. This conflict is not only leading to political debate but is now being considered in court. In the national forests, the conflict between forest officials and traders/commercial logging companies is very common. Such conflicts are resolved through negotiated kickbacks within the political-bureaucratic circle.

4.3.3. *Water-related conflicts*

Different kinds of water-related conflicts were reported in the study area. Source disputes, sharing of water for different purposes (for example, use for drinking water, irrigation, and water turbine), payment of compensation for damage caused while constructing canals and laying drinking water pipes, were frequently reported. Similarly, conflict over contribution for maintenance of the irrigation and drinking water systems, ambiguous roles and responsibilities of watchmen and their payments and role conflict among water users associations committees were other common water-related conflicts in the research area. Damage caused by the over flow of water from canals and conflicts due to the ambiguous roles of water technicians and officials were also quite frequent. Earlier studies (IMC, 1990; Pradhan *et al.*, 1997) have shown that water conflict is a normal phenomena if the same source is used for more than one purpose in the absence of clear provision of water rights. The occurrence and intensity of such a conflict is high when the water becomes scarce in the dry season. Inequitable and unreliable water distribution and excessive use of water in head section limits the supply (in terns of time and quantity) in tail section and often cause frequent conflict concerning the irrigation system. This is particularly serious when several irrigation systems operate upstream and downstream with limited water availability. The demand for irrigation water is increasing in the study area due to the introduction of improved varieties of rice, winter crops and changes in the cropping systems. The cropping intensity and cropping patterns are changing, together with technological innovations and the process of globalisation. In periods of water scarcity the frequency as well as the intensity of the conflict is high. It was also noticed that conflict resolution over two irrigation systems was easy when the same farmers own lands in the command areas of both irrigation systems. It is reported that the frequency and intensity of conflict is greater in joint managed irrigation systems than in ones fully managed by farmers (Gautam *et al.*, 1992; IIMI, 1990; 1997; IMC, 1990). The main cause of conflict in such systems was an unreliable water supply to tail end farmers during the winter and spring crop seasons due to an inability to implement proper water scheduling (IMC, 1990; Pradhan, 1989; Shivakoti *et al.*, 1996).

Earlier studies also showed that agency intervention in existing irrigation and drinking water systems worsens the water supply and gives rise to numerous conflicts (Pradhan *et al.*, 1997; IMC, 1990; Upreti, 1998b). This situation is discussed in detail in Chapter Five. The improper design of structural work and the quality of the construction result not only in inefficient delivery of water but can also lead to several conflicts (IMC, 1990). This type of conflict is discussed in detail in chapter six. Technical matters such as steep gradients of canals and laid pipelines caused an excess of water in a particular area and an inequitable supply. Flat gradients also caused silt deposits and reduction in water flow. Such technical difficulties had turned into the cause of conflict. In the agency developed systems constructed under contract arrangement, contractors are the major cause of conflict not only in new systems but also in the operation and maintenance of existing irrigation and drinking-water systems (Pradhan *et al.*, 2000).

In the study area most of the farmers managed irrigation systems (FMIS) practice some form of distribution rules and rotational water sharing, particularly in the peak water demand period. Therefore, they are effective in minimising potential conflicts. Community coherence among the water users is high in the FMIS and community managed drinking water systems and therefore community-managed systems are more effective in monitoring water distribution, maintenance and operation and in resolving conflicts, if any (Pradhan, 1989; Pradhan *et al.*, 1997). In the case of agency developed systems, users are generally unwilling to contribute to operation and maintenance (IMC, 1990; IIMI, 1990) because of a lack of any feeling of ownership and accountability. Within the particular irrigation or drinking water system conflict is frequently observed between tail-section and head-section users in sharing water particularly concerning the amount used and the time period. Basically, water availability determines the occurrence and frequency of conflicts. Generally, conflicts in the head-section, unlike those in the tail-section were not because of lack of water. Conflicts in the tail-section, in winter and spring were mainly due to water shortage. The magnitude of a conflict grows as the gap between the demand and supply of water increases. Unequal water distribution is generally linked with inadequate monitoring that allows greater access to head-section farmers. This is one of the major determinants of conflict concerning irrigation and drinking water.

In general, socio-economic, agricultural, organisational, and technical factors contribute to the emergence of conflicts. More precisely, availability, reliability, equity and seasonality of the water supply determine the occurrence and intensity of conflicts concerning irrigation systems that can have a direct impact on the performance of irrigated agriculture. Earlier research shows that there is clear relationship between irrigation conflict and crop yields. Conflicts and cropping intensities are also positively related as both are affected by the availability of water (IMC, 1990). Nevertheless, it is not always predictable. In some case farmers changed their existing cropping patters due to scarcity of water and increased benefits whereas in other cases their yields were decreased.

Local people use specific rules to determine the use of water. For example, if the water source is located in an individual's land, then they have full autonomy to use it themselves, but they have no authority to dictate who can use it for irrigation and how much to use within the community. However, in the case of stream water, which is common to all members of community, there is rule that all community members have equal rights to use it on a rotational basis. One of the respondents explained that: *"the source owner use Kuwapanikomul (a perennial water source located in his land) whenever he like. Only after he finishes his rice transplanting, then we get chance to use this water source. But we all community members share water from Chharekhola (a common stream) on the rotational basis".*

In several externally funded drinking-water projects

conflicts have erupted after a few years due to scarcity of water when the population increases in the village. While designing these systems, technicians generally ignore the potential future need for water citing financial and technical reasons. Engineers from the DWSO explained that they provide for future needs in their designs and estimates. However, in practice such provisions were not observed. Local people say that overseers refuse to consider the future water requirements of the community while constructing drinking-water projects in the village basing them on budgetary limitations. Another major conflict in externally funded drinking water projects is the location of the tap stands. Due to the influence of politicians or for their own hidden interests technicians locate the tap-stand close to the house of particular people (mainly rich and powerful, sometimes negotiated with a bribe), despite other villagers not agreeing. Similarly, sharing the source is another problem in such projects as they are decided on the basis of technical justifications ignoring the existing use patterns and social context. People may damage structures built in the source and cause the conflict to escalate.

On the issue of political interference in development projects, one Member of the Parliament explained that there would be no interference if the bureaucrats worked according to the bureaucratic rules, norms and ethics. Unfortunately they do not do so. If politicians do not interfere, then the poor and backward people suffer more from bureaucratic manipulations in development work. Therefore, to minimise these manipulations, politicians have to interfere in development projects implemented by bureaucrats in their village or district.

4.3.4. *Other Natural Resource related Conflicts*

Beside the three most common categories of natural resource conflicts mentioned above, there are several other ones observed in the study area. Prominent conflicts were on environmental and social dislocation issues. Similarly, there were several conflict on the environmental issues between local people and the Orient Magnesite Company; local people, government and contractors on slate stone excavation and trade; DDC and contractors about river fishing, local people and the Khimti Hydro Power Project on negative social impacts, villagers and development organisations on the alignment of a seasonal road and between DDC and illegal collectors of sand, stone and gravel from river beds.

4.4. Dominant Conflict Management Systems in Nepal

Conflict is of national importance in any country and therefore the state has different ways of dealing with them. Courts, conflict resolution bodies and anti-corruption bureau and the police are examples of these. In addition to state-led conflict management mechanisms, there can be several informal, unofficial local practices and procedures to deal with conflicts in society. Based on this framework, this section deals on both formal and informal common CM practices adopted in the study area. Formal practices are those which involve official procedures, guided by governmental rules, regulations and laws and handled by paid government staff. The most common formal practices in the study area are the activities carried out by the courts, police, district administration, NRM-offices (land, forest, water related offices) and VDCs. On the other hand, informal practices are those, which are locally developed and practised and enforced by communities. Informal practices may, or more likely, may not follow the governmental regulatory procedures. Local people or unpaid volunteers generally undertake them and the decisions are often not legally endorsable. However, both practices are directly and/or indirectly guided or influenced by each other, making it difficult to separate them completely.

It is noticeable that the intensity of conflicts as well as people's responses to them is changing over time and with changing circumstances. In the study area the willingness of local people to be actively involved in dealing with social conflict was directly related to the interdependence (intensity of use) of these natural resources. Such an interdependent relationship between the actors and resources was also demonstrated by several earlier studies (Upreti, 1998b; Thapa and Weber, 1994; Shivakoti, *et al.*, 1996; Rhoades, 1997).

There is a positive relationship between the active involvement of actors in managing natural resources and associated conflicts and the degree of their direct dependence on those resources. Successful management of community forests by FUGs, farmer-managed irrigation by WUAs in Nepal, forest resources conservation by Chipko Movement (hug tree campaign), local seed management by Beej Banchawo Andolan (Save Seed Movement) in India and the farmers field-school for integrated pest management in Indonesia are some of the prominent examples of community capacity to manage local resources. The globally the renowned Dutch water-management history is another example of how people use innovative sustainable management systems if and when they feel that their survival is closely associated with the success or failure of management of a particular resource.

Local people formulate informal conflict management practices by discussing the issues in public meetings. Sometimes such meetings became tense and even counterproductive. The whole environment became too emotionally charged to reach a solution. However, the same conflict was settled in the next meeting, after a time for reflection. For any negotiation local people use different strategies and options. Disputants' preferences for a particular forum to resolve conflict mainly depend upon their knowledge, affordability and interests at a specific time and in the particular circumstances as well as the availability and readiness of such forums (shopping forums). Different agencies or people became involved in conflict resolution when they saw some direct or indirect benefits from their involvement. It was observed that it was difficult to reach final negotiations when conflict cases were backed-up by political parties. The intensity of the conflict is also another important factor in drawing the attention of people to become involved. If the conflict is severe and seriously hampering the society then its members show their concern, but if the conflict is of a less severe nature people are generally less concerned. The jurisdiction of the forums also varies with the nature of the conflict (Benda-Beckmann, 1984). However, manipulation and local adjustment is common to establish the jurisdiction. Resolution of conflicts is also a means of establishing power and influence in the community. People only consider arbitration when the intensity of conflict is high and unmanageable, through mutual understanding, at their level. However, the majority of conflicts were resolved locally by mutual agreement and negotiation.

4.4.1. Informal Conflict Management Practices

In this section the common informal conflict-management practices adopted in the community to resolve social and natural resource conflicts are discussed. These informal methods and practices include the activities of *Dhami-Jhakri, Purohit*[4], *Mukhiya*, local leaders, and elderly people. The procedures applied in these practices, the quality of the resolutions, the implications and their relations with formal practices are discussed. The role of the specific time and context in informal conflict-management practices is also highlighted. For example, several conflicts were settled and several more erupted in the time of local and national elections.

In the study area the majority of conflicts (except complicated conflict cases such as rape, suspected or attempted murder, etc.) were resolved locally in informal

---

4. *The Purohit* is a culturally and socially recognised person to perform religious ceremonies and also acts as a bridge between villagers for information and communication. He (there is no provision of female *purohit*) has frequent house-to-house contact and good relations. Generally, his clients did not prefer to go against his arguments.

ways. Local elderly people often work as mediators to deal with conflict, though they have no legal status. Villagers commonly accept their settlements. Such informal CM practices are a blend of local customs, a sense of justice and religious feeling rather than official procedures. Generally no written records are maintained in informal CM practices. Elderly and socially respected people, traditional landlords, teachers, *Jhakri* (faith healers), *Purohit*, and *Mukhiya* are principal actors in resolving a wide range of local conflicts. These people do not only mediate social and natural resource conflict as neutral third parties but also generally decide terms and conditions for the negotiation process. They are not only mediators or negotiators as discussed in chapter two. The criteria to resolve conflicts were not legal evidence and documents, but religious faith (*Dharma Bhakaune, Tamo-Tulsi, Geeta and Saligram samaine*), historical considerations and practical realities. Only complicated conflicts, which were not possible to settle by informal means, go to the VDC. The police, other sectoral offices, and the DAO deal with only those cases, which can not be resolved by the VDC or for which they have no legal authority. Only those cases that can not be settled by these organisations, or are legally bounded to go to the court for resolution.

Most local negotiators do not charge a fee for their service in resolving conflict. However, they often expect some physical labour from the negotiating parties, perhaps for them to work on their farm. Some negotiating parties also voluntarily give them presents in kind such as ghee, chicken, vegetables, fruit, etc. Generally the winner party gives such presents and voluntary labour.

Disputants from ethnic groups strongly prefer negotiators from their own ethnic group. They only approach others if it is not possible for their ethnic leaders to solve the conflict. *Matwalis* are quickly drawn into conflict and immediately negotiate locally in contrast to upper-caste Bramin/Chhitri groups. Generally, conflict in extreme cases in *Matwali* groups turns into a physical fight. However, after negotiation they have no feelings of inferiority, hostility or deep-seated feelings of revenge. In contrast, Brahmin, Chhetri and Newar (other than the *Matwali* group) keep the conflict alive, even after negotiation is in a latent stage and look for future revenge. The majority of people, especially poor and backward ones, involved in conflict did not posses even a basic knowledge of formal laws and legal procedures. Only neo-elite such as school teachers, the VDC executive body and political leaders have such knowledge, which they use to manipulate conflict in their favour.

People learn negotiation skills through practice while being involved in community-level social conflict management practices. Those who had the time, credibility, temperament, willingness, articulation and vested interests were more involved in community level CM. Generally they carefully listen to the conflict story from both conflicting parties. They also inspect the place of conflict, if relevant, they also assess the past conflict tract records of the conflicting parties and consult neighbours as eyewitnesses, if applicable. If necessary they call meetings in public places (or some times in their own homes or even in the house of one of the conflicting parties, if the parties agree), to get the opinion of neighbours. Then on the basis of their assessment and judgement, they make their decisions. Conflicting parties in most of the cases accept such decisions. They use many cultural, religious and political proverbs (which highlights the importance to resolve conflict locally rather than to go to a formal process) to convince the conflicting parties. According to the context and situation, they also threaten, harass and even some time beat offenders to reveal the truth and/or to force them to accept the prescribed settlement. Occasionally, they also integrate their resolution measures with formal process. For example, sometimes the police are invited to execute the decision if the proven offender does not abide by it. Even in formal mechanisms sometimes the police or the VDC take the help of local mediators to resolve conflict instead of settling it themselves.

The main reasons expressed by people in preferring informal mechanisms are, trust in mediators, ease of settlement, maintenance of social harmony and lack of resources (money, knowledge and time) to use a formal conflict-resolution process. Nevertheless, particularly after 1990, the credibility of such informal conflict CM mechanisms is eroding fast, due to social and political changes (Khadka, 1997). Now even many people affiliated to political parties do not believe in these local negotiators/mediators/ arbitrators, questioning their fairness due to their potential bias to supporters of the particular political party with whom they are associated. Local CM capacity is also inhibited by the formal system.

In informal CM practices, male domination is common. However, the role of women is often instrumental in bringing conflicting parties to the negotiation table. In many conflict cases women had forced male members of their family to compromise to end the conflict. At local level, women are directly and actively involved in conflict and its management. In some cases, women acted as a mediator between husband and or other family members when they fell into conflict with neighbours. It is also found that women were used by male members of their families, as a means to get sympathy and favour from villagers. It was thought that if women were sent to the elderly people, local leaders and VDC heads to report the case that would make their case stronger[5] (Khadka, 1997). When people get into conflict each party tries to win the support of neighbouring villagers by telling the weaknesses and wrongdoings of the opposition. These types of misinformation and deceit may turn into malicious gossip and character assassination. Ultimately this creates an atmosphere of distrust, disrespect, and paranoia (Sandelin, 1997).

In several cases husbands were in a deep-seated conflict, whereas their wives have maintained a more normal relationship. It was also shown that men bring more conflict cases to a formal process of resolution than do women. The

---

5. It is a common belief in the study area that women do not report problems unless they are really victimised.

reasons expressed for this were socio-cultural restriction, fear of defamation, lack of decision-making authority and resources among the disputant women. However, women are frequently entangled in minor conflicts about crop damage by animals, children's quarrels and being suspected of cheating by their husbands. Women, generally from *Matwalies*, prepare and sell local liquors that often give rise to the arguments among the local drunkards. When customers have too much liquor, they may start to tease the women, antagonising their husbands or other members of their family or even occasionally their community, which often results in a physical fight. Due to several such incidences, women have banned alcohol in their village to minimise conflict and harassment of women. In both VDCs women were also harassed for being witches, leading to endless conflict in the community. For example, one woman (anonymity maintained) was severely harassed and almost discarded from the community as it was said that she was a witch, because her tongue was black, thought to be the perfect sign of witch. She said, *"I am poor, ignored by my husband who has taken another wife and is living far from me, isolated, living alone without support of any one, helpless and walk around in tatters. So all blame me, nobody speaks the truth. Neighbours behave inhumanely to me. I am seriously hurt but I have no choice other than to accept. I am treated as an outcast woman and people do not even drink water in my house. My two sons are labelled as witch's sons so they are very humiliated..".* Harassment to women is also clear from accounts of informants. Bhage Khatri, a renowned troublemaker in the village explains: *"several women are witches in our village, damaging our crops, making our children suffer and creating problems with the livestock. They have to be seriously punished but they are freely moving around".*

New Era (1988) from their conflict study in two districts show that the vast majority of conflicts were settled within the village by mobilising relatives, traditional leaders, village heads and friends. It was shown that several conflicts were deliberately kept active in a stage of grievance or hostility to maintain social relation. However, such unexpressed feelings of injustice hinder people's active participation in NRM. The approaches, strategies, procedures and results of local level CM vary according to the characteristics of the actors involved in the conflict, such as gender, caste, social status, networks, interpersonal relationships (Kaplan, 1995).

The importance of informal CM practices is reflected by the local saying: *"Deskalagi rajako niti chahincha tara goanko kam ma prajako riti thiti ko badi mahatto chha"* (King's policy is needed for the whole country whereas values and customs of local people are more important for managing village resources). Several CM activities carried out at local level are traditionally based on their values and customs (*riti-thiti*), which play a powerful role in binding people together for collective actions. The following paragraph presents a local custom-based method of resolution of conflict called *Sagun Garne* (reconciliation). *Sagun garne* (reconciliation) is a method based on cultural tradition. In this method, a gift is exchanged between disputants, in the presence of villagers, as a form of reconciliation. This exchange is performed after discussing the matter in meetings where villagers, negotiators and conflicting parties are present. When they reach a settlement then they start '*sagun garne*'. The conflict is declared as settled when both parties accept the gift. Then there is small celebration where all people take some *Jaad* (a type of fermented liquor). However, there are no written documents of such a settlement. The villagers, who are present at the *sagun garne* ceremony, are witnesses to the settlement. This practice is most common in Matwalis (Kami, Damai, Sarki) and Tibeto-Burman ethnic groups (Gurung, Mangar, Tamang, Jirel, Surel). The gifts are usually liquor, eggs, meat, etc. (Khadka, 1997). Some occasions are particularly important for informal conflict-resolution and reconciliation. For example *Dashain*[6] is traditionally used as an occasion to reconcile and strengthen relations by visiting each

---

6. A major Hindu festival in Nepal where all community members gather in public places and resolve pending conflicts, unsettled issues and decide collective community works.

other's houses, exchanging gifts and good wishes. Likewise *Tihar* (another important Hindu festival) is also used as an important occasion to promote harmony and reconcile conflict. *Ghewa[7] is another occasion to reconcile conflict. Many of the conflicts resolved in villages are verbal and not supported by written documents. When powerful people reactivate these cases the weaker party usually loses when the case goes to the formal process of the CM. The efficiency of the local procedure is context specific and mixed, some times effective and some times exploitative and ineffective.*

Local customs are not static. They are dynamic and responsive to wider social change and often congenial in promoting harmonious social relations (Oli, 1998). Other jurisdictions such as grazing land used by defined groups of users, the harvest of grasses, litter and wood from forests used by a particular community, upon which they have established their rights over time are respected by such customs. Nevertheless all customs are not effective in terms of equity and justice. Some of them maintain an unequal power structure in community.

The picture that emerges from this discussion is that dynamic, complex, successful and enduring local conflict resolution systems legitimately operated in community based collective values, visions and actions are disturbed by state intervention. It will be worth-quoting the conclusion of the research findings of Oli (1998:75) that "fundamental conflicts between the local people's perceived views and the government's view in regulating resource management is increasing. This is likely to continue until the government stops ignoring and impairing the role of local community in managing their resources".

4.4.2. Example of Resolution of Social Conflict through Informal Systems

Jhankri rakhne (exploration by faith healers): It is a method based on the belief that faith healers (witch doctors) have super-natural power from god to control particular

---

7. *This is a Tamang death ritual where people from the village gather and settle conflict between their community members.*

problems, most commonly conflicts related to allegations of witchery. The faith healers usually treats the culprits inhumanly (burning hairs, pouring hot water on the body, severely beating, etc.). Women are generally accused of being witches and men are always faith healers. This is the offensive method of conflict resolution in the study area. *Jhakri* also acts as a local doctor to treat several diseases and problems related to villagers in general and children in particular. In NRM *jhakris* are used to forecast rainfall, control or prevent forest fires, landslides, cure crops affected by different diseases and insects, etc.

Dharma Bhakaune (sacred test): It is a common informal method of determining the truth in managing conflict. This method is based on the principle of 'oath of innocence'. It is common when there is lack of other evidence. Common methods observed in this test are: taking contending parties to the local temples and asking them to undergo a test, asking conflicting parties to touch sacred materials such as *saligram* (a sacred stone), copper, sacred plants such as *Ficus religiosa* (peepal), *Ocimum sanctum*, (basil), *Cynodon dyctolen* (dub grass) sacred books and take an oath of innocence. Some time conflicting parties are asked to hold their children while performing such vows (Khadka, 1997). These tests take place in the presence of villagers, negotiators and conflicting parties. A feeling of sin, if the matter is falsified, plays a strong role in this method to find the wrongdoing. This method is also used occasionally in formal CM practices.

4.4.3. *Different form of Punishment in Informal Conflict Management Practices*

Various types of punishments were used in local conflict-management practices. Three examples are discussed here on how people punish wrongdoers in the community.

1. *Mafi magne* (public apology). A public apology by the guilty party for wrongdoing is a common method in the study area. The guilty party, in the presence of villagers and local elite, begs for pardon and swears not to repeat the offence. This is also sometimes accompanied with an additional fine and

other punishments. This method is also widely used in the formal conflict-resolution process.

2. *Jariwana* (fine) *and chhetipurti bharaune* (compensation): This practice involves reimbursement of loss (generally cash, and sometimes kind) by the guilty party and some extra punishment in the form of fines. This is very common in conflict related to crop damaged by animals, canal and drinking water-pipe damage, destruction or damage of public paths, physical fights, etc. If the community realises that one party has a considerable loss in property or sustained injury from the other party then the wrong doer has to bear cost for losses, other associated costs and medical treatment, if needed. In addition to the compensation for loss, a fine is generally collected, for use at the temple, school, guthi, or to repair a path or the drinking water.

3. *Pani kadne* (ostracise): This is a severe punishment, grounded in the orthodox caste system backed up by Hindu spiritual feeling. Though this is not applied in natural resource related conflict, it is still common in villages to deal with sexual conflicts. In this practice, the offender and his/her family are declared out caste and no-one maintains a social interaction and relationship with them. People stop visiting and eating in their houses and inviting them to their homes. This is a strong public sanction against the offender and common in molestation and illegal and immoral sexual relationships between unilateral kin groups based on either matrilineal or patrilineal descent. This punishment is legally prohibited by the law but still common in practice. Local people say that the threat of being ostracised is maintaining social harmony and limiting immoral sexual offences.

Geographical distance is also a crucial factor when opting for different forums for conflict resolution. If villages were from more remote areas, more traditional patterns of CM prevailed. This is also linked to network and social support. Those who have strong networks and social support get more benefits from conflict. The role of literacy in a conflict is more important in financial transactions. It is possible for those who can not read and write to be exploited by landlords and moneylenders when they make the relevant documents.

In the last few years, the Local Governance Programme, FECOFUN, Centre for Victim of Torture (CVICT) and Himalayan Grassroots Women's Natural Resource Management Association (HIMWANTI) like non-government organisations and projects are managing conflict differently than the former models and legal measures. FECOFUN is emerging as one of the important platforms in dealing with forest conflicts and defending interests and rights of the forest. In collaboration with different forestry-related projects FECOFUN is organising various activities in managing conflicts. HIMWANTI is another emerging forum created by women working in NRM to address their problems. Several NGOs are also being trained by various projects in conflict management. They are developing the capacity of people through learning and mobilising them to minimise conflict and resolve it locally. They are quite successful in managing conflicts in this way but scaling-up is the difficult and constraining part of these innovative practices.

4.4.4. Formal Conflict Management Systems

This section discusses common conflict management practices accomplished by formal organisations responsible for natural resources. The discussion considers issues of quality and efficiency of resolutions and their implications to poor people and NRM. This section also reports the role of power, influence of money and networks in resolving conflict. An effort is made to look at the assessment of the performance of the organisations responsible for conflict management, by different section of society such as people involved in conflict, politicians, general public, bureaucrats, etc.

Formal CM practice involves two major categories. The first category includes the court system and the second category includes governmental natural resource related offices, the police and the District Administration Office. These are all formally working under a governmental regulatory framework. Since 1998 the LSGA has empowered VDCs to formally deal with conflict cases and they are actively involved in CM. In the case of natural resource related conflicts, in addition to the Local Self-Governance Act, several other organisations are instituted by the government to look on sectoral issues such as DWSO for drinking water, DIO for irrigation, DFO for forest, DLRO for land, DADO for agriculture and DLDO for livestock related issues. In every region (between 3-5 VDCs) there are police posts to settle conflicts. The CDO and police have a mandatory responsibility to address all types of conflict issues. These organisations settle a large number of conflicts and only those conflict cases, which are not possible to solve there, go to the court.

NATIONAL ARENA

The national arena gives a bird-eye view of the situation of conflict in Nepal. Conflicts, which have eventually ended up in the courts, are discussed in this section. At the village level, there is no court and therefore, conflict cases go to VDC. Table 4.1 gives the overview of conflict in Nepal. This table demonstrates the filing of more than a hundred thousand conflict cases in court by their type and nature. This is a clear indication of the growing number of conflicts. It also indicates the weak performance of the informal conflict management system to resolve conflict locally. The conflicts presented in Table 4.1 are both civil and criminal cases. Natural-resource conflicts generally fall under civil cases and only occasionally turn into a criminal case. Land-related conflicts are the most serious in terms of occurrence in the civil cases. If disputes related to partition and inheritance, which are invariably related to land, are consider under the land-related conflict category the numbers are extremely high. The same Table shows that the trend of corruption related to conflict is in increasing. This trend suggests that the prevalence of corruption in Nepalese society is increasing over time (234 corruption cases were filed in 1995, which is more than a 100% increase, i.e., 486 in 1999). CDO, special police and Commission of Investigation of Abuse of Authority are primarily responsible for dealing with corruption issues and therefore only extremely complicated small numbers of cases not possible to resolve in these organisations go to court. It is interesting to note that almost all the corruption cases are won by the defendants because of faulty legal provision (these anti-corruption organisations have to present the evidence of corruption rather than evidence of innocence being presented by the defendants. It is not likely to have evidence of corruption by the defendants. Other factors affecting verdicts are political influence, money and power.

Table 4.1. Total Number of Conflict Cases Filed in all Nepalese Courts

Types of conflict	1995/96	1996/97	1997/98	1998/99	Total
Land	20978	31147	30712	27014	109851
Transactions	11678	14789	13970	12094	52531
Partition and family cases	14622	22278	20888	19825	77613
Forgery and cheating	9517	12621	12064	9367	43569
Looting	5806	6324	6017	6567	24714
Defamation	5282	3831	2969	2708	14790
Election	7	203	270	198	678
Assault	3868	5721	5390	4522	19501
Murder	2748	5301	4984	4953	17986
Theft	2381	3451	3413	2584	11829
Sexual offences	445	706	682	639	2472
Corruption	234	477	482	486	1679
Juvenile delinquency	21	12	3	23	59
Criminal abortion	90	159	203	376	828
Miscellaneous	16217	22765	23196	25660	87838
Total cases	93894	129785	125243	117016	465938

Source: CBS, 2000, P. 256 (adapted)

Though the figures in Table 4.1 indicate the wider existence of conflict; it is only a small part of the total conflicts. As explained earlier, only legally complicated and selected conflict cases reach to court. Large numbers of conflict cases are resolved locally or by other sectoral organisations such as DFO, DIO, DWSO, DLRO, etc. in districts, which are not reflected in this Table. A similar trend can be seen in the districts too. Though Dolakha is a relatively small mountain district with plenty of natural resources, large numbers of conflicts are observed. The following Table depicts the wide existence of conflict in this district.

Table 4.2. Number of Dispute Cases Registered in the Dolakha District Court, 1995-1999

Types of conflict[8]	1994/95	1995/96	1996/97	1997/98	1998/99	Total
Natural resource	401	552	425	176	143	1697 (41.12%)
Other	501	448	400	542	538	2429 (58.88%)
Total	902	1000	825	718	681	4126 (100%)

Source: Compiled from different records of the Dolakha District Court, 2000

Table 4.2 shows that conflict cases related to natural resources were increasing between 1995 and 1997 in the study district. About 41% of the total cases were related to natural resources. Large proportions of the natural resource related conflicts are land-related cases. This is mainly due to the cadestral survey conducted during that period. The conflict cases filed in court are only a small portion of the total as many cases were solved locally. However, after 1996, the trend is less. The decreasing trend is reported to be not due to the efficiency of the courts but due to the completion of the land survey and measurement programme in the district.

---

8. The registration book of the court has categorised conflict cases into *Dewani* (civil) and *Faujdari* (criminal). However, natural resource related conflicts belong to both categories. Therefore, I have categorised conflicts into 1) Natural resource related and 2) others, which include all the civil and criminal cases from the court's registration book.

In the case of research VDCs, secretaries of both of the study VDCs reported that 87% of households of Pawoti and 82% households of Sailungeshwor VDCs were engaged in conflict in 1990-91 when democracy was just restored. Occasionally such conflicts escalate to become violent when ignited by other forces such as political biases or personal revenge. For example, in 1991, the son of a powerful elite in Pawoti VDC was killed and 4 other family members were beaten mercilessly to death by a crowd of poor untouchable (*Damai*) people because the wife of a powerful member of the elite had acted callously (feeding human excreta to one of the Damai women) against them. These *Damai* were heavily exploited (routinely threatened, harassed, forced to work without wage, etc.) by these people in the Panchayat political system. Then, in the recently changed political situation they took revenge. According to the respondents, however, in recent years the frequency of conflict is decreasing in the study VDCs, mainly due to the frustration of people (disputants) with their respective political parties. Earlier, many of the conflicts were created for political benefit but as the disputants got no benefits from them, they now do not want to politicise their conflicts.

Table 4.3. Number of Complaints made in the Study VDCs during 1995-1998

Types of conflict cases	Pawoti VDC	Sailunge- shwor VDC	Total number
NR related conflicts	380 (55.15)	328 (51.99)	708 (53.64)
Irrigation	60 (15.80)	35 (10.68)	95 (13.42)
Drinking water	75 (19.74)	60 (18.30)	135 (19.07)
Pasture/forest	70 (18.42)	69 (21.00)	139 (19.63)
Land	175 (46.00)	164 (50.00)	339 (47.88)
Other conflict cases	309 (44.85)	303 (48.10)	612 (46.36)
Total	689 (52.20)	631 (47.80)	1320

Source: Compiled from various records of the VDCs. Numbers in parenthesis is percentage.

Table 4.3 shows that out of total number of conflict cases (1320) observed in the study VDCs 52.2% were reported in Pawoti and the remaining 47.8% in Sailungeshwor VDC. In comparing types of conflicts (natural resources related and others), 53.64% of conflicts are natural resource related in the study VDCs and the remaining 46.36% are other conflicts. Within the natural resource related conflicts, almost half are related to land, followed by forest and pasture (19.63%), drinking water (19.0%) and irrigation (13.42%) respectively. A comparison of VDCs shows that 55.15% of conflict cases in Pawoti and 51.99% in Sailungeshwor are related to natural resources and the remaining 44.85 and 48.10%, respectively, are other conflicts. It confirms that natural resource related conflicts are widely and inevitably prevalent not only in the study area but also as whole in Nepal. Based on the figures presented in Tables 4.1, 4.2 and 4.3 it can be conclude that Nepalese society is deeply interwoven with conflict.

From direct interviews with litigants coming to court, it was found that most of them were not aware of their legal rights and duties. Similarly, the majority of disputants did not contact lawyers because they could not afford the cost. Lawyers had rejected legal assistance to some disputants who were not able to pay legal fees. Often, even simple conflict cases take a long time, ranging from 2 to 5 years, to resolve which drastically increases the cost (New Era, 1988). There are no effective mechanisms for summary proceedings, which eventually limits access of poor people to the courts system (Oli, 1998). Nepalese courts are heavily clogged with pending litigation. The following statement of the Chief Justice of the Supreme Court indicates the situation. Addressing a three-day meeting of judges of the Supreme Court and appeal courts the then Chief Justice Mr. Keshav Prasad Upadhyay said *"over 82% of appeal courts' decisions ended up in the high court. Some legal and court procedures need to be simplified"* (The Rising Nepal, 25 July 2000). This issue raises a logical question why appeal courts' decisions are challenged in the Supreme Court? Are they unfair? Nepalese courts have a backlog of 64,700 cases, including 16,000 at the Supreme

Court, 14,000 at the appellate courts and more than 33,000 cases in the district courts. The pending cases increase by almost 13% each year (ibid.). This situation clearly justifies the popular statement in legal discourse that 'Justice delayed is justice denied' (Pickles, 1987). Recent research conducted by the Centre for Legal Research and Development shows that police and judges directly ask for bribes from litigants (Kantipur Daily, 11 Sept. 2000). From this evidences it can be argued that the legal service is not easily available to poor people and that it is slow and costly.

Earlier studies (Oli, 1998; New Era, 1988) also showed that court proceedings are quite lengthy and tedious. The following process noted by Oli (1998: 59) explains how complicated and lengthy is the Nepalese court procedure: "*if there is a conflict related to natural-resource management, or jure in re the parties set their case in what are called pleadings. The plaintiff files a particular claim. The defendant then files a defence and in some cases also a counter claim. The plaintiff then files a reply and defence to the counter claim. The defendant may blame party and bring into action through third party notice. The third party files a defence to that. The other side may ask for further and better particulars of any of these pleadings and this cause delay*". From this explanation it has become apparent that the time taken for a trial of a conflict case in court is remarkably lengthy, complicated and costly for poor and marginal people in terms of knowledge, time, and resources.

It was pointed out by the respondents that disputants have to wait up to five to seven years to settle disputes in court, by which time both plaintiffs and defendants have had to bear enormous physical, financial and psychological stress. Only lawyers gain remarkable benefits from such a lengthy process. It is also observed that lawyers and solicitors deliberately work in a complacent pace to maintain a continued source of income form the lengthy cases. Judges also support such lingering, as Pickles (1987) says '*we all are lawyers together and must stand together*'. There is not any evidence of persons responsible for delaying court proceedings being punished or being made to pay compensation to their clients for deliberately caused delay. In this context it will be relevant to quote that: *"hundreds and thousands of people spend sleepless nights in their homes and many more live in jail, anxiously awaiting the resolution of a conflict on natural-resource management"* (Oli, 1998:60). Other research findings (New Era, 1988; Kaplan, 1995) also demonstrated that wealthy and educated people obtained justice, from the formal system, more easily than poor people. The frequent and widening gap between rhetoric (rules, laws, policies) and real practices, the effect of differential legal knowledge, the high cost involved in obtaining justice and suspicion of fairness by the disputants are common problems in the formal legal system.

It has been observed that several formalities and technicalities in judicial administration caused an overload of conflict cases in court. Furthermore, court personnel lack the required technical knowledge and information related to natural-resource conflicts, which undermines credibility of the verdicts. Sangraula and Gurung (n.d.:3) state that *"In ordinary court house, a judge because of his/her legal background may not be familiar with the technical aspects of the case in hand. Half of the trial may be taken up explaining the technical aspects to a judge. Parties are lucky if, the judge is able to understand half of the issues explained. [..]. Technical expertise is not usually available in court proceedings"*. This situation makes for delay in rendering courts' decisions. In the legal system there is no efficient, amicable, expeditious and inexpensive mechanism to manage conflict and narrow down the areas of future potential disputes.

The settling of disputes by individuals appointed by disputing parties was formally started in 1956 under the Development Board Act, 1956. Enactment of the Arbitration Act in 1981 further strengthened legislation on arbitration. However, it is strictly limited to trade and commerce. Because of inappropriate and vague provisions, the arbitration act is not able to address the objectives for which it came into force (ibid:2). Litigation calls for frequent adjournments that make for delay in court process. The court, as stipulated in the Arbitration Act, is not able to maintain list of panels of arbitrators. Moreover, the tribunals constituted for arbitration are composed of lawyers, retired bureaucrats from governmental judicial services and retired judges, instead of being balanced by including experts in the fields concerned. It is also observed that there was no counselling in the conflict cases decided by courts, the police or the general administration.

From the reaction of the villagers arriving in district headquarters to accomplish different official tasks in different government organisations it was known that to obtain *tok-aadesh* (order-directive) to get things done it is necessary to mobilise *afnomanchhe* (*afnomanchhe* is a circle of family connections and relatives, externally developed by being extraordinarily loyal to a particular person, and with strong connections and interpersonal relationships with powerful people, who can be used if needed). It is also observed that a person having authority knows that there is no way to accomplish things other than by issuing *addesh* or paying bribes, regardless of their impacts. It is common to say to the customers in the government offices that *"addesh khai, mathiko tok aadesh chaincha, Hakim sable tok launu parcha, aile hundaina, bholi aaunu"* (Where is order? We need order/directive from the boss. It is not possible to do this work today, come tomorrow). This sort of dialogue is a veiled demand for a bribe/kickback. If customers offer a bribe to the official, then the necessary action is taken, but if not then he or she keeps them waiting for up to several days even for something that could be accomplished in a few minutes.

At the time of the local election, politicians and party cadres show an unexpectedly soft attitude towards disputants and therefore, many politically backed, unresolved conflicts were resolve instantly. For example, at the time of the parliamentary election in 1999, 155 unresolved social conflicts were resolved locally in the study VDCs. All resolved conflicts involved disputants, who were the supporters of the candidates of the parliamentary election. Similarly, 64 new conflicts were deliberately ignited to distract the voters from other candidates, in order to win the election. These new conflicts were between the voters from unidentified political affiliations or voters of other candidates. The VDC is becoming an increasingly important formal forum to resolve local conflict as the LSGA gives jurisdiction and defines the judicial procedures it has to follow. Most of the key informants (politicians, government officials, and local people involved in the conflict) stressed that the VDC is the most appropriate formal organisation to deal with community level natural resource related conflict. However, VDCs are not yet properly aware of their statutory authority, sometimes going beyond their jurisdiction and often being unable to use their statutory authority. If they work according to their jurisdiction, VDCs are the most efficient (in terms of access, familiarity, expenses and time) of the formal CM systems.

Provision of user groups and associations, made by different acts are used as legitimate forums to obtain financial and/or political benefits by different interest groups such as NGOs, political parties and local neo-elite groups. In practice, user groups and associations are not operating according to the ideals of these acts. For example, water is not used in the community according to section 7(1) 'priority order on the utilisation of water resources' of the Water Resource Act. Neither are conflicts related to water being settled according to section 7(2), nor are the payments of compensation to individuals, made for the use of their lands as stated in the act. The WRA makes provision for compensation to individuals to use or acquire their lands to construct dams, barrages, canals, ditches, water tanks, or for laying pipes, etc. but such compensation are given only if the eligible recipient is powerful enough to exert power. All forest disputes are also not settled according to the provision made in section 29 of the Forest Act, 1993. Well-informed people can manipulate the situation in their favour by use of the provisions of the acts. If people were better informed about these acts, policies and regulations, there would be less conflict and less exploitation. Some NGOs have started promising awareness raising activities but the scale is very small and therefore of little influence in terms of the wider impact. Even NGOs are marginalised and ignored by government offices. There is mistrust between NGOs and governmental officers as both blame each other for misuse of resources.

Referring to the earlier land measurement conflict, the Land Measurement Act (seventh revision) makes provision for demarcation and measurement of government and public lands, before the demarcation and measurement of private lands. However, in practice, measurement of public and government lands at the time of survey, under the name of powerful individuals was common. Those people who were well informed about the legal provisions and familiar with survey procedures could influence surveyors by bribery and were able to ensure that communal and governmental lands were measured under the names of their relatives and themselves. During the cadestral survey and land mapping in the study district between 1991 and 1996 these practices meant that large areas of communal and government lands were legalised under private ownership. The registration of public lands to powerful individuals was often supported politically and technically (using technical jargons and arguments by technicians). This has been shown by the more than 1300 cases on the land survey, filed in the district court. Article 10 of the Land Act classifies land into four categories based on the quality of land. The first category of land is called *Abal* (having irrigation facilities all year round, productive and fertile land with at least two crops a year). The second category is *Sim* (land with seasonal irrigation facilities, fertile soil with the potential for 2 crops a year). Third category is *Sim* (land with no irrigation facilities and based on rain-fed irrigation, a single crop per year). The fourth category is *Chahar* (dry poor quality soil, non-irrigated and only one crop a year). However, the surveyors, in consultation with local landlords and local politicians determined the category of land based on the amount of bribe instead of quality of land. The first category of land is that with a high valuation and the fourth category is that with a low valuation. Powerful people, wishing to have mortgages with banks or financial companies therefore want to raise the value of their poor quality lands. These practices demonstrate how government organisations responsible for NRM issues, operate in reality.

4.4.5. Assessment of Performance of Formal Conflict-management Systems

In interview with litigants coming to the different offices responsible for settling social and natural resource conflicts at district headquarters, a negative response was received on the performance of these organisations. To further

Table 4.4. Assessment of Performance of Formal CM System by Villagers Involved in Conflict

Assessment indicators	Response						Total
	Yes		No		No judgement		
	Number	%	Number	%	Number	%	
Political intervention in conflict	70	70	20	20	10	10	100
Good performance of judiciaries	10	10	60	60	30	30	100
Easy access to judicial system	10	10	70	70	20	20	100
Influence of money and power	70	70	5	5	25	25	100
Ambiguous role of GOs	40	60	30	30	10	10	100
Elite domination in CM	75	75	12	12	13	13	100
Transparency of CM process	6	6	74	74	20	20	100
Effectiveness of local CM practices	75	75	20	25	—	—	100
Need for reforming existing formal CM system	70	70	20	20	10	10	100

Source: Primary Data, 1998-2000.

understand the situation in reality, a simple-checklist type of questionnaire/survey-cum interview was carried out with different government officials, politicians and local people directly involved in conflict. They were requested to assess the performance of the formal CM system against nine given indicators. By and large their responses in this regard, which is presented in the following Tables (4.4, 4.5, 4.6) were frustrating in terms their performance. However, using the same assessment indicators the opinions of the people involved in the conflict were even stronger than that of government officials. The majority (70%) of them think that political intervention, influence of money and power and

Table 4.5. Assessment of Performance of Formal CM Systems by Officials

Assessment indicators	Response						Total
	Yes		No		No judge-ment		
	Number	%	Number	%	Number	%	
Political intervention in conflict	10	33.3	10	33.3	10	33.3	30 (100)
Good performance of judiciaries	5	16.6	10	33.3	15	50	30 (100)
Easy access to judicial system	10	33.3	20	66.7	—	—	30 (100)
Influence of money and power	20	66.7	10	33.3	—	—	30 (100)
Ambiguous role of formal GOs	5	16.6	15	50	5	33.3	30 (100)
Elite domination in CM	20	66.7	7	23.3	3	10	30 (100)
Transparency of CM process	12	40	15	50	3	10	30 (100)
Effectiveness of in-formal CM practices	20	66.7	10	33.3	—	—	30 (100)
Need for reformation of existing formal CM system	25	83.4	5	16.6			30 (100)

Source: Primary Data, 1998-2000.

elite domination in CM is high (Table, 4.4). The vast majority of the respondents agree that there is a strong need to reform the existing formal CM system. Likewise, both groups acknowledge that the informal CM is more effective than the formal one, due to the latter's inherent weaknesses. Furthermore, local people actively involved in conflict are not happy with issues of transparency involved in the formal CM systems.

Table 4.5 shows that government officials themselves are not satisfied with their role in CM. However, most of them

Table 4. 6 Assessment of Performance of Formal CM System by Politicians [9]

Assessment indicators	Response						Total
	Yes		No		No judge-ment		
	Number	%	Number	%	Number	%	
Political intervention	40	80	5	10	5	10	50 (100)
Good performance of judiciaries	15	30	30	60	5	10	50 (100)
Easy access to judicial system	5	10	45	90	—	—	50 (100)
Influence of money and power	45	90	5	10	—	—	50 (100)
Ambiguous role of formal GOs	30	60	15	30	5	10	50 (100)
Elite domination in CM	40	80	10	20	—		50 (100)
Transparency of formal CM process	25	50	20	40	5	10	50 (100)
Effectiveness of local CM practices	25	50	25	50	—	—	50 (100)
Need for reforming existing Formal CM system	50	100	—	—	—	—	50 (100)

Source: Primary Data, 1998-2000.

9. Politicians include: Members of Parliament, ex-ministers, DDC executive members, heads of the local political parties and chairpersons, vice-chairpersons and members of VDCs.

do not want to speak openly on sensitive issues such as performance of the judiciary and political interventions. The data indicates that there is lack of transparency in the dominant formal CM practices. More that 66% of respondents consider that the influence of money, power and elite domination in the formal CM system is common and therefore the performance of informal CM practices is viewed as more effective. Respondents acknowledge that the formal system, particularly the judicial system, is lax and not easily accessible to poor people and these people prefer the informal system.

Table 4.6 shows that political leaders are also not satisfied with the performance of the formal system responsible for dealing with conflict. They unanimously expressed the need for its reform to make it more responsive and effective.

The potential reasons given for the poor performance were the excessive influence of money, the blatant exercise of power and source-force, elite domination and party politics in the current system. Thought that the current formal system is not easily accessible to the general public. As can be seen in Table 4.6 the fair resolution of a conflict was a shattered hope or even a nightmare in the study area.

One of the government officials said that if the civil servants do not follow the instructions of politicians, instead sticking to the rules and regulations they have to face punishment or transfer into remote and difficult (mostly Maoist affected parts) areas. Immediately, politicians complain to more senior politicians of their party and/or concerned ministers to take action against the officials who have disobeyed their instructions. Ministers immediately take action if the person concerned has no countervailing power through *Afnomanche* in political and bureaucratic circles or does not offer a bribe. Such transfers have happened within 48 hours in some cases. So, it is better for the officials to obey illegal instructions instead of facing such punishment. More than 90% of respondents

Table 4.7 has an even more interesting story to tell. A total of 50 people who had won their cases in the formal CM system were asked to indicate the means they used to win the cases. Only 4% of the respondents won the cases without using any illegal means. The remaining 96% used illegal means such as bribes, the use of power or the mobilisation of *afnomanchhe* to win conflict cases. Among the different means used to win the case, the most common was a combination of bribery and mobilisation of political power and *afnomanche*, especially for complicated cases. Twenty percent of those who had won their cases only used bribes to win the case, 30% mobilised political power (leaders of the political party to which they are affiliated) and 6% mobilised their *afnomanche* to influence the case in their favour. This confirms that fair judgement and real justice is in serious question in the existing formal CM system.

Table 4.7. Means used by to win the Cases from the Concerned Formal CM Organisations.

Means used to win cases	Number	Percentage	Remarks
Use of Bribes[10]	10	20	
Use of political power	15	30	
Mobilisation of *Afnomanche*	3	6	
Combination of all three	20	40	
Fair, without any illegal means	2	4	
Total	50	100	

Source: Primary Data, 1998-2000.

During the interview, some staff of the offices responsible for formal conflict-management explained that Brahmin, Chhetri and well-informed people are more involved in conflicts in the district. Tamang (16%) is the second largest population group after Chhetri (34.2%) and Brahmin (11.4%) in the district (DDDC, 1999) but Chhetri and Brahmin are more

---

10. Bribes include both cash and kind. Kind includes, dehusked rice, fruit and vegetables, animals and animal products such as hides, ghee, milk, fish, honey, furniture, forest products such as wood, herbal medicines, clothes, gold and even occasionally land.

involved in conflict. The main reasons according to them are the level of awareness, affordability, and having *afnomanche*. The Tamang is third major group using the formal process of conflict resolution. I met a group of people in the district headquarters who had come to hear the verdict of the court on their land conflict with a local landlord. One of the group members expressed his frustration when they lost the case saying that *"Afnomanchhe chhaina, source-force chalcha, hami kharcha garna sakdainau ani ke mudha jitnu, gayyo tetiramro namari jagga sittaima. Tettiko tarik bokiyo insaf paiyela ki bhanera, faisala ta aarkai po bhayo"* (We have no people in power of our own, source-force is common and we can not invest money (for bribes), so how could we win the case; we lost our best land. We made regular appearances in court to get justice but the verdict was unexpected).

Source-force and *afnomanchhe* are very common practices in formal dispute-resolution practice in Nepal. Source-force is defined as having a contact (friends and relatives) who has the power to do what is needed. The strong belief is that every rule, law and procedure can be bent to one's purpose if an adequate source were at hand (Stiller and Yadav, 1979:120). If a person has *afnomanchhe* in authority or power he or she can force things to happen in their favour or negotiate when things get difficult (SNV, 1998). This can result in the opening of doors, instantly obtaining information, the completion of paper work on time, the bypassing of bureaucratic hurdles, saving unnecessary hassles and achieving a result in one's favour. In Nepal, source and force is universally applied for employment, promotions, transfers, scholarships, to win dispute cases, training, in fact for almost any activities. Competence, evidence of rights and wrong and justice become secondary in the face of source-force (ibid.). One intellectual person in this regard expressed his frustration with the Nepalese administration system saying *"one no longer believes that the Nepalese administration operates on the principle of what is fair and just but all believe that it is operated on source-force and corruption"*.

New Era reports that the court staff also accepted causes

for the poor performance of the legal system such as high attorneys' fees, a low level of legal knowledge and the complex judicial administration. The fairness of the Nepalese judiciary also depends on the personalities involved. In districts, politicians and administrators let the judiciary to know their wishes then these wishes are accommodated by the judiciary as much as possible (New Era, 1988).

It has become apparent from the expression of the then Chief Justice, reactions of politicians and people involved in conflict, earlier research findings (Kantipur, 11 Sept. 2000; New Era, 1988; Oli, 1998; Upreti, 1998b; Kaplan, 1995; Bhatiya, 1995; Khanal, 1998; Khanal, 1996; Shrestha, 1996a; 1996b) and empirical evidence of this study that the Nepalese formal CM systems are inefficient in timely resolving conflict cases and giving fair justice. This is due to several reasons such as the overwhelming numbers of conflicts arising due to faulty policies and procedures of the government and development organisations, lack of sufficient manpower, bribery and kick-backs, the complicated litigation process, lack of transparency, influence of power, politics, money and *afnomanchhe*, ambiguous and contradictory laws, regulations and tasks of government officials.

4.6. Comparison with Reference Groups

The comparison of the findings from the study area with reference groups confirmed that the sorts of community level CM practices are largely identical. It became clear that attempts to politicise conflict for political benefit, elite domination in NRM and conflict resolution, inaccessibility and complications of the formal conflict management in general and the court system in particular to poor villagers were similar in all reference sites. The comparison also indicated that the accommodative nature of people engaged in social and natural resource related conflicts, the change in the social organisation and power relationships in the village after democracy and their impacts on conflict management are largely similar. Intensity of conflicts and their transformation were affected by time. This characteristic was common in both research area and throughout the reference sites. In the reference groups of ethnic homogeneity, an accommodative strategy of CM was higher than in hetero-geneous groups.

4.7. Changing Power form and its Impact in Conflict Management

As I discussed earlier, the post Rana period (1951 to 2000) in Nepal experienced the following power forms, which are more influential in dealing with conflict and CM practices in the study area. Due to rapid political (3 major political changes in 1950/51, 1996, 1990), economic and technological changes the power forms have also changed accordingly.

(a) Cultural and religious power was more influential before 1970. During that time people were using cultural norms and religious rules to deal with most of the conflicts. However, this means was also used to exploit poor people. Religious rules were strictly applied and violators were severely punished. Social relations were based on cultural and religious norms.

(b) Economic power was more influential during 1970-1990. Gradually the religious power in the study area was reduced and the influence of money and wealth was increased and that became the basis for the development of social relations and resolution of conflict. Rich people influence poor people by lending them grain and cash. The determinant factors to escalate and/or resolve conflict then become money and grain.

(c) Physical power was more influential during 1990-1992. During the popular movement in 1990 and immediately after that the physical force became more prominent in villages. Physical attack and fear of physical fights greatly shaped social relationships and the pattern of conflict.

(d) Knowledge, information and party political power was more influential during 1992-2000. The physical power base has changed to knowledge, information and ideology based social relations in the community after 1992 when the political parties took control over from a "free riding" situation. The election was accomplished, majority government started to rule the country. The escalation and resolution of conflict as well as exploitation and discrimination all were based on party ideology.

4.8. Conclusion

Several conclusions may be drawn based on the quantitative data and qualitative information presented in this chapter. Similar characteristics of social and natural resource related conflicts across the country is by far the most important explanation for the observed widespread prevalence of political intervention and the influence of power and money in CM. Fairness, ethics, the rule of law and judgement play minor roles in determining CM. This suggests that the existing socio-political system, more than anything else determine the outcome of conflict. In other words, the formal CM system is not responsive enough and needs prompt reform.

At the same time there is no assurance whatsoever that the formal conflict management system assures a fair resolution of conflict. The conflict analysis alone, without reference to the broader socio-political system and social organisation of the society, does not provide a real image of the dynamics of power and politics in CM. It also provides no real evidence of a fair role being played by state instituted organisations or of fair dealing by the political leaders and party workers to resolve conflicts.

The multi-temporal comparison of influential power forms that created or escalated conflict between 1950 and 2000 shows that traditional power structures are changing fast and new power forms are emerging and influencing CM. There appears to be little supportive evidence of the claimed, effectiveness (NPC, 1998) of the existing linear top-down approach of CM through huge rigid structures and legal procedures. Given the large numbers of conflicts observed and the ineffective roles of existing organisations dealing with CM, an alternative approach for more effective CM (Chapter 9) is definitely needed. In agreement with the thinking of Warners and Jones (1998), Doughorty and Pfaltgraff (1990) and Buckles (1999), the evidence put forward in this chapter suggests that a new means of CM is essential for positive social change. However, there seems to be little evidence of an alternative CM emerging to break the rigid socio-political impasse. Neither are there any indications that the existing conflict management approach is changing its pattern to adjust to changing needs. What makes the alternative CM responsive to address these issues and contribute to enhancing non-coercive positive social conflict is the topic of chapter nine. The forth chapter also examined indigenous CM practices in their religious and cultural contexts. Some of these practices can be improved for lager scale situations. Specifically, positive aspects of local CM practices can be integrated into an alternate CM. This chapter also demonstrated that the dynamics of conflict in society do not allow for linear, specialist based conflict resolution procedures.

Embeddedness is a distinct characteristic of social and natural resource related conflicts. Based on the socio-cultural context, people use their own criteria to classify conflict. The major criterion is the effect of conflict on social relationships. Conflict is only categorised as severe when it disrupts social relationships.

CHAPTER 5

Creation, Escalation and Resolution of Conflict—Empirical Realities

5.1. Introduction

The previous chapter discussed the general situation of social and natural resource conflict in Nepal and their management practices. The chapter four shows that conflict is an integral part of society and influenced by the socio-cultural, political and economic situation and temporal and spatial factors. In this chapter I present three specific conflict cases, one related to farmer-managed irrigation, one related to forest and pastureland and another related to drinking water. These three cases are closely interrelated. This chapter not only explores how and why conflicts arise, but also analyses their interlinkages and transformations. It demonstrates that conflicts create problems but can also promote co-operation, generate alternative resources and change unequal social relationships in society. Diagnostic symptoms of conflict were reflected in distorted communication and information, anger, aggressive and defensive actions and other unusual social behaviour. The nature and causes of conflict suggest that it is a part of a dynamic process of social change.

5.2. Conflict on a Farmer-managed Irrigation System

A local elite through Janashramdan (what is known as people's 'voluntary labour' constructed the 2.5 km Andherikhola Farmer-Managed Irrigation System (AFMIS) in 1934. Its original command-area was 150 ha in the fifth, sixth and seventh Wards[1] of the Pawoti VDC. Farmers had managed this canal themselves, abiding by some specific rules and regulations. The function of daily management was assigned to the *Kulo Rekhdekh Samiti*. There were no major conflicts concerning the irrigation system and the water turbines.

This irrigation system was expanded later in 1970, to cover an additional 200 ha, using a governmental development grant. Earlier 70 households had been using the canal, but a further 100 households were added after the 1.5-km extension. This extension introduced severe conflicts in village due to the misuse of financial resources and water sharing by head- and tail end farmers. After the external intervention, poor operation and maintenance, weak management, an unreliable water supply, inequalities in water distribution, seasonal migration and misuse of funds were observed which had not been noticed earlier. The new beneficiaries, the old users and the local politicians became locked into a long lasting conflict.

In 1970, a powerful local political leader, who was also the *Mukhiya*, in consultation with the then *Pradhanpancha* (Head of the Panchayat elected by eligible voters. VDC chairperson replaced the term Pradhanpancha after 1990), obtained a government development grant and extended this canal to make irrigation water available in this area. The hidden aim of the extension was twofold, to terrace and sell public grazing and forestlands and to irrigate their unirrigated land located in the extended section. The sale of public lands by powerful people (generally from the Brahmin and Chhetri caste groups) to poor people was common at that time. Their position as elected political leaders and the fact that they came from a higher social strata, meant that the (unhappy) head-section farmers (mainly from the Tamang ethnic group and some Brahmin, Chhetri and Newar) did not openly

---

1. A VDC is divided into 9 segments for administrative purposes and each segment is called a Ward. An elected chairperson who is the executive member of the VDC heads each ward.

oppose their decisions. The extension of the canal was completed mainly by induced 'volunteer labour' from the tail-end farmers. After its completion several upland farms at the tail-end section were converted into irrigable lowland farms. There was fast encroachment of pasture and forestlands by powerful people, which until then had been used by the community. These were cultivated and sold by local political leaders. As the political leaders and village elite had a strong relationship with staff of the Land Reform and Land Revenue Offices in the district headquarters, they made the necessary legal documents for these public areas to be sold to the individuals. A small amount of the money earned from selling these lands was sufficient to keep these staff in their support. Because of the increased area under irrigation due to such terracing, large volumes of water were diverted to the tail-end section to meet the increased water demands. This led to the head-end farmers having water shortages in the peak agricultural season. Then the head-end farmers raised issue of water shortage and their riparian and seniority water rights. The tail-end farmers argued that the extension of the canal using government funds, gave equal rights over this AFMIS to all farmers within the command area, in contrary to the claim of the head-end farmers of riparian, seniority and investment rights.

Those farmers whose l. nds were used for the alignment of the canal made several access outlets in the canal and opposed sharing water with tail-end farmers. They also blamed the tail-end farmers for damage to their crops by water leakage, due to the large volume of water being taken to the tail section. However, the head-end farmers maintained good personal relationships with some powerful people of the tail end, by not protesting when they took water. This meant that most of the general tail-end farmers faced water scarcity problems. When the head-end farmers blocked the water supply, it escalated into a lasting conflict. In the prolonged drought in May and June the conflict escalated and led to frequent water stealing, physical confrontation and damage to the intake of the canal. These confrontations were concerned with access and control of water for water turbines, down-stream canals, and were between the head and tail end farmers of this irrigation system. In this way the previously, effectively managed irrigation system became dysfunctional. Rules of the Kulo *Prabandha Samiti* (Irrigation Management Committee) were not respected. Before the extension of the canal the *Kulo Prabandha Samiti* was composed of representative of all local farmers and all local farmers were themselves involved in the repair, maintenance and distribution of the water.

Rules Made and Executed by the Kulo Prabhandha Samiti before 1970

- Farmers of the head section have to finish their rice transplanting before the last week of June, after which other farmers have access to the water (from the first to the last week of July),
- Before every rice transplanting season all users must compulsorily repair the canal
- Chairman of the Kulo Rekhdekh Samiti should regularly monitor distribution of water, using a sancho (wooden water gate) in periods of water scarcity,
- Every user should pay four Pathi rice (approximately 14 kg) per hectare of rice field irrigated by the canal to pay for the caretaker,
- If conflicts arise amongst the users, they should report first to the Kulo Rekhdekh Samiti. If the Kulo Rekhdekh Samiti fails to resolve the conflict then they should go to the formal authority,
- If any one violates the rules for the first time (s)he should pay a fine, decided by the Kulo Rekhdekh Samiti. If (s)he repeats the same violation a second time (s)he will not be allowed to take water from the canal

Source: Upreti, 2001a

After the extension, operation, maintenance and water allocation activities were assigned to the *Kuruwa* (Caretaker, it is also known as Heralu, Choukidar, Naike) appointed by the local leaders. Due to the conflict with the head-end farmers, regular surveillance was felt necessary to bring water to the tail end. Otherwise, the head-end farmers could frequently stop the water supply. However, this did not function properly, due to non co-operation from head-end farmers. The existing conflict escalated again over the repair of the canal when its intake was damaged by flood in 1980 and the head section of the canal was damaged by big a landslide in *Kamare* area in 1986.

The tail-end farmers called a meeting between themselves and head-end farmers to settle the problem. At the meeting they agreed to share the water. They also organised a meeting with the users of downstream canals and water turbines to resolve the water scarcity problem. They made an unwritten agreement to share water rotationally. It was agreed that in the peak rice transplanting time water would not taken by the water turbines (as they need large volumes of water to run the turbines). This did not function properly because the owners of the water-turbines took water, when their customers came to grind grain, in disagreement with the negotiated agreement.

In 1986, the *Upapradhanpancha* (vice-chairman of the Panchayat) received forty-three thousand Nepalese rupees (US $ 632, at the exchange rate of Rs 68 per US $ in 1999) from the development grant of the District Panchayat to repair the problematic parts of the canal. It is a common practice to provide money as development assistance to the supporters and followers of the leaders of DDC. The hidden agenda in giving money under this arrangement is to financially support their followers. Some critical development examiners say that more than 90% of such a budget is misused. Therefore, he shared this money with another elite from the head section, to minimise the pressure from his political opponents and to mobilise the head-end farmers for volunteer repair. Consequently, only a small amount of the total budget was invested in repairing the canal. The real problem concerning the canal, which had caused conflict, was a lack of proper rules and regulations for access, distribution and rights over the water rather than repair and maintenance. The chairman and the *Mukhiya* were politically in opposition of the vice-chairman and therefore they brought the issue of misuse of money into the public domain. The vice-chairman was severely criticised for giving money to other people instead of fully invested it in repair work. After some years, the canal at the tail end was not able to support a full flow of water. Only a few active and powerful people from the tail end, who received water, were interested in being involved in further repair of the canal.

In 1995, the VDC again provided one hundred thousand rupees (US $ 1470, Rs 68 per US $ in 1999) under the popular *Afno-Gaon-Afai-Banau* programme to repair the canal. *Afno-Gaon-Afai-Banau* was a very popular (political) development programme presented by the CPN-UML government during its nine-month first ruling period in 1995. Afno-Gaon-Afai-Banau stands for Built-Our-Village-Ourselves. This was the first time in Nepalese history that local government had received financial resources directly from the central government to undertake a development programme. An active member of the ruling political party from the VDC got the repair contract. Repair was extremely badly needed at the tail section of the canal but work was carried out at the intake where there was no major problem. By doing this he saved a large portion of the total budget, which would have all been needed if the tail section had been repaired. Apparently, opposition leaders and villagers strongly raised the issue of misuse of money, which then turned into a political conflict. The opposition lodged complaints against the contractor to the VDC but no action was taken. Opponents also approached the DIO. The DIO avoided the problem citing that this project was out of its mandate. The DIO argued that their own technicians should monitor the fund provided by the VDC. In this case, the reaction of the contractor was different. He says: *"According to the grant condition, local people have to contribute to the project. It was absolutely impossible to complete the repair work without the participation of local people but they did not co-operate. In such a situation how is complete repair possible? The problem was only created for political gain and was a clash of personal interests. Whatever work has been done is according to the prevailing laws and regulations of the government. The misuse of resources is only a reflection of Nepalese political culture".*

Some frustrated tail-end farmers changed their cropping patterns and some farmers looked for alternative sources of irrigation and constructed other small canals from these sources instead of getting entangled in the AFMIS conflict. Some farmers even started rainwater-harvesting practices and others stopped working in the agricultural sector and migrated seasonally to Kathmandu and other areas to earn a wage. Heavy seasonal migration had already begun in the mid eighties when the Swiss funded 110 km Lamosanghu-Jiri Road Project was constructed mainly by using manual labourers. Labourers got far more wage from this project, which strongly encouraged people to change to wage labour. Khimti Hydro-Electric Project, Busti-Khimti Road Project, Arniko Road Maintenance Project, Kharidhunga Oriented Magnesite Project, etc. like big infrastructure projects in surrounding areas also used heavily pooled labour forced from the agricultural sector in the study area (Upreti, 2001a). A few farmers from the middle section bartered their turn of water for grain with poor farmers of the head section. Eventually, the remaining tail-end farmers negotiated with head-section farmers and made an agreement to share the water. According to this agreement tail end farmers were allowed to take water from the last week of June. Nevertheless, this agreement also did not function properly.

One of the respondents explained that: *"... Before the extension the users of the head section were united and acted together. All canal-related works were performed from voluntary labour. Leadership was unanimous. The Kulo Rekhdekh Samiti has properly solved all water-related conflicts. When political leaders received money the first time and extended the canal to irrigate their land, to sell grazing and forestlands then the problems started. Because of the money obtained several times for the extension and repair, not only* the performance of the functional canal became poor (also in head section) but also several conflicts escalated in the village. *The village elite and elected leaders used their power and position to force us to volunteer a contribution but they misused the budget obtained for this purpose. This situation made us prudent towards their activities. Many times we villagers have raised our voice against the misuse of money but nobody was ready to listen us, neither the district administrators, VDC, nor politicians. We are tired of the repetitive misuse of resources obtained from external sources. This has even increased after the restoration of democracy, which was supposed to improve this situation. So far, all major political parties have ruled the country but none of them show their responsibility to the poor rural people. They are not even ready to listen to the voice of villagers. Many small farmers and tenants have left agriculture and seasonally migrate to cities. Even after the negotiation some of the head-section farmers are reluctant to share water according to agreement. The big conflict in the forest and pasture land was the direct result of this extension"*.

Again in 1999, the VDC chairman from the same political party (who gave a grant to party workers to repair the canal earlier), planned to repair the extended section of the canal and submitted a proposal to the DIO to obtain funds from the ADB funded Second Irrigation Support Project (SISP). All the documents were already prepared and the project was in a stage of negotiation, when his local political opponents arranged a delegation of villagers to oppose this project and lodged a complaint at the DIO. They argued that it was not necessary to invest money in the canal, which was entangled in several conflicts. They proposed to repair another canal above the AFMIS that had not been functional for 25 years. However, the VDC chairman did not accept the alternate proposal citing the possibility of escalating the earlier resolved conflict about the canal alignment. The DIO decided to keep the proposed project pending and asked the interested parties to negotiate and come with a unanimous proposal. Since then there have been several arguments and counter arguments, blame and lobbying about this proposal which so far has not moved any further.

5.3. Conflict in Forest and Pastureland

This case describes the local dynamics involved in a conflict related to pasture and forest resource and the process of negotiation. Historically, the majority of pasturelands were governed under a common property regime, co-operative management of pasture by local communities who used that resource for their livestock. The Pastureland Nationalisation Act, 1973 empowers government to nationalise pastureland under traditional ownership with provision for delegating the use and management of such land to local village boards. Since then the dominant communal pasture arrangement has changed. The conflict in this case was related to the ownership issue and access to and control over of the community-managed forest and pasture land. The disputed forest and pasture site is popularly known as Matarkopakho. This 50 ha forest land surrounded by farms has been virtually always used by 40 households for grazing, collection of litter for animals, alignment for irrigation canals and as a place of worship. They possessed valuable knowledge about the management and utilisation of this land for a common purpose.

In 1971, a powerful politician who was also the *Mukhiya* (the same person involved in the first case) terraced and cultivated the Peepalkobot, Bhotekokuwa, mahankal-kopakho and Tirtirekodharo, different segments of the *Matarkopakho* forest-pasture area, with the intention of selling them after first using them for cultivation. The *Mukhiya* and the *Pradhanpancha* extended the Andherikhola Farmer-Managed Irrigation System up to this area to increase the value of the newly terraced areas. The *Mukhiya* and his joint family members claimed that this land was the property of his forefathers. Earlier, 110 years ago his great-uncle had terraced this land for cultivation because of his ownership rights over this land. But after a few years, when he fell ill, he left it uncultivated. He believed the terracing of the grazing land was cause of illness and he kept the land for grazing as usual. Some elite people of the village supported the *Mukhiya*'s argument. However, the farmers who had used this forest and pastureland for a long time claimed that this land was fully common pasture, owned by the community and that the great- uncle of the *Mukhiya* had encroached it for cultivation. They had obtained the *Lalmohor* (special approval from king or his designate) 100 years ago to use this forest as communal grazing land.

Other people who were supporting the encroachment also started terracing the remaining segments of that pasture area adjoining their fields. During that period it was common for local powerful people to encroach public lands. This case became more complicated because the villagers protested the intrusion. Such opposition was not common in the village at this time, due to fear of the powerful people. The protesters appealed to those encroaching the land to leave part of it to stop the conflict but this proposal was not accepted. In fact the protesters were threatened and tension between the two groups mounted. Due to the availability of irrigation from the Andherikhola Farmer-Managed Irrigation System extension, the value of land as well as land transaction had been increased. The *Mukhiya* wanted to get maximum benefit from this situation selling more barren, grazing and forest lands.

In the 3 years following the first encroachment the protesters made several unsuccessful attempts to negotiate with the invaders. Ultimately the protestors opted for a legal solution. Among the protestors 5 households were not ready to protest the encroachment because of potential risks, 7 households had morally supported the protest but did not wish to be actively involved and the remaining 28 households strongly opposed the invasion. After a series of confidential meetings and discussions they formed a *Sangarsha Samiti* (Committee formed to take action against land invasion) under the guidance of the *Kaitebuda*, an elderly and respected member of the community. Finally, the protestors lodged a written complaint to the *Sarba-Sampana-Daudaha*. This is a powerful administrator appointed by the central government at that time to inspect districts and settle the local people's problems on the spot. He had authority to punish any wrongdoers instantly. He immediately decided the case in favour of the protesters and issued a warning to the *Mukhiya* to leave the encroached public land straight away. However, *Mukhiya's* lineage brother was the head of the District Panchayat, his father was a powerful *Laptan* (a title given by Rana Prime Minister, the literal translation is lieutenant) and his relatives were in various powerful positions. By using this family power-network the invader did not leave the disputed land. The protesters changed their strategy to take the land back through compromise. They approached the *Mukhiya's* mother, elder brothers, *pandits* (master of religion) and *purohit* and mobilised them to force him to leave the invaded land. Heavy religious pressure was exerted over him. At the time of local election the users also mobilised other villagers in their favour forming a coalition. There were many dissatisfied land taxpayers under the *Mukhiya's* tax administration because they had not only to supply free labour during the agricultural season but also had to pay milk products, fruit, vegetables, potatoes, goats, etc. regularly to the *Mukhiya as Koseli*[2] *and Mukhiyoli*[3]. *Taking advantage of this situation, the Sangharsha Samiti* discussed issues with these taxpayers to form a concerted alliance. They announced that they would only vote for the *Mukhiya's* allies if he left the invaded land. Ultimately, from the pressure of his relatives, religious leaders and election tactics an agreement between the protesters and the invader was made in 1976 in which he had to return the major part of the encroached land. He was only allowed to keep a small part of land near his farm to limit crop damage from the grazing animals. This agreement also exempted any of the land he had already sold.

Before the intrusion, villagers were following the norms they had developed to use and manage this forest and

---

2. Koseli is an unofficial arrangement where the taxpayers have to give presents to the Mukhiya every season. Koseli items are generally goats, milk products, fruit and vegetables.

3. Mukheuli is an informal norm developed by the Mukhyia for all taxpayers under his land tax administration to contribute physical labour for his farm.

pasture land. There were no major problems in the use of the forest and pastureland. They had not considered an invasion of their grazing land was likely because once before another invader had left the invaded land due to religious beliefs. The following parable of a member of the *Sangarsha Samiti* reflects the situation: "*All of a sudden, our pasture land was terraced and cultivated. Thorn was kept in our doorstep[4] by invading our pastureland, which we had been using since time immemorial. We were totally dependent on this land for grazing and fodder collection. It was not our intention to go against the Gaonko Malik[5] though we did because we had no alternative. Many people were very afraid when we decided to protest the action of powerful politicians, Mukhiya and landlords from higher social strata. The Mukhiya felt insulted due to our protest and threatened us. But due to the creative ideas of my uncle Kaitebuda, and our continued protest over five years we were successful in having our land returned. That was one of the great successes in my life. If we had not fought for this land, it could have been turned into rice fields before 30 years.*"

Several times during the conflict the *Mukhiya* and his supporters threatened the members of the *Sangharsha Samiti* and once even the leader of the *Sangharsha Samiti* Mr Dhakal was physically attacked in a public place. They were constantly creating different legal and practical problems for the protesters. The *Mukhiya* refused to accept the land tax from these users. The problem faced by one of the protesters is quoted as: "*I had to purchase a rice field. I decided to sell my other land to make money. I approached him to get clearance but he refused to receive the land tax. Then I went to district headquarters and paid the land tax. At the beginning Malpot Addaka Karmachari (staff from the Land Revenue Office) harassed me and tried to force me to go back and pay the tax to the Mukhiya, but later, after listening to my problem, they accepted it. I obtained a land tax clearance certificate*

---

4. To keep throne in the door is a strong superstition causing a loss of all property and one's home and a collapse of future generations.
5. A local term which indicates the respected position of local elite in the village. Its literal meaning is the boss of the village

and purchased the intended land. Next year, I again approached him to pay the tax respecting his position but he refused. However, now we have a normal relationship".

While I was discussing this conflict with him, the *Mukhiya* was open in explaining his perspective about this conflict. He said: "*At that time there was an increasing trend to cultivate barren public land. The Pradhanpancha and Upapradhanpancha sold more than 1000 ha public land and almost half of the forest that existed in the VDC. Many people encroached and fenced barren lands adjoining their farms. This land was the property of my great-uncle. He left it uncultivated because, after dreaming that a white cow grazing in there had kicked him in his face[6], he left it uncultivated to graze cows. But the ownership did not cease. Of that land I had cultivated a small portion inserted in my field. The section of land, which I terraced, was not suitable for grazing because it was surrounded by cultivated land on three sides. Many time animals grazing in this part of land severely damaged my crops. Villagers had suggested me to cultivate this inserted part but only a few had created problems. Being a senior politician of the VDC it was not appropriate for me to go against my own villagers and therefore I was ready to compromise locally. However, they complained to the Sarba-Sampana-Daudaha but did not get any satisfaction. Nevertheless, because of my compromising strategy negotiations took place and the conflict was settled locally.*"

The *Pradhanpanch* was reluctant to talk about this conflict. He said: "*I have faced more than 100 cases of this type in my 45 years of political life. This was only one small case in the past 30 years, which I can no longer remember fully. What I remember is that part of this grazing land was cultivated by the Mukhiya. From our efforts, part of the cultivated land was returned to its original use. The leader of the protection committee was responsible for unnecessarily creating and prolonging the conflict but due to the understanding of other users and efforts of local elderly people, negotiation became possible*".

---

6. According to local legend if a cow kicks in the face of someone this means something very bad, such as death of the dreamer happens. To prevent this happening part of their own land should be kept uncultivated to graze cows.

During the process of negotiation, animals of the members of the Sangarsha Samiti damaged standing crops of the Mukhiya and other farmers. Children from the age of 8-14 were given the task of grazing their animals and collect firewood together. When the children gathered in one place to play, animals damaged the crops of the surrounding farms. On several occasions the farm owners caught the animals and punished the children, which led to conflict between the owners of the animal and farms. To resolve this conflict all household heads including the Mukhiya gathered in the Chautati[7] to discuss the problem. After several meetings they came to a unanimous decision to take turns (Gai Herne Palo[8]), one adult going daily as a cowherd to guide the children and watch properly to prevent crop damage by the animals. This platform created a congenial environment to discuss the forest and grazing-land related conflict with the Mukhiya and significantly contributed to the successful negotiations. "The success of returning land from the Mukhiya weakened the deep seated patron-client relationship, established a sense of group identity and disqualified the 'might is right' type of control of local natural resources", says an elderly man (user of this disputed land and brother of the invader).

After the successful negotiations, as a second step, the forest and pastureland users looked for a long-term solution to protect the land from future invasion and to regenerate the forest. Therefore, they decided on afforestation of the land. Their motive for afforestation was to involve government agencies and so minimise the risk of invasion. When the government is involved, villagers generally do not go against its action. Afforestation was a government-initiated programme and the DFO had the authority to give severe punishments in cases of offences in the afforestated or forest areas. During the 1980s there was strong governmental

---

7. A place with social and cultural value where people gather to discuss problems and pertinent issues in the village.
8. Local term to indicate the adults taking turn to go as a cowherd to monitor the activities the cowherd children to prevent crop damage by animals.

emphasis on afforestation and all forestry-related projects, the IRDPs and government offices were heavily involved in this task. This was a massive programme came to address the forest destruction crisis created by political leaders and smugglers in 1979/80 to protect the partyless Panchayat political system. Almost half of the valuable forest of the nation was destructed and exported to India. In 1984, Integrated Hill Development project (IHDP) provided seedlings, fencing, watering materials and technical support for the afforestation in the disputed land. During the afforestation, the son of the *Mukhiya* protested against transplanting forest seedlings in the part of the land returned earlier. A meeting was called and both parties agreed to transplant forest seedlings in all the disputed lands without considering the voice of the son of the *Mukhiya*. Then the elder son of the *Mukhiya* removed some plants from the land, which he had formerly protected.

After that event, the project and the users decided to control the forest area by appointing a watchman. The project sponsored to appoint one watchman. The watchman was appointed from the nearby village for strict surveillance of the forest area. This proved unsuccessful because even for very minor cases such as the removal of a few forest seedlings from the boarder of farmlands to construct a boundary, the watchman submitted written complaints to the DFO to take legal action. At that time DFO was legally very powerful having the authority to fine, jail and even to shoot forest offenders on the spot. This power was very much abused by the forest authority to collect illicit revenue. As a result the conflict between farmers having lands surrounding the forest areas and the watchman himself increased due to his biased intention to take legal action against the villagers. When the project was phased out and the DFO took responsibility for supporting this forest, it did nothing except threaten villagers, based on earlier reports of the watchman. Ultimately, the Forest Protection Committee changed the earlier approach of forest protection and asked a local NGO to support them. The local NGO helped them through different training programmes, meetings and problem solving discussions. They also ran courses to develop leadership whereby people got an opportunity to demonstrate their leadership qualities and the ability and capacity to handle local level conflict and manage the forest. They have developed rules and regulations themselves for the management and utilisation of the forest. To overcome the contested ownership claims, this disputed land was counted as public forest and pastureland during the time of land survey and measurement in 1994/95. Although the wife of the *Mukhiya* objected to this action raising the issue of her ownership to the negotiated land, her voice went unheard because of the domination of her opponents in the decision making process.

In 1996, conflict among the users was instrumental in obtaining the chairpersonship of the Forest Protection Committee. Many people were interested in holding the position, as it was a good means to motivate villagers, and persuade them to give their support in elections and other public activities. Potential candidates for ward chairperson and other positions, of different political parties were interested in being included in the protection committee. New users (other people from the same community who had not previously participated in protesting the land invasion) were pushed by political workers to claim inclusion in the beneficiaries group. However, old users, who had fought to conserve the land, had planted the forest and taken care of it, were not ready to recognise them as users and share benefits with people who were originally against their land protection campaign. Political workers wanted to include all the people hoping to obtain their votes to win the election. In the midst of the conflict the ranger from the government's forest office verbally granted primary users' rights to new users against the claim of old users. The tension erupted when there was strong competition for the position of chairperson of the Forest Protection Committee in February 1997. Both groups (new and old users) presented candidates for the election of chairperson. Though the candidate supported by the old users won the election the conflict between them remained unresolved. By using the conflict situation as an opportunity, the wife of the *Mukhiya* cut a few trees and cultivated a small part of the forest area, which she had contested earlier. She forced her husband and relatives to claim their ownership in that part of the forest. She was able to do this by using the situation of a changing power structure in the village and this was a small success for the *Mukhiya* family.

Earlier local leaders of the CPN-UML had a strong hold in the village and had been against the land encroachment. However, all family members (except one younger son) of the *Mukhiya* were supporters of the NC party, the main opponent of the CPN-UML. When the younger son (who was a UML supporter) of the *Mukhiya* was nominated by the CPN-UML as the candidate for the post of VDC chairperson, then the *Mukhiya* and his wife supported the CPN-UML. The son of the *Mukhiya* in his election campaign declared to the voters that settlement of the conflict over forestland encroached by his family would be his first priority if he won the election. After winning the election he did little to settle the conflict due to the pressure of his family. When the CPN-UML was divided into two fractions (CPNUML and CPNML), the hold of the CPN-UML became relatively weak in the village and the situation became favourable for the *Mukhiya* family. The tensions between new splinter groups increased and the people who were earlier protecting the forest politically divided into two groups, working against each other. The VDC and the DDC, both ruled by the CPN-UML were not ready to listen to the complaints of users because the majority of them were in the splinted fraction, i.e., the CPN-ML, which had become a serious opponent of the CPN-UML.

5.4. Conflict in Spring Source for Drinking Water

This case deals with the conflict between people of two hamlets in sharing a water source for drinking water. This case is basically the by-product of the forest-pasture land conflict described in section 5.3 and it demonstrates how one conflict links with another, how people deal with such conflicts and how they learn to negotiate locally for the effective use of the available water resource.

NARRATIVE DESCRIPTION OF THE CONFLICT CASE

This conflict is related to a spring-water source locally known as *Gofle Bhoteko Dharo* located in Ward seven of the Pawoti VDC. The people entangled in this conflict were Brahmin, Chhetri and Tamang. The area was densely populated (500 people per square km) and only three spring sources provided drinking water for more than 100 households. Among them, *Gofle Bhoteko Dharo* was a spring-water source located in the land of an individual and serving only a few households (hereafter referred as the "permanent users") mainly for drinking water and partly for irrigation. The source owner belongs to the Chhetri caste group with a relatively weak economic position. Villagers from the lower part of the village (who until then had no access to the water from this source and are hereafter referred to as the "claimants") who were all economically relatively well off and socially from higher strata, suffered from a lack of sufficient drinking water. The educational level, access to information and power centres of the claimants was higher than that of the permanent users. Water scarcity became more prominent when the number of households in the village increased. In 1970, two rich households from the claimants group decided to take part of the water from that source. The father of the source owner agreed to provide part of the water. However, due to the high investment required to construct the tank and lay down the pipe they cancelled the project. Later in 1989, the claimants again explored the possibility to appropriate part of the water from this source and discussed this issue with the source owner[9] and the permanent users. In the beginning, the source owner and the

9. His father had earlier agreed to share the water source, but as he was already dead the source ownership in this book denotes his son. Land invaders and many potential users were supporters of the panchayat political system, which made it easy to obstruct negotiations.

permanent users agreed. Accordingly, the claimants decided on location of the tap stands, collected stones, transported the hardware fittings and construction materials such as cement, polythene pipe, and fittings, given by the District Panchayat from the district headquarters. They also dug out the position for laying pipes from the water source to the area of the claimants. Due to the democratic movement in the country to overthrow the Panchayat political system the construction process was stopped for about 2 years. In early 1992, the claimants again started to construct the project.

At that time, the source owner refused to give water. He cited the problems of water shortages in the dry season for irrigating his field surrounding the source. The hidden reason behind this disagreement was rooted in the earlier forest-pasture conflict between villagers. The source owner was the nephew of the chairman of the forest-pasture land protection committee; the majority of the claimants were relatives of the land invader whereas the majority of the permanent users were relatives of the source owner. Therefore the son of the protection committee chairman pushed the permanent members and the source owner to protest at sharing water[10]. A few people from another area, who wished to take water from this source and had different political allegiance from the leaders of the claimants, also supported the son's action and convinced the source owner to refuse to share water. In the midst of the conflict, one of the claimants threatened the source c.vner by saying they were determined to appropriate water from this source at any cost. The resulting anger of the source owner and the permanent users contributed to escalation in the conflict.

The political differences among the villagers have greatly accelerated the conflict. According to other neutral villagers this water source was sufficient for both groups of people for drinking water as well as for irrigation. Lack of water was not the real cause of the conflict. The root cause of the conflict

---

10. The situation was very favourable to manipulate or obstruct development work at that time because of the freedom due to political change.

was the forest and pastureland conflict and exacerbated by misunderstanding and political differences between the permanent users and the claimants. The claimants argued that drinking water should get priority over irrigation. They had used this argument with the district authorities, DDC, and VDC. However, these organisations were not interested in getting involved in this conflict because of the political backing of the case. They decided to seek a local solution and approached the Ward Chairman (WC) to start negotiations about the conflict. Then, as a problem solving strategy, to technically disqualify the argument of the permanent users and the source owner about the lack of water in the source, the WC invited a technician (overseer) to measure the capacity of the source. The overseer verified that the source was sufficient to meet the needs of both groups of users.

One of the active women from the claimants group, who was also the initiator of the negotiation process, said that fetching water was the main responsibility of women. Women from every household have to daily collect approximately 200-400 litres of water for household consumption. Generally, it takes about 50 minutes to collect water from the source. The available water source was small and far from their area. The drinking water problem was primarily related to women. Therefore, the women of the claimants informally talked several times with the wife of the source owners and the permanent users and convinced them of their arguments. The women had intensively discussed this problem on various occasions, during Mela-*parma* (an exchange of labour to perform main agricultural activities) and *Pani-pandhero* (every morning and evening many women gather at a water source to fetch water). They also discussed the issue during *Ghans-daura janda* (villagers go together to the forest to collect firewood and grass) and *Hatbazaar* (an informal forum where people weekly or fortnightly gather to sell or buy different goods and to settle many practical issues). The occasion of *Bibaha-bratabandha* (religious ceremonies for marriage (*bibaha*) and sacred thread (*bratabandha*) given to the male to be eligible for marriage) were other forums where women made intensive efforts to convince the wife of the source owner and the permanent users. Women also have to work together to prepare materials for these occasions.

To resolve the conflict, a local NGO was invited by the claimants as a third party mediator. This NGO organised different training on communication, problem solving, source conservation, community participation, and conflict resolution as well as formal and informal meetings and discussions. Relatives of the permanent users and religious leaders were also mobilised to convince them to negotiate. The Brahmin priest called *Purohit* was actively mobilised by the Ward Chairman and ENAP to convince the permanent users. All these efforts made it possible to form a Mediation Group-*Madhesthata Samuha* (MG) from within the community. The MG proposed the following suggestions to resolve the conflict on the use of the water source:

Either the source owner sells the land where the source is located to the claimants on condition that the source would be accessible for both groups of users, or the owner allows water appropriation under the following conditions:

1. The claimants should construct a reservoir tank close to the source to collect water,
2. Water should be collected in the reservoir tank mainly at night time,
3. If, in case of water shortage for rice transplanting, water should not be collected in the reservoir tank during that time,
4. The claimants should take the responsibility for the conservation of the source,
5. The source owner and the permanent users should inform the claimants and the MG before using the water for rice transplanting,
6. Both groups should apologise for the past blame and misunderstandings,
7. If misunderstandings emerge, then the users have to inform the MG.

This proposal was thoroughly discussed in successive meetings with the permanent users, the source owner, staff of the local NGO, other villagers and the claimants. After almost two years of efforts the proposal with the above conditions was accepted and an agreement was made to use the source by both groups of users under the second category of conditions. During the negotiation meeting it was also agreed to explore the possibility of another drinking water project. As a result, representatives of both groups together with VDC approached the Drinking Water Supply Office and DDC and were able to obtain large drinking water project enough for four villages in this area.

5.5. Issues in Conflict an Analysis

This section analyses the issues raised by conflicts. The open and hidden causes for the emergence of conflict were rights to resources, power, political support, government money in connection with government intervention, etc. These conflicts were inter-linked with each others and were transformed into other social conflicts over time. The process of conflict management and their outcome were governed by various factors.

Basically all conflicts were manifested in the issue of access to and control of natural resources. The hidden reasons behind these conflicts were different, ranging from obtaining money from government grants to establishing rights over resources. However in all cases the issue of ownership was important. In the first case head-end farmers claimed their riparian and seniority right and the tail-end farmers also wanted to establish their rights. In the second case a member of the powerful elite wanted to establish his ownership rights in the pastureland, whereas the villagers wanted to prevent loss of their community ownership. In the third case the claimants wanted user-rights over the spring source against the claim of the source owner. These issues are discussed in greater detail in the following paragraphs:

The cases demonstrated that the entitlement of rights are generally related to an individual's involvement in managing natural resources, or in creating infrastructures such as expansion of the canal, or have an historical association such as grazing rights in the community owned forest and pasture land. When existing rights are not taken sufficiently into account while recognising or creating new rights, conflict is inevitable (Pradhan *et al.*, 1997). These cases illustrate that while political intervention is a generic problem and resource scarcity pertinently exists, their manifestation frequently changes and negotiation is required not only on use of resources but also on power sharing. Ownership and property right issues are dynamic concepts and change over time due to changes in the social structure, political process and power relationships.

Both physical factors as well as political forces are crucial to create and maintain rights over natural resources based on negotiation and re-negotiation. For example, the water turbine owners needed to be entering into negotiation in order to obtain water to run their water turbines and to minimise the feelings of uncertainty of their clients about the operation of the turbines. Similarly, the changes in land-use patterns in the tail-section in the first case also changed the claims for water rights.

In the context of community based NRM the important issues are who have access and who have control, how much and when one can appropriate resources (Bromley, 1992). They are generally based on the rules that relate to rights and benefits and obligations. Importantly, communal right (in the farmers manage irrigation case) was the general right to use the forest and pastureland by a certain group of people, which itself became a source of conflict. However, if grazing land is abundant this may not create conflict. In the case of grazing land the property right issue was associated with the authorised use of grazing land agreed upon and recognised by a group of people and the community. The claim of users on the pastureland was based on the agreed pattern of use in the community, accepted since time immemorial. This claim was also based on their efforts to protect and invest to sustain and manage the forest-pastureland.

All these three cases show that property rights are not only between people and natural resources, but are also a social relationship between people, because who uses, who controls and who are excluded is defined by social arrangements and sanctions. It was shown in all three cases that the claim of rights was changing over time with the change in local context, social organisation and power relationships. Those seeking new rights contest the existing rights in the changing circumstances.

The cases show that legal rights, like existing users have senior right and priority over new users. The vicinity of the water source land has a prior right (Khadka, 1997) but this does not always function rigidly. Rather, rights function on the basis of negotiation and agreement (Benda -Beckmann, 1999). It is important to note that the context (e.g., the presence or absence of rules about the uses of resources, alternatives to appropriate resources, ways of monitoring and controlling the behaviour of users, etc.), content and time factors alter rights. A matter of debate among the villagers was the control of water by individual on the basis of land rights or the right to use water publicly. Therefore, the debate is not only about water rights but also related to land rights. In the case of the spring water source conflict villagers wanted to transform the private ownership to communal access rights whereas they wanted to protect the communal access right in the forest and pastureland case.

In the irrigation case upstream farmers claimed their seniority right to use the water as *sabik* (old) as the water source belonged to their *chauhaddhi* (command area). They were therefore reluctant to share the water with other farmers. They also took care of the canal against potential damage of floods and landslides, which gave them a further reason to claim their rights. Many head-end farmers claimed their rights based on land rights since the irrigation canal passed through their lands. Similarly, tail-end farmers claimed their rights based on their physical investment during the time of expansion and also based their argument on the legitimate decision of the local government to extend this canal.

In the forest and pastureland case the property claim of both groups was based on historical association. All these arguments and counter arguments of farmers about access and control of resources make the property rights issue complicated and greatly contested. This implies that no clear property rights in natural resources can be deduced straightway from a single legal principle (Pradhan *et al.*, 1997). Acquisition, allocation and distribution of natural resources and their procedures are crucial factors, since they delineate these resources to users in terms of time and adequacy. They determine how much resource is available to supply to individual users in relation to their need and demand.

As noted by Benda Beckmann *et al.*, (1996), the behaviour of people towards access, control and transfer of resources and resolutions of associated conflicts are not completely regulated by state regulations alone. In practice, local people have their own cultural, social and customary practices, organisations, laws and procedures to address these issues. Customary practices and regulations, religious rules, local norms, economic opportunities and technical advancement have a great deal of influence on human behaviour in relation to control, use and management of natural resources. In the second case when new users became the primary users after the interference of rangers and politicians, these new users did not have much of an affinity with the forest. They contributed less to forest management and harvested more than allowed by the rules made by the previous old users. In this way, ignoring the traditional system, formal agencies are not only introducing conflict in the community but also promoting an unsustainable use of existing common property resources, previously sustainably managed by the communities themselves. Not recognising traditional rights of existing users' and excluding them from the decision making process does not achieve sustainable management of common property resources (Ostrom, 1990; Oli, 1998; Bhatiya, 1997).

5.6. Factors Affecting Conflicts and their Management Practices

Several factors played a role in the emergence, escalation and resolution of conflict. Among them the role of the local power structure and social relationships among the disputants and formal organisations and informal institutions played a crucial role in this process. In addition to these factors non-social issues of seasonality, scarcity of water, topographical proximity, and natural calamities such as landslides were important factors affecting the conflict management process.

5.6.1. Local Power Relations

The role of power is complex and problematic in these cases as the community was divided into factions based on power, family relationships and political ideology. The cases show that power relationships determine success or failure of management of community level natural resource related conflicts. Differences in wealth, gender, caste and ethnic background influence power relations in the community. Political preferences, differential access to power centres, rights and obligations of the community members determines collaboration or conflict over natural resources (Upreti, 1999b; Warner and Jones, 1998). Local political processes, values and differential power exercises influenced conflicts in all the three cases. That conflict should be triggered by the relationships of power is hardly surprising (Warner, 2000)

Villagers consider long-term effects while negotiating about conflicts. Local people only considered arbitration if the conflict became intense. The primary sources for arbitration were neighbouring villagers, local leaders, relatives and religious leaders. Only if negotiation is not possible at a local level, they do approach formal sources such as the VDC and DDC, police, district administration and courts for resolution. Some people and organisations become involved in conflict resolution for their own future benefit (for example, the members and head of the VDC become involved in a negotiation to gain support in an election). Nevertheless, the magnitude and dimensions of a conflict increase when people handle the cases with political interests. In such situations, the conflicts usually remain unresolved because the actions of local powerbrokers in dealing with the conflict are controversial and directly affect the established local interests.

The institutional basis of power possessed by overseers, local elite and the Ward Chairman gave them legitimate authority to influence the situation. Two characteristics of a person play an important role in issues surrounding any conflict (Warner, 2001). The positional character of the person, which an individual has by virtue of their particular social position (e.g. as the authority to take certain decisions) and their personal idiosyncratic character (features of personality, personal biography e.g., linkage with influential elite, etc.). The cases studied demonstrated that the idiosyncratic characters of local leaders and politicians played an important role in creating conflict. Power relationships within a community have certain characteristics, existing or evolving over time and space. It is important to realise that there are deliberate interventions of power brokers to influence or alter the conflict situation. In contrast to the role of power brokers, general villagers do not get entangled in conflict for the sake of power. Even when villagers are engaged in conflict, they show collective, associative and bonding behaviour. All these cases demonstrate that unequal power, legitimised in the established social system hinders resolution and promotes status quo and eruption of conflict.

Political allegiance is increasingly intruding into the creation and/or resolution of conflicts in Nepali villages (Kaplan, 1995, Shrestha, 1996a, Upreti, 1999b). Earlier conflict studies show that several conflicts may have arisen simply because the individuals involved belong to different political parties. Party politics serve to focus power alliances, which are an endemic part of Nepal's rural life (Bhatiya, 1995; Kaplan, 1995). Political allegiances are overriding the traditional basis for allegiance. Choice of alliance is not solely influenced by particular situations but also by the intention and pre-existing characteristics of the individual. Feelings of group identity (i.e. elite, powerful, powerless, rich, poor, landlord, tenants, etc.) psychologically forces people to form alliances. Contending parties seek alliance with other people of similar characteristics, intentions and interests. In 1970, the owner of the spring-water source agreed to provide part of that source to two powerful people because of their strong influence in the village. Allegiance to political parties in Nepal is an important condition for enhancing and/or inhibiting the processes of conflict resolution. Earlier studies also noted that political allegiance is the dominant and decisive factor in creating or resolving conflicts in Nepal (Khadka, 1997; Oli, 1998; Upreti, 2000b; Khanal, 1998; Shrestha, 1996a). When they fall into serious conflicts with others, people learn to ally themselves with strong political groups if their own position is weak. When they are active members of a strong political party and an unfavourable outcome is anticipated they can exercise political power to modify the outcome in their favour (Upreti, 1999b; Kaplan, 1995).

The political power of a disadvantaged group grows at the time of an election when they are able to vote. They can use this voting right as an opportunity to bargain with powerful people (generally only powerful people stand in elections). Social change through work of NGOs and civil society organisations are also empowering disadvantaged groups of people. Such empowerment efforts are also gradually being incorporated into the political process.

5.6.2. *Social Relation and Conflict*

Social relationships are an important factor in the resolution of community level conflicts. The cases studied demonstrated that relationships are based on socially shared values and power structures. Community level negotiation and re-negotiation are the central pivot of the water, forest and pastureland conflict conflicts. These negotiations in themselves are criteria that can be used to analyse CM in the power-unequal situation. Negotiation at the community level on resource use is predominantly a concrete social process defined by the relationships between the actors concerned. These three cases all show distinctly that there is not a well-defined single procedure or criteria to deal with CM. Many locally evolved situation-specific criteria help in community-level negotiations about the use of resources. These criteria are developed, tested and adapted in a specific social, ecological and cultural situation.

The cases show that the social relationships have a direct and influential role in CM. If social relations are good among the community members the greater the possibility of resolution of conflict. The cases have identified that the resolution of conflict is difficult if greed, vested political interests, and vertical power relationships dominate over altruism, generosity, co-operation, and tolerance. In such a situation CM is essentially a challenging and tedious task. An effective and lasting resource-use agreement is very difficult to declare and agree upon or implement in such a situation. Community conflict management is a constant learning and building process through unceasing efforts to encourage solidarity, altruism, civic spirit and respect for diversities and different social realities. Nevertheless, the cases have indicated that there are many threats to the accomplishment of successful resource-use negotiations. They are constantly under siege by power brokers and local elite, who wish to manipulate and distort them for vested interests and political gains.

5.6.3. Development Organisations, Informal Institutions and Conflict

The effectiveness of management of natural resource related conflicts depends to a large extend on the way in which farmers, technicians, politicians and bureaucrats are involved (Sidaways, 1996). Farmers usually co-operate with any external interventions if they are assured about the benefit (such as reliable and predictable delivery of water or ensured grazing) (Rhodes, 1997). Supply-led development interventions (the extension of the canal, for example), generally do not espouse the principle of democracy, equity and social cohesion (Pandey, 1999). Often, they support an unequal power structure within a community and ultimately they often fail on that social ground (Rhodes, 1997). The role of formal organisations in resolving the conflict in all three cases was not conducive in creating a win-win situation.

When there are multiple actors with their own interests, perceptions and objectives in any CPR then it becomes difficult to resolve the conflict. In all these cases political leaders wanted political benefits whereas general farmers wanted undisturbed access to resources (e.g., regular availability of water to irrigate their field, availability of grazing land, undisturbed access to drinking water). Political organisations were looking for a political advantage and a strengthening of the positions of their own party workers. The role of the *Sarba Sampana Daudaha* in the first case seems important in resolving conflict but the solution did not prove to be effective in the long term. In the second and third cases the role of the project, local NGOs and indigenous institutions were crucial whereas the roles of governmental organisations were ambiguous. It is may be concluded from all the cases that the role of the state instituted agencies in CM was ineffective compared to their official task and were influenced by local power relations and vested interests.

The religious connotations imbedded in the perception of people could help in resolution of some conflicts. Local norms, values and beliefs sometimes appear ubiquitous and usually have a practical significance in the conflict resolution process (Deutsch, 1973; Furtze and Stafford, 1994; Bottomore, 1996). Drinking water and pastureland were very much religious and cultural concepts in the study area. These cases demonstrate that the role of local customs in management of conflict related to natural resources is still significant. Indigenous institutions such as *Chautari, Mukhiya, Pako Manchhe, Sangharsha Samiti, Purohit, Mela-parma, Bibaha-bratabandh, Hathazaar* still have important roles in the conflict resolution process.

Legal provisions dominate the government's approach to conflict resolution in Nepal and therefore the importance of local knowledge is less acknowledged. Culture is a source of local knowledge that is developed overtime by sharing and interpreting experiences (Brenes, 1994). Local knowledge is the knowledge possessed by local people and contains a rich and untapped source of information about CM strategies and practices. Local knowledge encompasses specific characteristics and qualities, methods and ways of processing or transforming information for effective CM for sustainable management and utilisation of available natural resources. In the study area, not to provide drinking water or to encroach grazing lands are considered sins. As a norm, it does not matter who owns the source, drinking water should be accessible to the general public and should get priority over irrigation. Strong religious beliefs promoted by the *Purohit* that '*to provide drinking water is to pave the path to heaven and to create obstacles to drinking water and damage the grazing land of cows is to prepare to go to hell after death*' are still shaping the behaviour and actions of many villagers towards these resources.

Local approaches use tools and procedures that are moulded by the local people's own particular economic, social and cultural contexts. They provide a range of techniques with logical meaning and conditions for their own self-realisation. These cultural and social conditions are inherited from previous communities. I am not arguing that all indigenous and customary practices are better than the formal ones, but it should be emphasised that the positive aspects of indigenous approaches need to be properly utilised to manage conflict effectively.

5.6.4. Time and Space in Conflict

Spatial factors are one of the prime sources of conflict where resources are scarce. Proper resource allocation and distribution procedures and monitoring mechanisms minimise conflict and ensure fair access and control over natural resources in these situations (Axinn and Axinn, 1996). Physical proximity gives farmers more access and control of resources (Mollinga, 1998; Chambers, 1988). For example, in the first case farmers from the head section because of their closer access to the source were able to use more water by making extra outlets from the canal (both frequency and amount) at the cost of the tail-end farmers.

Time (seasonality) is another important factor in natural resource related conflict as there are no problems concerned with access to water during the water abundant period. The frequency of conflicts increases in the summer when the need for irrigation water in the paddy fields reaches a peak. Therefore, the differential access demand for water between farmers of different geographical areas, lack of proper control mechanisms and disproportionate access to irrigation water (improper water scheduling, uncontrolled water allocation, unreliable water supply, etc.) in times of water shortage are major sources of conflict.

Siltation, landslides, intentional damage to canals, seepage and leakage all contributed to escalating conflicts in the AFMIS but the effects were not severe and gradually ceased within a few weeks. Water distribution, in principle, should be based on matching the crop water requirement (Mollinga, 1998; Parajuli, 1999). However, in practice proximity and power, are more important factors determining water distribution than the water requirement of the crops. Furthermore, water requirement is a subjective judgement and influenced by factors such as the soil condition, efficiency of water application, the season and the specific crop variety. These are open to different interpretation (IMC, 1990; Parajuli, 1999). Water availability and frequency of conflict are correlated, the degree of water availability determining the occurrence and frequency of conflict, if other factors remain the same (Sukla *et al.*, 1997). Farmers have their own strategies to cope with water scarcity in the study area. For example, to prevent prolonged drought they worship the *Nag* (snake) on serpentine day (*Nagpanchami*) and *Indra* (king of the haven) believing that they give rain. *Indrajatra* and Serpentine day are the rituals of the ancient Hindu religion to bring balance to rainfall and to overcome water related calamities, which are still prevalent in the study area. *Nagpuja* and *Indrajatra* express people's gratitude to divine energy. Farmers also alter cropping patterns, the land-use system, rain water harvesting, delay cropping, change crop varieties and land management (mulching, early hoeing, minimum tillage, etc.) to cope with water scarcity.

At a time of water shortage, in the absence of a clear arrangement for water distribution, conflict seems to be a normal phenomena when the same source is used by more than one system (within and between irrigation and or drinking water systems), or for more than one use (drinking water, irrigation, water turbines, etc.). However, the occurrence and intensity and/or severity of the conflict varies with the seasonality, local power relations, availability of alternatives, contradiction of norms and regulations, cropping systems, etc. As was explained in Chapter Four, unlike other social conflicts, natural resource related conflicts, even though the frequency is high, do not generally turn to violence. Rather, they commonly limited to dissatisfaction and disagreement and generally locally negotiated and re-negotiated to keep the situation working. In all three cases temporal and spatial factors played important roles in escalating as well as managing the conflict. In the first case the deep-seated conflict became weak and transformed into an opportunity to opt for exploring alternatives. In the second case the time factor significantly contributed not only to resolving the conflict but also to creating a dense forest resource. In the third case the time factor played a crucial role in escalating and resolving the conflict. In all three-conflict cases the degree and intensity became less, as the conflict became old, but increased again with changing power relationships in the village.

5.6.5. *Public Preference in Conflict Management*

People involved in conflict use various strategies and options to influence the outcome in their favour. In all three cases the conflicting parties mobilised their networks, local instituti-ons, indigenous knowledge, community norms and values as well as formal legal regulations. Mobilisation of *Purohit*, religious arguments, complaints to the governmental mobile administrator, mobilisation of relatives and friends to convince the opposition, approaches to projects and NGOs all were example of diverse strategies used by people in a conflict. In a conflict situation people use laws and rules as resources to influence the outcome. The local norms such as seniority rights were used to justify their arguments. Formal laws were also equally used in the process of making arguments and counter arguments in all three cases.

5.7. Gender Role in Conflict Management

The role of gender itself is a social construct, which has to be seen in the particular social and cultural context. The important issue of who have access to resources and more importantly, who controls them is governed by social and cultural framework (Upreti, 1995). Gender discrimination in Nepal is clearly reflected in ideological, legal, political, religious, cultural, and social practices. These cases have also indicated that women had very little role to play in CM except in negotiating in the spring-water source conflict. Though the Constitution of Nepal does not directly discriminate against people, it still indirectly supports unequal power relationships by declaring Nepal a Hindu State. This is because the Hindu religion through various rituals, religious rules and customs is by and large discriminating. The respondents explained the causes of low involvement of women in CM as: i) not being able to express their feelings because of social suppression, ii) being afraid to go against *Thulomanchhe* (local elite and village landlords were respected in the village because of their wealth, power, exposure, relationships with politicians, police and government bureaucrats and coming from higher social strata), iii) not being allowed by their family members to go to the meetings and discussions and iv) being very busy with household chores. Some of the men strongly suppressed women's opinions saying *Pothi Baseko Ramro Hundaina* (a local legend which explains the superstition that 'if hen produce the same sound as a cock this will be unfortunate'). Because of such restrictions women have very little decision-making power. Even if women participate in meetings their opinions are not listening to or respected and the reaction of their male partners is more important).

Key women informants said that, earlier women had only shared their opinions with their husbands in their own houses, but did not participate in any meetings and discussions. The overwhelming predominance of men and the limited role of women in CM can explained some of the disruptive social practices in rural areas. The second case clearly indicates that as time and context changed the role of women also changed and they gradually became more involved in decision processes (for example, the wife of the *Mukhiya* who became a key decision-maker in the later stages of the conflict). Sensitivity to gender issues was an external concept and at the beginning, contradictory to the customary norms of the majority of users. Several studies (Rhodes, 1997; Bhatiya, 1997; Thapa and Weber, 1994; Ghale and Gurung, 1998; Upreti, 1995) as well the cases described here, have shown that over time the concept of gender issues is gradually being incorporated in NRM strategies and practices.

In the hill and mountain regions, women are the key persons and a rich source of indigenous knowledge and skills for NRM (Ghale and Gurung, 1998). If they are given the chance they effectively utilise all available options to resolve conflict. For example, the third case indicates that women used different forums to discuss their drinking-water problem and were able to create a favourable situation for water use. Many women also participated in the training provided by the NGO. Especially older married women were far more co-operative than the male members in resolving local level conflicts because of their ability to accommodate differences. Women respondents explained that men were less sensitive to drinking water problems than to those related to irrigation because they do not fetch drinking water. The male members were involved in the conflict, but the women were creating a positive social pressure to resolve it. The political groupings and biases were less important for the women compared to male members in the community. Party-led political bias did not hinder women from sharing ideas and discussing the problem. However, social status such as the higher position of their fathers or husbands, caste and class (education, economic condition, etc.), marital status, and other positional socio-cultural characteristics greatly influence the role of women in CM.

5.8. Learning from Conflict: Conclusion

Several researches have shown that rural communities in Nepal are far more capable than governmental organisations, in sustainably managing their natural resources (Upreti, 1999a, 1999b; Oli, 1998; Bhatya, 1997, Rhodes, 1997). Successful CM empowers local people based on social justice and utilises local institutions or creates new ones, if necessary, based on local conditions (Pendzich *et al.*, 1994). It can indeed be concluded that conflict can be a means of learning and a source of empowerment of villagers in general. These cases have shown that effective management of natural resources is mainly determined by needs and interests, coping strategies, adapted procedures and the initiatives of resources users. Despite the investment of local government (DDC, VDC) in water (in both irrigation and drinking water) in the study area, such efforts are not able to give satisfactory outcomes. Rather they are exploited by power brokers and are implanting and enhancing conflicts.

The cases have illustrated that conflict can teach people how to manage resources. The afforestration in the second case, the exploration of alternative sources for a larger drinking-water project in the third case or the rain-water harvesting initiative in the first case are evidence of local people's ability to learn. The harnessing of such local collective learning by institutions is vital in addressing natural-resource conflict.

All the cases demonstrated that even though the villagers become entangled in conflict they do not opt for violence and serious fight because they have learned from their own experience and from their ancestors to live in coexistence in their community. That can be seen from the commonly used local parable in the study area: *"Desko Deuta Bhanda Gaon ko Bhut Kamlagchha"* (the ghost of one's own village is more useful than the god of far distance). Villagers were adaptive and accommodative in their behaviour and make utmost efforts to negotiate locally.

The facilitation of a persuasive extension approach (which develops the capacity of conflicting parties to solve conflict by learning and adaptation) is crucial in CM, as was demonstrated by third case. Here the approach followed by a local NGO in mobilising people for collective learning and action was most effective in resolving the conflict. In such cases not only the local people learn to co-operate but also the facilitating organisation learns (Van den Ban, 1997) how to facilitate negotiation. The NGO facilitator's role in negotiating the drinking-water conflict proved that 'facilitation' is a pragmatic approach to enhance flexibility, adaptation and interactive learning (Röling, 1996; Röling and Wagemakers, 1998; Maarelveld *et al.*, 1997). The facilitation process either starts locally or from the help of external organisations. Many learning theorists highlight the fact that 'learning provides alternatives for problems' (Röling, 1996; Hamilton, 1995) and therefore learning is the means of problem solving.

When parties in a conflict realise the cost of it is too high and the benefits too low the length of it can be shortened. Among many positive changes brought by conflict in the study area, an important one was a change to the feudalistic relationships. The cases show that challenging the existing social structure and practice promotes reform. However, it is important to note that if conflict is not handled properly it not only wastes time, energy and resources but also causes the disintegration of harmonious social relationships, promotes insecurity and in extreme cases causes violence. The democratic methods of conflict resolution and normalisation of relationships through participation of both parties involved in conflict, the capacity for local mediator and leadership development, transparency, learning, communication, fair application of laws and regulations are vital for alternate CM which is described in detail in chapter nine.

All three cases show that villagers are not only active negotiators and mediators of conflict but also active managers of natural resources. They seek relationships with different people to exchange knowledge, information and experiences and to build alliances to develop and implement new ways of managing conflicts, even in a hierarchical unequal society. Local people, although not always recognised as such in Nepal, are the principal managers of local natural resources (Rhoades, 1997) and negotiators of the natural resource related conflicts.

I realised that learning from experience, joint decisions and purposeful collective action, communication and (in)effective use of information and local networks highly affect local CM. These cases have indicated that different groups (local elite, general villagers, and government officials) react very differently to the same problem. This leads to the conclusion that conflicts on natural resources are not neutral, but culturally and socially defined. It logically follows that a community is not guided by a unitary legal system and rules do not always shape the behaviour of people (Benda-Beckmann *et al.*, 1996, Spiertz, 2000). These rules are modified locally by people to adjust their needs and claims.

Based on the empirical evidence presented in this chapter, I argue that natural resource related conflicts create a lessening of mutual regard, disagreement, hatred and hostility but society does not disintegrate. Many times conflict strengthens truth and explores realities and opportunities. The cases show that usually the repressed parties bring conflicts to light but they keep within the tolerance limits whereby armed violation or seduction is prevented. Although many conflicts remain unsolved for extended periods of time a workable relationship between the parties involved is common. Major sources of conflict in natural resources are changes in traditional use pattern, vagueness of laws, misunderstandings among users, political interference and external interventions. Greed is the most important factor that aggravates conflicts. The study shows that conflict is more common if the parties involved belong to different political, caste/ethnic and economic groups. Such associations are a triggering force in conflict. It is obvious that the duration of the conflict and its resolution depends on the severity and complexity of the problem. Such resolutions are influenced by the skill and approach of the mediator/ negotiator and the benefit derived from the conflict. Effective communication and use of network/linkages promote willingness of conflicting parties to negotiate.

Local level resource-use negotiation and CM are not just issues of a formal mechanical arrangement but more importantly the process of accommodation of multiple interests and power differentials. It is important to realise that every one is biased and has their own perspective and interpretation of a particular conflict, which is based on their own social background, understandings and intention. These perspectives and world-views provide direction, help to explain and give order and perceive to the conflict and provide the potential for negotiation. Being aware of their own perspective allows them to agree or refuse to negotiate. Parties in conflict bring with them a whole range of rational, emotional, corporal and sensual diversities. They negotiate and become involved in the process of conflict resolution, not only because there are rational reasons to do so, but also because they get hunches, insights, have preferences, visions, dreams and hopes (Brenes, 1994).

This chapter has outlined 3 conflict-related cases and examined the strategies, mechanisms and practices of local-level management of conflicts concerned with the use of resources. These conflicts may erupt for several potential reasons such as diversity and inconsistency in application of customary practices and formal legal procedures, different perceptions of ownership and rights, management differences, top-down external interventions and other social variables. The chapter reveals that local people have their own strategies, mechanisms and approaches to utilise the available limited natural resources and resolve conflict. Furthermore, this chapter discussed the role of norms, values, beliefs, knowledge, power, communication and facilitation, feeling of ownership and property rights and temporal and spatial factors which have a profound effect on CM in Nepal.

CHAPTER 6

External Development Intervention— Source of Social Conflict

6.1. Introduction

In the fifth chapter I discussed the dynamics of conflict in a farmer-managed irrigation system, a community managed forest-pastureland and an individually owned drinking water source. That chapter clearly demonstrated that external development interventions, if not implemented properly, could introduce new conflicts into a community. This is discussed in this chapter, together with the role of various interest groups in igniting the conflict. To examine conflict created by external intervention I took the case of the Asian Development Bank funded irrigation development project called the Upper Andherikhola Irrigation System (UAIS). This chapter explores the extent to which an intervention without assessing the local socio-technical feasibility and social settings can make an irrigation-development project a complete failure. This chapter also analyses the effects external intervention can have on local social relationships within a community causing conflicts.

Recently there is growing governmental interest in the increase in food production through expansion of irrigated areas (NPC, 1998). Hence the government is increasing assistance to develop new irrigation systems as well as rehabilitate FMIS to enhance agricultural production and productivity by increasing the water supply and improving its reliability. It is expected that such intervention will result in expansion of the irrigated area and crop intensification. To achieve this objective the government has obtained foreign loans and grants from ADB, WB, and several other donors to develop several large and small irrigation projects, one of which is the UAIS.

**Table 6.1. General Overview of the
Upper Andherikhola Irrigation System**

S.n.	Parameters	Characteristics	Remarks
1.	Date of Survey	1990	By DIO
2.	Start of construction	1993	By DIO-WUC
3.	Date of completion	1996	
4.	Total investment	Rs. 8109959 ($ 119264)	Revised from original Rs 6575883
5.	Command area	447 ha	Pawoti and Sailungeshwor VDCs
6.	Target farmers	540 households	Pawoti and Sailungeshwor VDCs
7.	Length of canal	6 KM	
8.	Financial support	Asian Development Bank	Irrigation sector Support project II
9.	Implemented by	District Irrigation Office	With WUA/C
10.	Current status	Non functional	Severe conflict existed

Source: Upreti, 2001a.

The case study area is situated at an altitude range of 1500 to 2250 metres above sea level. The communities of the research site are different castes and ethnic groups such as *Brahmin, Chhetri, Tamang, Damai, Kami, Sarki,* and *Newar.* The socio-economic status of the people in the study area is very diverse with a large segment of population composed of the economically poor and some people being very rich. Economic status and feudalistic social arrangements mainly dominate social relationships.

6.2. Background of Conflict

In 1982 a powerful member of the village elite group, with the recommendation of the *Pradhanpancha*, formally applied to the Department of Irrigation (DoI) to construct an irrigation canal from the Andherikhola. Respondents explained that the motive behind this was to irrigate his newly purchased semi-irrigated land. The DoI conducted a survey and prepared a report. However, due to a lack of follow-up in getting approval from Kathmandu, this project was not executed. When the District Irrigation Office was established in the district headquarters in 1989, the Department of Irrigation forwarded them the survey report. As a newly established office, the DIO found this one of the suitable projects to start immediately. Therefore this project was activated. The ADB provided a loan to the government to develop the irrigation sector through the Irrigation Sector Support Project (ISSP).

Dolakha was also one of the districts covered by ADB-funded irrigation project (ISSP). An active local politician (hereafter referred to as the initiator) from the Sailungeshwor VDC had started to work with DIO as a contractor in another irrigation project whereby he established a 'relationship of special intimacy[1]' (Wade, 1982) with DIO-engineers. The DIO engineers suggested the reactivation of the UAIS with a fresh application, linked with the former one, to be submitted by another member of the elite with the earlier recommendation of the *Pradhanpancha*. Accordingly, the initiator submitted the application to the DIO with signatures of some villagers. The DIO conducted a detailed survey and made a budget estimate under ADB/ISSP and forwarded it for approval. The Regional Appraisal and Approval Committee (RAAC) granted approval without any difficulties. RAAC is formed under the chairmanship of the Director of the Regional Irrigation Directorate to appraise and approve irrigation projects which cost less than Nrs 10 million, on the basis of the recommendation of the District Appraisal Committee (DAC) and to provide guidelines for the smooth implementation of the project. The DIO chief is the convenor of the DAC.

---

1. Bargaining for bribes is more direct and surreptitious between contractors and engineers who have developed a relationship of special intimacy (Wade, 1982).

The first conflict between local villagers and DIO/initiator concerned alignment of the canal, when local people found out that the originally proposed alignment of the canal was changed at the time of the survey by the DIO-technician on the suggestion of the initiator[2]. Many people were not aware about the survey of this project, so no organised efforts had been made to construct the canal from an earlier proposed alignment. The villagers only objected later when they realised about the change in alignment. However, the feasibility study of the project was already completed so their opinion was ignored and the conflict between local people and the DIO remained unsettled. Immediately the project was approved, a WUC was formed of supporters of the initiator in 1992, under the guidance of the irrigation technician, to meet the criteria[3] of the Irrigation Sector Support Project without discussing this with the other villagers. The person, who had earlier initiated the process for this project, was nominated chairman and the initiator himself became secretary of the WUC. The VDC chairmen of both Sailungeshwor and Pawoti VDCs were not consulted during the whole process. After the formation of the WUC, the DIO released 1.5 millions rupees (22059US $ @ 68 rupees per dollar in 1998) for the first year to start construction. When local leaders and chairmen of the two VDCs knew that 1.5 millions rupees was released for this canal they were anxious to be actively involved in the WUC because it had the authority to take all decisions related to the project. However, the WUC did not respond to their sudden interest. The VDC chairmen felt their roles were being undermined if such a big project was implemented in their VDCs without their active involvement. They therefore raised the issue in public and deliberately created problems for the WUC. Their supporters from the down-stream canals of Fasku and Pawoti

---

2. According to the respondents the motive for the change in alignment of the canal was to increase the total cost of project.
3. According to ISSP criteria, the implementation of the project should be carried out by WUA/C (DoI/ADB, 1997).

VDCs then actively raised the issue of water rights (prior or seniority rights) and water scarcity in the existing downstream-irrigation systems (2 in Pawoti and four in Fasku VDCs) and several water turbines. They argued that if water is was taken from the proposed intake of this canal the downstream canals and turbines would suffer from water scarcity. This then became an issue of prestige and a power struggle between the two groups of people. Ultimately, a delegation of the disgruntled people led by the VDC chairmen went to the District Administration Office to stop the construction. To resolve the conflict the Chief District Officer organised negotiations involving both groups of people of all three VDCs. Finally, an agreement was made between the chairmen of all three VDCs and WUC to a) share water by placing a *sancho* (gate), b) include people from Fasku VDC (nonusers) in the WUC and c) divide the three positions of WUC (chairman, secretary and treasurer) as well as construction work between the three VDCs. As a result the WUC was reorganised and expanded from an 11 to a 19-member committee with the DIO overseer as an advisor. All construction work was divided between the three VDCs under the discretion of the VDC chairmen who were also added members of the WUC.

After these negotiations, DIO provided the earlier released 1.5 million rupees to the WUC (not spent the previous year because of the conflict) to start the construction. According to the project agreement, the users would provide 0.5% cash of the total project cost as a 'security deposit 'and a 15% labour or cash contribution. Villagers were not prepared to contribute so large an amount because of the growing conflict. The WUC in consultation with the DIO-technician decided to construct one section of the canal (which was mainly earthwork) with an estimated cost of 3 millions rupees. They gave the work to 70 local contractors on the condition that they accomplish all the given work and share the available 1.5 millions rupees. The local contractors completed the assigned work without knowing that the WUC had made a profit of 1.5 million rupees from the work, which should have cost 3 million rupees. In this way the WUC could pay for additional work equivalent to 1.5 millions rupees and this was interpreted as the user's contribution. By doing so the WUC was able to meet the financial criteria (total 15.5 percent contribution of users) of the Irrigation Sector Support Project. After meeting the ISSP financial requirement, the DIO technician and the WUC announced that the remaining construction would be assigned on a tender basis. In this tender arrangement only the registered professional contractors with defined minimum experience, having defined equipment and technical manpower are eligible to undertake construction work in contract basis where local contractors can not qualify. Therefore, small local petty contractors were not able to meet the tender criteria and were automatically removed from the construction process. In accordance with the earlier negotiated agreement, the WUC divided the remaining construction work into three sections and allocated it to the key leaders of the three VDCs. Most of those who got the construction work contracts were not beneficiaries of the project and so not very interested in the quality of construction. Hence, the quality of the work was extremely poor. Those landowners who had strongly protested placing the canal in their land either received a cash payment or were given work in this project. The technology used in the UAIS was complicated (cemented structures, masonry, etc.), expensive and local people were generally not conversant with the technology. The DIO overseer and the WUC members were able to manipulate the quality of work to save money, what Wade (1982) calls 'saving in the ground'.

The key informants (mainly contractors) explained that there are open-secrete norms of kickbacks in the construction industry. If a project is implemented under a tender arrangement contractors have to pay 10%, if implemented under a quotation basis they pay 20% and if implemented via WUC they have to pay 15% kickback to the concerned irrigation officials. This is the minimum kickback standard based on the project's total cost estimate. In this case, the

WUC fixed a 22% kickback (15% for higher authorities[4], 2% for the field technician and 5% for the WUC fund). The technician, generally the overseer, deputised for this project was primarily responsible for extorting the money. The entire irrigation development process in this case was systematically interconnected with rake-off, extortion and kickbacks. It is common in Nepal that if an overseer deputised for a particular project is not able to fulfil his obligation (collection of specified amounts of money) to his boss he will be transferred to an undesirable place, what Wade (1982) calls 'dumping ground'.

There was a water mill right below the intake of this canal. The mill owner, a powerful local elite and politician, had strongly protested the construction, citing the problem of water scarcity in running his water mill if the water was diverted to the canal. The WUC made an agreement with the mill owner and paid 75 thousands rupees from the WUC fund to move his mill to a suitable position on the canal to operate by canal water. The WUC also provided money to different people as compensation for crop damaged during the construction process. These payments were decided on the basis of personal relationship and/or by power exercise. The WUC chairman provided a monthly remuneration to his son for working in a government office, keeping account of the project. Final approval from the DIO about the accomplishment of the project was required to receive the final payment. To obtain this the WUC placed corrugated zinc sheets in some parts of the canal so that water flowed in it at the time of the inspection by DIO engineers. At this time the mill owner announced that he was ready to move his mill to the agreed location providing there was water in the canal. Unfortunately the canal was still not in operation because of several serious problems such as poor structures, structures being damaged in several places and landslides in more than 20 places.

---

4. Generally higher authorities use field technicians to extort money from district level projects.

The conflict between two groups (or even many sub groups) still continues in this project and the WUC is completely dysfunctional. With all its accompanying conflicts and tensions the 8.12 million rupee ($119264) project was officially completed in 1996. Immediately after the official declaration of completion of the project the technician was transferred to another district.

Villagers were unhappy with the performance of the WUC. At this time the first communist government in Nepal drastically changed the broadcasting programme of Radio Nepal and ran special awareness rising programmes against corruption, social inequalities and exploitation. This mass media campaign increased the negative feeling of the villagers towards the corrupt behaviour of WUC.

In the middle of the construction period some disgruntled persons registered a complaint with the special police[5] authority about the poor quality of the structural work and misuse of money. The special police investigated the case but it was dropped after laboratory examination of a sample of the structural work. Special relationship between the technicians, WUC members .(contractors) and the investigator presumably influenced the outcome of the laboratory examination. The investigation report was used as evidence by the WUC to take work in this project as a standard.

There was serious conflict between the existing WUC (which was under the control of the Nepali Congress Party supporters) and the supporters of the CPN-UML. It is very common to include party workers (especially of the ruling party) in all types of users committees. The bureaucracy always works for the political interests of ruling party and creates an environment favourable for them. It is very hard

---

5. In the district the authority of the special police is assigned to the CDO. In special cases, such as bigger corruption scandals the special police department sends their own investigators. These investigations are highly affected by source-force, *afnomanche* and bribery.

to find neutral members in most of the user committees in Nepal. As a result the conflict between two powerful political parties, the disgruntled supporters of the CPN-UML formed another parallel WUC in 1997 to deal with this non-functional canal. The interest behind the formation of WUC in the non-functional canal was to obtain the fund to repair this canal. It was estimated that almost half of the budget of the original canal construction is required to repair and maintain this project. They approached the CDO to dissolve the existing WUC and register their new one. According to the Water Resources Act, 1992 the District Administration Office is authorised to register water users committees, if some one wants to make use of water for collective benefit. The registered WUA/C is an autonomous and corporate body having perpetual succession. The CDO asked them to show evidence of the resignation of the existing committee members. As this of course was not possible their application to replace the existing WUC was rejected.

Villagers also expressed their concern and dismay on environmental issues. This project created many environmental problems such as several landslides, cracking and shrinking of boggy lands, soil erosion and damage of cultivated lands and public paths. Landslides damaged individuals' lands and crops during and after the construction period. The victims blamed the WUC for this damage and this caused further severe conflicts. Villagers argue that it would be more environmentally friendly, more user-responsive and less controversial if the canal was constructed from the originally proposed alignment.

According to the key informants (contractors, technicians, political leaders and users from the project areas) the performance of 80% of other ADB/ISSP funded projects in the Dolakha district is similar to this case, and all are entangled in severe conflicts. Only two projects (Khanikhola and Buling Irrigation Projects) out of ten are properly functioning and the other remaining (*Namdu, Saharetar, Mirge, Fadkekhola, Ghyang, Marbutar, and Andheri*) irrigation projects are problematic. The common problems reported in these projects were misuse of funds, poor quality of structural work, conflicts between local members of different political parties, poor performance of WUC, ambiguous role of DIO/technicians, extortion of money and political intervention. Earlier studies (IMC, 1990; Sukla *et al.*, 1997) also showed a similar situation in irrigation systems due to formal interventions. The following Table summarises the main conflicts and their major causes in this irrigation project.

Table 6.2. Summary of Conflict in the Upper Andherikhola Irrigation System

Conflict on	Major causes
Financial resource use	• Competition to handle money
Alignment of canal	• Preference differences among the actors
	• Change on original alignment
Formation of WUC	• Competition to be included in WUC
	• Ignorance of voice of people by WUC
Sharing of water source	• Problem raised by people of another VDC
	• Water turbines compete for water
	• Other FMISs objected to use the source
Use of technology	• Expensive and complicated
	• Poor quality of construction
Land ownership	• Farmers protested at digging the canal in their lands
Working procedure	• Non transparent procedure,
	• Top-down and secret decision making
	• Exclusion of local people
Role of irrigation bureaucracy	• Ambiguous, controversial and corrupt

Source: Primary information from the field, 1998-2000.

6.3. Issues in Conflict

This case study indicates that irrigation development and management is based on social relationships and negotiated interests. These interests are a combination of physical, technological, institutional and infrastructural systems. Irrigation is therefore a social system (Mollinga, 1998) which creates a platform (Röling, 1996) in the form of an emerging organisation (i.e., WUC) to deal with conflict related to water acquisition, allocation, distribution and utilisation in a particular socio-cultural and political setting. Vincent (1996:43) states that *"with the societal framework, one can study the social outcomes of irrigation systems in terms of the conditions and relationships between direct and indirect resources. Struggle between groups can be explored explicitly, as can partnerships in negotiation, and the operation of social networks and key actors within them"*. Irrigation as an organisational system is a product of collective action in terms of resource mobilisation, conflict resolution, people's participation, water distribution and benefit sharing (Uphoff, 1986). Various causes and consequences of the conflict of this irrigation canal are discussed in the following sections.

6.3.1. Catalysts of Conflict

Different factors play a catalytic role in the initiation of conflicts in this irrigation system. The conflicts were manifested in 3 major categories: i) conflict between the users of different resource systems, ii) conflict among the users within the shared resource system and iii) conflict between users of a particular resource system and external agencies concerned. All three categories of conflict are observed in this case. According to the custom in rural Nepal, outsiders are traditionally treated as guests with special privileges and bounded in ritualised social behaviour. This was one of the reasons that at the beginning some local people, who were aware of the survey as it v as carried out via their lands, did not raise their complaints with the irrigation technicians even when they realised their work was unjustifiable. The irrigation professionals interpret this treatment as their legitimate privilege. The village elite uses this ritualised behaviour of people as an opportunity to manipulate the situation in their favour. However, due to ambiguous roles and top-down decisions of a vicious circle of local elite and irrigation bureaucrats, local people gradually lost interest, developed apathy, became frustrated and finally became antagonistic. The conflict created by such feelings and the underlying causes led to the complete failure of this project. Local knowledge, skills and community interests were largely ignored right from the beginning of the feasibility study up to the construction period and this worked as a catalyst to initiate and escalate conflict. To ignore these local dynamics is to ignore self-supporting mechanisms in the development and continued operation of an irrigation system as well as inducing different sorts of conflicts (Laurent and Foaguegue 1999; Yoder, 1994; Pant, 2000).

At the beginning of the construction process gossiping, dissatisfaction, disagreement, haggling and protest were widespread. These dissatisfactions were suppressed by the efforts of powerful elite, administrators and irrigation bureaucrats. Generally it is observed that many projects often fail on social grounds because they neglect the existing social differences (e.g., class, gender and ethnic differences, historical legacies, political rivalries, hidden interests, etc.) (Pant, 2000; Shivakoti *et al.*, 1996; Upreti, 2000c). Farmers, local politicians and external interventionists belong to different social groups with different interests and priorities, experiences, expectations and status quo, which pose communication difficulties. In this case a lack of understanding, social behaviour and priorities amongst them were the bottlenecks of co-operation that became a source of conflict.

The Increasing number of formal interventions in the natural resource sector is also leading to more conflicts (Pradhan *et al.*, 1997; Upreti, 1998b). One of the major causes of such conflicts is that these interventions are implemented without much knowledge of or insight into the functioning of existing systems, local norms, rights and obligations related to local-level water and land use practices. In this context the statement of Benda-Beckmann *et al.*, (1996:2):*"pre-set technocratic and bureaucratic notions of how irrigation systems ought to be managed are forced upon water users, who are lured into co-operation with the bait of large credit facilities. New organisations, Water Users Associations, have to be formed by all potential users within the command area, without considering what this might mean for prior users. Large irrigation projects that showed little sensitivity to the existing rights and to the needs and wishes among the local population have methodology with overt or tacit resistance"* is more relevant. However, some local people (mostly village elite and political leaders) invite external interventions (the government sometimes comes with various development interventions without a request from local elite) for two purposes: i) a genuine reason to improve the village situation, and ii) a veiled reason to obtain direct personal benefit (mostly financial) from such interventions.

6.3.2. Political Interference and Conflict

Some key politicians from the main local political parties, some teachers and selected village elite from the 3 VDCs have obtained direct financial benefit from this project. Those people who were deliberately excluded from the construction process by the WUC led the dissatisfied villagers in protest against the work of the WUC. Political leaders in the earlier Panchayat political system created several severe problems to the anti Panchayat activists and opponents. After the restoration of democracy these anti-Panchayat activists and opponents emerged as mainstream political leaders in the village. Due to the tension between these two groups the social setting of the village was heavily disturbed. There was a deep 'confidence crisis' in the village. Each small non-political issue was deliberately linked with party politics for political gain. Different levels of conflict were also observed within members of the same political party. Everyone tried to influence people in their favour to the disadvantage of others. This irrigation system became a suitable platform for such political manoeuvring and served as a catalyst for the initiation of conflicts.

6.3.3. Water Sharing, Water Rights and Conflict

Water acquisition and sharing were other catalytic forces in the escalation of conflict. People from the downstream canals and water turbines complained about scarcity of water right from the beginning of the project. The politicians effectively used this issue of water rights to defeat the arguments of the initiator and the irrigation officials. The opposing party claimed that the source was big enough and that the intake was located far enough from the other canals and turbines so that there would be no significant reduction of water. Initially, this issue was just raised as a political issue but during the negotiations it became one of the crucial points to be agreed. Placement of a *sancho* (gate) in the intake of this irrigation canal was agreed in a tripartite meeting held to discuss the sharing of water. Water acquisition deals with having access and control over water in a natural source (Yoder, 1994). The supporters of this canal wanted to acquire water from the highest part of the stream. Water sharing implies a fair distribution of the available water and an agreement was reached over this by involving non-users in the water users committee to balance the power and negotiate the conflict (political dimension). Water rights among users sharing the same source are generally contested (Spiertz, 2000; Benda-Beckmann *et al.*, 1996). The objections of downstream-water users in this case became the central locus for conflict when local water-sharing rules were broken. There is an accepted local norm that diversions are not asked for or allowed within a specific distance upstream if the available water is insufficient for all systems.

6.3.4. Imposed Participation, Top-down Decision Making, Lack of Transparency and Conflict

The situation was interesting in that neither general villagers had demanded this project from that alignment nor were they consulted during the feasibility study and implementation process. The canal was constructed in the high altitude area (about 7000 feet) where rice cultivation is not common and there is no practice of irrigating other winter crops, if they are grown. Villagers argue that if local farmers had been consulted during the feasibility study they would have opted for the original alignment whereby conflict would have been minimised and the area under irrigated agriculture could have been increased. The fact that the farmers' priorities had been ignored, by excluding them from the project planning, meant that their participation in implementation was virtually zero and also raised severe conflicts and tensions. The farmers' concerns were not taken into account and the process lacked a plan for solving conflicts. This resulted in suspicion, hostility and a lack of co-operation. Although a meaningful participation of users is clearly stated in the irrigation policy documents, in reality such participation was virtually nil in this case.

The case demonstrated that participation of beneficiaries and transparent decisions making are crucial for sustainable development and management of irrigation systems. The qualitative participation of users in decision-making and the implementation process and the need for proper assessment survey design and effective monitoring of the irrigation system are the key determinants of success (Uphoff, 1986; Turrel, 1995; Korten and Siy; 1989; Pradhan, 1989). This case has demonstrated that qualitative participation depends on the interests of local people and other actors involved in the irrigation development process such as technicians, bureaucrats and politicians. However, interests vary due to differences in power and position. Wealth, caste and ethnicity, status, authority and political and ideological preferences also governed interests in participation (Uphoff, 1985, Chambers, 1988; Pant, 2000).

Farmers' participation represents an important part of the larger process of irrigation management (Uphoff, 1986). People's participation is more predictable and productive when it is mobilised through appropriate organisations of users which was distinctly lacking in this case. A user organisation (as structure) is important for successful irrigation development activities (as process). Organisational aspects of the project such as planning, decision-making, resource mobilisation, CM and co-ordination were performed without involving users, which ultimately created severe problems during implementation. In this case both the social and physical structures were very weak. The decision-making process was top-down and not transparent. The irrigation technicians viewed themselves as the supplier and the real implementers and local people were viewed as the passive acceptors of the governmental largesse. Both the WUC members and the technicians were aware that involving users in the construction process from the beginning addresses local interests and concerns, leads to an understanding of the public values associated with these issues and concerns, and ensures the long-term sustainability of the project. However, they were also equally aware that such involvement could reduce much wanted illicit revenue. This was their main reason for not involving people in the decision-making process construction project.

The case demonstrated that formal interventions generally use existing social differences (such as class, gender, caste, ethnicity, historical legacies, power, occupation and political rivalries) as an effective means of accomplishing objectives (hidden and stated) in the direction of their desire. They mobilise very few people of the upper strata of a society to achieve that. The village population is composed of rich and poor, powerful and weak, educated and illiterate. However, in order to gain legitimacy, the external agencies mainly operate in a non-transparent way through politicians and traditional power brokers from the higher social strata. This eventually excludes the interests and concerns of women, real water users, the poor and people from lower socio-cultural strata. It is also interesting to note that such interventions mainly focus on technical concerns, rather than on equity and social justice. They consider the interests of just one articulate elite group rather than the heterogeneous population. This biased view of the power and social relationships ultimately leads to contradictions and conflict in the village community. This case proved that when people perceive that bureaucratic decisions are unfair, distrust develops and the any ultimate decision is more likely to be rejected.

The VDC executive members and secretaries explained that increased political interference and social conflicts in the village are also due to the lack of a comprehensive irrigation resource inventory in the village. This would make it easier to make a choice between creating new irrigation systems and making better use of the existing irrigation ones and would minimise arbitrary decisions, if such inventory were available. In this case technical and social information was lacking and non-transparent top-down decisions were imposed. According to the respondents the major cause of the conflicts in this irrigation development process was the lack of transparency. By keeping the process non-transparent, irrigation technicians and the WUC members could ensure that any extortion would go smoothly without any interference from the general public. A transparent process bestows legitimacy, minimises controversy and increase people's participation (Pandey, 1999). Regardless of the importance of the project, a lack of transparency results in conflict and opposition, minimises democratic values and nearly always leads to the failure of the project.

6.3.5. Distorted Communication, Incomplete Information and Conflict

Lack of communication and information among the villagers was one of the major sources of conflict. Most of the villagers did not know about the feasibility study, the source of financial assistance, the conditions and procedures of implementation or the responsibilities and authority of the WUC. Many people only knew about this project when the resulting conflict became public. Information was strategically limited to maintain secrecy and opposition from the villagers was ignored.

Considering the conflict scenario in this case it should be stressed that communication, information exchange, and the use of a common language are very important in making people aware about intervention, in seeking their co-operation and in reducing conflict. Keeping myriad villagers uninformed or providing distorted information creates confusion, suspicion and disagreement, which virtually always leads to more conflicts and the ultimate failure of the project. In section 6.2 it was discussed how conflict at the time of implementation was often the result of a communication gap, information distortion and a lack of awareness. Providing correct information and having proper communications can enhance the development of mutual understanding, clarify misunderstandings and eradicate suspicion.

6.3.6. Poor Functioning of Water Users Committees and Conflict

Several studies have shown the great importance of social and organisational aspects in enhancing the effectiveness and efficiency of irrigation systems (Pant, 2000; Ostom, 1992; Benjamin *et al.* 1994; Mollinga, 1998; Parajuli, 1999; Chambers, 1988; Uphoff, 1986). This is clearly reflected in this case. It became apparent from the case described in section 6.2 that there was a crisis in confidence, resulting in hostility and frustration amongst the villagers. A lack of interest about genuine responsibility of the WUC was due to hidden economic interests, which forced the WUC to deviate from the standard WUC governing rules. This meant that the role of the WUC became a persistent source of conflict. The WUC, which was the hub of the whole irrigation development process, was brought into being to serve the objectives of two groups of actors (i.e., irrigation technocrats and local elite). Entire procedures, strategies and action plans of the WUC were focused on achieving these objectives. It is interesting to note that all necessary documents were correctly produced and submitted to the concerned authorities for legal evidence.

The role of the WUC is crucial in managing irrigation systems. Ideally, the WUC is responsible for construction, operation, maintenance and repair of canals. It should ensure the equitable distribution of water, collect and make use of irrigation service fees, take the necessary action against the contravention of rules, resolve conflict if any should arise and develop and execute rules and regulations. A registered WUC is an autonomous corporate body according to the Water Resources Act, (Khadka, 1997). However, the role of the WUC in this case was controversial and became a source of conflict.

It is widely recognised that sustainability of irrigation is ensured when state intervention promotes qualitative involvement of farmers in planning, construction and maintenance is increase (Pant, 2000; NPC, 1998). This is recognised in the Water Resource Act, and the Irrigation Policy, 1995. All irrigation and water management documents emphasise the role of water users associations and committees. Now–a-days the use of such rhetoric is becoming the fashion in Nepal. The Department of Irrigation emphasises that irrigation projects should be implemented through the WUC working within the given framework. For example, Irrigation policy emphasises irrigation management transfer to WUA. Irrigation Development and Management Plan of the Ministry of Water Resources highlights the importance of management transfer of irrigation system of less than 500 ha in hills and less 2000 ha in Terai to enhance the performance of irrigated agriculture. However, it is reported that irrigation management transfer is not operating according to ideals in Nepal. Major problems identified by the Central Co-ordination Committee of the WUA in this regard are: poor farmers are not able to pay water tax, not sufficient water available, payment of tax without getting water, no clear provision of punishment in Water Resources Act to those who damage or break the canal to get water illegally, lack of market linkages to sell the agricultural product and misuse of resources. However, in reality, these provisions are not translated accordingly. The provision of WUC is rather used by irrigation technocrats to manoeuvre as the ultimate responsibility lies with the WUC and they can escape referring to WUC when problems occur. Powerful people in the village always wanted to be included in the WUC in order to gain access to large amounts of money[6]. So, in fact WUC

---

6. Of all the sectoral village level development activities, irrigation is the first one to bring large amounts of money to the village from outside sources.

arrangement is more the platforms for manipulation instead to ensure sustainability of the irrigation projects. Another important issue in WUC is the application of externally imposed rules. Such externally imposed rules force people to alter their normal behaviour to meet the necessary conditions defined by rules. For example, a compulsory 15% contribution from users encouraged the WUC members and irrigation technicians to manipulate petty contractors (asking them to work double of what they were paid for) and the local community.

Taking all these issues relating to the WUA/C together it can be concluded that local institutional arrangement (WUC) becomes weak when it does not represent the real users and works only to meet the criteria of a project (for example, a registered WUC is a precondition to obtain ADB/ISSP assistance). Interventions, even when they operate through WUA/Cs, are not sustainable if complex interlocking social dynamics are ignored. New institutions created by the external interventions generally do not function if they are not compatible with the existing ones (Pant, 2000).

6.3.7. *Technology and Conflict*

Technology provides the knowledge and techniques to make water available to irrigate lands and physically control its delivery to the fields, influencing plant bio-mass, soil property and the ecosystem as a whole (Mollinga, 1998; Chambers, 1988; Parajuli, 1999; Yoder, 1984; 1991). However it also creates ample room for conflict and corruption (Wade, 1982; Korten and Siy, 1989; Upreti, 1998b). In this respect irrigation can be seen as a resource in two ways. First, it is an input for plant growth and development (Vincent, 1996) and secondly, it is a means of extorting money and other associated benefits for bureaucrats and politicians.

Technology not only greatly influences the sustainability of an irrigation system but also serves as a source of conflict. The main focus of the design (high technology based expensive structures) is often to increase the cost of the project so that technicians and WUC members can increase their profits. To increase the costs of this project the site for the canal alignment was chosen so that a large numbers of complex concrete structures were needed. Local people argued that the same canal could be constructed with far fewer structures if the originally proposed alignment was accepted. Many structures were severely damaged because they were not constructed according to the design, what Wade (1982) calls 'saving on the ground'. Farmers prefer to construct canals without heavy cement structures, arguing that canals constructed with low cost measures run for longer periods with fewer problems than those constructed using high technology like this canal. However, irrigation technicians mostly prefer to design canals with many structures. These require more investment for construction so increasing the opportunities for extortion (Upreti, 1998a). This also necessitates a regular maintenance budget, which is also at their disposal.

Obviously high technology and structural work should not be ignored. However the quality of the technical construction work is basically the responsibility of irrigation engineers and this needs to be controlled honestly. Wherever possible local technology should be used to sustain the system after external intervention has ceased. Quality assurance of the physical structures depends upon execution of the project according to the design specifications (for example, the ratio of cement used). It is a well accepted fact that irrigation systems require locality-specific technical designs (e.g. canals have to have the material strength and spill facilities to cope with hydraulic forces, and appropriate control structures to deliver water, etc.). However, the problem is how these designs are translated into practice. Location specific inexpensive designs and incorporation of local knowledge and experience in designing irrigation systems would minimise conflict, address local people's need and help in operating and maintaining them later. However, kickback extortion and 'savings on the ground' are becoming guiding factors in choosing technology and design structures in construction projects in Nepal, rather than the principles involved and the technical merits. The Report of the Nepal's

Administrative Reform Task force, 1999 explicitly mentioned the widespread existence of organised corruption in irrigation, road and drinking water projects from village to national level[7]. DIO engineers need to be accountable to the users to ensure the quality of work. All details of the particular project need to be transparent to the beneficiaries of that project to ensure 'getting the process right' (Uphoff, 1986). Based on the above discussion, it is logical to conclude that technology in itself is neither good nor bad but its context specific application is very important. This can be used as a source of extortion, manipulation and conflicts, if applied wrongly.

6.3.8. Corruption and Conflict

Corruption is a framework that helps in understanding how public roles and private interests of technocrats and politicians are in conflict and how power relationships and cronyism influence irrigation development process. It gives answers to the questions of how illicit revenue collection and rake- off work in bureaucratic and political circles accomplishes and how village leaders and local politicians are mobilised in this extortion process in any projects that are externally funded and implemented under the guidance of irrigation technicians. As noted by Wade (1982) in his study on canal irrigation in India, it is also common in Nepal for irrigation bureaucrats to collect illicit revenue and pay senior bureaucrats and politicians to secure them transfer to high-earning projects and so buy advantageous positions again and again. During the tenure of any irrigation technician they need to recover the amount they paid to obtain the position, the extra money used to pay the superiors and politicians to keep them continue in high earning projects, as well as needing to make a lucrative profit for themselves for taking risks (for example potential corruption charges and protests

---

7. See the draft report of Nepal's Administrative Reform Taskforce 2055 Chaitra (1999) Page 49, clause no 5.3.3 for the strong existence of organised corruption in Nepal.

from public for extorting money from the project). It is interesting to note that irrigation professionals (particularly assistant engineers and overseers) express their feelings, and talk about how they extort money, how much and when they gave money to seniors (to obtain particular work or to get support from politicians and seniors by extortion) or what problems they faced from seniors when they failed to fulfil their expectations, when they are drunk. It is common practice that their own group (generally they do not include people other than overseer/engineers in their drinking, gambling or casino group) goes to relatively expensive and good restaurants of that area (mainly district headquarters) to drink and share secrete issues with each other. Sometimes they also ask politicians to drink with them to develop and finalise extortion strategies or to ask them to force concessions from the senior technocrats in the particular project where they are working. I visited such restaurants several times as an ordinary customer sitting in separate corner and listening to their conversations. This helped me to gain insights into these issues that I was not able to get from other sources.

The Report of the Nepal Administrative Reform Task Force, 1999 and 'Good Governance' a Quarterly Bulletin of the ProPublic (a NGO) have provided evidence consistent with the issues raised in this book on corruption. ProPublic (2000:9) found that corruption persists in the following layers of construction works in Nepal: a) While making the estimate of the construction works, b) Bargaining on the rates of commission while awarding contracts, c) Compromises on the quality of works d) Claiming more work than actually carried out, e) Lack of adequate competition, f) Contractors fixing who tenders for the project by having deals amongst themselves, so avoiding competition g) Claiming extra payments under the pretext of price increases or other excuses, h) Extending projects unnecessarily and in a pre-planned way, i) Corruption through consultancies, j) Corruption under the pretext of maintenance or other reasons.

Power in this case was mainly used to achieve personal financial gain, distinctly against the interest of the majority of villagers. The formally recognised positions and associated power of the WUC members, the DIO technicians and the VDC members legitimised the irregularities in the construction process. In this case position and authority (e.g. the decision of the WUC to collect 22% commission, that of the DIO to remove local contractors), personal relationships and links (e.g. the relationship between the DIO engineer and the initiator) and interests (e.g. negotiation of two groups for their own economic benefits) were used to achieve personal gains. These all were abuse of different power forms.

The irrigation technocrats (mainly the head of office) have wider discretionary powers to allocate, reallocate and cut-off a budget of a particular irrigation project, appoint contractors, transfer subordinate technicians and make decisions in favour of politicians who support them. Irrigation bureaucrats use such power skilfully to create an environment favourable for extorting money from irrigation projects. In the case described above the WUC was compelled within that discretionary power to provide 17% of the total budget as a kickback and therefore the quality of the work deteriorated. It is a common practice in Nepal to collect money from development projects for the senior bureaucrats and politicians. The collected money has to be distributed to different layers of concerned authorities (bureaucrats and even politicians if the amount is large). These different layers of people are collectively known as 'above'. Technicians responsible to construct this canal should have fulfilled their responsibility (to pay to seniors) to retain in the project. As noted in section 6.3.4 technicians use technical jargon and administrative procedures to manipulate resources for their benefit, things about which villagers have little idea.

In general, villagers, politicians and technocrats have different reasons for taking part in an irrigation project. Interests of bureaucrats are related to obtaining money and promotion whereas politicians want to gain more power. Neither group is interested in the issues of irrigation per se.

However, the interest of the farmers is mainly to have regular water available from the canal to irrigate their land. The patronising attitude of irrigation professionals leads to conflict and hinders the building of relationships with the community. Irrigation technocrats have often developed idiosyncratic feelings of superiority due to their social status and education, power and contacts. In recent years it is almost impossible for the children of poor people to get access to Engineering colleges because of extremely large amount of additional (capitation) fees and the inability to compete in entrance examinations with those students who come from expensive high quality boarding schools. Even if they succeeded in the entrance examinations they are not able to invest in 5-6 years of expensive engineering colleges. In the few cases where someone from a poor background completed an engineering education, it is extremely difficult for them to find appropriate and relevant work without *afnomenchhe,* source force or the use of bribes. The engineering coming from such background see local farmers as a part of the problem and themselves as the source of the solution. They always want to maintain special close relationships with local power brokers in accomplishing construction projects. Therefore, their official contacts in the village are the head of the village, political leaders and power brokers, who it is hoped can minimise potential trouble from them later.

Technicians develop special relationships with local power brokers mainly by paying for hospitality. Only those brokers, who have a good relationship with the chief of their office can hope for some of the share from the project implemented in their villages. Technicians also give work on the project to the favourites of power brokers to maintain their special relationships. Technicians regularly send money to senior politicians and more especially to senior bureaucrats. They also send crockery, furniture, goat, ghee or material for dowries to their married daughters to ensure their compliance in any extortion or to prevent their transfer to a bad posting such as the Maoist influenced area. I talked with one engineer, who was school friend of mine, about this issue. He said *"extortion of money and corruption is an inevitable part of the professional life of engineers in Nepal. It is necessary to fulfil the demands of senior officials and politicians if any engineer wants to survive professionally (to get better opportunities in terms of training abroad and education, posting in big earning projects, and not being posted in the Maoist area or other dumping ground)"*. It is also interesting to note that those people who are the master of corruption always say that the practice of extortion is wrong and morally reprehensible. The engineering profession is dominated by corruption despite the public expression (more especially by politicians rather than bureaucrats) of their remorse and shame at the situation. However, their speeches have no credibility with the general public.

Politicians are interested in new irrigation projects since such projects are a means of gathering financial resources and consolidating political support at elections as well as strengthening the influence of their party at the local level (ProPublic, 2000; Pandey, 1999; Upreti, 1998b). This powerful motivation of politicians is strategically utilised by technocrats and contractors to extort money. As a result the institutional and technical performance of such projects deteriorates. In contrast, FMIS perform better and function properly, mainly because they have well recognised principles supported by social sanctions and flexible criteria (Pradhan, 1989).

Contractors are one of the major perpetrators of corruption in construction projects in Nepal. They increase their net benefits by paying bribes to government officials and politicians. Technocrats assist them by saving on the estimates, saving on the ground (Wade, 1982), revising estimates to increase the amount needed and adding extra money. Engineers generally become involved in increase the benefit from contractors for themselves, their bosses and politicians. In some cases, even if the project needs to be approved by the Cabinet the minister concerned makes sure this is achieved promptly. Many engineers also work with these contractors in an anonymous partnership to increase the shared benefits. Large contractors have strong immediate influence over senior politicians and ministers or senior government bureaucrats. For this reason engineers, unless they also have bargaining powers, are wary of such contractors in case they organise their transfer to non-earning projects or remote areas.

Media Service International under the support of the Westminster Foundation carried out a comprehensive study in Nepalese corruption practices for Democracy. Findings of this study show that 21% of the surveyed respondents thought the most corrupt officials were civil servants, 20% indicated politicians, 19% ministers, 18% police and 11% judiciary. The remaining 11% see other people such as workers of corporations and NGOs as the most corrupt. Among the respondents 30% see politicians as being primarily responsible for such corruption followed by civil servants (28%) and traders (15%). Thirteen percent of the respondents considered the political system itself is primarily responsible for such rampant corruption. Of the total 1197 respondents consulted, 75% gave bribes to accomplish their work. 23% said that they had never accomplished any work without bribery and 44% said they occasionally resorted to bribery to accomplish work. Some 61% respondents excused the use of bribery by explaining that it is not possible to accomplish work without its use. Research findings indicate that the most corrupt offices are the LRO, Custom Office, Police Office, courts, District Administration Office, Tax Office, Forest Office, Electricity Office, Telecommunication Office, Municipalities, Road Office, Drinking Water Office, Irrigation Office, Hospitals, the army and the Land Measurement Office (Nepal Samachar Patra Dailly, April 25, 2000).

As noted by Uphoff, (1986) improving irrigation management requires critical thinking about farmers' organisations, political neutrality, and active participation of local people and implementation of a transparent process. This is generally lacking in projects implemented and designed with the interests of politicians' and bureaucrats' in mind.

Lack of co-operation, weak social relationships, mistrust, and even recrimination were the product of this irrigation development process. Villagers blamed DIO officials and politicians for their corrupt role in abusing the available resources. On the other hand irrigation officials argued that farmers themselves have to take responsibility for the failure of the project. They further stressed that it is necessary to educate and control the villagers to follow the technician's instructions.

Based on the empirical evidence it is realistic to say that the interests of many external interventions in the development of irrigation systems are not for the better performance of irrigated agriculture[8] but rather to raise larger amounts of illicit revenue from the project for irrigation bureaucrats and politicians. All in all, irrigation bureaucracy together with politicians capture a large portion of the resources allocated for irrigation development at the cost of social conflict and the resulting failure of the project in question.

6.4. Learning from conflict

From the foregoing discussion it has become apparent that statutory, administrative and technocratic authorities are the major factors in irregularities and corruption. These authorities in this case modified rules and procedures, to exploit the local situation and create a favourable environment to extort money. Their personal interests and behaviour play a significant role in (mis)use of resources and (ab)use of power, irrespective of governmental laws, rules and regulations, and professional ethics. In relation to that

---

8. The improved performance of irrigation systems enhance the wellbeing by increasing benefits from irrigation, such as productivity, equity and productivity in terms of costs, and adverse social, health, environmental and other effects (Chambers, 1988)

the statement of Benda-Beckmann *et al.,* (1997:229) is illustrative. They state: *"socio-legal studies in the field of law and behaviour have generally demonstrated that the mere existence of legal rules and principles, whether originating from government legislation, tradition or contemporary local law making, do not justify to draw direct conclusions with respect to behaviour of people. They only become significant when people- farmers, government officials, project managers- orient their behaviour towards these rules..."*. In this case, a comprehensive and well illustrated operational procedural manual and its recommendations and the irrigation department's policies and guidelines were deliberately manipulated. Hence the construction process was used for the self-interests of bureaucrats and WUC members. The important question of how these greed-based behavioural changes can be directed towards shared goals based on socially learned understanding remains unanswered.

Farmers-managed irrigation systems function better in Nepal than the jointly managed irrigation systems (JMIS) because farmers in FMIS themselves make locally interwoven rules and monitor and effectively enforce. It has become clear from this case that farmers do not feel any ownership in JMIS because the irrigation systems were built, financed and regulated by outsiders to serve their own interests rather than the need of local people. Differences in interests hindered co-operation, raised conflict and virtually assured the failure of the irrigation project. A lesson we can learn from this conflict case is that the degree of failure of externally funded projects is directly correlated with local people's feelings of exclusion.

Taking all the raised issues together it can be argued that conflict can be minimise if the activities of irrigation professionals and water-users committees is kept transparent and away from local politics, following a bottom-up approach to planning and construction of irrigation projects. If WUC were politically unbiased it would be possible to mobilise local human resources and social capital to improve the performance of irrigation systems, increase accountability and reduce conflicts. One of the most important lessons learned for effective management of irrigation systems is the development of a feeling of ownership among the users which gears them toward responsibilities and rights (Shivakoti *et al.*, 1996). If they consider the system is theirs they become involved in its care and management. To ensure accountability is to actively involve people in the whole process.

Strengthening the capacity of villagers by providing accurate information, giving awareness training on departmental financial regulations related to irrigation projects, giving advice on the most vulnerable points for extortion, and developing their skill and confidence to deal with irrigation engineers would perhaps help to improve the performance of irrigation projects. Furthermore, regular monitoring and periodic evaluation, timely auditing by the concerned authority could minimise the conflicts created due to financial irregularities and corrupt practices. Proper application of financial regulations and the fair use of a reward and punishment system coupled with a code of conduct, rights, duties and obligations of civil servants as defined by the Civil Servant Act could help to reduce bribes and extortion.

In conclusion, it may be generalised that an integration of both the soft-side of irrigation (institutional, managerial, and organisational issues; CM, resources mobilisation and utilisation, people's participation) to get the social process right and the hard-side (hydrological and hydraulic issues, construction technology, structural designs) to get the technical engineering process right (Uphoff, 1986) is essential to improve the performance of the irrigation sector. From the scenario of the Nepalese irrigation situation presented elsewhere in this chapter it is clear that irrigation is not only a major input for agricultural productivity and a significant source for personal income but also a major source of conflict that alters the existing social relationships.

This case illustrates the general characteristics of the Nepalese socio-political system and functioning of government bureaucracy in general, and in particular makes it possible to understand the development process of irrigation systems through formal intervention. The causes of under performance of the project include technical (design and implementation), institutional (WUC), political and bureaucratic factors. It is clear from the case that corruption is not only an inseparable part of the irrigation development process in Nepal but also a major source of conflict. Most often, human relationships are ignored in irrigation development and management, which undermines institutional, managerial, technical, socio-political and economic dimensions with hard core engineering. Unless the human dimension receives due consideration conflicts and ultimate failure of irrigation system will common.

Formal interventions do not always operate according to written irrigation policies, procedures and guidelines. Rather negotiations take place at local level to meet different interests. Powerful elite and politicians change the established pattern of development processes by negotiation and restoring administrative, regulatory, political and bureaucratic connections and links. Power relationships, social linkages, resource mobilisation and the actions of WUC are all shaped and legitimised by the self-interests of the actors. In this context it is not surprising to see that corruption is a distinct feature of formal intervention which characterise the general scenario of operation of the Nepalese administrative and political system. One can further argue that an irrigation system executed by outsiders in the name of users, which does not assist in the development of their institutional and organisational abilities leads to conflict and undermines local human potential (Upreti, 1998a).

From the empirical findings it is appropriate to say at this point that successful irrigation development depends on to what extent farmers are organised in participation, resource mobilisation and decision making. The principal objective of implementation of irrigation projects is to increase production and productivity of crops, to improve economic conditions of farmers and raise their livelihood. But the case studied indicates that all irrigation projects, in reality, are not implemented to achieve this novel objective, but are guided by hidden objectives such as an individual's monitory earnings, political gain, extortion and the accumulation of power.

External development interventions provide avenues for illicit practices through construction, maintenance and extension of irrigation systems. In this process, farmers, government agencies, and village elite are directly and or indirectly involved in their own ways by using technological means, customary norms, scientific jargon and formal laws and rules. As a result, in many cases, intervention in irrigation has been counterproductive. On the whole, it can be emphasised that irrigation is not only an on-farm activity, crop water management and hydrology but also has a whole dynamic of culture, politics economy, customary practices, people's perception, government's actions and learning and mis-learning.

A significant implication of this irrigation development process is the raised awareness of the villagers. After this project, villagers learned the potential ways to minimise misuse of externally obtained resources. Their level of confidence to deal with such issues has been increased. Due to this case people are now aware of the implications in the implementation of externally supported projects in their area. They actively wish to know the details about such external projects (budget, benefit, effects, etc.) before taking any decisions.

CHAPTER 7

Dynamics of Land Conflict—
A Reflection of Reality

7.1. Introduction

Chapter six examined the social implications of external interventions in society. It was shown how external development intervention has become controversial, promoting conflicts in the complicated web of power, political party strife and socio-economic relationships in society. The need has been recognised for a more facilitative and supportive role of formal interventions in NRM, which gives more attention to cultural, economic and political issues and is completely impartial (Warner and Jones, 1998: Buckles, 1999). However, much still remains to be done to carry this out in practice. This chapter examines the dynamics of land conflict within the broader framework of land reform, land rights and power struggles. The case study in this chapter deals with the conflict between tenants and landlords to control ownership rights. The case highlights the process of how the parties in the conflict responded to it, why they approached the courts and why they returned from court adjudication to local compromise. This chapter starts with the introduction and description of the conflict. This is followed by a short analysis of the dynamics of conflict and negotiation. Finally, specific conclusions are drawn about the extent to which negotiation is possible even in a situation of an unequal power relationship.

The case presented in this chapter is related to *Guthi* land.

Guthi is a type of land tenure system, which grants right over land to religious or charitable organisations. According to the Trust Corporation (*Guthi* Sansthan) Act, 1976 *Guthi* is defined as 'endowment made by any philanthropist through relinquishment of their title to movable or immovable property or any income-yielding fund for the construction, operation or maintenance of any temple, rest-house, road-side shelter, inn, well, tank, bridge, school, house, or institution, in order to run a monastery or celebrate a religious occasion, ceremony or festival or any religious and philanthropic purpose' (Oli, 1998: 41). The same act divides *Guthi* lands into 3 categories viz.: *Raj Guthi* (owned by the *Guthi* Corporation), *Chhut Guthi* (a concession made by the government to individuals over *Guthi* property) and private Guthi (Guthi owned by individuals). Such endowments were made with the specific purpose of maintaining these organisations. The people who manage *Guthi* are called *Guthiars*. *Guthi* grants were safer from confiscation by the state than other forms of land tenure because of concessions to their religious nature. Both state and individual landlords have established *Guthi*. Individuals established *Guthis* because of the protection against confiscation and the restriction on alienation. *Birta* holders kept part of their lands for the *Guthi* as a means of protecting portions of their holdings from possible confiscation or preventing future generations from selling them. Often the earning from *Guthi* lands was in excess of the amount needed to fulfil the religious or charitable purpose. In such cases the excess was simply appropriated by the individual *Guthiars* for their own use (New Era, 1988). The case described in this chapter belongs to the category of private *Guthi*.

7.2. Background of Land Conflict

The people engaged in the land conflict were from Deurali village. The Deurali village is situated in the Pawoti VDC. It is relatively densely populated. The population composition of the study area is Sarki (cobbler), Kami (blacksmith) Chhetri, Newar, Tamang and Bramin. However, more than 60% of population is Brahmin and Chhetri. The socio-economic condition of the village is poor, most inhabitants being poor tenants. Until 1990 social relationships were skewed with a patron-client mode of power structure in the village. A few Brahmin and Chhetri landlords own more than 70% of the different categories of agricultural land in this area. The local categories of land classifications reported in the study area were 1. Khet land (low land) - a) bagar land (land reclaimed from stream/river), b) kholakhet (located by the river/stream), c) simkhet/gairikhet (poorly drained fertile land), d) tarkhet (usually dried and located on slopes above river/stream terraces), e) kanlekhet (khet consisting of small terraces), and f) surke khet (long narrow strips of terraced land located on steep slopes). 2. Bari land (upland) - a) ghar-bari (*bari* land located around the house), b) *Patabari* (large broad terraces), c) *Kanle bari* (fairly narrow terrace), d) *Surke bari* (very narrow strips of terraces), e) *Khoriyabari* (shrub/forest land cleared to make bari), f) *Kharbari* (steep land where thatch grass is grown), g) *Dandabari* (land located on the top of a hill) and *Dhungyan bari* (bari with stony soils). The disputed land represents all these categories. Many farmers are tenants and some Brahmin, Chhetri and Sarki people are landless. Food insecurity and forced agricultural labour are common. However, in recent years, the power structure in the village has begun to change as democratic change has allowed the poor a voice.

More than 150 years ago a high cast Hindu Brahmin family allocated about 350 ha of the Deurali village as a private *Guthi* to run rituals, to worship god and maintain the temple. At that time, several well-off devotees (mainly landlords) donated lands to gods and goddesses because of their religious faith. Land was not scarce, and the *Guthi* owner rented out the *Guthi* land to 40 tenants of the Deurali village. The fixed rent was generally collected in the form of grain, an arrangement that had been running for generations without major problems. As well as paying rent, tenants also provided free agricultural labour and artisan services to the *Guthi* owners.

After the overthrow of the Rana regime in 1951 initiatives were taken to reform the feudal system of land accumulation. As part of this reform process, in 1959 the leader of the *Guthi* owners (administering the *Guthi* land on behalf of the present 50 *Guthi* owner families), collected money (equivalent to the rent of five years) from all the tenants to transfer the ownership rights of the *Guthi* land to them. However this was not carried out due to reluctance from the *Guthi* landowners. This became the first cause of conflict between the *Guthi* owners and the tenants. Although the tenants became dissatisfied the conflict did not escalate mainly because of the influence of the landowners. Tenants provided wood and trees from the *Guthi* land to the *Guthi* owners hoping for a future settlement of the pending issue of ownership transfer. Later, together with the emergence of the Panchayat political system in 1962 some *Guthi* landowners became powerful, obtaining a lot of statutory powers, when they were nominated as members of the village council and head of the Village Panchayat. By using these statutory powers the landowners were able to suppress the dissatisfied tenants, who continued to give free labour and *koseli* (presents). The majority of the *Guthi* landowners had many times more land than the ceiling made in the Land Act and tenants have to give free labour to cultivate these large areas.

The newly established Panchayat political system brought the Land Act under the Land Reform Programme in 1964. The government made an inventory of the existing ownership arrangements and tenancy status all over the country. All landowners and tenants should have registered their association on particular land to claim ownership rights over that land later. The role of the village council and its head was crucial to facilitate the registration process. During the process of registration the leader of the *Guthi* owners again collected money from the vast majority of tenants to register the land under their ownership. Because of the failure of the earlier promise some tenants did not pay, and only those who gave additional money were able to register the land. However, the tenancy arrangement was continued and transferred to the tenants' offspring. *Guthi* landowners wanted to keep the tenancy arrangement unchanged and tenants wanted to establish their rights over the tenanted *Guthi* lands. After some years tenants stopped paying rent, arguing that they had already paid money twice to transfer ownership rights and should not have to pay rent any more. The *Guthi* landowners first tried persuasion in an attempted to collect rent locally, but this failed due to resistance of the tenants. After this the *Guthi* owners mobilised force to collect the rent. Use of force in Nepal is manifested in the mobilisation of police and other powerful people to influence conflict in their favour. People having access and good relations with officials of the District Administration and Police Offices instantly mobilise the police to pressure (physically and psychologically) another party to drop or alter their claims irrespective of whether they are right or wrong. The landlords threatened to take tenants to the CDO office, and bought in the police to threaten them. However, all these strategies did not work. Finally, they made an appeal to the *Guthi* Corporation Office against the tenants. The *Guthi* Corporation Office is a special office set up by the government to administer the *Guthi* property, to settle disputes related to them and conserve these properties. The *Guthi* Corporation Office pronounced in favour of the *Guthi* owners. As a result, an agreement was made, according to which the *Guthi* owners would transfer ownership to the tenants immediately after receiving 60000 rupees from the tenants to run the *Guthi* rituals. The tenants immediately paid the money but again the ownership was not transferred. Although the tenants had already stopped paying the land rent they were still providing free agricultural labour to *Guthi* owners in the peak agricultural season. The social relationships in the village were too important for either side to ruin them. The landowners needed tenants as agriculture labour to run their agriculture and tenants wanted to borrow money and agricultural products from the landlords.

When the CPN-UML led minority government ruled the country for 9 months in 1995, Radio Nepal started to broadcast "pro-poor" programmes and urged Nepalese people to organise against socio-cultural exploitation and to protest their rights over feudal elite and landlords. This media propaganda significantly strengthened the determination of villagers and tenants and they became more organised to legally fight the *Guthi* owners to establish their land rights.

The conflict between the two groups was in a stalemate for several years. Meanwhile, a 5-km Ghangkhola Irrigation canal was constructed under 'royal decree' (*hukumpramangi*) by the central government investing 6.7 million rupees to irrigate the 200 ha of adjoining area of Deurali. Before restoration of democracy in Nepal King had promulgated such directives frequently. In 1955 one Brahmin elite member attempted to construct a canal (2 km above the present Ghangkhola Irrigation Canal) but local people disagreed and complained to royal palace to stop the construction of the canal stating that if this irrigation canal was constructed it would affect two villages by increasing the likelihood of landslides. So this project was not approved earlier. One person from the same village working in the Royal Palace submitted a second application (*Binti patra*) as follow-up. Ultimately it was approved with change in the intake of the canal and construction was completed in 1980. However, the canal did not cover the disputed Deurali area. The villagers from the Deurali village interpreted that as a deliberate attempt of the leader of the *Guthi* owners to exclude them from irrigation. They protested strongly to the engineer as well as the leader. Professional troublemakers (some people in the village were always willing to create and be involved in conflict for their own personal benefits) used this as an opportunity to start additional conflicts between the two villagers arguing that Deurali villagers opposed the irrigation of their lands. This resulted in conflict between Deurali Villagers and other people of the irrigation command area. The conflict became serious when the engineer rejected a request from the Deurali villagers for the extension of the canal, based on technical, economic and political reasons.

Realising the complexity and the gravity of the conflict some people from the irrigation command area discussed the problem with the Deurali villagers and made a verbal agreement to unofficially extend the canal after completion of the project.

When the canal was completed and running under the management of a users committee another serious conflict emerged. When the irrigation system came under the management of users, local politicians claimed credit for the canal as a means to win local support. There was competition to be involved in the WUC. Few elite members dominated the WUC and obtained more benefits from the canal (e.g., operation of the water mill). There was also conflict on rehabilitation and maintenance. Maintenance of the canal intake by all the users was agreed, as it was considered *Budhiwol* (as parental property where all have common right and responsibility) and the remaining canal length was divided into segments and allocated to sub groups in their area. However, this arrangement did not function. There were also no written rules for water distribution and maintenance. The Chairman of the Water User Committee installed a water mill, which used water from the canal. Users then asked him to contribute a small part of the profits he earned from the mill to the users' committee fund. When he refused to pay, all users unanimously removed him from the post of the users' committee's chairman. He then started to urge the Deurali Villagers to extend the canal and helped to escalate the latent conflict between the two villages.

Relatives, local traditional leaders, *purohit*, elderly people and political workers have all made several attempts to resolve the *Guthi* land conflict, especially after the leader of the *Guthi* owners collected money for a second time and tenants stopped paying rents. These efforts made before the leader of the *Guthi* owners filed a case in the court. But they were unsuccessful in resolving conflict. *Guthi* owners were confident about the legal verdict in their favour because the *Guthi* Corporation Office and Land Survey Office had earlier made decisions in their favour. They had legal documents, and also had influence with bureaucrats and powerful politicians. Tenants strongly organised themselves under the leadership of one of the local tenants of the *Guthi* land to get title of the land, because their survival had been dependant on that land for five generations. During the entire period of conflict the leader of the tenants organised tenants in protesting against landlords and developing links with different people, party leaders, and organisations. By using his leadership skills he was able to keep tenant groups intact and united, to argue, counter argue and effectively and convincingly present their problems. As a result the tenants virtually succeeded in establishing their ownership rights over the tenanted *Guthi* land.

In 1990 the Panchayat political system was overthrown and local power relationships changed again. In 1991 the government in the Dolakha district implemented the cadestral survey for preparing land-related information. The survey was very important to reconfirm ownership rights according to the government's land reform programme. Both parties therefore made utmost efforts to measure the disputed lands according to their own interests. This situation gave plenty of scope for surveyors to manipulate the situation. However, the political situation was not favourable to the *Guthi* owners due to their strong affiliation with the recently overthrown Panchayat political system. The majority of the tenants were active supporters of the 1990's democratic movement. As a result, the *Guthi* owners were not in the position to influence land surveyors and 120 tenant households were able to include the *Guthi* land in their own ownership in the registration book. Nevertheless, some of the main leaders of the *Guthi* owners gradually became affiliated with a big right-wing political party and regained their lost power. The majority of the tenants gained the support of another left-wing political party. As a result, after 1990 the disputants were clearly divided into two major opponent political parties and the conflict became a bipartisan political one. *Guthi* owners then filed a case in the Land Survey Office (*Napi Goswara*) claiming that the tenants had encroached the *Guthi* land. The Cadestral Land Survey Office ruled in favour of the *Guthi* owners and the tenants responded by filing a petition in the district court against the *Guthi* Sansthan, the Cadestral Survey Office and the *Guthi* owners. The situation now became very complicated due to a strong organisation of tenants, a power struggle between two powerful political parties and the involvement of governmental organisations such as the *Guthi* Corporation and Land Survey Offices. The *Guthi* owners, realising that it would not be possible to evict 120 households from the village even if they did win the court case, expressed their willingness to negotiate with the tenants. Ultimately, the negotiations resulted in an agreement being made between the two groups. According to the agreement, all 120 household tenants, in addition to the amount already paid by them, would have to pay one hundred thousands rupees to the *Guthi* owners. This was to establish a trust fund (*akchheyakosh*) to run the rituals and maintain the temple. For their part the *Guthi* owners would have to permanently transfer ownership of the land to the tenants. Accordingly the litigation case was withdrawn from the court and negotiations were returned to a local level. Tenants paid the agreed amount of money and the ownership of the disputed lands was permanently transferred. This transfer of the land was legalised by the district court. In this way the long lasting conflict was settled in 1998 after 39 years of conflict. However, conflict among the *Guthi* owners erupted when the money received from the tenants was not deposited in a bank account, so that the interest would allow the trust fund to cover the costs of worshipping as agreed.

Due to this land conflict power relationships in the VDC were changed. The general public gained confidence to defend their rights against the powerful elite. The exploitation of the tenants by village landlords and powerful elite was reduced and a new form of social relationship was established.

To create a favourable environment to bring the *Guthi* conflict to the negotiation table the chairman of the VDC (who was also a leader of the *Guthi* owners) extended the disputed *Ghangkhola* Irrigation Canal in 1996 up to the stream called *Chandanekhola* from where small irrigation canal connects to the *Deurali* area. This canal extension strategy helped to reduce the tension between villagers and bring tenants to the negotiation table.

Though the extension of the irrigation canal was a by-product of the land conflict it had a very positive impact on both villages. As a result of the canal the cropping pattern changed (maize-fallow to rice-wheat), the cropping intensity increased (1 crop a year to 2-3 crops a year), the existing land use pattern changed (upland to rice field) and new varieties of cereals and vegetables were introduced. The water use pattern was also changed. The availability of irrigation water directly provided drinking water facilities for villagers (for 35 households in head section of the canal) and indirectly served to recharge several drinking water sources located below the canal[1]. Use of irrigation to kitchen gardens is now common. The use of water for sanitation (cleaning clothes, houses, bathing, use in toilets, etc.) and for animals was increased. Respondents also informed me that the village air is cooler since the canal has been open and the intensity of diarrhoea and cholera has been reduced. Sufficient vegetables are being produced in the dry season to increase the villager's income level and health condition. Farmers are producing more food, vegetables and milk and are looking for external markets and the Local Governance Programme is trying to develop new market linkages. The value of the land has increased considerably and out migration has decreased. According to the respondents, parents of other villages are eager to marry their daughters to boys of their area. The villagers' workload, especially that of the women has increased due to the increase in crop intensity. This is especially true for rice cultivation where only women

---

1. When water is flowing in the canal in the dry season the volume of water in the downside spring sources was increased.

transplant rice seedlings. The water mill has also changed woman's working patterns. Before the canal was operational women had to work at night to dehusk rice (*dhan kutne*) and grind the flour (*pitho pidhne*). These jobs are now carried out in the water mill and women are engaged in other activities.

7.3. Factors Contributing to Conflict

After 1951, together with political change a number of significant changes occurred in the theory and practice of land ownership in Nepal. These changes include the abolition of the *Brita* and *Jagir* tenure systems and initiation of the land reform programme. Such changes reflected a new, more democratic spirit in the land reform efforts. This new democratic spirit brought several consequences to land tenure arrangements and ownership patterns. The *Deurali* land conflict is a direct product of these changes. The following section presents a brief analysis of the conflict dynamics.

7.3.1. Effects of Wider Social Change and Transformation of Conflict

The case description pointed out that the historical context is important in land conflict in general and *guthi* land in particular. As discussed above the land dispute began in 1959 and continued unabated for 39 years. It was only settled in 1998 after a long and bitter battle both in the village and the court. During these 39 years the *guthi* land conflict was extended and transformed or linked to several other issues such as extension of irrigation, water use, land inheritance and other social and political conflicts.

From the standpoint of conflict transformation the 39 years of the *guthi* land conflict can be looked at as having different phases. The socio-political system in the village was more feudal when the land conflict erupted for the first time in 1959. Conflict was suppressed during the realm of the feudal landlords. The situation in terms of balance of power was not much changed even after the emergence of the Panchayat political system. The tenancy rights of the *Guthi* tenants were raised but not strongly enough. Landlords influenced the voice of tenants over tenancy rights by strategically giving them hope of gaining their rights later. They used the tenants as free agricultural labourers on their farms. During this phase two processes were at work, one the hope and wisdom of the tenants and the other the elite's manipulations. These tenants also rented other lands from the *Guthi* owners and village landlords. Meanwhile conflicts between landlord groups over power sharing were observed within the village. This situation allowed the *Guthi* tenants to raise their voice and politely protest the exploitation of the landlords. This became clear in 1980 when a national referendum (to change or reform the then political system) gave the tenants an opportunity to have their voices heard. Opponents of the existing political system effectively raised the issue of exploitation of tenants and poor farmers by local landlords under the protection of the existing political system. This situation helped the tenants to stop paying rent to the *Guthi* owners.

The 'national democratic movement' in 1990, which aimed to restore democracy in Nepal was an important time for the tenants. During that period tenants and poor people were organised under the leadership of anti-Panchayat activists and started to protest the manipulation of the *Guthi* owners and village landlords. After this people's movement the power relationships in the village was changed and landowners became softer towards tenants and decreased their exploitation.

During the 39 years of conflict the parties concerned had opted for several forums to help in its resolution. Among them the Village Panchayat, the District land Reform Office, the *Guthi* Corporation Office, the District Police Office, District Court and the Land Measurement and Survey Office, were some of the major formal organisations. The *Purohit, Mukhiya* and local social networks of friends and relatives as well as political parties were other forums used to settle the conflict. Both groups used both formal and informal procedures and both used formal laws as a resource to resolve the conflict in their favour.

7.3.2. *Power Differential and Social Relations*

The owner/tenants relationship in the *Guthi* land conflict is characterised by cleavage and interdependence. The split between the groups has extended and expresses the social and legal confrontation over *Guthi* land; it is evident in the attitudes of hostility and is reinforced by the deep political divisions between the two groups. Interdependence derives from the separate but complementary roles the two groups play in the community. The interrelationship between the landowners and the tenants is therefore primarily understood in terms of their differential rights and interests in the land as well as the socio-political configurations created by land conflict. These rights and interests and so the relationships between the two groups have altered mainly in the course of the past four decades. During the period of the *Guthi* land conflict a variety of economic and political changes occurred leading to a fundamental transformation in the relationship between the two groups. The willingness of the leader of the *Guthi* landowners to negotiate by offering an extension of the irrigation canal is an example of the change in social relationships. As the leader of the *Guthi* owners had been a very powerful person in the VDC for more than 3 decades, it was less likely for him to give up his claims if the social relationship in village was unaltered. The Deurali land conflict indicates that the local power structure has changed over time from a land-centred feudal system to party based politics and knowledge centred power relationships.

In as much as a struggle of the tenants for the land undoubtedly changed group relationships, we might ask; 'why didn't the land struggle erupt into violence'? The answer is the 'accommodative', 'interdependent' and tolerant behaviour of the disputants. Although the disputants were dealing with land conflict their social relationships had not ceased. Tenants were working on agricultural farms belonging to the *Guthi* owners and the *Guthi* owners were providing loans and mediating in other local conflicts between tenants. Such interdependence helped to bring them to a negotiated settlement. Despite the widespread conflicts, a certain sense of accommodation and social harmony was still prevalent in the village. One can argue that as a result of the tolerant and accommodative behaviour of tenants and the unchallenged social relationships, powerful elite people were able to exploit them by collecting money several times without transferring ownership rights. This is against the spirit and legal provision of the Nepalese Land Reform Programme and is unfair to the tenants. Nevertheless, irrespective of the legal provisions, tenants would not have got ownership rights over *Guthi* land if they had not organised a continuous peaceful struggle.

The case clearly indicated that land conflict should be finally dealt with in court, to ensure recognition and legitimacy, even if it is negotiated locally. The reasons cited by respondents for an inability to resolve land related conflict at the community level were that the complicated land related conflicts must be decided by courts in order to receive formal recognition. Similarly, anecdotal evidence of respondents, local leaders, lawyers, judges and the Supreme Court's annual report (Table 4.1) confirm that a higher percentage of land related cases goes to court than of other natural resource related conflicts because of the issue of their legitimacy. This case also demonstrated that land conflicts are generally dealt with in court irrespective of the size of landholding of individual households. This is in contrast to other conflicts where rich people and those with a reasonable standard of living commonly take conflict cases to court. Poor people mentioned that VDC level conflict resolutions are cheaper and quicker than outsider organisations. Sometimes poor people also use the court strategy to legitimise their claim over land.

In the existing practice, acquiring a registered title on land by poor and landless people seems in practice extremely difficult and costly. The concern here is not only the issue of *Guthi* land but also the credibility of government bureaucracy and public administration. As discussed elsewhere in this chapter the powerful elite, in consultation with governmental bureaucrats deliberately manipulated the *Guthi* land conflict.

The decision of the Guthi Corporation and Land Reform Offices in favour of the landlords is an example of the influence of power in such a conflict. Such manipulation favours the local elite, who has higher political connections, in getting benefits from land conflict, taking advantage of the poor knowledge of tenants about legal provisions related to land.

7.3.3. *Rules v/s Behaviour: Difference in Rhetoric and Reality*

Does a rule or legal framework govern the behaviour of individual people? Are there discrepancies in what ought to be done (rhetoric) and what is happening in reality? These questions are particularly important in this *Guthi* land conflict. The state provides legal measures through the *Guthi* Corporation Act and regulations to govern *Guthi* land and to resolve associated conflicts. The Land Act, 1964, Land Survey Act, 1962, Land Administration Act, 1967, Soil and Water Conservation Act, 1982, Muluki Ain (Civil Code), 1963 Land Acquisition Act, 1977, Land Revenue Act, 1977 and the Agriculture Development, Act 1966 also deal with *Guthi* land related conflicts. However this case shows that these laws and regulations are not able to secure the rights of tenants. Landlords and the village elite class have largely controlled the *Guthi* land property regime. The exploitation of the tenants by the people who were close to political power centres, who were well informed about the legal provisions and able to influence bureaucracy, either in an open fashion or in a more indirect and subtle way is evident in this case. Private appropriation of income from *Guthi* lands by powerful politicians and privileged local landlords, which were traditionally allocated to run the rituals of the lord *Mahadev* is an example of how powerful elite manipulate common resources.

In this case the provision of a ceiling on land holdings made in the Land Act, 1964 was not effectively executed because the majority of the *Guthi* owners had more than the ceiling. The section 3, article 7(1) of the land related Act, 1964 has made provision for a ceiling on land ownership. The ceiling made for Terai households was 25 bigha (for cultivation) + 3 bigha (for homestead) (1 bigha or 0.67 ha) per family, 50 ropani (for cultivation) + 8 ropani (for homestead) (1 ropani or 0.05 ha) per family in Kathmandu valley and 80 ropani (for cultivation) + 16 ropani (for homestead) per family in Hills. All landlords have far more than the defined ceiling. Sons from the age of 16 and the unmarried daughters from the age of 37 can have such rights. Therefore all landlords registered their excess lands to other members of family to prevent confiscation of land above the ceiling. The *Guthi* owners also did not respect tenancy rights, the amount of rent and family limits on ownership of agricultural land defined by the land act. Those tenants who were renting land from landlords were not granted tenancy rights. The right of tenurial security and rent control to tenants of *Guthi* lands defined in the Land Act was also not applied in practice. These were all negotiated locally between tenants and landlords. The old provision of *Mukhiya* (*taluk*-if responsible to collect tax of upland and Jimwal-if responsible to collect the tax of low lands) made by the act to collect land revenue was exploitative. One of the *Guthi* landowners was the *Mukhiya* in that area and this fact legitimised the actions of the *Guthi* owners. Though section two, article 3 of the fourth revision of the act abolished the provision of *Mukhiya*, this arrangement was still operating in the village and significantly affected this conflict. Section 7 article 25(1) ensured tenancy rights (50% of the tenanted land) to the tenants, but the *Guthi* land tenants were not able to demand their tenancy rights because they were not able to get receipts for payment of the rent from landowners. Earlier the tenants have to pay 50 percent of the total produced, but later it was lowered to the 50 percent of the main harvest only. The tenants had some obligations to the tenanted land. They should not damage or decrease the value of rented land. Landowners who have no other residence and wish to build house on the land which (s)he will occupy and cultivate, are permitted to resume a portion or all of the rented land from tenant. In such a case the landowner has to compensate the tenants at least 25 percent of the market value of the cost of the land (New Era, 1988).

According to the Land Act, 1964 tenancy right should be granted to those tenants who are actually cultivating lands if they register as tenants and these rights should include security of tenure so long as they pay the stipulated rents. Earlier studies (Zaman, 1973; Regmi, 1976; 1987a; 1978b Malla, 1997) and the case study show that these provisions are not effective to ensure tenancy rights. Rather, they are frequently altered, manipulated and locally negotiated. Therefore, land related acts are not able to guarantee the right of the *Guthi* tenants. They only give an ideal framework in which people have to negotiate. In practice, rhetoric (even precisely written legal texts) is changed, modified, and/or ignored by powerful actors. Tenants also attempted to use acts and regulations as resources for their land right but with less success.

It is interesting to note that even if the land acts and regulations were not fully translated into practice, these provisions made a difference, affecting the behaviour of both *Guthi* owners and tenants. Both groups tried to use the law as a resource in their struggle and to legitimate their claims. Although it took a long time, the tenants eventually had success in getting their ownership rights based on their legal claim. The tenants would not have had ownership rights without the legislative provision.

7.3.4. *Role of Time and Context in Conflict*

From the narrative description of the *Guthi* land dispute it is clear that the role of time and context was crucial to the emergence and transformation of the conflict. Whenever there is a flexible situation, be it a time of National Referendum of 1980 or the Popular Political Movement of 1990, poor farmers in general and the *Guthi* tenants in particular raise their voices against their exploitation. Similarly, the *Guthi* land conflict escalated and became the issue of bargaining at the time of local elections where the leader of the *Guthi* owners was a candidate for the post of the

Head of the VDC. At that time he was more soft towards the *Guthi* tenants, made several promises to resolve the Guthi land_conflict and even committed himself to support Deurali villagers to obtain a loan from the Agricultural Development bank. However, after the local election such promises and commitments were not fulfilled and the villagers also became less assertive in raising these issues later.

When the leader of the *Guthi* owners failed to collect rent even mobilising the police force and using threatening tactics, the landowners filed cases in the *Guthi* Corporation Office and Land Reform Office. He approached these formal organisations because his position was weak at that time in the village due to recent political change. If and when the influence of elite people in the village is strong they suppress their opponent villager's activities and do not allow them to seek a formal resolution of any conflict. But if the local situation is not in their favour due to specific circumstances (such as organised protests from the opponents, backed up by another powerful political party, political movement, etc.) they themselves take cases to a formal conflict resolution process. In most of the cases formal process are resolved in their favour as they are able to mobilise networks and use their special relationship with bureaucracy.

The land survey and measurement became crucial in escalating as well as resolving conflict. The survey in the study district was conducted during the politically sensitive time when the former political system had just been overthrown. The stable (though unequal) power relationships in the village had been changed and mainly inexperienced, ambitious younger people were dominating the political scene. These politicians supported the tenants out of revenge against allies of the former political system. Tenants themselves overwhelmingly supported the multiparty democracy of the popular anti Panchayat movement and felt a strong stake in the new political system. Government staff from the land revenue and land survey offices felt insecure due to this political change because they had actively exploited the villagers, collecting bribes under the protection of politicians of the Panchayat. They wanted to ingratiate themselves with the new politicians by showing their loyalty and keeping their distance from the politicians of the past political system (though most of the government officials were strong supporters of *Panchayat*). The traditional locally based revenue officials like *Mukhiya, Jimuwal* were unhappy with the political change. They felt they were being humiliated, shown no respect and even threatened by the political leaders and workers of the new system and therefore their influence in the village at that time was insignificant. All these related factors worked in the tenant's favour in acquiring their ownership rights. However, supporters of the former political system soon joined one of the powerful parties and regained part of their lost power. Political change redefined the local power relationships and social system of the village.

It is interesting to note that an increasing number of conflicts were observed after the abolition of the partyless Panchayat political system. This was probably due to more freedom of expression in the new political system and ideological differences of the political parties. This shows again the importance of particular context and time factors in escalation or settlement of conflict.

Cultural and social shaping of Nepalese society in general, and society of the study area in particular, especially up to the end of the Rana regime period (1950) and to a lesser extent up to the end of the Panchayat regime (1990) was guided by the process of Sanskritisation. Sanskritisation is 'the process by which a 'low' caste or tribe or other group takes over the customs, rituals, beliefs, ideology and style of life of 'high' and in particular, a twin-born caste (Caplan, 1970). This also gained constitutional support when Nepal was declared a Hindu State as the Hindu religion is strongly based on Sanskritisation. Essentially, it was a means whereby a subordinate group in society recognises the superiority of Hinduism by emulating its cultural practices. After changes occurred in the political context such influence decreased.

Political attitudes and activities within the study area are influenced by the wider national political context. Therefore, not only disparities between the country's legal and regulatory framework related to land, but also political and power relationships are manifested in this conflict case. The complicated nature of negotiation, local initiation to resolve it, preference of disputants to go to litigation in court and finally return to a local level compromise were all shaped by the political nature and social power relationships.

7.3.5. *Ownership and Property Rights*

When the *Guthi* land was tenanted earlier, there was no population pressure and therefore the land had less economic value. Therefore, the *Guthi* owner gave land to tenants to prevent loss of efficiency, as he was not able to cultivate it himself. In those circumstances, the issue of property rights was not as strong as when it was raised later. When government passed the Land Act, 1964 the property right issue became highly contested and debated (NPC, 1998). Nepal's present socio-economic structures show that land is the main property and source of income of Nepalese people. Due to the vertical social structure and a highly stratified economic condition local elite had earlier accumulated large portions of land. Some elite members, who were more spiritual and religious in nature, allocated part of their lands as *Guthi* using the earnings of the land in worshipping god and providing land for tenants to cultivate. Later, when the amended Land Act, 1964 was passed to eliminate dual land ownership manipulation was drastically increased. There are several loopholes and weaknesses in the land related acts and the Deurali *Guthi* land conflict is rooted in their manipulation. The whole dynamics of the Deurali land conflict, its spread to other conflicts and final resolution is centred on legal ambiguity, local power relationships and political manoeuvring.

7.4. Compromise as a Pragmatic way to Manage Conflict

In this case, the tenants were organised, better informed about each other's behaviour and were in constant interaction about the problem. They had effective communication and information networks, which helped them to organise strongly. The effective communication between them facilitated collective understanding and gave a feeling of group identity because of their common interests and intertwined relationships. The tenant group was strongly organised because it was absolutely impossible to go against the powerful elite on an individual basis. This is also reflected in the study of Wade in a South Indian village. He states *"villagers will deliberately concert their actions only to achieve intensely felt needs which could not be met by individual responses"* that is *"they will straightforwardly come together to follow a corporate arrangement"* (Wade, 1988:185-188). It illustrates that the collective effort started within a social group in response to a collective need to regulate the allocation of land resource under conditions of scarcity. It is still a general tendency in rural Nepal that villagers are inward looking and suspicious of outsiders and outside involvement (New Era, 1988). This situation is clearly reflected in the book entitled 'Dangerous Wives and Sacred Sisters' written by Bennet where she discusses the importance of local village leaders in conflict resolution. She states that *"such internal solutions seem to be common-indeed the elder men in the village say they can't remember a single case were villages actually went outside Narikot* (a village close to Kathmandu) *to the police or the government courts"* (Bennet, 1983:8). Such an influential role of local leaders to resolve community level conflict is gradually disappearing with changing circumstances.

One old tenant deeply involved in this *Guthi* land conflict said, *"up to a certain extent I wanted to avoid going to court to resolve the conflict because of the complicated and expensive process and non-objectivity. It is meaningless to go to a formal process because it is almost not possible to get justice there due to the heavy influence of money and favour, political loyalties, and personal relationships"*. His statement clearly reflects the suspicions and reluctance towards formal organisations involved in conflict resolution. Other villagers also frequently expressed similar suspicions and distrust. This is the reason that disputant villagers first approached certain respected local leaders and elderly people to mediate. This is a clear example of the 'forum shopping' strategy used by local people and the preference and mobilisation of certain institutions to resolve conflict. It is interesting to note that such mediators are always male or groups of men and generally from higher caste or social strata. They are locally called *Panchbhaladmi* (literally five gentlemen), *Budhapaka* (elderly men), *Ganyamanya* (counted among the honoured), and *Gurupurohit* (teachers and priests), etc. Earlier, most conflicts in study area were mediated informally by men who are regarded as notables (Bhaladmi). Bhaladmi achieve notability with age, wealth, and increasingly with education and are expected to be fair and impartial when hearing disputes, and to possess the influence to make the decision acceptable to all the disputants (Caplan, 1970).

The simple nature of land conflicts means that people firstly seek resolution at a local level and complaints and decisions are generally oral. If a disputants feel that they cannot get a fair hearing from the traditional local leaders or they are from the same political party as the VDC head and hopes for favour then they approach the VDC. If the parties in conflict suspect the decision of the VDC or the decision is not in their favour, then they approach the police, CDO, Land Revenue Office, and finally if all else fail they approach to court. It was revealed that the VDC chairpersons and executive members were ignorant of the details of their official or formal authority and jurisdictions. They were not well informed about conflict resolution provisions envisioned in the Local Self-Governance Acts, 1998 and regulations. However, VDC secretaries were more informed and aware of these provisions compared to the elected representatives of VDCs. Only in conflicts concerning serious crimes and complicated land conflicts do people approach judicial bodies directly.

In all common land related conflicts such as land inheritance and partition, boundary encroachment, title irregularities such as fraudulent sales, competing claims to the same land and registration of the title, local VDCs and institutions are not able to settle the conflict legally. The reasons for this inability, according to the lawyers and the judges, are the complex nature of land issues, on which these local organisations could not give a legal recognition. Many times the Land Revenue Offices themselves are actively involved in the land fraud and irregularities. One example of such a dispute is the registration of public land under the ownership of *Balgram-* (Children Park) in Pokhara to the name of an individual based on bribery (later the court ordered to cancel the registration).

7.5. Conclusion

Land conflict also embodies water, forest and agriculture, three of the most contentious issues in contemporary natural resource related conflicts. Land in general and *Guthi* land in particular, in the study area is becoming an effective means to alter the feudalistic power relationship and effect wider social change. Land conflict is also a good source of illegal earnings for those people who have the authority to deal with it, as is clear by the prevailing corruption and bribery.

Legally regulated land management under the Guthi Corporation Act was expected to promote socially beneficial effects, increase efficiency and effectiveness of *Guthi* land, give tenural security and increase incentives for investment in land improvement. However, this case demonstrated that *Guthi* land management measures are not able to meet these expectations and such optimism is still diluted by the powerful lust for land.

From the foregoing discussion, the picture emerges that a land reform programme provides mechanisms for the political and technocratic manipulation of lands for economic and political benefits. Given the economically and socially highly stratified Nepalese society, extremely skewed land distribution and the ambiguous role of bureaucracy it is very difficult for the poor and marginalised people to get benefits from such a land reform programme (Ghimire, 1992; Badal,

1999; Karki, 1999; Bista, 1991; UNDP, 1998, New Era, 1988). Rather it increases conflict and gives advantage to powerful people. The influencing of powerful people on the bureaucratic and judicial decision making process is a common phenomena where land-related conflicts have to be resolved. This means that it is unlikely that poor people will get justice or gain a feeling of security. Such a failure increasingly defames the credibility of the legal system of the nation state.

The outcome of the adjudication process, especially the decision of the Guthi Corporation Office created insecurity and caused a feeling of injustice to develop among the tenants leading to their alienation. However, this is not only the responsibility of the surveyors or the Guthi Corporation Office. Surveyors had also faced difficulties such as excessive land fragmentation with ownership of numerous very small parcels of land, multiple claims and disputes, direct and indirect pressure from politicians and local elite. It would be therefore inappropriate to conclude that discrepancies and conflicts arise only as a result of the actions of surveyors and bureaucrats. The socio-cultural context, politicians and local people are equally responsible in promoting conflicts and discrepancies. None of the actors acted according to the legal system. Contradictions between the provisions relating to private Guthi land made in the Guthi Corporation Act, Land Act, Land Acquisition Act and Tenancy Right Acquisition Act created the core of the conflict in this case. These provisions were open to different interpretation, which led to various uncertainties and a failure to resolve the conflict. The land laws themselves fail to gain popular support and became another source of conflict. Institutional mechanisms were unresponsive in addressing the issues involved in the conflict. In summary, the impact of the formal legal system and administrative measures for the fair settlement of land-related conflict is minimal and they are even becoming a source of further conflict themselves. It is therefore not surprising that thousands of land disputes are pending in courts. It is relevant in this context to remember the popular saying in the law discourse 'justice delayed is justice denied' to the poor and marginalised section of society.

Despite the availability of various acts and regulations, state instituted organisations and the focus of government policies and programmes on land reform in general and *Guthi* land management in particular, conflicts over land are increasing. It is safe to say at this point that conflicts related to land resource arise due to the disrespect or violation of an individual's jurisdiction in order to take over the rights and duties of others (Oli, 1998). One of the major sources of land conflict in Nepalese society stems from institutionalised massive corruption perpetrated by politicians and bureaucrats and inequality caused by widespread mass poverty (Ghimire, 1992; Oli, 1998). Despite the legal mandate of different organisations to effectively manage conflict, lack of commitment, competition among themselves to maintain their supremacy, bribery and corruption are ruining their performance. It is not an exaggeration to say that these organisations themselves are becoming the source of natural resource related conflicts, instead of a means of their resolution. The Deurali land conflict is an example of such inefficiency.

On a wider level the most desired political change of 1990 in Nepal has also done little to bring about much needed land reform for the vast majority of Nepalese people. Since 1990 all major political parties either in the form of majority, minority or coalitions have led the government but there has been very little change in the land reform and management system. There is a wide spread agreement that more effective land reform is urgently needed to reform agriculture and to transform society (to achieve the goal of social justice, poverty alleviation, gender and equity concerns) (UNDP, 1998; Ghimire, 1992). However, the lack of political commitment and willpower of the politicians and the poor performance of bureaucratic institutions threaten the prospects of land reform.

CHAPTER 8

Complexity in Managing Social and Natural Resource Conflict in Nepal

8.1. Introduction

Chapters four to seven have discussed the empirical findings about social and natural resource conflicts, their interrelations and transformation patterns, characteristics and resolution measures. The empirical chapters demonstrated that conflict is a dynamic and integral part of society and their resolution practices in Nepal are becoming increasingly inadequate and expensive. In this chapter I will analyse the reasons behind conflict and their resolution practices based on the analytical framework discussed in the second chapter. In my theoretical and methodological approach, I based myself on perspectives developed in legal anthropology and communication and innovation studies. A legal-anthropological perspective focusing on legal pluralism is used to analyse the diverse effects of laws in conflicts and a conceptual roadmap derived from the social learning perspective is used to explore the scope for their improvement.

I put forward the thesis in the first chapter that Nepalese society is facing several conflicts and challenges due to a lack of conducive policies and institutional arrangements, weak implementation of existing policies and regulations, rampant corruption, abuse of power and political interests. The economic motive of powerful people for irrational exploitation of economic and natural resources is another paramount factor promoting conflict in the community. In the context of this problem several efforts have also been made from both the formal and informal sectors to address these conflicts. This chapter has attempted to analyse these conflicts and the efforts to manage them. To explore social and natural resource conflicts and their management practices, the study was accomplished under a complex, multi-actor NRM problem context where multiple governmental organisations, NGOs and local powerbrokers were engaged in dealing with natural resource conflicts by using various state, customary, religious and normative rules. In this chapter I argue that most of the formal and informal CM practices, while resolving social and natural resource conflicts, mainly favour powerful and resourceful people (cf. New Era, 1988; Oli, 1998; Kaplan, 1995). In the following sections I analyse specific causes of conflicts, their management practices and specific factors affecting the process of conflict management in Nepal.

8.2. Causes of Conflict and Transformation Patterns

8.2.1. *Temporal and Spatial Issues in Conflict Transformation*

Chapters four to seven demonstrated that conflict occurs in various stages. Empirical findings indicated that conflict starts with a stage of personal and social antagonisms over certain issues such as transaction, sexual and marital reasons, political interference, extension of canal, encroachment of communal pastureland, sharing of water source, location of intake and resource-use and establishment of water right over land, etc.. The same conflict enters into a latent stage at some point in time (e.g., lesser degree of antagonism). It enters an ignition stage at some particular time (such as the visit of the government's mobile administrator in the pastureland case, the start of pipe laying in the spring water source case or release of money from the DIO in the ADB-funded irrigation case) and then escalates to the active manifestation stage. At some point in time it enters a stage of termination and reconciliation (as discussed in the spring-water source conflict, negotiation of the Guthi land conflict). Transformations of conflict from one issue to other issues (e.g., transfer of ownership right to extension of irrigation in the Guthi land conflict, political conflicts between local political parties) are common. Conflict can be transformed from one stage to another (latent to ignition to escalation to termination) in a cyclic fashion (e.g. in the Guthi land case) but most of the time its interlinkages do not follow a clear cyclic pattern. Analysis of causes of conflict shows that their intensity and transformation potentials differ with different circumstances. Based on the discussion of the second part of the book, I have summarised the major causes of conflict. They are:

- (a) opposing interests and divergent beliefs (in forest-pastureland conflict),
- (b) lack of basic understanding or ignorance of interdependence between people and natural resources (as discussed with respect to general conflicts in chapter four),
- (c) ignorance of relations of solidarity, sense of identity and belonging, relations of trusts, common rules and sanctions (in all five conflict cases)
- (d) influence of social, political, cultural, technological and economic interests (ADB-funded irrigation case),
- (e) differences in perceptions, work styles, attitudes, communication problems and social exclusion (general conflicts in chapter four),
- (f) contradictory legal provisions and ambiguity over responsibility and authority, and
- (g) vested political interest and monetary greed (both irrigation cases).

In conflict situation, one party wants to influence or control the behaviour of another party whose actions and counter-actions are mutually opposed. Social conflicts are endemic in every day life in Nepalese society where social structures and power relationships play a crucial role. Though these social structures and power relationships favour powerful people they, in turn, are more disrupted by the escalation of conflicts than ordinary people (cf. Sidaway, 1996).

Social conflicts are not only involved with the use of natural resources but are also directly related to or originated from policies, new technologies, laws and socio-political interests. Therefore, it is difficult to demarcate the boundaries of social conflict. Nevertheless, a sociological approach of analysis of conflict (from the knowledge of collective behaviour, social structures and institutions) combined with a psychological way of analysis (from the behaviour of individuals) greatly helps to understand the dynamics of social conflicts, even if there is no clear demarcation.

8.2.2. *Common Interests as a Basis for Negotiation*

All the cases presented seem to suggest that the elite's manipulation of conflict has resulted in an increased ability of tenants and villagers to defend their rights, to protest against manipulations and to negotiate. An essential prerequisite for defending their rights and bargaining at negotiations was 'a common interest' framed under a specific context and time. Therefore, conflicts are not necessarily always socially irrational and dysfunctional and contribute to changing local social relationships and helping to build the capacity of local people.

8.2.3. *Access and Control of Resources as Causes of Conflict*

Chapters three to seven illustrate that access, allocation and distribution of natural resources and power relation were some of the major issues in conflict. Differential access and control, changes in access patterns and inequitable access frequently caused conflicts. Conflicts also arose about the fulfilment of obligations (application of rules and implementation of policies, resource mobilisation, and participation). Similarly, regulations and responsibilities of government organisations involved in natural resources and manipulation by powerbrokers were central issues in creating conflict. The irrigation and *Guthi* land conflicts confirmed that bureaucratic inefficiency and manipulations had greatly helped to accelerate conflicts. Chapter four clearly indicated that conflicts between users themselves and between users and government agencies were frequent. These conflicts were linked to gender concerns, resource degradations, value differences (staff/bureaucrats v/s communities), insecurity (seasonal scarcity of resources), etc. New and expanded development projects (such as irrigation and drinking water systems, demarcation of forest boundaries, land measurement, etc.) have altered the existing resource use patterns and given rise to numerous additional conflicts.

8.2.4. Interdependence, Identity and Conflict

Empirical data have shown that complex 'interdependency' and 'identity' are unique features of natural resource conflict. For example, tenants residing on the *Guthi* land had a special identity and economic base and therefore they engaged in a peaceful struggle with the powerful elite group to maintain this identity. The powerful elite members used locally available natural resources as a means to establish a stronghold in the village. Ordinary people in a community also use natural resources as a means for identity and survival. Therefore, the relationship between natural resources and people was shaped and reshaped by interdependent relationships in a particular context. Polarisation of economic and political interests between privileged classes and poor people and rapid changes in political and economic activities in Nepal has resulted in competition for, conflict over and encroachment of natural resources by various interest groups. It has also led to corruption. Whether it was a *Guthi* land conflict or spring-water source conflict or conflict on the extension or new development of an irrigation canal, ignoring this interdependency ultimately promoted conflict. The farmers-managed irrigation conflict, the forest-pastureland conflict and the *Guthi* land conflict cases illustrated that historical background, time and space were other important aspects of natural resource conflict. During special periods of time such as an election or the restoration of democracy, conflict suddenly increases or in some cases conflicts may be resolved instantly. This indicates that the time factor and the specific context affect the intensity of conflict. This means that the life cycle of a conflict determines the management or resolution strategies.

8.2.5. Property Rights, Ownership Issues and Conflict

Ownership and property right issues were, among others, central concerns in natural resource conflict. Contradiction of legal provisions, differences in legal arrangements and their actual applications, ambiguity over responsibility and authority of government organisations and unequal resource distribution greatly enhanced conflict over natural resources. With some justifications (such as historical or religious association and linkages) people may claim their rights over common natural resources. The pastureland conflict case shows that forest and pastureland was managed as a common property resource[1] according to community norms and values. Members of a particular community exclusively shared the right of access, allocation and exclusion. The spring-water source case also illustrates that ownership, access and control of a particular natural resource lie with community members. The issue of rights to prior appropriation and riparian rights were strongly raised at the time of the extension of the farmers-managed irrigation system (construction of the new canal and the encroachment of forestland) (cf. Khadka, 1997). People also construct rights on the basis of their historical association (in farmers managed irrigation case) and cultural basis (spring-water source case). For example, the claim of the source-owner over water rights was based on the argument that the source was located on his land. Similarly the community's claim on ownership over pasture and forestland was based on historical association. In the farmers-managed irrigation

---

1. See Steins (1999), Berkes and Tanghi (1989), Ostom (1990), Benda-Beckmann and Benda-Beckmann (1996), Torton *et. al.*, (1998); Berkes (1996) for a detailed discussion about common property resources.

system, forest and pastureland and spring-water cases, property rights were also claimed based on prior use. In the forest-pastureland case, it was also based on the investment of resources. In the fifth case property was established by payment of money. Changes in resource-use patterns (change in cropping pattern/systems, irrigation schedule, rotational grazing, etc.), changes in the mode of operational arrangements (land transfer to descendants, FUG, WUA, etc.) and changes in infrastructure (availability of new canals, forests, etc.) are all contributing to changing the rights of different groups and are bringing new conflicts in natural resources.

The case described in chapter seven clearly indicates that the demand of farmers to register individual title emerged from their feeling that such titles would secure their right of ownership and give pride, dignity, identity and a source of livelihood. Such feelings are interconnected with local rituals, cosmovision and religious and spiritual meanings (cf. Regmi, 1978a). This continuous struggle of the tenants to establish their ownership was based on these feeling of security, rituals, and identity. For the tenants acquiring ownership rights over the *Guthi* land was the principal form of insurance against economic hardship and financial crisis as it was their only valuable asset, which they could sell or mortgage to get some money.

Nevertheless, this insurance function of land is making the vast majority of poor people landless (Ghimire, 1992; Blaikie *et al.*, 1983) because landlords give money for a mortgage with extremely high interest rates. When the borrowers cannot repay the loan the landlords foreclose and take possession of the land. There is not sufficient protection from such foreclosure by rich and powerful people because the judicial system is under the influence of the political establishment. It is too costly for poor people to access and more importantly they have no faith in the fairness of the judicial system (Kaplan, 1995; Ghimire, 1992; Bhatiya, 1997). A land-related study in Africa by Platteau (1996) also demonstrated a situation similar to that in Nepal. This means that such manipulation of the land is a common characteristic of developing countries.

8.2.6. *Ignorance of Local Needs, Interests and Experiences and Conflict*

Natural resource management is the key interface between local knowledge/interests and scientific knowledge. Local knowledge and experiences are manifested in the day-to-day actions of villagers. Local knowledge can only be properly integrated with knowledge brought by external actors when NRM is accomplished in a collegiate pattern (Shivakoti *et. al.*, 1996). As discussed in chapter six barriers to the incorporation of local knowledge/interests into the irrigation project implemented by DIO includes their social and political agendas and the professional and cultural background of the staff. The failure of this project is evident, irrigation technocrats having designed it on the basis of behavioural factors without allowing the involvement of local people. Needs, interests, knowledge and experiences of the local community were mainly ignored. This case also indicates that outsiders are often not adequately trained to recognise and deal with unacknowledged professional and cultural agendas, which may underlie interactions between outsiders and a community. The formalised, mandatory process of co-ordination between the actors involved in the irrigation project was lacking. Formal intervention in the farmers' managed irrigation case has increased conflict because local rules and regulations were ignored and even replaced. Development interventions give rise to conflicts when villagers/users believe that their prior rights are overridden. Misappropriation of project assets intended to benefit the general public, was another point of contention in the study area. When the consequences of intervention are not carefully considered by development organisations and when local ideological factors are not respected a subtle form of hostility increases, ultimately leading to conflict. There is a growing consensus that the creation of enormous conflicts, related either to land, forest, water or any other natural resource, are due to external interventions based upon the hidden agenda and vested interests of external actors (Kaplan, 1995; New Era, 1988; Oli, 1998). As has been observed from the farmers managed irrigation, ADB-funded irrigation project and the *Guthi* land conflict cases, privileged classes take more advantage of government initiated NRM programmes and this often creates social conflict. For example, the ADB-funded irrigation project created a vicious spiral of discord and initiated several conflicts in the village. In the *Guthi* land case, it is not surprising that the relationship between the land registration/reform process and conflict is indisputable and that land-measurement favoured powerful people.

8.2.7. Technological and Development Interventions and Conflict

Technology is one of the important causes of conflict especially when external development interventions introduce new and sophisticated technologies, incompatible (in terms of skills, knowledge, financial resource requirement, etc.) with the local situation. The technology used in the ADB-funded irrigation system was one of the major sources of lasting conflict in the community because it was expensive, required a lot of external input such as cement, construction tools and local people had no knowledge or skills to work with the new technology. Properly designed/created structures and institutions (either by resource users themselves or external intervention) and a combination of new technology with local knowledge and experiences encourage people to work together. Physical structures (such as an intake of a canal, canal damaged by flood and landslides, etc.) not only create conflict but also inspire people to work together and encourage them to carry out regular monitoring. The faulty design of NRM projects is a strong source of conflict. There is a strong relationship between the technical design and the organisation of users to create and or resolve natural resource conflicts.

8.3. Understanding Conflict-management Options and Procedures

Unless the conflict is linked with other destructive structural causes people involved in natural resource conflict do not opt for violent action. The degree, intensity and violent effects in social and natural resource conflict are less than in ethnic and other violent conflicts. People involved in social and natural resource conflicts, especially conflicting parties from the same community, are generally accommodative. Wherever possible they adopt a tolerant strategy rather than one of confrontation and therefore demonstrations, active sabotage and violence are not common in natural resource conflicts in villages. They first opt for accommodative methods (bargaining, negotiation, etc.) and make the utmost efforts to prevent confrontation. If the conflict remains unresolved, then they approach their preferred political parties before seeking legal measures. In the study area conflicts were mainly resolved locally. Religious ceremonies and festivals such as marriages, worshipping, and public gatherings *in Dashain* and *Tihar, Chautari and hatbazars,* etc. were common forums to discuss problems and in most of cases reach a consensus or majority decision on specific options. Outcomes of these resolutions could be both permanent and temporary. Social and natural resource conflicts also create new institutions (e.g., mediation groups, protection committees, tripartite committees in UAIS, etc.) and physical structures (e.g., construction of other small irrigation canals, alternate grazing provision, etc.). Local people have several options to settle conflicts, and they pursue a particular one based on their faith and knowledge about them. Settlement of natural resource and social conflicts (especially land-related conflicts as most of the lands are occupied by landlords) is shifting to the formal legal system and official litigation proceedings, which are more advantageous to resourceful people.

Chapters five to seven suggest that endurance (wait, let things mature, gain value and resume negotiation) was a common feature in community level conflict. Such endurance replaced stagnant inaction with constant, persistent and creative efforts to resolve the conflict (cf. Pendzich, 1993). The spring-water source conflict case shows that parties involved in conflict have creative ingenuity rather than passive complacency. Such ingenuity and endurance also generated local mechanisms (e.g., *Sangarsha Samiti*, Mediation Group) and enabled local people to work together in order to manage local conflict. Willingness of users to develop the forest, get drinking water and irrigate their fields were important motivating factors to initiate collective action. They have generated mechanisms for firm and persistent efforts to make the best from the conflict situation. Their adaptive management strategy to learning from the process was successful in seeking new ways of managing conflict in natural resources (cf. Lee, 1993).

The analysis of conflict management practices adopted by formal (operating according to government's regulatory provisions) and informal (operating according to local arrangement with or without following government regulations) organisations/individuals brought an important question about their effectiveness and credibility. Empirical chapters clearly indicated that both practices are methodologically inadequate, economically expensive, administratively difficult, pro-elite (biased) and structurally inaccessible to poor people. Nepalese formal CM practices (except VDCs) are biased in favour of power centres and entangled in pervasive corruption. They are the product of a long history of social stratification, cultural tradition and undemocratic political processes and tend to discriminate against powerless and vulnerable people. However, some hope can be placed upon the emergence of local organisations such as the FUGs, WUA, and local NGOs to deal with growing community level conflicts in Nepal. The redefined role and willingness of VDC is another emerging area of hope. Poor people have started to raise their voice in VDCs. Since 1990, VDCs are becoming more responsive to the concerns of local people in order to win their vote in periodic elections. In managing community level conflicts these local organisations have demonstrated that they can mediate, negotiate and manage conflict far better than the state machinery.

It is observed that in an informal CM process disputants first go to local negotiators (generally local leaders) to make an oral complaint naming the wrongdoers and presenting evidence. The negotiators then summon both parties to present their evidence and witnesses in the presence of villagers at a public hearing. The negotiators then render an "on the spot" decision based on the testimony and other evidence. Such decisions may be compensation in cash and kind, a fine, a public apology or a warning or referral to the CDO, police or court. In some conflict cases there may be no concrete evidence linking the defendant to the wrongdoing and only tenuous circumstantial evidence which may not work in court proceedings. Legal procedure and rules of evidence do not restrict local negotiators, who know the past behaviour and present actions of the conflicting parties, to make local negotiation ways. From a pragmatic point of view, even though evidence is obviously important in investigating truth in a conflict, it should not be the single determining factor for its fair resolution.

In formal CM practices the decisions made by the formal bodies are, at least in principle, enforceable through legal provisions. However, as shown in chapter four most of conflicts that are resolved through informal processes are not always enforceable by legal provisions. They are however subject to daunting social sanctions to those who disobey the resolutions. The cost of disobedience could be social disapproval or ostracism or a threat to testify against that party in future proceedings. When the conflicting parties realise that villagers will testify against them they generally comply with the local resolution. This arrangement is helping society to manage several conflicts locally. To give importance to local relationships and accommodate differences, villagers used a cultural legend "*Des ko deuta bhanda gaon ko bhut kamlagchha*" (Ghost of own village is more useful than the god from far distance). When external intervention occurs, new rules, regulations and procedures, which replace, ignore or do not give sufficient attention to local norms, values and rules ultimately create conflict in society.

Societies have developed procedures based on local values and beliefs to resolve conflict. Local conflict-management practices (chapter four), which are accessible to all members of the community and in which local people have confidence are based on these procedures. Nevertheless, such local community based practices have some inherent weaknesses because their resolutions generally favour powerful people in the village. Weaker sections of societies (women, minorities, powerless, etc.) in many cases get fewer benefits from the solutions offered by these practices. Written documentation is also lacking in these practices and they are not able to deal with conflict related to new technological issues. Therefore, conflicting parties engaged in do not depend only on local CM practices. They approached both informal and formal forums if they were favourable. Political forums are actively used in conflict. Local political parties want to be involved in conflict resolution so as to convince conflicting parties that they should vote for them in any election. All five cases demonstrated that parties in conflict used several formal and informal forums instead of relying on a single forum and a unitary method of conflict resolution. In the recent past, the frequencies of middle level people going to district-based formal forums for the resolution of conflict is increasing. Poor people are still reluctant to approach district-based forums. Ordinary people only opt for litigation when the conflict is serious and has lasting consequences such as land inheritance or when one of the parties in the dispute wants to take revenge on their opponents. To take a conflict to the courts or to any formal legal process is mainly interpreted in the village as being for revenge, rather than seeking justice. This is because more affluent people often take the conflict to a formal process in order to force their opponents to surrender to them. Powerful people often start a formal process (or threaten to do this) to justify their importance in the community and validate their act in the village. In most villages there are professional troublemakers who start legal proceedings in false cases just to punish those who do not respect or satisfy them. The aim of these professional troublemakers is to gain financial rewards (cash or kind), to punish to those who do not follow them and to raise/maintain their social status. They have good networks and relationships with politicians and government officials in the district, and are well aware of the legal rules and procedures as well as having strong personal relationships with lawyers. By using these privileges they are able to manipulate conflict cases to their benefit.

Several conflicts were not completely resolved but managed to keep the situation working. After some time many such conflicts transform to other forms (e.g., the *Guthi* land case conflict was linked to irrigation, the forest and pastureland case conflict was linked with the spring-water source and exploitation of *Mukhiya*). Chapter four demonstrates that transformation of a conflict from some specific issue to a more general form is more common (e.g., water to land to social conflict). Most of the conflicts begin with resources use (access to, control over and exclusion) and become linked with other social and political conflicts. Vested political interests overwhelmingly influence them. They are also occasionally linked with issues such as; lending and borrowing, family feuds, witch-hunts, molestation, alcoholism, crops damaged by animals, and casting of votes to a particular political party.

The organisational culture of organisations working dealing with conflict has contributed to creating and or resolving conflict (e.g., culture of irrigation technicians, foresters, land surveyors and contractors, culture of organisations in treating political leaders differently than the general public, etc.). It is observed that there is no proper interaction between the authority deciding the conflict case and the parties involved in the conflict because of a feeling of supremacy and associated authoritarian behaviour. These organisations have their own preconceived ideas, interests, priorities and procedures that govern the conflict resolution process and ultimately the outcome.

This book argues that conflict management involves various diagnostic processes, decision-making procedures, interpersonal efforts, argument tactics and negotiation options (cf. Hellriegel *et al.*, 1999). Emotional behavioural responses of people engaged in conflict do not generally ignore any negative consequence while dealing with conflict. Potential negative consequences become secondary when conflict becomes severe as in the farmers managed irrigation case. In such a case, distributive bargaining (competitive, zero sum, win-lose) is more common than integrative negotiation. In a distributive situation there are fixed resources to be divided so that the more one gets, the less the other gets, therefore, one party's interests opposes the others. The concern in this case is to maximise one's own interests by manipulation, forcing, and withholding information. In contrast, in integrative bargaining (collaborative, win-win or creating value) the main concern is to maximise joint outcomes through co-operation, sharing information, mutual problem solving and creating resources (develop feelings that they have greater value than before). The decision-making process and its outcome also affects the behavioural responses of the parties involved in conflict. As discussed in chapter four local conflict resolution decisions are more socially endorsable in a community. People were less assertive in endorsing decisions made by formal organisations compared to local decisions. Similarly, powerful people are less likely than the general public to respect decisions of formal litigation. The major options used by actors to manage conflict in the study area are summarised below.

8.3.1. Compromise

Compromise was one of the most common options used in managing conflict in the community. Compromise is a trade-off between disputants to manage conflict. Disputants feel that they have to relinquish something but socially their position is strengthen (Warner and Jones, 1998). In this option the continuing relationship with the other party is valued. Compromise in the forest and Guthi land cases demonstrated that when there are normal relationships between the disputants the outcomes of conflict resolution are mostly win-lose. Requesting, manoeuvring, pressuring and demanding are commonly used strategies in this option. This option can enable disputants to be advantaged if no agreement is reached.

8.3.2. Collaboration

Collaboration was one of the options used in resolving social and natural resource conflict in the community. The spring-water source case is an example of collaboration where people's behaviour became assertive at a later stage to bring about a win-win situation and maximise joint outcomes (cf. Warner and Jones, 1998). In this case conflict was utilised to create better resolutions (e.g., collection of wastewater in the tank at night, exploration of alternate sources for larger drinking-water scheme, etc.). Parties in conflict using this option perceive that both groups are benefiting. Sharing, examining and assessing the causes of the conflict is a prime action in this option to create alternative resources/solutions. Psychological feelings to maintain the interpersonal and social relationships push the disputants to collaborate (spring-water source case). The degree of collaboration was less in the resolution of the grazing land, AFMIS and *Guthi* land conflicts.

8.3.3. Withdrawal

Withdrawal is basically an avoidance option for those parties who prefer to avoid confrontation. Chapter four shows that disputing parties mainly used the withdrawal option, to prevent the worsening of personal relationships. Powerful people use this option over powerless people to maintain the existing status quo. They benefit more by withdrawing their claim and showing they can be humble to poor people. Powerless people often use this option because they fear defeat, as they feel unable to compete with powerful people (feeling of helplessness). Pressuring, threatening, and entreating are common methods used in this option.

8.3.4. Force

Force was one of the options used in the study area, which is coercive by nature and largely based upon power, linkage and *afnomanche*. In the pasture and forest conflict the powerful *Mukhiya* used physical force to threaten protesters and in the *Guthi* land conflict the landlords used the police force against their opponents. Both cases indicated that the use of force develops deep feelings of injustice that prevents co-operation and disputants look for revenge when the power relationships in the village change. However the amount of force used was limited and in most cases people were tolerant and opted for other options such as withdrawal, collaboration and compromise.

8.3.5. Consensus

Consensus was another strategy in managing community level social conflict. In a consensus option synergy of collaborative negotiations is used to widen the basis for decision-making, thereby avoiding trade-offs altogether. It is more than simple agreement. It is also called as collaborative or win-win or integrative CM. However, it was not possible to make consensus in complicated social conflict cases.

8.3.6. Accommodation

Accommodation was another characteristics of local level conflict management. In this strategy party value a strong and continuing relationship with one or more of other parties above the attainment of its own goals. In these cases the party may elect to 'accommodate' the other parties, withholding to all or some of their claims. Although such outcomes may look as the result of 'force', the difference is that rather than losing outright, the accommodating party perceives itself to have gained by securing good relations, accompanied by 'good will' and the option to achieve some greater goal at a future date

(Warner and Jones, 1998). Self-actualisation plays greater role in this strategy.

In all these strategies one or all of the four elements such as redirection of behaviour, reallocation of resources, reframing perspective and realigning structural forces are acting (Fisher, 1997). In managing social conflict educating and appealing to rules are more useful than coercion, manipulating and threatening. Options like stealing, cheating, lying, requesting entreating, manoeuvring, pressuring, threatening, demanding, monitoring, arguing by rules, staying neutral, exploiting are other alternative strategies use in CM.

8.4. Understanding the Factors Influencing Conflict Management Practices

Myriad of factors contributes to creation or resolution of conflict. They were: political interests, power relationships, bureaucratic influences, laws and regulations, government's policies and strategies, corruption, the influence of local social structures, customary norms and values, leadership quality, gender relationships and differences in understanding or perception. I also observed the intimate connection between conflict and communication, information and their inter-linkages in the resolution or escalation of a conflict. Among them the following factors are identified as the most crucial in social and natural resource conflicts and their management practices:

8.4.1. Top-down Linear Perspective

From the beginning my thesis maintained that government, policy makers, planners, donor agencies and politicians mainly look upon conflict management in Nepal from a top-down, reductionist and linear perspective. I have argued throughout the book that conflict management is neither linear nor single discipline based. Rather it is complex and requires new practices and processes, which provide forums for collective learning and concerted action (Röling and Wagemakers, 1998). My arguments on the failure of Nepalese conflict management is because of a lack of understanding of local perspectives, lack of coherence in policy and legislative provisions, lack of commitment and devolution of power (cf. Pandey, 1998; Dahal *et al.*, 1999). These weaknesses are the important sources of conflicts. Empirical evidence has demonstrated that integration of local perspectives and learning from local experiences is weak in contemporary CM practices in Nepal. All the cases detail that conflicts between community and external interventions were exacerbated by the ignorance of local interests and manipulation by powerbrokers. Chapters three and four put forward evidence that the existing formal CM practices in Nepal are mainly relied on by the police, local administration and courts and they are lengthy, slow, costly and inaccessible to poor and marginalised people.

8.4.2. *Formal and informal laws*

The role of law has been a central concern in CM practices and its fair execution in Nepal is a highly debatable issue. Law in the context of conflict is used as a fundamental resource to negotiate conflict (Benda-Beckmann *et al.*, 1997). Exercise of laws and regulations dealing with conflict takes place in a specific context and they are only one among many conflict resolution measures. The contradictions and inconsistencies between different formal legal and policy provisions have caused several problems in implementing development projects (Chapters three and four). Therefore, the co-existence of different legal forms has diverse implications for social and natural resource conflicts. The fifth case showed that though a formal land-related legal arrangement had good intentions, its abuse by the influence of power at the time of its execution caused insecurity to tenants instead of providing security. Powerful people were able to manoeuvre formal regulations. This stresses the point that whatever promises are made in legislation they have to actually be transformed into practice to give justice. Both irrigation conflict cases show that development interventions were based on a formal legal framework and they either ignored or undermined the local context. This not only enhanced conflict in the village but also promoted misuse of resources as shown in the farmer-managed irrigation and *Guthi* land cases. It can be seen from the spring-water source conflict case that people make local rules themselves, modify existing ones and maintain these rules with specific interests, what Moore (1973) describes as a 'semiautonomous social field'. In the context of conflict, laws therefore should not only be understood as those laws, which are recognised and enacted by the state, but also as the rules operated in a semiautonomous social field. This demonstrates the important role of legal pluralism in studying conflict in society.

Legal CM practices were often based on the belief that legal mechanisms are the only appropriate means to resolve conflict. Formal CM practices commonly view local people as conflict creators and the legal institutions as the solutions of these conflicts. As indicated by both the forest-pasture and *Guthi* land cases implementers of legal intervention assume that legal enactment forces people to resolve (or hide) conflict by threatening punishment. They also interpret law as an ultimate instrument for social engineering, an effective means for homogenising a heterogeneous society and resolving all conflicts (cf. Nader and Todd, 1978). However, the important question is how laws are translated in reality. For example, irrigation regulations in Nepal grant legal recognition to water-users groups as autonomous entities and envisage the rights and duties of users. In reality, as discussed in chapter six, these provisions are not properly translated into practice. Similarly, implementation of a full cadestral survey in Nepal was aimed at developing effective land related information system and minimising potential land conflicts. Empirical evidence suggests that conflicts were increased by the survey. Enacting more laws and imposing more regulations does not always change people's behaviour. Such legal engineering is only one aspect in shaping people's behaviour. The Irrigation Sector Support Project had clear criteria, rules and norms to implement ADB-funded irrigation projects. But they were interpreted and modified by implementers based on their own interests.

From this study it can be argued that the existence of legal rules and principles does not necessarily always shape the behaviour of people. These rules and principles can be relevant only when people respond and behave accordingly (Benda-Beckmann *et al.*, 1997). Many people rely on legal rules or look for a legal basis to legitimise their claims when property rights become problematic or contested. In this situation disputing parties generally look for different options. Either they want to justify their claims with formal authority (i.e., the court, police, and local administration), who usually decide such complaints by reference to legal principles, rules and procedures. Alternatively, disputing parties move to a more informal but socially recognised institution or forum such as the *Mukhiya, Jamindars*, and priests and village headmen, who negotiate such disputes on the basis of customary norms and local practices (cf. Spiertz, 2000). The interpretation of laws by authoritative experts (for example, judges, administrators, project personnel, etc.) was different from local people. Such differential interpretations become a powerful means for promoting or defeating specific interests. From the discussion with lawyers and observations of case proceedings in court it became clear that the Arbitration Act is not contributing to management of natural resources and social conflict. Section three of the act severely limits the scope for making arrangement that any disputes under contract or agreement are resolved through arbitration. Community level social and natural resource related conflicts are not falling under any bilateral or multilateral agreement. Therefore this act is practicably inapplicable to dealing with other social and natural resource conflicts.

From the analysis of the empirical material in chapter four it is realised that costly, lengthy and unfamiliar procedures are a disincentive to pursuing disputes in the formal system. This is further exacerbated by political bias and source-force (Khadka, 1997). The picture that emerges from this argument is that a broader reform is needed of the legal system to make it more flexible, accessible, cheaper and faster to ensure fair justice.

8.4.3. *Caste, Ethnicity and Social Relations*

Caste/ethnicity is an important factor in conflict. People from a higher caste and social strata (e.g., Brahmin, Chhetri and Newar) prefer to conceal conflict (created by their vested action) instead of going to the court or semi- judicial organisations. They opt for a formal process only when they are sure that the outcome will be in their favour. People from low caste/ethnic groups and from lower social strata generally prefer not to go to the formal process because it costs money, hampers work, requires time, is an unfamiliar procedure and they doubt the fairness. Even when lower caste people occasionally want to approach formal organisations for conflict resolution, they are not able to do so independently. They have to take help from political leaders of their party, local teachers, etc. If both conflict parties are similar in their status but they are from different political parties, conflict is more likely to become intense. Comparison of the influence of caste/ethnicity and socio-economic status of people involved in conflict, shows that people from lower socio-economic status, irrespective of caste/ ethnicity, suffer more from exploitation and manipulation. Even poor people from a higher caste suffer more from manipulation by rich and powerful people of a backward ethnic status. In a conflict, the socio-economic status is more important than caste/ethnicity in manipulating the situation.

Local social relationships have great bearing on conflict and its management in a community. As discussed in the chapter three, there are some exclusionary social institutions in Nepal, which promote unequal social relationships and the partitioning of specific cultural, economic and political processes in relationship to particular social groups. Social institutions express the organisation of social, economic and political activity, which is followed by the majority of the members of a society. Such exclusionary social institutions include the family, the education system, a system of religion, a political and economic system and the more general patterns of community norms and values (Furtze ¬and Stafford, 1994). They even inhibit democratic values and the enhancement of human capabilities and constitute a social liability. The empirical evidence indicates that there is distinct lack of interaction between government staff working in offices responsible for handling conflicts and poor people. However, these staff have strong relationships with powerful people, local elite and politicians. Staff of these organisations (including staff of DDC and VDC) play crucial roles in resolving conflict and such resolutions are greatly affected by the aforementioned social relationships. DDC and VDC are the organisations headed by elected political leaders but with a strong influence of the government appointed bureaucrats. However, the role of bureaucrats in these organisations is not decisive, they manipulate the conflict situation using legal-procedural jargons, regulations and norms of government which are beyond most poor people's understanding.

The farmers-managed irrigation system, forest-pastureland and *Guthi* land conflict cases show the mode of interaction and relationships between power brokers and poor people. These cases indicate that there is a better interaction between VDC members and poor people as compared to the bureaucrats. Poor people have no access to government bureaucracy. If poor people want to establish a relationship with bureaucrats they mainly have to go via power brokers or use other means (bribery, *afnomanchhe*, etc.). In such cases manoeuvring by bureaucrats and power brokers is common and they consider such relationships as normal. However, such relationships and influence uphold, recreate or even exacerbate social deprivations and maintain unequal power relationships.

When the state established several natural resource related agencies equipped with authority and responsibility and armed with a diversity of policies, rules, and regulations an unequal patron client relationship was generated. As examined in chapter four several conflicts emerged due to the contradictory roles of government organisations and ambiguous boundaries, which differed between traditional ones and those drawn up by government agencies.

Conflict management, as observed in the empirical chapters, takes place within a context of social relationships. Some groups gain more benefits using political and economic power, physical force and use of knowledge and networks in a conflict situation. A reciprocal relationship is found to be very important in resolving conflict. This reciprocity is a strong characteristic of local level CM when the parties in the conflict are equal in their strength. Horizontal social relationships are more favourable in resolving conflict than vertical social relationships. Economic relationships help resolve conflicts but deals are made in a trade-off manner. Rich people provide cash and kind to poor people to influence the decision/outcome. Political relationships (voter-winner and party leader-member relationships), political structures (party units, positions as heads of wards, VDCs, etc.) increasingly dominate CM after 1990. A party specific ideological bias and political interpretation of all local issues are overwhelmingly creating wider gaps between individuals affiliated with different political parties and a confidence crisis in the village. The quality of the relationship, interpersonal relations, communication and information and social networks play crucial roles in CM. These relationships are based on a common set of expectations (e.g., to gain) a shared set of values (e.g., elite's characters), and a sense of trust between the actors (e.g., approach one's own party for the resolution of conflict). Even rural people use conflicts as opportunities to develop new relationships or strengthen existing relationships with political leaders, local elite and landlords to obtain financial and social benefits or to obtain public support in their favour. Local people also use conflict as an opportunity to bargain with political parties for their nomination as a candidate for local election. According to the election procedure in Nepal, 47 candidates for each VDC have to be first nominated by concerned political parties, if the candidate wants to contest the election on the behalf of a political party. There are strong interests of political leaders within the political party to nominate candidates of his/her favour, as the nominee, if elected, entertains resources and authority. When the political party issues the letter of nomination then the candidate can register his/her application to contest for the particular post in the election with the election commission. The willingness of people to be involved in CM or to keep their distance depends on social relationships and the effects of conflict to them.

Political relationships have a great impact on the negotiation process. Political relationships are now increasingly replacing traditional social relations. The general public (except supporters of particular political party) suspects the role of political leaders in solving conflict fairly because of the differences in what they say (generally right things) and what they do (generally guided by vested/ political interests as discussed in the farmers-managed irrigation, forest-pastureland and ADB-funded irrigation cases). The establishment of a political balance is now a new way of managing relationships in a village (this is reflected in all village level activities such as forming water and forest users groups). Some government staff are increasingly involved or are being forced to become involved in conflicts. Many village level conflicts were evolved as bilateral conflict (involvement of only two parties) but when professional troublemakers intervene these conflicts became multi-lateral and complicated. When this happens the real causes of the conflict is often sidelined.

8.4.4. *Power and Politics*

Political ideology is a powerful variable in any social conflict, which influences the whole CM process at different levels. Power in a conflict can influence the outcome by the efforts of a few actors, contrary to the interests of the majority of actors (Liebert and Imershein, 1977). When power is mobilised in conflict resolution the result is mostly win-lose. The farmers-managed irrigation, ADB-funded irrigation and *Guthi* land cases clearly indicated that the use of power often creates a resentful, fearful and unfavourable attitude in a conflict situation. At present *Mukhiya, Purohit, Pandit, Dhami-Jhakri* have no formal authority and are not recognised by the formal law as such but in practice they still have an influential role in the escalation or resolution of a conflict at the local level. However, after 1990, the influence of feudal power has decreased and the patterns and forms of domination are being transformed to the party political process and being taking over by the newly emerged neo-elite group. Earlier, local elite people were rich and their domination was mainly based on economic parameters, socio-cultural values and religious status but now domination and manipulation are based on knowledge, information and political ideology. The resolution and escalation of conflict are greatly influenced by these power forms. Earlier cultural and religious power was stronger in the community. Conflict resolution was based on a religious framework. This was changed to an economic power base and negotiation and renegotiations of social actions were mainly guided by economic power. At the time of political change in 1990 the existing power base was heavily disturbed and physical force became more prominent in shaping relationships in the village. People were very afraid of possible revenge and physical action against them as a result of the freedom obtained from the restoration of democracy. This form of power base did not last long and changed to knowledge, information and political ideology based power forms (cf. Dahal *et al*, 1999).

In my discussions with Members of Parliament, Chairpersons of DDC and VDC and senior political leaders of various political parties, they accepted the increasing level of politicisation of conflicts and political interference in CM. They claim that intervention in a conflict by political parties/ leaders is essential to ensure justice to poor people due to the failure of government organisations to give this justice. The forth and fifth cases have also illustrated how politicians influence bureaucracy to work in their favour. Technocrats and bureaucrats are forced to consider that rural people are unimportant compared to powerful politicians. It is a very common practice in Nepal that when political leaders (especially from the ruling party) feel that bureaucrats are not respecting their instructions and not supporting them they approach a higher authority and transfer them to a remote area or a less beneficial sector. If bureaucrats are from the families or relatives of senior politicians they could prevent such transfer. Otherwise, they have to bear a sort of punishment for not working in favour of politicians. Hence almost all civil servants work according to the instructions of the politicians from the ruling party irrespective of the rules and regulations. Such a psychological perception in bureaucracy leads to a weakened functioning of organisations. Comparatively, political interference is reported to be less in courts and therefore the performance of courts in resolving conflict is said to be better than other organisations involved in dealing with natural resource conflict. Regarding the political interference in conflict, an environmental activist from a local NGO explained that: *"Political interference in development activities is a common feature. Local political leaders always interfere even in minor issues and manipulate for their political benefit. Many times leaders of different political parties forced us to direct our activities according to their interest but that was not possible for us. Then they blamed our organisation and staff as supporters of communists and created a very hard environment in our working area. Always politicians interfere in both GOs and NGOs to work in their favour"*. A sweeping generalisation commonly prevailing in the political sector in Nepal is that poor people and the tenants belong to the communist category. This is because the manifesto of the communist parties is aimed at poor people and tenants who make up the vast majority of Nepalese people. These people generally cast their votes for the communist parties.

When people engage in conflicts in study area, they usually have allegiance to a political party. They are affiliated to one of the major political parties and are therefore protected from the potential risks. If by any circumstance, conflicts arise in the village, local political workers of major parties intervene for their political benefit, particularly to win the local election. Even many small issues become the source of conflict simply because the individuals involved belong to different political parties. Chapter four outlined that many such conflict cases were resolved by local leaders before the local election on the condition that the contending parties vote for their candidates.

8.4.5. Network and Linkage

Networking is an exchange of knowledge, information and experiences between different people to build an alliance to develop and implement specific work. Networks are both formal and informal and durable relational patterns that emerge as a result of these exchanges (Engel and Salomon, 1997). As discussed in chapter four people lacking networks and linkages suffered more than the people having a strong circle of *afnomanchhe*. The *Guthi* land owners, who had a strong network of powerful people and bureaucrats succeeded in bringing the decision of the *Guthi* Corporation and Land Reform Offices in their favour even when the tenants had already paid for the land twice. Networks became effective in handling the spring-water source conflict. Local networks also help to minimise betrayals, develop adjust to changing circumstances, enhance reciprocity and trade-offs and bring the conflict to the negotiation platform. The feeling of belonging to a particular category in the community psychologically helps people to make an alliance. As observed in the pastureland conflict case when interests and objectives of people came close to their common grazing problems a concerted alliance developed to collectively protest the pastureland encroachment. When stalemates or escalations of conflict occur, progression is achieved by establishing networks and linkages (spring-water source case).

8.4.6. Corruption and Irregularities

Corruption is becoming an increasingly important factor in resolution of conflict in Nepal (cf. Kaplan, 1995). Table 4.7 in

Chapter Four clearly indicates that corruption is an integral part of formal conflict management practices. The use of bribes, mobilisation of *afnomanchhe*, use of political power and a combination of all of them were common methods used to win the conflict cases. Out of 50 respondents 96 percent had used these three means to win the conflict cases. The lack of faith of local people towards the staff dealing with conflict management was reported to be caused by their arrogant, indifferent and corrupt behaviour (Chapter Four). The lack of collaboration of local people with the personnel of government agencies in the ADB-funded irrigation case was due to a lack of faith. No matter how professionally and academically competent they are, if they are entangled in corruption a fair resolution of the conflict is unlikely. The present widespread corrupt behaviour of a large majority of staff working in governmental organisations has undermined the few co-operative, proficient, ethical, hard working, scrupulous and sincere bureaucrats and technocrats. The extension of the farmers-managed irrigation system, invasion of pastureland, change of originally proposed intake in the ADB-funded irrigation project, and manipulation of *Guthi* land were all the reflection of corrupt behaviour. Chapter four analysed the lack of trust, exacerbated corruption, the mobilisation of *afnomanchhe*, dualism and an absence of abiding by the law by powerful elite as common features of formal conflict management practices in Nepal. An important inference I made from the observation of social and natural resource conflicts is the risk of degradation of the natural resource base, social imbalance and inequality, if the state does not prevent corruption and abuse of rules and regulations by powerful people.

8.4.7. Communication and Conflict

The media played a crucial role in escalating conflict. The first CPN-UML government broadcasted an awareness programme against corruption and social inequalities from Radio Nepal. This programme caused the development of a strong negative sense towards malpractice observed in both the ADB-funded irrigation project and the *Guthi* land conflict cases. It is widely said that the media in Nepal are not autonomous and operate under the political camps wiping out credibility, integrity and professionalism (UNDP, 1998). UNDP Human Development Report-Nepal 1998 shows that Nepalese media distorting communications by reporting biased news items to justify the actions of their political camps and to contribute to the survival of their patrons which ultimately promotes confusion, suspicion and conflict in the community. However, though biased towards the UML policy and programme, at that time the media played an important role in organising users and tenants to protest against the manipulative actions of *Guthi* landowners and WUC.

Scholars of conflict have long acknowledged the central role of communication in conflict management (Folger and Johns, 1994). In case of the ADB-funded irrigation project, communication became ineffective in understanding the interests and objectives of the villagers and finally the communication system became dysfunctional. Similarly, specific language for communication (words, jargon, etc.) and discourses used by technicians in both irrigation and land conflict cases isolated villagers and became a source of conflict. By using such discourses politicians and bureaucrats established their strong hold in a conflict situation. The spring-water source conflict case clearly demonstrated that networks, regular meetings and discussions improved communication between parties involved in conflict and led to a win-win resolution. From the experiences of the cases it can be said that establishment of an effective interpersonal communication among the users is crucial to settle conflict because it promotes understanding, mutual interests and co-operation. Listening to others, understanding the views of others, identifying needs, interests, concerns and fears of disputants, getting agreement on rules, constructive discussions, creative problem solving and building relationships were important elements in the resolution of the spring-water source conflict (cf. Tearfund, 1998). As shown in the spring-water source conflict, interaction is an effective tool to seek common ground for negotiation. Regular interaction in specific issues often creates new ideas to resolve conflict, enhances self-assessment of local people and external actors, their roles, status and ability to generate solutions and promote social learning. This is the alternative way of managing conflict based on communicative rationality. When there is proper communication and information sharing, doubts, uncertainties and misunderstandings become clear and even if the outcome does not meet their expectations they are more likely to accept it. Conflict due to confusion and misunderstanding can be resolved by putting all the relevant information to the actors involved in the conflict. Distrust and feelings of exploitation and injustice can be minimised by improving communication.

8.4.8. *Use and Abuse of Information*

Strategic use and abuse of information serves as a basic starting point for escalation or resolution of conflict. In the spring-water source conflict, the effective use of information served to develop a constructive relationship between the parties involved in the conflict. In contrast, in the ADB-funded irrigation conflict people fell into a pattern of mutually aggressive behaviour, hiding or twisting information to minimise the opposing party. As all the cases demonstrate the lack or misuse of information was one of the prime factors in creating conflict. From the analysis of all the five cases it can be generalised that one of the major causes of creation or escalation of conflict is a lack of correct information and manipulation of information by well-informed people. Similarly, language (technical words and jargon) is an important factor in conflict.

8.4.9. *Emergence of New Local Organisations*

On a small scale, local level community organisations are evolving as important forums and are working in participatory principles to organise people for their own benefit. These 'new institutional arrangements are emerging as community-based grass-root organisations such as forest users groups, water users associations, women's self-help groups, mother's club (*Ama Samuha*), small farmers' groups, etc. and providing a mechanism, whereby local people can participate in resolving conflicts. Some of these local organisations are even expanding to the national level through their networks such as the Federation of Community Forest Users Group-Nepal, Himalayan Grass-root Women' Natural Resource Management Association, National Federation of Water Users Association, etc. Such community-based arrangements could provide local forums, promote accountability and a feeling of security to local people and create a safe and continuous space for negotiation. They could also play an important role in minimising political and legal manipulations, reducing fear and anxiety and avoiding the marginalisation of poor people. They demonstrate that institutional arrangements can emerge through institutionalisation of actor's practices when they become patterns of action and interaction. These institutional arrangements are the outcome of networks in which several people and users groups are organised for the common interest. It is a process of building relationships and creating interactions among users. These organisations are actively involved in managing social conflicts in their community and so far they have proved to be far better than formal CM practices. Even national networks of these organisations are dealing with governmental ministries and departments to establish their rights and identity. The roles of external organisations, in this context, have to strengthen such initiatives, instead of expanding their own regime, to provide sustainable and long-term conflict resolution mechanisms.

8.4.10. *Leadership*

Leadership seems to be a crucial factor in resolving conflicts in the community. The role of elderly people in the second case to organise and guide the *Sangarsha Samiti* and the unanimous leadership role of the chairman of this forum as well as the successful leadership role of the leader of *Guthi* land tenants distinctly exemplified the paramount importance of leadership in conflict. People who are willing to contribute as much as possible to resolve conflicts in favour of majority will evolve as leader (chapter four). Styles and strengths of leadership determine the quality and relationships between the conflicting parties. In the study area older, respected and trust-worthy persons mediated conflict effectively. Contending parties called upon them and in return they were honoured and their status was confirmed. Their judgements were usually followed, but they had no recourse except to moral persuasion of their fellow villagers. The capacity of local leaders to resolve conflict depends upon how group members listen and support them. The fifth case shows that to win the faith of the members, leaders have to be able to secure their interests and create a positive environment for interaction and collective action. The fourth case of irrigation conflict exemplified that if there is no strong leadership escalation of the conflict is more likely and it becomes more difficult to resolve. The spring-water source case demonstrated that leadership emerges from the context and local situation. It depends on the degree of organisation of users through appropriate facilitation by the support of neutral organisations. A carefully built interactive learning and action process facilitated by local NGOs became effective in resolving the conflict in the spring-water source case. When parties in a conflict perceive that their current problems cannot be solved without collective action, then this psychological feeling encourages them to engage in meaningful interaction and concerted action that eventually increases the possibility of resolution (for example, the *Guthi* land conflict). Basically motivation, behaviour and the context are responsible for escalating or resolving conflict in society. Change in the extension of the irrigation canal (context) affected the existing pattern of use of irrigation water in the head section and developed feelings of injustice and cognitive distrust that led to an aggressive response such as stopping the water flow in the tail section. Leadership plays an important role in such a hostile situation to keep conflict under control.

8.4.11.Gender Relationships in Conflict

There is very little documentation on the role of gender in CM. However, in practice women play a crucial role in resolution of social and natural resource conflict at the community level (cf. Upreti, 1998b). Women's heavy involvement in NRM activities encourages them to become involved in related conflicts and their management. User groups appear to be generally a more promising avenue for women's involvement in CM. Nevertheless, it is critical to consider the workload (increase or decrease) of women when participating in conflict resolution as women are already overloaded compared to men (Ghale and Gurung, 1998; Upreti, 1995). The gender relationship in a community is not, by any means, static. Gender relations in general and gender roles in CM in particular are often tightly associated with political, cultural, social and economic changes taking place in society. The spring-water source case has demonstrated that even when men have significant scepticism and resistance to resolve conflict, women take the initiative to enter into negotiations. The accommodative nature of women and their problems of fetching water were the motivation and interests of such an initiative. Little or no involvement of women in conflict management in the farmers-managed irrigation, ADB-funded irrigation and Guthi land cases indicate that men generally do not acknowledge and support women's involvement in CM, as the decision-making authority of rural women is limited. But women as members of society cannot be isolated from the wider social environment. However, it is hard to generalise the profound role of women in effectively managing conflict based on the success story of only one case. It needs further research. Based on the role of women in the spring-water source case, it can safely be argued that women's involvement in local CM practices provides ample opportunities and advantages to negotiate conflict locally.

Women's involvement in local CM offers important advantages. These advantages are:

(a) women's active involvement provides a cheap and flexible means of conflict resolution to those women who have no resources to invest in a formal process;

(b) it helps to give justice to those women who are not able to express their feelings and problems to men due to cultural and other social reasons (Chapter Four) and

(c) equity and justice to poor and backward women increases if the problem is dealt by women as they are more familiar with the problems of women.

Responsive CM needs sensitivity to gender aspects. Conflict can be effectively managed only when the CM process acknowledges the importance of the gender role. The low level of involvement of women in managing conflict in all cases (except the spring-source case) indicates that rural women are socially constrained. Pervasive and deep exclusion of women has a direct bearing on their active involvement in social activities such as CM. Women were found to be more accommodative in negotiating conflicts locally than men in all socio-economic groups. The role of women in effective negotiation is mixed, effective in small and simple conflict but indifferent in big and complex ones. Building social trust and mutual understanding are important elements in CM.

To answer the question why women are not actively involved in CM, one has to analyse the socio-cultural construction of gender relations. A woman's life, according to the Hindu tradition, is incomplete without entering into a lifelong relationship with a husband (this is a very dependent relationship) and the separate independent identity of woman is not acknowledged by the Hindu cultural and religious framework (UNDP, 1998). Women are taught this from their childhood, which severely limits them having an image of the future as independent and equal members of society. In recent days, however, gender relations are gradually being reconstructed due to the constitutional assurance of equality, external pressures such as donors conditions and the influence of technology, access to information, NGO advocacy and women's initiation.

8.5. Wider Implications of Conflict

Considering conflict as an opportunity it helps to reduce existing conflicts, presents ways to prevent new ones emerging and provides for crisis management as and when conflicts arise (Walker and Daniels, 1997). Conflict over the role of external interventions gave lessons on social inclusion of beneficiaries in project planning and the CM process. It also indicated the need to bring disenfranchised actors and marginal people into the interaction for collaborative negotiations. By having 'pro-poor' NRM practices less exploitative forms of negotiation can be promoted at the local level. Finally, it can be a means to bring about an equitable NRM and responsive CM approach. After experiencing conflicts brought about by formal interventions in NRM, villagers became more aware of the misuse of resources and started to become actively involved in externally funded new development projects. Such awareness and participation of local people increased accountability and a feeling of ownership to achieve sustainable NRM.

Conflict has also important impacts on land management and tenure systems in the study area. For example the intensity and frequency of conflict is more in the tenanted irrigated lands. Tenants with an insecure claim to the land they cultivate are generally unwilling to contribute to permanent capital investment in irrigation systems and land management as the landowners expect or even force them to. Due to such a conflict the proper exploitation and management of the land resource and ownership feelings over tenanted land are lacking. A conflict situation in natural resources forces local people to utilise the existing resources optimally or efficiently, create new resources or search for different alternatives. Some farmers after the irrigation conflict in the farmer-managed irrigation case started rainwater harvesting, off farm activities within the village and the majority of them seasonally migrated to other areas for employment. In the second case, people looked for an alternate management option to develop the community forest and protect it from encroachment, practised rotational grazing and set up an effective surveillance procedure. In the spring-water source case collective efforts were made to bring a large drinking water project in that area and effective rules were made to utilise water at night. In the forth case people explored several alternatives for irrigation such as the use of local small streams, collection of running water from natural water taps, change in cropping patterns and nature of crops grown and an alteration in the land use pattern. In the fifth case efficient utilisation of water available from the extended canal and a change in land use systems was observed. Productivity of the *Guthi* land was increased after the transfer of ownership rights. Because of conflict local people have developed coping strategies (e.g., stall feeding of animals after protection of forest area, exploration of alternate irrigation source and construction of small canal, change in farming systems, etc.). This also enhanced the resources use efficiency. All these are the innovative NRM practices adopted by farmers due to conflict.

Every society establishes, maintains, or even changes its social values, principles and procedures. It is observed that significant correlation exists between performance of existing socio-cultural structures and conflict in society. Social differences such as ethnicity, economic status, positions have influenced the conflict situation. Before political intervention only males were overall decision-makers in NRM but later women also started to participate in CM and played important roles in decision making related to NRM. The ability of women to participate in meetings, sharing their opinions, expressing their concerns and putting forward arguments was increased (spring-water source case). In this way gender roles and relations started to change. Conflict had also created scope for interaction in articulation of goals and seeking solutions of the problems. In this process people examine existing social structures, organisations, power relationships, legal complexity and their own role within the society. This ultimately helps to develop their capacity and redefine their roles, leading to constructive resolution of conflict. Many conflicts are not possible to resolve by independent individual efforts and require collaborative action. That gives opportunities to work together as seen in the farmer-managed irrigation, spring-water source and Guthi land cases (cf. Röling, 1996). That also helps to establish new relationships and modify behaviour.

Grassroots organisations are evolving in the NRM sector to address conflict issues. They are raising their voice to reform/democratise governmental organisations working in the NRM-sector. The issues of corruption, transparency, accountability and efficiency are being frequently raised. In recent years VDCs are increasingly involved in conflict management. Poor people are approaching and starting to raise their voice with VDCs. Alternate resource generation (obtaining different NRM-projects such as drinking water, irrigation from outsider agencies, plantation of forests, rain water collection, etc.) is increasing in the study area. The capacity of the general public to raise it's voice against exploitation by powerful elite is increasing. People are organising in different forums such as *Shangarsha Samiti*, Mediation Groups, and users' groups and participating in different capacity building activities whereby their level of confidence is increased. People directly involved in conflict developed a fairly good legal knowledge and confidence to deal with courts, the police and the district administration. Very exploitative economic relationships between local elite and villagers manifested in the form of *Koseli* (free gifts from their farm products) and *Mukheuli* (free labour service) to be given to *Mukhiya* have been stopped. The Patron-client type of social relationship in the village has changed. The pattern of communication and sharing of information is moving towards party lines and used as a means for political gains. In this way after these conflicts some quite substantial changes were observed in the study villages.

8.6. Conclusion

In this section I am concluding the gist of the whole book. The central focus of this book has been to examine social and natural resource-related conflicts and their management practices in Nepal and their effects on NRM and society. Writing this study started with a certain confusion, frustration and ambition. The confusion was how to analyse the complex and problematic social conflicts. The frustration was for the poor performance of the existing conflict management system in Nepal. The ambition was related to achieving some pragmatic solution to effectively address social conflict in community. From the outset, I have emphasised that conflict is increasing in society and their management practices are becoming problematic in Nepal. Through taking an ethnographic approach, I was able to examine social and natural resource related conflict and local people's perception within a wider socio-political context.

It can be concluded that the dominant formal legal conflict resolution processes widely practised to resolve conflicts in Nepal do not recognise the local capability to resolve or manage conflict and that integration of new innovations in their conflict resolution process are lacking. A regulatory and legal framework narrowly guides them. Relationships of people involved in conflicts with their biophysical and socio-economic conditions are important aspects but they are ignored in the formal resolution process. Technical knowledge and aspects essential to fairly decide the cases are lacking. If conflict in natural resources is to be managed in a more equitable and egalitarian way, the approach should be more flexible, diverse, not relying only on regulations, but also focused on collaborative action and experiential learning (Jiggins and Röling, 2000). Conflict resolution requires special mediation and arbitration skills and negotiation techniques for a higher degree of success. The effectiveness of CM and the achievement of sustainability of NRM depend crucially on the active involvement of actors in the CM process. To achieve that a people-centred, action oriented, learning-based locally available alternative approach is essential

By looking at the dynamics of conflict, I came to the conclusion that there is no single form and model for handling conflict in the community. Rather it is a broad, dynamic and complex process constantly evolving and responding to changing circumstances. So long as the present dominant methods of addressing conflict in the country continues, conflict will increase more in the future together with the expansion of development interventions. It became clear from both the empirical evidence and theoretical background that conflict is ubiquitous. Conflict, far from being static, is evolving under the pressure of growing resources scarcity, faulty execution of policies and procedures, excessive political interference and political, bureaucratic and administrative corruption. Conflict can be positive because its management or resolution often leads to creative options and innovation. When people are entangled in conflict they search for ways and means to change the situation. Protection of pasture and forest land, proper utilisation of the spring-source of water, exploration of alternate irrigation sources and rain water harvesting, the increased motivation of people to participate actively in externally funded or implemented development activities, securing entitlement and ownership of land in a non-coercive way in this book demonstrated that conflict can be a stimulus for positive change and a source of learning. Such changes are more durable and acceptable in terms of resource management, social relationships and community organisation. Nevertheless, conflicts can also have serious negative effects. If not addressed timely and appropriately, it may deplete resources, affect psychological wellbeing and can result into anxiety, tension and resentment that ultimately damage social relations, promote violence and disintegrate society.

By critically examining the existing Nepalese CM methods and practices, by exploring the weaknesses and areas of improvement I have provided some food for thought to reform the existing conflict management practices. The empirical chapters sufficiently demonstrated that accountability, transparency and effectiveness of the formal practices of CM are seriously undermined by their inherent characteristics such as feudalistic, elite-biased expensive and authoritarian modes of operation. Informal practices also favour powerbrokers. These are the most important reasons for their administrative and ideological reform. The ability of this exploration to generate discussion and debate among the Nepalese actors is for the future. I am aware that by critically examining the formal CM practices, I will be criticised. People who gain from these practices will be threatened and reactive. I believe, however, that constructive criticism generates discussion and debate and provides ample room for reformation. If such reaction and debate is generated one of the objectives of this research is met.

I want to emphasise that management of conflicts reflects complex dynamics that must be understood in order to design successful NRM interventions. Therefore, policy makers must look beyond existing policy and regulatory prescriptions to successfully manage conflicts. If CM efforts are to be effective in managing natural resource and helping poor people to reduce poverty, then it is axiomatic that the CM approach needs to reconsider the structural and procedural limitations (e.g., access, time, legal complexity, etc.) and include powerless people in the mainstream CM process. Given the limited access to legal services and relevant information available to most poor people, the existing conflict management practices can not ensure fair justice to all members of community. There is a danger in assuming that the poor are getting justice by enacting laws and regulations. Clearly, giving effective justice to poor and powerless people requires great sensitivity to and respect for their voice, background, objectives and circumstances. CM practices to give justice to powerless people need to avoid imposing solutions developed in an ivory tower.

The empirical cases show that social and natural resource conflicts are complex in nature with enormously high transformation potentials (cf. Warner and Jones, 1998; Walker and Daniels, 1997; Yordan, 2000). The forest-pasture and the

Guthi land conflict cases demonstrated that they are also powerful catalysts to change established patterns of interactions, power relationships and social structures in the community. These conflicts influence social, economic and political aspects in a rural community (cf. Jandt and Pedersen, 1996). Social conflicts were reflected in disagreement (spring-water source conflict case), hostilities (AFMIS case) and social or personal dislocations (ADB-funded irrigation project). These conflicts also frequently switched to latent and active phases. Conflict management is a mixture of balancing political, social and legal power relationships (e.g., the *Guthi* land case) characterised by trade-offs and negotiations where weak groups of people generally encounter obstacles and difficulties.

I conclude that existing Nepalese CM practices are not able to address growing conflict. Political influence and monetary power (corruption) have greatly contributed in making formal processes and practices fail to give justice to the general public. Therefore, the existing formal conflict management practices can not be taken for granted, as an excuse not to analyse their weaknesses and contextual factors affecting their performances. The empirical cases in the study provide ample evidence for this. The question is how to make the inaccessible accessible and ineffective effective. It needs greater reform of administrative and procedural aspects of adversarial forums (e.g., police, administration, courts, etc.) at the national level and promotion of the role of collective learning-based, context specific, locally operated alternative forums (e.g., local mediation, interactive negotiation, etc.) at the community level (actual practices). The administrative and procedural issues at the national level rest with the state. However, those who are intimately involved in dealing with conflicts can implement the promotion of alternative practices at the community level. The final chapter deals with the role of ICM.

CHAPTER 9

Interactive Conflict Management—
An Alternative

9.1. Introduction

In the first chapter I explained that one of my objectives in carrying out this study was to develop an alternative methodological approach to address community conflicts. The analysis of social and natural resource conflict presented in the empirical chapters demonstrates that conventional CM practices, both formal and informal, are inadequate to address conflict in community. Due to their in'.erent weaknesses they are unable to resolve the ever-growing conflicts. In this chapter I present my attempts to develop a learning-based and action-oriented method called 'Interactive Conflict Management (ICM)' to address community-based conflicts in more accessible and practical ways. An account is given of ICM; its ideas and logic, need and relevance, implementation strategy and step-wise procedure. I identify potential actors promoting ICM, its institutionalisation procedure and opportunities and challenges. In this approach I propose a three-tiered strategy to address social and natural resource conflicts (preventive measures, actual management of conflict after occurrence and referral to legal options). I identify the determinants of success and failure of ICM and propose areas for future research in relationship to conflict management.

There are two strong interconnected bases for proposing ICM as a practical method to address social and natural resources in community. The first basis is the successful implementation of an ICM style of conflict resolution procedure by local NGOs in third case (and other similar success stories of local organisations such as FUGs). In the spring-water source conflict I have discussed how people gather together to discuss problems, how they trained to deal with conflict, what they did to develop mutually acceptable rules, how they sought the solution collectively and how they were able to manage conflict effectively. The second basis is my practical experience-based confidence in implementing such procedures. I have intensively used similar procedures in community-level rural development and NRM project planning. Mechi Hill Development Programme (MHDP), a community development project has implemented pro-poor focused and gender-sensitive development activities in three remote hill districts in eastern Nepal. The working area was very much power-skewed and economically and socio-politically highly stratified. With the participatory need assessment, joint project planning and implementation, and process monitoring, community development/ NRM activities succeeded in bringing rural poor and backward people and women into the mainstream development process. By doing so, their needs, concerns and interests were properly incorporated into the project activities implemented in their communities. Well-trained community facilitators have implemented this process in more than one hundred villages. Targeted community members actively participated in various activities such as community planning, local resource management, conflict resolution, non-formal education and users group training. The important aspect of this process was collective learning from joint planning and action. The feedback and the lessons learnt from the first cycle were integrated in the next cycle. The contents, methods and process itself were continuously revised, based on the experiences and knowledge people gained from the action process. Although powerful people resisted at the beginning, they were ultimately supportive in promoting this process because they were also mobilised in the process.

Recently, CIVICT has also successfully implemented 15 community mediation projects in Ilam, Jhapa and Saptari districts. CIVICT has focused conflict and mediation in the framework of human rights in these area to ensure safety, security and access to justice to women, poor and marginalised group of people. These right-based community mediation initiatives are becoming increasingly successful. CIVICT also devised community level training manual on mediation, trained community members on mediation skills and the committees were mobilised under the regulative framework of Local Self-Governance Act (CIVICT, 2001, Prasain, 2001).

From these success stories and experiences, I am fairly confident that this type of people-centred, learning-based and community-led method can be one of the pragmatic alternatives to effectively manage social and natural resource conflict.

9.2. Weaknesses of Existing System—Basis for Interactive Conflict Management

It is not sufficient to state that formal practices are expensive and inaccessible especially to the weaker section of society and informal practices mainly favour powerful people. The next step is to critically examine the practical bottlenecks, which make these existing practices expensive, inaccessible and power-biased before proposing an alternative. The important question is why are the present methods not able to properly address community-based conflicts and how do they differ from normative ideological bases to actual practices. One of the main causes of exploitation noticed in the field was related to the lack of knowledge of rural people about legal provisions and their legal rights. This knowledge gap led to an increase in ineffective enforcement of laws and misuse of legal provisions by elite and powerful people. If local people had proper knowledge about their rights and legal protection there would be less manipulation by the elite. In this sense legal knowledge is one of the important resources in dealing with conflict. Mediation, negotiation and facilitation skills were lacking in existing conflict resolution practices. The provision of proper information and communication with local people especially at the time of planning of externally funded NRM projects in their area was lacking. The willingness of the VDC, community based organisations (such as WUA, FUG, mothers' clubs, small farmers' groups, etc.) and local NGOs in resolving natural resource conflict in collaboration with local people was constrained by a lack of practical CM methods. Interaction between district-based organisations working in conflict and village-based resource users was lacking because of methodological limitations such as non-involvement of local people in any decision process related to CM. Positive aspects of local CM practices were not integrated in mainstream CM practices. People involved in traditional CM practices expressed a willingness to engage in interactive conflict management but they lacked the appropriate skills. The ability and willingness of women to resolve community level conflict was shown in their active involvement in the resolution of the spring-water source conflict. The existing conflict resolution methods do not permit them to become actively involved, so excluding a large segment of society from CM practices. Formalities and technicalities of judicial processes are unfamiliar to ordinary people. The bottlenecks or constraints can be grouped into two categories when deciding the intervention strategy to resolve social and natural resource conflicts. They are: a) Broader structural, legal and political constraints for which actions are needed at the national level. Reformation of bureaucracy, revision and enactment of laws, national policies and procedures are essential to overcome these bottlenecks. ICM has only little role in overcoming these constraints (although as people gain confidence they may demand the reform of these structural and legal constraints at national level) and b) Specific, locally based limitations and constraints in the management of conflicts where ICM has a greater role to play. Many of the above mentioned bottlenecks are directly related to methods and can be improved through application of appropriate methods at the local level. Therefore, ICM aims to provide a method for community-level management of conflicts. Nevertheless, this method may not be able to address all conflicts caused by different externalities or conflicts caused by the legally structured situations in a community. However it can certainly minimise a large number of conflicts caused by procedural and methodological difficulties.

9.3. Conceptualising Interactive Conflict Management

Basic elements of ICM are derived from social learning (Röling and Wagemakers, 1998), conceptual basis of collective cognition (perception, emotion and action) (Capra, 1996) and adaptive management (Lee, 1993), as discussed in chapter two. Chapters five and seven clearly indicated the importance of collective learning and mobilisation of collective power of people to resolve social conflicts in their community. Collective learning is a new concept to deal with social conflicts, which draws on what is called soft systems methodology (Checkland and Scholes, 1990), an alternate way of learning and action. Collective learning encourages villagers and experts to learn issues in conflict and explore alternatives together to address them. Collective learning is transformative in nature and there is more emphasis on a process to make incremental improvements to mutual understanding for concerted action (Röling and Wagemakers, 1998). Collective learning promotes effective listening and dialogue amongst all the parties. It essentially seeks to empower them and helps to improve their ability to effectively communicate with each other, to understand and analyse problems and use the outcomes to make informed collective decisions. Parties involved in the collective learning process acknowledge their strengths and limitations, goals and interests and construct solutions around their common understanding. In the learning theory 'learning to learn' draws attention to single loop and double loop learning. In single loop learning people learn from experiences to adjust their actions. In double loop learning negative feedback from experience leads to adapting and examining the underlying assumptions and rational behind behaviour. Through double loop learning people learn how to learn, and begin to understand the process of learning itself and the behaviour and strategies which inhibit or facilitate it (Ramirez, 1997).

The empirical chapters show that local people's collective action led to the protection of grazing land, generated forest and established their rights against power-based exploitation. The forest and pasture and spring-source cases are also examples of collective actions for effective management and prudent use of local natural resources to meet the needs of the present, without affecting the needs of future generations. To scale-up such success stories, a learning based approach is essential. Interactive conflict management is a repeated cycle of learning and action jointly undertaken by concerned actors. Actors in this context are individuals or collective groups (both formal and or informal) who are intentional (engaged to realise an objective), sense makers (construct their life world) and having agency (capacity to make difference in a context) (Long and Long, 1992) such as VDCs, users groups, local NGOs, community leaders and the general public. The focus of ICM is to make conflict management forums easily accessible to rural people and to minimise dependence on adversarial forms of conflict resolution. Both the pasture and *Guthi* land cases demonstrated that when the stakes (e.g., interdependence, common threats, etc.) are high, collective efforts are increased. Success and failure of resolution of conflict depends on a fuller understanding of interdependence by people. The focus should be on the process of interaction to recognise such interdependence. Interactive conflict management is based on the realisation of interdependence. If this interdependence is not appreciated then interventions need to focus on enhancing the feeling of mutual interdependence (Leeuwis, 2000). As observed in the case of the spring-water conflict when people started to consider potential solutions for their problem, arrays of potential alternatives were formulated. The interaction process led to an agreement on rules for managing conflict.

Such interaction in the spring-water source conflict helped to remove the sources of conflict before they escalated to severe disputes. The important bottom-line in CM is to manage conflict in an effective and efficient way, not to suppress conflict and not to let it escalate out of control (Smith, 1997; Drew *et al.*, 1997; Vayrynen, 1991).

Table 9.1. General Differences between Informal, Formal and Interactive Conflict Management

S.n	Characteristics	Informal practices	Formal practices	ICM
1.	Underlying assumptions	Local culture and values shape behaviour and action	Formal legal rules shapes behaviour and action	Negotiations shape beha viour and course of action
2.	Perspective orientation	Positivist	Reductionist/ Positivist	Construc- tivist
3.	Role of (in) formal law/ legislation	Customary rules dominant	Formal law dominant	Both suppor- tive and Contextual
4.	Role of learning	Contextual	Minimal	Fundamental
5.	Mode of learning	Single loop	Single loop	Double loop
6.	Methodologi- cal orientation	Semi-flexible	Structured	Flexible
7.	Enabling forces	Social sanction Local rules	Laws, regulation	Interaction dialogue
8.	Responsibility allocated to	Local elite Powerbrokers	Government apparatus	Joint (external facilitators and local people)
9.	Gain	Mostly powerful	Mostly one party	Both parties
10.	Resource view	Negotiable	Fix pie	Expandable
11.	Main actors	Local elite and powerbrokers	Government officials	Facilitators and local people
12.	Value to relationship	High	Low	High

9.3.1. Emphasis on Social Learning, Interaction, Communication and Concerted Actions

From the analysis of the conflict cases in the preceding chapters, it became clear that interaction, communication, learning and facilitation were some of the crucial factors lacking in existing conflict management practices. Communication facilitates meaningful dialogue among people to address their problems by linking messages and discourses and exchanging views on a problem. Influence, manipulation, exploitation, persuasion, threats, all are accomplished through communication. Communication between conflicting parties widens understanding of each other's needs, drains frustrations and transforms negative stereotypes and images to learning opportunities. Therefore, ICM aims to improve communication and interaction. From the ICM process, actors generate knowledge, skills, confidence, trust, resources and insights to deal with community-level social and natural resource conflicts. Distorted communication or wrong information, as discussed in chapter six, helps to develop a negative sense. Regeneration of forest in the disputed pastureland has shown that people learn to take corrective measures through concrete experiences. In this case they assessed the advantages, risks and opportunities in opting to act concertedly for afforestation. The afforestation case suggests that concerted action is based on collective interests and mutual interdependence to manage complicated natural resources for the collective benefit. Concerted action is a result-oriented concept, which emphasises the collective agency in tackling complicated conflicts that can not be solved by individuals. It includes formation of common forums for collective decision and action.

Röling's notions of 'soft side of land' (1999b) and 'platforms for management of collective natural resources (Röling, 1996) provides a conceptual basis to resolve conflict through concerted action. The case of the ADB-funded irrigation project demonstrated that inappropriately facilitated external NRM interventions can lead to mistrust resulting in increased non-compliance. The reasons for mistrust in this case were a lack of communication and sharing of information and a lack of proper facilitation of the planning process so that local people could make informed choices on mutually acceptable irrigation options. The spring-water source conflict demonstrated that people involved in conflict not only create the rules and opportunities by which they organise their relationships with one another but also effectively utilise these rules and opportunities to maximise any resources for a common benefit.

The Deurali *Guthi* land as well as the grazing-land conflicts highlight that when one group of people place a high value on their own interests ignoring others' concerns then conflict often results. In contrast the spring-water source case indicated that when people also value the interests of other people then the outcome is 'collaboration'. Chapter four clearly pointed out that the pro-elite biased, legal centric and learning-ignored conflict management practices can not resolve social conflicts appropriately. Therefore, a learning-based, issue-specific and democratic approach is needed to minimise these weaknesses while resolving conflict in community.

Analysis of all conflict cases shows that managing conflict involves managing social relationships. Conflict management therefore should not only be visualised as a regulative idea but also as a means of developing the ability of people to improve social relationships. The empirical information has demonstrated that conflict is both a negative as well as a positive social phenomenon. It can be constructive as well as destructive, depending on how it is dealt with. Therefore, conflict is both an input to enhance social change if managed non-violently and a 'liability' to society if it is allowed to go out of control (Walker and Daniels, 1997; Drew *et al.*, 1997).

9.3.2. *Emphasis on Capacity Building of Local People*

The efforts of NGOs in making the Mediation Group capable of resolving the spring-water source conflict in a consensual way proved that if local people are helped to develop their knowledge and skills they can effectively manage conflict in community. Local capacity building in conflict management starts with participatory conflict analysis. It seeks the synergy and creativity among actors and ensures the full implementation of commitments made in a negotiated agreement, based on joint conflict assessment. Local peoples' integration into decision making in NRM itself results in less conflict because of the developed feelings of ownership and incorporation of local knowledge and experiences. Interests of local people can be insured and their experiences can be integrated in CM procedures by involving them in the conflict management practices. External interventions must instigate a partnership based on mutual co-operation. Though capacity building is a lengthy and continuos process, it enormously helps to settle conflict in a positive way.

From the cases presented in chapters four to seven it is clear that the lack of peoples' ability to defend their rights causes exploitation by powerful people. Capacity building mainly focuses on developing confidence of community members through various training, improved communication, legal awareness and shared learning practices. As observed in the third case peoples' confidence was developed by an exchange of information and ideas as well as regular dialogues and interaction processes. In this case people discussed problems intensively to come to a negotiated agreement. This is also an adjustment process in which options are exchanged and explored according to the logic of acceptance and consequences.

9.3.3. *Emphasis on Skill Development to deal with Conflict*

Appropriate training on negotiation, facilitation, communication, conflict analysis, mediation skills, legal awareness, etc. help to develop peoples' ability to be actively involved in conflict management to resolve conflict locally. Such training can be used to strengthen the useful existing customary, institutional or legal approaches or to help establish new mechanisms (Warner and Jones, 1998; Warner, 2000). Agencies working in local NRM projects and programmes are investing huge resources in training and planning. The issue is only how to integrate content and method of conflict management in their regular training programme. The best way to incorporate skill training in their training/planning activities is through co-ordination of organisations working in the village by the VDC.

9.3.4. Emphasis on Integration of Experts' Skills and Community Experiences

One of the main focuses of ICM is to integrate positive aspects of external knowledge/skills and local knowledge/ experiences in dealing with conflict. Such integration leads to increased effectiveness and accountability of conflict management. In the ADB-funded irrigation project villagers were treated as just a crowed of people to be manipulated. The decisions of the authority were imposed. It was expected that people would legitimatise and endorse what the irrigation authority had already decided. This paternalistic attitude caused serious conflict in this case. If irrigation bureaucrats had acted as facilitators, designing the project together with the community, serious conflict could have been avoided and the canal would now be functional.

9.4. Interactive Conflict Management Complements Formal System

Interactive conflict management is not a complete alternative to the formal organisations working in conflicts. It complements them if integrated into their CM practices. It helps formal organisations to legitimise their decisions by incorporating the perspectives and opinions of local people into their CM resolution practices. Neither is it a "tip-of-the-iceberg" forum to which conflicts are brought after all other attempts to manage them have failed. Instead, it reduces the burden of the increasing numbers of conflicts dealt with formal organisations. It is also not a sort of "flying doctor" having a magic remedy to solve all conflicts. It is a pragmatic methodology to ensure accessibility to local people, which allows to resolve conflict in community and minimises the large number of lawsuits to go to police, administration and court. With this approach the local community, VDC, users groups, local NGOs, and projects working in the area themselves decide on interventions when the actual conflicts occur or the potential for a conflict is seen to be present.

9.5. Three-tier Strategy in Interactive Conflict Management

ICM adapts a three-tier strategy to deal with social and natural resource related conflict in community.

1. Preventive measures: Minimise potential conflicts through facilitation, raising awareness and cognitive realisation. Interaction among the community members and external intervening agencies is the basis of minimising potential conflicts.
2. Addressing actual conflict at community: Manage or resolve actual conflict locally after its emergence. The procedure stated in section 9.4 is used to manage or resolve conflicts.
3. Referral to legal resolution: Refer to judicial (legal) regulatory (government offices) options with proper counselling only if unable to resolve conflict locally by alternate ways. Local people have already developed their capacity by being involving in the procedure stated in section 9.4, so fewer manipulations are expected when formal legal options are needed.

9.6. Implementation Procedure

To translate ICM as a methodological concept into practice, a clear procedure is essential. From the analysis of conflict cases in chapters four to eight and the ideas of different scholars working in conflict issues (Susskind and Cruikshank, 1987; Pruitt and Carnevale, 1993; Ury *et al.*, 1989; Gray, 1989; Buckles, 1999; Leeuwis, 1999 and 2000; Warner and Jones, 1998; Warner, 2000; Warner, 2001), I proposed the following 4 step procedure to facilitate ICM. In all these steps all parties (e.g., VDC, NGO, users groups, local people, etc.) involved in CM bear responsibilities. However, facilitators of the process (be they staff of NGOs, GOs, VDCs, members of user groups or villagers) have a crucial role to play in every step. When specific responsibilities are assigned, then in the second step particular persons have specific roles to play. The four-steps are interrelated with each other. The activities outlined in one step may be necessary to undertake the following step and all listed activities may not be necessary in every conflict case. They are content specific and may need to be adapted according to the specific situation to settle a particular conflict.

These four steps are:

Step 1: Joint conflict assessment/analysis
Step 2: Intervention strategy and action plans design
Step 3: Actual implementation of action plans
Step 4: Reflection and modification

9.6.1. *Joint Conflict Assessment/analysis (step 1)*

As observed in the spring-water source conflict case, entering into participatory conflict analysis begins with the critical process of building rapport with the community. This underpins any successful CM. Effective negotiation is only possible when sufficient trust and effective communications have been developed among the conflicting parties, and/or between facilitators and these parties. Participatory conflict analysis needs to continue until a plan is finalised that outlines the way in which the conflict will be managed (process design). This process design considers the overall strategy of CM by combining various options. Understanding what constitutes the essence of the negotiation process is a major concern in this step. Socialising skills and ability, knowledge about local context, experiences of handling conflict situations, communication skills and the ability to handle emotions are some of the important qualities of the facilitators (negotiators/mediators) to accomplish these tasks. To assess the conflict the following actions needs to be taken.

1. Raise issues
2. Discover interests
3. Generate opinions
4. Develop agreements

Complete analysis of a conflict situation (whole complexity of socio-political relations and their effects on natural resource conflicts) before engaging in implementation of any agreements is essential. From the joint conflict assessment, people understand the fundamental causes of conflict and potentials and limitations for its resolution. As observed in the third case, conflict assessment is fundamentally about the assessment of people, their aspirations and relationships based on investigation of all related issues, gathering all relevant information from all sources, analysis, synthesis and reintegration (creation of new constructs and patterns) (Ramirez, 1997). Findings of the assessment bring alternative choices for concrete action to settle the conflict.

Based on this study and the literature the following points should be considered while conducting conflict assessment:

1. Establish rapport with disputants/villagers and develop understanding of the local system.
2. State the objectives of conflict assessment.
3. Prepare conflict map exploring the following:

   - Identify the people involved in conflict (who is affected, who can influence outcomes, past history of the parties in conflict, etc.), people having leadership quality, willingness and faith of people (they can be mobilised later in the implementation stage) and interdependency between conflicting parties.
   - Identify incompatibility of goals, values, feelings, interests and underlying needs and fears of people, determine whether the disagreement represents underlying assumptions, values, and attitudes. Separate feelings from facts.
   - Identify substance/content and nature of problems, their boundaries and look how the conflict is developing and transforming (historical background, sparking issues), identify magnitude and connectivity (linkage of conflict with other social issues).
   - Identify risks, potential social impacts, costs of conflict, scope and incentives for co-operation and immediate issues that reduce conflict.

- Identify relevant governmental policies and legal arrangements (jurisdictional and legal constraints and potentialities).
- Explore cultural differences, power relationships, knowledge and information gaps, communication barriers and geographical distribution of conflict.
- Find commonalties between parties in a conflict.
- Explore potential to mobilise available local resources.
- Distinguish between procedural, substantial and relational conflicts and prioritise them based on severity.

Participatory rural appraisal (PRA), appreciative inquiry, focus group discussion, key informant interviews, brain storming, observation, etc can be used to accomplish this step. All these explorations give ideas on how to design the intervention strategy and action plans. An extremely important question in analysing conflict is "why?" Why do disputants feel so strongly about this? Why do they have such serious arguments over this issue? Why do they think in that particular way? These "why" questions clarify the reasons and thinking of the parties in conflict. Such conflict maps assist in revealing fundamental reasons for the conflict and the range of possible options and relevant choices for intervention. Such options are generally innovative, flexible and may go beyond a legalistic approach to settle their differences and develop future orientation (Warner, 2000; 2001). Conflict mapping is a kind of learning based soft method, which promotes structured dialogues to improve the conflict situation in natural resources (Walker and Daniels, 1998). Through the conflict mapping process facilitators and villagers acquire a means to deal with substantive, relational and procedural issues in conflict. Joint conflict assessment helps to examine their goals, positions, and underlying interests and explores the best alternatives and a fair and reasonable deal. It explores what is the minimum one party can accept and what is the maximum another party can offer. A joint conflict assessment exercise lets villagers engage in interactive dialogue to generate creative ideas and explore acceptable options. This is also a vision building process of how to transform various interests to gain common benefits.

9.6.2. Design of Intervention Strategy and Action Plans (step 2)

The second step is to narrow down the problem into a workable scope and define specific activities for conflict management. The jointly developed objective criteria based on principles and the result of analysis helps both parties to come to an agreement (spring water source case in this book).

Due consideration of CM planning based on participatory conflict assessment leads to effective CM. It is important to realise that failing to plan is planning to fail in CM. While developing CM strategy, intervention priority should be given to one of the 3 integral components of conflict i.e., substance, procedures and relationships (Walker and Daniels, 1998). I suggest the following activities in the second step in shaping the ICM trajectory.

- Identify the key actors (who can do what) for the prioritised conflicts and assign responsibilities.
- Jointly define criteria (inclusion or exclusion) for resolution. Establish ground rules on procedures, role of individual actors, time frame, dealing with sensitive and confidential issues, recording and documentation process, etc.
- Decide and agree on various training activities and associated agreements.
- Decide particular intervention options (withdrawal, force, accommodation, compromise, and/or a combination of them), which options in which conditions.
- Identify favourable governmental policies, rules and local customs, which support the intended resolution, if relevant.
- Decide a specific time frame (when) and forums/places (what and where).
- Develop a concrete agenda for action and forge agreement with actors on the prepared action plans.
- Make arrangements for external inputs (knowledge, skills, etc.), if needed.

The same methods mentioned in the first step can also be used to accomplish the second step. One of the major challenges for ICM practitioners in this step is to facilitate the convergence of the different knowledge processes of the actors involved in disputes by bringing them to common platforms for collective action (Röling, 1996) and joint learning (Pretty, 1994; Röling and Wagemakers, 1998).

9.6.3. Implementation of Action Plans (step 3)

Based on the outcome of the second step, implement the activities defined to manage/resolve the conflict. In this stage mainly selected actors are involved in the conflict management process. While implementing intervention plans, separate people from problems, address problems not personalities, look for an integrative solution (possibility to create additional resources), which allow disputing parties to co-operate and promote interaction. Implement various training activities to develop capacities of people to manage conflict. Consider the following points while implementing a CM process:

- Put rigid issues to one side and start with simple issues to brainstorm for other ideas while starting the process. Often conflicts arise when people think that there is only a limited solution. A break through happens when people discover alternate ways to resolve conflict (Susskind and Cruikshank, 1987; Warner, forthcoming).
- First deal with principles and concepts. Sometimes people in conflict who do not agree about the details can agree on a concept or goal. The details can then be sorted out later. Look for a multi-step process to resolve conflict, if it cannot be resolved straight a way (Urey *et al.*, 1989).
- Discuss issues in relation to a wider policy environment to enhance feelings of interdependency by introducing external and internal examples.
- Link resolution and reconciliation between religious, cultural values, norms and customs, if needed.
- Deal with relational problems first and focus on concerns and interests rather than positions and personalities.
- Involve trusted people (may be outsiders or community members) to monitor the progress and ensure compliance.
- Start with low cost, simple procedures.
- Exchange proposals, counter proposals and their revisions

where both parties are expected to make offers and concessions.

- Communicate (verbally or non-verbally) effectively to exchange information related to the process and share information about the success stories and causes of failure from other areas. Use argumentation tactics. Make messages simple and understandable. Also make language patterns (discourse style, question-answer sequence, timing of message, symbolic and ritualistic dimensions, degree of consequences of verbal and non-verbal communication, etc.) simple because it is the vehicle for exchange of meanings to positively influence conflict management.
- Stress holistic improvement (situation) rather than a short-term solution of the specific problem and emphasis progress if it is not possible to achieve a specific outcome.
- If the CM discussion is exhausting adjourn the meeting temporarily for relaxation. This helps people to rethink through an issue and come up with new ideas for agreement. If discussions go in the wrong direction, stop the discussion. Create a special group meeting environment where people can argue, disagree (break meetings into smaller discussion groups).
- Ensure active participation of all people involved in meetings. If the personal behaviour of particular people is creating problems, it is a good idea to communicate privately. Avoid putting the blame on individuals.
- Document all achievements (what agreed so far) during the meeting.
- Refer to higher formal authorities (e.g., district administration, police, court, etc.) with proper counselling, if not able to resolve/manage conflict locally.

Parties involved in conflict either do not wish to resolve/ manage conflict or do not realise it is in their best interest to achieve an agreeable solution. During the CM practice sometimes the atmosphere becomes charged with anger, frustration, resentment, mistrust, hostility, and a sense of futility. Communication channels close down or are used to criticise and blame the other and the original issues become blurred. New issues are added as the conflict becomes personalised. Even if one side is willing to make concessions often hostility prevents agreement. In such a conflict, perceived differences become magnified, each side gets locked into their initial positions and each side resorts to lies, threats, distortions, and other attempts to force the other party to comply with their demands. In such a situation take the following corrective measures:

- Divert hot issues for the time being by starting games, jokes and story telling, which reduce tension.
- Increase the accuracy of communication and provide extra information.
- Depersonalise the conflict--separate the issues from the people.
- Establish commonalties (look for greater common goals and focus on what people have in common).
- Find ways to move forward (by mobilising close allies, supporters, friends, relatives, etc.).
- Make an acceptable proposal, refine and reformulate, assess potentiality for trade off.

In general, the implementation process starts by identifying the best and worst possible outcomes and exploring trade-offs for the key issues. Try to create additional resources or options (if possible) to satisfy both parties and offer non specific compensation (one side gets what it wants and the other side is compensated on another issue). This is an adaptive dynamic learning and a joint decision making process to find common agreement to resolve conflict. It is also a psychological process, which influences perceptions and expectations of people in conflict.

Another important aspect in the implementation stage is the use of influence and persuasion. The implementation process tries to change the belief of conflicting parties. A persuasion strategy should be used to achieve an acceptable agreement. While doing so consider personal conditions (personality, risk taking personality, self esteem, co-operative response, authoritarian behaviour) information conditions (information on the situation, the context, what is at stake, other party's needs, goals, means of actions, personality and value) and structural conditions (networks of issues and relationships, legal and socio-political complexity of the process) (Buckles, 1999; Walker, forthcoming).

9.6.4. Reflection and Modification (step 4)

This step constructively reviews the corresponding activities undertaken, process and procedures followed and outcomes achieved so far and explores desirable and feasible changes in next cycle of conflict management. This process looks forward, considering the desirable changes to make an improvement next time (Wilson and Morren, 1990; Walker and Daniels, 1998). Mutual gains are the prime concern in this step.

9.7. Facilitators of Interactive Conflict Management

As discussed earlier, all organisations working in the community are dealing with conflicts. Governmental offices, NGOs, CBOs, users groups and federations or local political bodies such as VDCs and Wards are all actively engaged in conflict management in community. Some of them have mandatory legal provisions to address local conflict and others are active due to their own interests. However, the methodologies used by them are not responsive enough to deal with conflict in fair and effective ways. Therefore, learning-based, action-oriented and people-centred methodology greatly helps to improve their performance in conflict management. In this context ICM relevant and it is not a separate package to be implemented in addition to their normal methodological procedures. It is only essential to use concepts and stepwise procedures of ICM in their existing conflict management practices. All organisations and individuals involved in CM at the community level could use an ICM methodology. Discussions with various CBOs, NGOs, VDC and users groups indicated that thy are eager to implement new methodology in dealing with conflict.

9.8. Institutionalisation of Interactive Conflict Management

One of the major challenges of any new methodology is its

institutionalisation. How to sustained such methodology and by whom? What sort of legal, institutional and financial arrangements are available to operationalise ICM? To answer these questions, among others, we should refer to the Local Self-Governance Act (LSGA). The LSGA in Article 34(1) and Section 8, article 70 and 71 provide legal authorities and functional responsibilities to VDCs to deal with community level conflict cases. Therefore, the first condition is to incorporate ICM method under the conflict resolution procedure of the VDC. This act also made provision for manpower and financial resources. VDCs have already started to work according to these provisions. Separate legal enforcement is not needed when ICM is incorporated into the VDC conflict management procedure. The avenue provided by LSGA is suitable to facilitate ICM in villages to develop the capacity of local people, to improve communication and to share information. LSGA gives a mandate to the VDC to co-ordinate and monitor those organisations (NGO, GO, CBO, etc.) that are implementing development projects/activities in that VDC. In that aspect ICM can be incorporated into all the activities of organisations working in NRM issues in a village. As the VDC is a permanent political structure there is no risk of donor or project dependency, once incorporated into the VDC system. As indicated in the chapter four, VDC is a local organisation based on the support (vote) of the general public. It is more concerned with local people and therefore actively engaged on several local platforms, working together with the public to resolve conflicts. Critiques say that VDC is also generally controlled by the local elite and it is also a heavily politicised unit and therefore it is not feasible to implement such type of democratic methodology. I do agree with this fact but if we want to non-coercive change we have to start somewhere. Other local structures like government office are far more rigid, top-down and unaccountable to general public. NGOs and CBOs have even less influence and are not mandated to deal with conflict. In this ground the only way is to start with VDC. Some VDCs have demonstrated excellent performance and many expressed their willingness. So I firmly believe that VDC should be the point of intervention to democratise them and mobilise to resolve local level conflicts.

All those who are engaged in CM practices are investing money, resources and time. In this respect there is no need for a separate budget, manpower or the creation of new organisations. What is needed is the training of facilitators engaged in conflict resolution issues. Several NRM projects are interested in supporting such a single-investment capacity building aspect to develop local capacity. Therefore training facilitators should not be the major constraining factor in promoting ICM.

9.9. Opportunities and Challenges

Conflict management is a sensitive issue and dealing with it requires special skills. There are always risks of ICM being applied in a mechanistic fashion when its methodology provides a stepwise procedure. If facilitators fail to understand the underlying principles of ICM, success is less likely. ICM as a methodology has to address context specific conflict with continuous adaptation. Therefore, ICM itself is not a mechanical package to be uniformly used in all conflict situations. Success or failure of ICM depends on the facilitation process. Facilitators should have an active strategy, good skills, credibility, trustworthiness, resources and willpower to make ICM successful. Effective facilitation enhances flexibility, adaptation, information gathering, utilisation and interactive learning to resolve conflict.

During the implementation of ICM process several unpredicted and unintended consequences may arise. At that time facilitators have to be able to tackle such a situation. The four-step methodology proposed here should not be used as a blueprint to be strictly adhered to. It should be adapted, modified and used as a methodological outline. Only proper facilitation and context-specific adaptation ensures resolution of conflict in community. If facilitated properly it develops the capacity of local people to effectively manage social and natural resource conflicts.

Power brokers and village elite may feel threatened because of the empowerment led procedure of ICM, which challenges their manipulation of the conflict situation. Therefore, they could create obstacles to implement ICM. In such a situation weaker actors have to be strengthened by forming coalitions, using conventional policy instruments such as legal rules and communication campaigns (Warner, 2000; Leeuwis, 2000). Success of ICM is also based on interaction and effective communication. If this is hampered there is less chance of success. Mobilisation of local resources is another important determinant of success or failure of ICM.

OPPORTUNITIES

VDC is recognised by the state as one of the effective decentralised bodies to deal with local conflict. Therefore, VDC has legally defined conflict management roles to play at the local level. As discussed in chapter four, although the performance of VDCs in conflict management is not satisfactory, they are far better than other formal options in terms of accessibility, cost and time. Elected representatives of the VDCs are more accountable to the local people and more likely to listen to the views of poor people. VDC has also given financial resources to implement various activities under the arrangement of LSGA. For the first time in the history of Nepal, the UML government gave three hundred thousand rupees to VDCs in 1995 to implement development activities. Since then the central government provides an annual budget to VDCs to implement various activities in villages. The amount of the annual allocation has now been raised to half a million rupees. After this budgetary provision VDCs are actively involved in local development activities in their villages. There is a willingness by VDCs to engage in dealing with natural resource conflicts as stipulated by the LSGA. All NGOs, CBOs and projects working in the particular VDC have to work in co-ordination with the VDC. This means that there is self-regulated provision to deal with conflict in a village. The part lacking is the appropriate methods to carry this out. ICM provides a badly needed alternate method.

The study has clearly demonstrated that there are several local methods and practices to deal with conflicts. Some of them are more useful and practical and some favour local power relationships. There is tremendous potential for using these positive aspects of locally available experiences, methods and repertoires of conflict management by adapting ICM at the community level. In formal methods there are some legal limitations to incorporate these local practices, but in ICM these practices are an integral part of the process.

The emerging civil society organisations are advocating the promotion of capacity building of local people as advocated by the democratic constitution of kingdom of Nepal, which endorses people as the ultimate source of power. Many laws and regulations contradictory to the constitution are being revised to ensure the spirit of the constitution. In several cases civil society organisations and local communities are working collaboratively to minimise conflicts in the community.

Even within the government's legal sector there is growing concern over the need for a locally based decentralised conflict management approach rather than relying on legal systems Some aspects of ICM can also be applied to court proceedings. When mediation is part of the legal proceedings then ICM could play an important role.

In recent years several local users organisations such as the forest and water-users groups, FECOFUN, HIMWANTI, mothers' clubs, etc. have emerged at community level to deal with NRM and related conflicts. They are very useful forums accessible to all users and working to ensure fair resolution of conflict. NRM projects are also giving support to institutionalise them. Such decentralised organisations need appropriate methodology to deal with conflict.

CHALLENGES

There are not only good prospects for the use of ICM in the community, it also raises several challenges and problems in translating the concept into practice. The most important challenge is the power-based social structures and elite influence in a village. Generally the village elite want to maintain the patron-client relationship in resolving conflicts. Interactive conflict management wants to break such a relationship by empowering local people and organisations. People's empowerment is enhanced when people actively participate in conflict analysis, interaction, discussion and legal arguments to solve conflicts. Therefore, local powerbrokers will not co-operate in promoting ICM. Even if it is not possible for them to stop ICM being incorporated into the activities of all organisations working in conflict, they will try to create barriers.

Translation of ICM as a methodological principle into a specific operational activity remains highly circumscribed by skills in conflict analysis, communication, negotiation/ mediation and facilitation as well as the conceptual clarity of the actors involved in the CM process.

Scaling up ICM to a wider level is another challenge and largely depends on the success or failure at the community level. There is good chance of countrywide scaling up if it works properly under the procedural framework of VDC. If a few NGOs and grass-root organisations only apply ICM it may be difficult to promote it at a wider level. The legitimacy of ICM is another concern. As it is a methodology framed under the legal arrangement of LSGA, there may not be problem of legitimacy as it does not challenge the legal arrangement of the state. It rather helps to improve performance and increase their efficiency.

9.10. Conclusion

ICM is based on a social learning perspective. It is a community-focused, learning-based and action-oriented methodological approach to resolve/manage conflict to improve the performance of NRM. It moves beyond the structurally designed, compartmentalised blue print approach of conflict resolution. It is an approach that steps back from the natural resources stand and focuses on the continuous interaction between people, between people and their position in the broader socio-cultural setting, in order to integrate socio-political and biophysical dimensions of NRM. ICM acknowledges the knowledge, skills and experiences of the community as social capital to help manage conflict. Diversity embedded in the local community can be mobilised to resolve/manage conflict.

SUMMARY

Management of Social and Natural Resource Conflict in Nepal— Realities and Alternatives

This book is about social and natural resource conflicts and their management systems in Nepal. It is based on the research carried out between 1997 and 2001 in six districts of Nepal with detail case studies in Dolakha district. The information was collected at two levels (general information and specific and in-depth information from the case study sites). The case studies have especially focussed to five inter-connected conflict cases related to irrigation, land, drinking water and forest and pastureland. The study was conducted mainly using qualitative research methods. The aims of this book are to understand and analyse the dynamics of social and natural resource conflicts and their resolution measures, and to seek far suitable alternatives to improve conflict management practices at local level. It is hope that this book will stimulate debate on need to reform existing conflict management systems to bring broader non-coercive social change in Nepal.

Conflicts are an inevitable part of the social process in society. Therefore, this book has embraced conflict as a source of learning to create opportunities for non-coercive social change and rural transformation. In this Book I have used theoretical perspective of legal anthropology and social learning to analyse the dynamics of conflict. The performance of existing formal and informal conflict management systems have been analysed. Inter-linkages of various conflicts with broader socio-political contexts are examined. Based on the findings an alternative methodological approach of conflict management is proposed. Access and control and political, environmental and economic motives were found to be the driving forces in creating social and natural resource related conflict in society. An uneven distribution of resources has created scarcity, competition and conflict in Nepal. This book argues that competition and conflict are increasing due to the lack of a conducive national policy and legal and institutional arrangements, and a top-down approach. Feelings of injustice have greatly contributed to develop conflict in community.

This book is arranged in nine chapters. In the first chapter the problem context and methodological issues are discussed. In this chapter I have argued that the behaviour of people is shaped and reshaped by a specific context and local power relationships. The existence of plural legal systems in the community itself is a source of conflict. Different and even conflicting perspectives, values, objectives and knowledge of local people are manifested in the specific context and shaped by social relationships. Any particular conflict is linked with historical, cultural, political, economic and institutional issues, as well as the social context and is affected by norms, values and daily practices.

In the second chapter theoretical issues are presented. In this chapter theoretical concepts such as mediation, negotiation, arbitration, adjudication, litigation, legal pluralism, property rights, forum shopping, constructivist perspective, soft system thinking, cognitive system, communicative rationality, platforms for negotiation and adaptive management are discussed. In the third chapter general overview of Nepal is presented. In this chapter a brief socio-economic, cultural, political, and historical overview of Nepal are discussed. The political economy of natural resources and a brief review of Nepalese NRM policies, laws and regulations are presented.

Chapters four to seven of the book are devoted to empirical investigations. In the forth chapter general social and natural resource conflicts and their characteristics are documented. Most common formal and informal conflict management systems are discussed. In the fifth chapter three specific conflict cases are presented. The first case relates to conflict between old and new users on an old farmers-managed irrigation system. The second case highlights the conflict between a powerful elite group and general villagers to control forest-pasture land. The third case deals with the conflict between two groups of people to access and control a spring water source for drinking water. In all these three cases local social relationships, ownership issues, the ambiguous role of external development organisations, effects of time and space, and gender issues have greatly contributed to escalate and manage the conflict. The sixth chapter presents an Asian Development Bank-funded irrigation project where severe conflicts erupted in the process of its planning and construction. This case shows that formal intervention, if not implemented properly, not only fails to appropriately develop and manage local natural resources but can also cause severe conflict in a society. The conflict issues in this case were analysed in terms of participation, decision making, transparency and corruption, working practice of the water users committee, the role of technology, communication and information. The seventh chapter presents the conflict between landowners and tenants over religious land to control ownership rights. The effects of socio-political change, practical applications of state rules and laws, effects of time and context, peoples' initiatives and the importance of social relationships are analysed in relation to escalation, transformation and resolution of conflict.

Borrowing and transactions, external development interventions, family matters, party politics, character defamation, prostitution and sexual abuse and religious differences were common social conflict in society. Identification of users, the sharing of benefits, access to the forest products, payment of royalties, illegal exploitation of non timber forest products, participation and contribution of users in managing forests, and leadership were the most common issues in forest-conflict. Sharing the water for different purposes, contributions for maintenance of irrigation and drinking water systems, ambiguous roles and responsibilities of water users committees were the common sources of water conflict. In land related disputes inheritance, demarcation, ownership and rights, tenancy issues, encroachment, payment of land tax and rents were all frequent contentious issues. In all types of conflicts, bureaucracy, corruption and misuse of resources and the abuse of power and authority played significant roles. All these conflicts crosscut and in practice it is not possible to draw a clear demarcation between them. Conflict is more common if the parties involved belong to different political, caste/ethnic and economic groups and these associations may be the triggering force in conflict. When the conflicting parties realise the cost of the conflict is too high and the benefits too low it can often be shortened.

Based on the theoretical references discussed in chapter two chapter eight analyse conflict at broader level. Dynamics of social natural resource conflict are analysed and common conflict management options used in the study area are discussed. The analysis is framed under property rights issues, the role of formal and informal laws, caste, ethnicity and social relationships, power and politics, external interventions and issues of corruption, communication, information and networking, leadership and gender issues. Based on the overall analysis, chapter nine presents an alternative approach called interactive conflict management (ICM). This alternative methodological approach provides ways to overcome the weaknesses of existing conflict management practices and proposes a learning-based and action oriented procedure. Based on the analyses of opportunities, challenges and limitations for its institutionalisation, ICM provides a step-by-step procedure to accomplish conflict resolution in community.

Management of conflict is not only limited to linear, legal-focused conflict resolution procedures. Conflict management is a dynamic process of adaptation and action and resolution depends on the effectiveness of interaction and actions governed by values (willingness to resolve conflict), context (possible challenges and difficulties) and perspectives.

The book highlights that government sponsored natural resource management systems do not adequately value local practices and therefore create numerous conflicts. State laws, regulations and legal principles were contradictory, inadequate, expensive or inappropriately applied and therefore not effective in properly addressing conflicts in society. A legal-centric interpretation of government policies and procedures (treating them as the only solution of all conflicts) gave rise to several conflicts instead of resolving them. The politicisation of conflict, elite domination, inaccessibility of formal conflict resolution systems and procedures to poor villagers and complications accompanying these procedures were very common. The general public questioned whether formal conflict management practices played a fair role in settling social and natural resource conflict. These procedures themselves became a source of further conflict. The Deurali land conflict is an example of such inefficiency and bias. As shown by both the forest-pasture and religious land cases, the legal approach assumed that legal enactment forces people to resolve conflict by threatening them with punishment. The legal approach interprets the law as the only ultimate instrument for social engineering and effective means of homogenising a heterogeneous society and for resolving all conflicts. Staff of formal organisations commonly viewed local people as conflict creators and themselves as the best means of solving of these conflicts. These feelings mean that the formal conflict resolution approach widely practised in Nepal does not recognise the local capability of resolving or managing conflict. There is also a lack of integration of new innovations in the process of conflict resolution. Allegiance to political parties in Nepal is an important factor in the enhancement and/or inhibition of conflict resolution processes. Political ideology is a powerful variable in social conflict, which can influence the whole conflict management process at different levels of social aggregation. When power is mobilised in conflict resolution it usually results in a win-lose situation. Political power exerts substantial influence in any conflict. If a conflict arises in a village, local political workers of major parties intervene for their own political benefit, particularly to win a local election.

I have highlighted in this book that resolving a conflict is also a means of establishing power and influence in society. In Nepal majority of the conflicts have been resolved locally in informal ways. Redirection of behaviour, mobilisation of networks, linkages with power centres, differential interpretation of laws and regulations and the use of force are some of the major strategies used by local people to negotiate or resolve conflict. Local people use various locally existing forms of social networks, shopping forums and platforms to deal with conflict issues. People first use local forums to discuss conflict issues at the community rather than opting for a legal solution. This was because such platforms and forums were accessible, cheap and based on local knowledge and experiences. Local negotiators use cultural, religious and ethical proverbs highlighting the importance of resolving conflict locally to convince conflicting parties. At the local level, women are directly and actively involved in conflict and its management. In several community-level conflicts, children were the source of conflict as well as an effective means of its resolution. An intimate connection was observed between conflict and communication, information and their inter-linkages in its resolution or escalation. Transformations of social conflict to political, temporal manifestation and intensity of conflicts varied depending on political interference and power relationships. Power relationships determine success or failure of management of community level conflicts. Local political processes, values and the differential power base influenced conflicts in all cases. Time and space are very important determining factors for escalation of resolution of the conflict. During special periods of time such as elections and the restoration of democracy, conflicts suddenly increased and several others were resolved instantly. The intensity of the same conflict changes over time and its life cycle determines the management or resolution strategies. Having a natural resource conflict in their community forced local people to, utilise their existing resources optimally or efficiently, create new resources or search for different alternatives.

All the cases seem to suggest that elite's manipulation of land, water and forest conflicts has increased the ability of tenants and villagers to defend their rights, to protest and negotiate in situations of conflict. Generally, the degree, intensity and antagonistic effects were less marked in natural resource conflict. Local people as far as possible follow accommodative strategies rather than confrontation. Although many conflicts remain unsolved for extended periods the existence of a workable relationship between parties involved in the conflict is common. In natural resource related conflict the situation is usually, less antagonistic because of the accommodative nature of the people involved. Villagers consider social relationships as an important factor in managing conflict in community. People use their own criteria to classify conflict based on the socio-cultural context. The major criterion is the effect of the conflict on social relationships and a conflict is only categorised as severe when it cause these to be disrupted. Compromise was a commonly used strategy in managing community-level conflict and this was based on trade-offs between disputants. Analysis of all conflict cases shows that managing conflict is managing social relationships. Empirical information demonstrated that conflict is both a negative as well as a positive social phenomenon.

The focus of ICM is to make conflict management forums easily accessible to rural people and to minimise dependence on adversarial forms of conflict resolution. Developing local capacity in conflict management starts with participatory conflict analysis. Appropriate training on negotiation, facilitation, communication, conflict analysis, mediation skills, legal awareness, etc. help to develop the ability of people actively involved in conflict management to achieve a local resolution. ICM acknowledges the knowledge, skills and experiences of a community to manage conflict. Diversity embedded in a local community can be mobilised to resolve/manage conflict. The success or failure to resolve a conflict depends on a fuller understanding of the interdependence by people. With the ICM process actors generate knowledge, skills, confidence, trusts, resources and insights to deal with social and natural resource conflicts at community-level. Conflicts that arose due to confusion and misunderstanding can be resolved by putting all the relevant information to the actors concerned. A complete analysis of a conflict situation (whole complexity of socio-political relations and their effects on society) is vital before any negotiated agreements are implemented. Assessment of such an analysis gives people understanding of the fundamental causes of conflict and the potential and limitations for resolution.

References

ActionAid Nepal, 2001. *Vidayakharuma Bedartawal Mohiharuko Anurodh (Request of Unregistered Tenants to the Parliamentarians).* Kathmandu: Success Nepal and ActionAid Nepal.

AAN (Action Aid Nepal) (1997). *Country Strategy Paper II 198-2000. An Abridged Version.* Kathmandu: Action Aid Nepal.

Acharya K. P. (1998). *A Review of Foreign Aid in Nepal.* Kathmandu: Citizen's Poverty Watch Forum.

Acharya R. N. (1993). *The Economics of Share Cropping: A Study of Two Terai Villages of Nepal.* Malasiya: University of Pertanian.

Adhikari R., N. Belbase and Y. Ghale (2000). *Seed of Monopoly: Impacts of TRIPs Agreement on Nepal.* Kathmandu: Action Aid-Nepal and ProPublic.

Alasuutari P. (1998). *An Invention to Social Research.* London: Sage Publications.

Anderson J., J. Clement and L. V. Crowder (1997). *Pluralism in Sustainable Forestry and Rural Development: An Overview of Concepts, Approaches and Future Steps.* Proceedings of Pluralism and Sustainable Forestry and Rural Development, 9-12 December 1997, FAO, Rome. Pp. 17-28.

Ansari N. and P. Pradhan (Eds.) (1991). *Assistance to Farmers-Managed Irrigation System: Experiences from Nepal.* Kathmandu: Department of Irrigation.

APROSC and JMA (1995). *Nepal Agriculture Perspective Plan: Final Report.* Kathmandu: National Planning Commission.

Axinn N. W. and G. H. Axinn (1996). The Human Dynamics of Natural Resources System. In: Shivakoti, G., G. Varughese, E. Ostrom, A. Sukla, and G. Thapa (Eds.) *People and Sustainable Development: Understanding the Dynamics of Natural Resources*

System. Kathmandu: IAAS/TU, Indiana University, FAO Farmer-Centred Agricultural Resources Management Programme and Winrock Institute for Agricultural Development.

Badal K. (1999). *Nepalma Bhumisudhar, Krishikranti Ra Arthatantrako Vikas* (Land Reform, Agricultural Revolution and Economic Development in Nepal). Kathmandu: Bhrikuti Academic Publications.

Baral L. R. (1998). *Crisis of Governance or Callous Elite Attitude towards Problems*. A Paper presented in the Seminar on Democratic Conflicts and Crisis of Govermentaility, organised by CNAS, Kirtipur, TU. 17-18 Nov. 1998, Kathmandu.

Basnyat B. B. (1995). *Nepal's Agriculture, Sustainability and Intervention: Looking for New Direction*. Published PhD Dissertation. Wageningen: Wageningen Agricultural University.

Bawden R. (1995). On the Systems Dimension in FRS. *Journal for Farming Systems Research-Extension*. 5(2): 1-18.

Beck U., A. Giddens and S. Las (Eds.) (1994). *Reflective Modernisation: Politics Tradition and Aesthetics in Modern Social Order*. Cambridge: Polity Press.

Belbase N. and D. C. Regmi (1998). *Comparative Analysis of Decentralisation and (Community) Forestry Legislation*. Kathmandu: International Centre for Integrated Mountain Development.

Bell D., H. Raiffa and A. Tversky (Eds.)(1989) *Decision Making: Descriptive, Normative and Prescriptive Interactions*. Cambridge: Cambridge University Press.

Benda-Beckmann F. (1999). *Between Free Riders and free Raiders: Property Rights and Soil Degradation in Context*. Paper presented in International Workshop on " Economic Policy Reforms and Sustainable Land Use in LDCs: Recent Advances in Quantitative Analysis", June 30 to July 2, 1999. Wageningen: WUR.

Benda-Beckmann F. and K. Benda-Beckmann (1999). A Functional Analysis of Property Rights with Special Reference to Indonesia. In: van Reije T. and F. von Benda-Beckmann (Eds.) *Property Rights and Economic Development: Land and Natural Resources in South East Asia and Oceania*. London: Keyan Paul. Pp. 15-56.

Benda-Beckmann F., K. Von Benda-Beckmann and L. L.J. Spiertz, (1997). Local Law and Customary Practices in the Study of Water Rights. In: Pradhan R., F. Benda-Beckmann, K. Benda-Beckmann, H.L. Spiertz, S. K. Khadka, and H. Azharul (Eds.). *Water Rights, Conflict and Policy.* Proceeding of Workshop held in Kathmandu, Nepal. Jan. 22-24, 1996. Pp. 221-42.

Benda-Beckmann F., K. Benda-Beckmann, R. Pradhan, and H. L. Spiertz. (1997). Introduction. In: Pradhan, R., F. Benda-Beckmann, K. Benda-Beckmann, H.L. Spiertz, S. K. Khadka, and H. Azharul (Eds.). *Water Rights, Conflicts and Policy.* Proceeding of Workshop held in Kathmandu, Nepal. Jan. 22-24 ,1996. Pp. 1-11.

Benda-Beckmann K. (1984). Forum Shopping and Shopping Forums: Dispute Settlement in a Minagkabau Village in West Sumatra, Indonesia. In: Benda-Beckmann K. (Ed.). *The Broken Stairways to Consensus: Village Justice and State Courts in Minangkabau,* Dordrecht: Foris.Pp. 37-64.

Benjamin P., W. C. Lam, E. Ostrom and G. Shivakoti (1994). *Institutions, Incentives and Irrigation in Nepal.* Decentralisation: Finance and Management Project Report. Burlington: Association in Rural Development.

Bennet L. (1983). *Dangerous Wives and Sacred Sisters.* New York: Columbia University Press.

Berger P. L. and T. Luckmann (1967). *The Social Construction of Reality: A Treatise in the Sociology of Knowledge.* Garden City.

Berkes F. (1996). Social Systems, Ecological Systems and Property Rights. In: Hanna, B.Y. S., S. C. Folke and K. G. Maler (Eds.). *Rights to Nature.* Washington D.C.,: Island Press. Pp 87-107.

Berkes F. and M. Tanghi (Ed.) (1989). *Common Property Resources: Ecology and Community Based Sustainable Development* London: Belhaven Press.

Bhatia A. (Ed.) (1995). *Seminar on Conflicts Resolution in Natural Resources.* Kathmandu: Nepal Mediation Group/ICIMOD. Participatory NRM Programme.

Bhatia A. (1997). *Power, Equity, Gender ad Conflict in Common Property Resources in the Hindu-Kush Himalayas.* Issues in Mountain Development 7/97. Kathmandu: ICIMOD.

Bista D. B. (1991). *Fatalism and Development: Nepal's Struggle for Modernisation.* Culcutta.: Orent Longman Ltd.

Blaikie P., J Cameron and D. Seddon (1983). *Nepal in Crisis*. Delhi: Oxford University Press.

Bottomore T. (1969). *Sociological Theory and the Study of Social conflict*. Publisher unknown.

Brenes C. (1994). Perfecting Utopia-Extension in Times of Participation. *Forest, Trees and People Newsletter*. No 25 October 1994. Uppsala: Swedish University of Agricultural Sciences.

Bromley D. W. (1992). *Making the Commons Work: Theory, Practice and Policy*. California: Institute of Contemporary Studies.

Buckles D. (Ed.) (1999). *Cultivating Peace: Conflict and Collaboration in Natural Resource Management*. Ottawa/Washington: IDRC/ World Bank Institute.

Bush R. A. (1995). Dispute Resolution- the Domestic Arena: A Survey of Methods, Applications and Critical Issues. In: John A. Vasquez, et. al., (Eds.). *Beyond Confrontation: Learning Conflict Resolution in the Post-Cold War Era*, Michigan: The University of Michigan Press. Pp.9-37.

Bush R. A. B. and J. P. Folger. (1994a). *The Promise of Mediation: Responding to Conflict through Empowerment and Recognition*. San Francisco: Jossey-Bass Publishers.

Bush R.A. B and J. P. Folger. (1994b). Ideology Orientation to Conflict and Mediation Discourse. In: Folger J. and T. Jones (Eds.). *New Directions in Mediation*. London: Sage Publications. Pp. 3-25.

Campbell A. (1992). *Taking the Long View in Tough Time: Landcare in Australia*. The Third Annual Report of the National Landcare Facilitators. Canberra: Australia. National Soil Conservation Programme.

Caplan L. (1970). *Land and Social Change in East Nepal: A Study of Hindu-Tribal Relationships*. Berkeley: University of California Press.

Caplan P. (Ed.) (1995). *Understanding Disputes: The Politics of Arguments*. Berg: Oxford Providence.

Capra F. (1996). *The Web of Life: A New Synthesis of Mind and Matter*. London: Harper Collins Publishers.

CBS (1995). *Statistical Year Book of Nepal 1995*. Kathmandu: Central Bureau of Statistics.

CBS (1998). *Nepal in Figures 1998*. Kathmandu: Central Bureau of Statistics.

CBS (2000). *Statistical Pocket Book Nepal.* Kathmandu: Central Bureau of Statistics.

CBS (1996). *Statistical Pocket Book Nepal.* Kathmandu: Central Bureau of Statistics.

Chambers R. (1988). *Managing Canal Irrigation: Practical Analysis from South Asia.* New Delhi: Oxford University Press.

Chandhoke N. (1995). *State and Civil Society: Explorations in Political Theory.* New Delhi: Sage Publications.

Chapagain D. P., K. Kanel and D. C. Regmi (1999). *Current Policy and legal Context of the Forestry Sector with Reference to the Community Forestry Programme in Nepal. A Working Overview.* Kathmandu: Nepal UK Community Forestry project.

Checkland P. (1981). *Systems Thinking Systems Practice.* Chickester: Wiley.

Checkland P. and J. Scholes (1990). *Soft Systems Methodology in Action.* Chicester: John Wiley.

Citizen's Poverty Watch Forum, 2001. *Impacts of Foreign Aids in Nepal.* Kathmandu: Citizen's Poverty Watch Forum.

CIVICT, (2001). *Community Mediation Report : Quarterly Report June-August 2001.* Kathmandu: Centre for Victim of Torture.

Dahal K. K., K. P. Acharya and D. R. Dahal (Eds.) (1999) *Development Challenges for Nepal.* Kathmandu: Nepal Foundation for Advance Studies.

Daniels S. E. and G. B. Walker (1997). *Rethinking Public Participation in Natural Resource Management: Concept from Pluralism and Five Emerging Approaches.* Proceedings of Pluralism and Sustainable Forestry and Rural Development, 9-12 December, 1997, FAO, Rome. Pp. 29-48.

DDDC (Dolakha District Development Committee) (1999). *District Development Plan 1999/2000.* Charikot: Dolakha District Development Committee.

Denzalay Y. and B. G. Garth (1996). *Dealing in Virtue: International Commercial Arbitration and the Construction of a Transnational Legal Order.* Chicago: University of Chicago Press,

Denzin N. K. and Y. S. Lincoln (Eds.) (1998). *The Landscape of Qualitative Research: Theories and Issues.* London: Sage Publications

DOI/ADB (Department of Irrigation/Asian Development Bank) (1997). *Operational Procedural Manual Second Irrigation Sector Project Loan No 1437 NEP (SF)*. Kathmandu: NIA Consult Inc. Manila Philippine in association with EastConsult (P) Ltd. Nepal.

Dougherty J. E. and R. L. Pfaltgraff (1990). *Contending Theories of International Relations*. London: Harper Collins Publisher.

Dreu C. K.W. and E. van de Vliert. (1997). *Using Conflict in Organizations*. London: Sage Publications.

Engel P. G. H. and S. M. L. Salomon (Eds.) (1997). *Facilitating Innovation for Development: A RAAKS Resource Guide*. Amsterdam: KIT Press.

EPC (1993). *Nepal Environmental Policy and Action Plan: Integrating Environment and Development*. Kathmandu: Environment Protection Council/HMG-N.

Felstiner W. L. F., R. L. Abel and A. Sarat (1981). The Emergence and Transformation of Disputes: Naming, Blaming and Claiming. *Law and Society Review* 15.

Fisher R. (1997). *Beyond Machiavelli: Tools for Coping with Conflict*. Boston: Harvard University Press.

Folger J. P. and T. S. Jones (Eds.) (1994). *New Direction in Mediation: Communication Research and Perspectives*. London: Sage Publications.

Furtze B. and C. Stafford (1994). *Society and Change: A Sociological Introduction to Contemporary Australia*. Melbourne: Macmillan Educational Australia.

Gautam U., N. Agrawal and R. Subedi (Eds.) (1992). *Nepal Managing Large Surface Irrigation projects: A Participatory Review*. Study document NEP/89/006. Kathmandu: Department of Irrigation, HMG/Nepal.

Gellner D, J. Pfaff-Czarnecka and J. Whelpton (Eds.) (1997). *Nationalism and Ethnicity in a Hindu Kingdom: The Politics of Culture in Contemporary Nepal*. Amsterdam: Harwood Academic Publishers.

Ghale Y. and J. D. Gurung (1998). *Role of Women's Group in Watershed Management*. Paper Presented in the Mid Term Workshop of PARDYP at Almora, India. 2-7 March 1998.

Ghimire K. (1992). *Forest or Farm? The Politics of Poverty and Land Hunger in Nepal*. Delhi: Oxford University Press.

Gilmour D. A. and R. J. Fisher (1991). *Villagers, Forest and Foresters: the Philosophy, Process and Practice of Community Forestry in Nepal.* Kathmandu: Sahayogi Press.

Goldstein H. (1981). *Social Learning and Change.* New York: Tavistock Publications.

Gray B. (1989). *Collaborating: Finding Common Ground in Multiparty Problems.* San Francisco: Jossey-Bass Publishers.

Griffiths J. (1983). The General Theory of Litigation: A First Step. *Zeitschrift Fur RECHT-SOZIOLOGIE.* (2): 145-201.

Guba E. G. and Y. S. Lincoln. (1994). *Fourth Generation Evaluation.* London: Sage Publications.

Gulliver P. (1979). *Disputes and Negotiations: A Cross Cultural Perspective, Studies in Law and Social Control.* New York and London: Academic Press.

Gunderson L. H., C. S. Holling and S. S. Light. (Eds.) (1995). *Barriers and Bridges to the Renewable of Ecosystems and Institutions.* New York: Columbia University Press.

Habermas J. (1989). *The Theory of Communicative Action.* Vol. 2. Boston: Becon Press.

Hamilton N. A. (1995). *Learning to Learn with Farmers: An Adult Learning Extension Project.* Published PhD Dissertation. Wageningen: Wageningen Agricultural University.

Hardin G. (1968). The Tragedy of Commons: *Science.* 162: 1243-1248.

Hellriegel D., J. W. Solocum and R. W. Woodman (1999). *Organisational Behaviour* (Sixth Edition) New York: West Publishing Company.

Himal (1995). *Rajnitik Bhumarima Nepalko Jalshrot Bibad* (Nepalese Water Resource Conflict in Political Turmoil). Year 5, No. 3, 2052 Kartik-Poush. Kathmandu: Himal Association.

HMG/N (His Majesty's Government of Nepal) (1989). *Master Plan for the Forestry Sector.* Kathmandu: Ministry of Forest and Soil Conservation.

HMG/N 1992. *National Report on United Nations Conference on Environment and Development.* Kathmandu: His Majesty's Government of Nepal.

HMG/N (1999). *Draft Report of Nepal's Administrative Reform Taskforce 2055 Chaitra.* Kathmandu: His Majesty's Government of Nepal.

Hoftun M., W. Raeper, J. Whelpton (1999). *People Politics & Ideology: Democracy and Social Change in Nepal*. Kathmandu: Mandala Book Point.

Holling C. S. (1995). What Barriers ? What Bridges ? Chapter 1 In: Gunderson L. H., C. S. Holling and S. S. Light. (Eds.) *Barriers and Bridges to the Renewable of Ecosystems and Institutions*. New York: Columbia University Press. Pp. 3-37.

Idris S. M. M. (1998). *Why ? Why ? Why...?*. *Half of the Sky: The Struggle of the women in the Third World*. Malaysia: The Third World Resource. No 94. 1998.

IIMI (International Irrigation Management Institute) (1987). *Irrigation Management in Nepal: Research Papers from National Seminar*. Kathmandu: International Irrigation Management Institute-Kathmandu Office.

IIMI 1990. *Assistance to Farmers-Managed Irrigation Systems*. IIMI Country Paper-Nepal-No 3. Kathmandu: International Irrigation Management Institute-Kathmandu Office.

IMC (Irrigation Management Centre) (1990). *Water Use Conflicts and Their Resolution in Selected Irrigation Systems in Nepal*. IMC Applied Study Report No 13. Pokhara: Irrigation Management Centre.

Jandt F. E. (1973). *Conflict Resolution through Communication*. New York and London: Harper and ROW Publishers.

Jandt F. E. and P. B. Pedersen (Eds.) (1996). *Constructive Conflict Management: Asia Pacific Cases*. London: Sage Publications.

JHPIP (Johns Hopkins Population Information Programme) (1998). World Report of Johns Hopkins Population Information Programme. Baltimore: Johns Hopkins Population Information Programme.

Jiggins, J. and N. Röling (2000). Adaptive Management: Potential and Limitations for Ecological Governance. Article accepted for publication in the *International Journal of Agricultural Resources, Governance and Ecology* 1 (1): 28-43.

Kantipur Daily, 11 September, 2000. ULR: http:// www.nepalnews.com.np/kantipur.htm

Kaplan P. (1995). Nepal Community Mediation Study. In:. Bhatiya, A. (Ed.) *Seminar on Conflict Resolution in Natural Resources*. Kathmandu: ICIMOD.

Karki A. K. (1999). *The Politics of Poverty and Movement from Below in*

Nepal. A procedural paper submitted to School of Development Studies, University of East Anglia (revised version, 2000).

Karki M. D. (1998). Lackluster Participation. *The Kathmandu Post* Daily, 2 September, 1998. Kathmandu: Kantipur Publication (P) Ltd.

KC, D. B. 2001. A Study of Bounded Labour System in Western Nepal: A Case Study of Bhimapur Mauja, Rajapur, Bardiya. MSc Thesis. Wageningen: Wageningen University-Research Centre.

Khadka N. (1994) *Politics & Development in Nepal, Some Issues*. New Delhi: Nirala Publications.

Khadka R.J. (1997). *Sources of Conflict and Methods of Resolving them in Sindhuli, Nepal*. Proceedings of Conflict Management Workshop. Hawaii: East West Centre.

Khadka S. S. (1997). Water Use and Water Rights in Nepal. In: Pradhan, R., F. Benda-Beckmann, K. Benda-Beckmann, H. L Spiertz,, S. K. Khadka, and H. Azharul (Eds.). *Water Rights, Conflicts and Policy*. Proceeding of Workshop held in Kathmandu, Nepal. Jan. 22-24, 1996.Pp 47-62.

Khanal D. R. (1998). *Conflicts Between Local Organisations and FUGs in Community Management and Solutions for Conflict Resolution*. Paper presented at the "Widening horizons workshop" organised by ICIMOD , 16-20 March, 1998.

Khanal M. P. (1999). Political Improbity and Moral Turpitude. *The Kathmandu Post*, Nov. 22, 1999. Kantipur Publication, Kathmandu, Nepal.

Khanal R. (Compile) (1996). *Report on Conflict Resolution Workshop*, Dhulikhel, 11-13 August 1996. Kathmandu: Nepal Madhysthata Samuha (Nepal Mediation Group).

Kolb D. (1984). *Experiential Learning: Experience as Source of Learning and Development*. Prentice Hall, New Jersey.

Korten F. F. and R. Y. Siy (Eds.) (1989) *Transforming a Bureaucracy: The Experience of Philippine National Irrigation Administration*. Manila: Anteneo De Manila University Press.

Kremenyuk V. (Ed.) (1991) *International Negotiation: Analysis, Approaches, Issues*. Oxford: Jossey-Bass Publisher.

Lamers H. A. J. M. (1994). *Report Writing for Science Technology and Management*. Sixth edition. Wageningen: Wageningen Agricultural University.

Laurent N. and A. Foaguegue (1999). Understanding Conflict

between Farmers and Researchers-The Camroon Experience. *Forest People and Tree Newsletter* No 39. August 1999. Uppsala: Swedish University of Agricultural Sciences.

Lee K. N. (1993). *Compass and Gyroscope: Integrating Science and Politics for the Environment.* Washington: Island Press.

Leeuwis C. (Ed.) (1999). *Integral Design: Innovation in Agriculture and Resource Management.* Mansholt Studies 15. Wageningen: Wageningen University-Research Centre.

Leeuwis C. (2000). Reconceptualizing Participation for Sustainable Rural Development: Towards a Negotiation Approach. *Development and Change.* 31(5): 931-959.

Liebert R. J. and A. W. Imershein (Eds.). (1977). *Power, Paradigms and Community Research.* London: Sage Publications

Likert R. and J. C. Likert (1976). *New Ways of Managing Conflict.* New York: McGraw-Hill.

Long N. (Ed.) (1989). *Encounters at the Interface: A Perspective on Social Discontinuities in Rural Development.* Wageningen Studies in Sociology-27. Wageningen Agricultural University.

Long N. and J. D. Van der Ploeg. (1989). Demythologising Planned Intervention. *Sociologia Ruralis.* 29 (3/4): 226-249.

Long N. and A. Long (Eds.) (1992). *Battlefield of Knowledge, the Interlocking of Theory and Practices of Social Research and Development.* London: Routledge.

Lubchenco J. (1998). Entering the Century of Environment: A New Social Contract for Science. *Science 279:* 491-496.

Maarleveld M., and C. Dangbegnon (1999). Managing Natural Resources: A Social Learning Perspective. *Agriculture and Human Values* 16 (3): 267-280.

Maarleveld M., N. Röling, S. Seegers and C. Van Woerkum. (1997). *Social Learning for Collective Natural Resource Management: Facilitation, Institutions and Policies.* Technical Proposal. Department of Communication and Innovation Studies, Wageningen Agricultural University.

Malla Y. (1997). *Stakeholders Response to Changes in Forest Policies.* Proceedings of Pluralism and Sustainable Forestry and Rural Development, 9-12 December, 1997, FAO, Rome. Pp. 253-276.

Martinelli D. P. and A. P. Almeida (1998). Negotiation, Management, and Systems Thinking. *Systemic Practice and Action Research.* 11 (3): 319-334.

Maturana H. R. and F. J. Varela (1992). *The Tree of Knowledge, the Biological Roots of Human Understanding.* Boston Sambala Publications.

McCay B. J. and J.M. Acheson (Eds.) (1987). *The Questions of the Commons: The Culture and Ecology of Communal Resources.* Tucson: University of Arizona Press.

Mitchell J. C. (1983). Case Study and Situation Analysis: *The Sociological Review.* 31: 187-221.

MoF (Ministry of Finance) (1998). *Economic Survey, Fiscal Year 1997-98.* Kathmandu: His Majesty's Government, Ministry of Finance.

Mollinga P. P. (1998). *On the Waterfront: Water Distribution, Technology and Agrarian Change in a South Indian Canal Irrigation.* Published PhD Dissertation. Wageningen: Wageningen Agricultural University.

Moore .S. F. (1995). Imperfect Communication. In: Caplan P. (Ed.) Understanding Disputes: The Politics of Arguments. Berg: Oxford Providence.

Moscovici S. and D. Willem (1994). *Conflict and Consensus: A Grand Theory of Collective Decision.* London: Sage Publications.

MoWR (Ministry of Water Resources) (1992). *Irrigation Policy 2049 BS.* Kathmandu: Ministry of Water Resources.

Nader L. and H. F. Todd (1978). Introduction, Chapter 1. In: Nader L. and H. F. Todd (Eds.). *The Disputing Process- Law in Ten Societies.* Columbia University Press, New York. Pp. 1-40.

Nepal Samacharpatra Daily, April 25 2000. Kathmandu.

New Era (1988). *A Study of Legal System and Legal Situation in Rural Areas of the Kingdom of Nepal.* Kathmandu: Friedirich Naumann Foundation.

NGO Forum-Nepal (NFN) (1999). *Assessment of Nepal's Performance in Implementing the World Social Declaration on Social Development 1995.* Kathmandu: NFN Secretariat, Rural Reconstruction Nepal.

NPC (National Planning Commission) (1985). *Seventh Plan 1985-1990.* Kathmandu: National Planning Commission (Nepali Version).

NPC (1998). *Ninth Plan 1997-2002.* Kathmandu: National Planning Commission.

NPC (1992). *The Eighth Plan 1992-1997* (Unofficial Translation).

Kathmandu: National Planning Commission, HMG/Nepal.

NRA (National Research Associates) (1999). *Record of Nepalese Development: District Profile*. Kathmandu: National Research Associates.

Ohlsson L. (Ed.) (1995). *Hydropolitics: Conflict over Water as Development Constraints*. London and New Jersey: ZED Books.

Oli K. P. (1998). *Conflict Resolution and Mediation in Natural Resource Management*. Kathmandu: IUCN-Nepal.

Ostrom E. (1990). *Governing the Commons: The Evolution of Institutions for Collective Actions*. New York: Cambridge University Press.

Ostrom E. (1992). *Crafting Institutions for Self-Governing Irrigation systems*. San Francisco: ICS press.

Ostrom E. and P. Benjamin (1993). Design Principles and the Performance of Farmer- Managed Irrigation Systems in Nepal. In: Manor, S. and J. Chambouleyron (Eds.) *Performance Measurement in Farmer-Managed Irrigation Systems*. Proceedings of an International Workshop of the Farmer-Managed Irrigation Systems Network held at Mendoza, Argentina from 12-15 Nov. 1891. Oxford: Oxford University Press.

Panday D.R. (2001). *Corruption, governance and international co-operation: essays and impressions on Nepal and South Asia*. Kathmandu: Transparency International Nepal

Panday D.R. (1999). *Nepal's Failed Development: Reflections on the Mission and the Melodies*. Kathmandu: Nepal South Asia Centre.

Pant D. R. (2000). *Intervention Processes and Irrigation Institutions: Sustainability of Farmers-Managed Irrigation Systems in Nepal*. Published PhD Dissertation. Wageningen: Wageningen University Research Centre.

Parajuli U. R. (1999). *Agro-Ecology and Irrigation Technology: Comparative Research on Farmer-Managed Irrigation Systems in the Mid Hills of Nepal*. Published PhD Dissertation. Wageningen: Wageningen University Research Centre.

Pecock J. L. (1986). *The Anthropological Lens: Harsh Lights, Soft Focus*. Cambridge: Cambridge University Press.

Pendzich C. (1993). Conflict Management and Forest Disputes A Path out of the Woods. *Forest, Trees and People Newsletter*. No 2 April 1993. Uppsala: Swedish University of Agricultural Sciences. Pp. 4-9.

Pendzich C., G. Thomas and T. Wohlgenant (1994). *The Role of*

Alternative Conflict Management in Community Forestry. Resolve Working Paper No 1, Forest Tree and People Programme. Phase II, FAO, Rome. Uppsala: Swedish University of Agricultural Sciences.

Pickles J. (1987). *Strength from the Bench: Is Justice Just?* London: J.N. Dent and Sons Ltd.

Platteau J-P. (1996). The Evolutionary Theory of Land Rights As Applied to Sub Saharan Africa: A Critical Assessment. *Development and Change* 27: 29-86.

Pradhan P. (1989) *Patterns of Irrigation Organisation in Nepal: A comparative Study of 21 Farmer Managed Irrigation Systems,* Country Paper No.1. Colombo: International Irrigation Management Institute.

Pradhan R. (2000). Land and Water Rights. In: Pradhan, R., F. Benda-Beckmann and K. Benda-Beckmann (Eds.) *Water Land and Laws: Changing Rights to Land and Water in Nepal.* Kathmandu: FREEDEAL.

Pradhan R. and U. Pradhan. 1996. Staking a Claim: Law Politics and Water Rights n Farmers Managed Irrigation Systems in Nepal. In: Spiertz, J. and M. Wiber (Eds.) The Role of Law in Natural Resource Management. VEGA Publications. Pp. 61-76.

Pradhan R., F. Benda-Beckmann and K. Benda-Beckmann (Eds.) (2000). *Water Land and Laws: Changing Rights to Land and Water in Nepal.* Kathmandu: FREEDEAL.

Pradhan R., F. Benda-Beckmann, K. Benda-Beckmann, H.L. Spiertz, S. K. Khadka, and H. Azharul, (Eds.) (1997). *Water Rights, Conflicts and Policy.* Proceeding of Workshop held in Kathmandu, Nepal. Jan. 22-24, 1996. Kathmandu: International Irrigation Management Institute.

Prasain, D. (2001). *Community Level Dispute Processing in Rural Nepal* (draft report). Kathmandu: Penal Reform International.

Pretty J. N, (1994). Alternate Systems of Inquiry for a Sustainable Agriculture. *IDS Bulletin* Vol. 12, No. 2. London: Institute of Development Studies. Pp. 37-50.

Programme on Humanitarian Policy and Conflict Research-Harvard School of Public Health (PHPCR-HDHP) (2001). *Conflict Precention Initiative. Setting Priorities for Preventive Action in Nepal: Final Report of the Web Conference.* Harvard: Harvard School of Public Health.

ProPublic (Forum for Protection of Public Interest) (2000). *Good Governance.* Quarterly Bulletin. Vol. 2, No. 3, January 2000. Kathmandu: Forum for Protection of Public Interest.

Pruitt D. J. and P. J. Carnevale (1993). *Negotiations in Social Conflicts.* Buckingham: Open University Press.

Rafia H. (1991). Contribution of Applied Systems Analysis to International Negotiation. In: Kremenyuk, V. (Ed.). *International Negotiation: Analysis, Approaches, Issues.* Oxford: Jossy-Bass Publisher.

Ramirez R. (1997). *Participatory Learning and Communication Approaches for Managing Pluralism: Implications for Sustainable Forestry, Agriculture, and Rural Development.* Proceedings of Pluralism and Sustainable Forestry and Rural Development, 9-12 December 1997, FAO, Rome. Pp. 117-152.

Rana P. S. J and D. N. Dhungel (Eds.) (1997) *Contemporary Nepal.* New Delhi: Vikash Publishing House.

Rapoport A. (1985). Thinking about Home Environment: A Conceptual Framework. In: Altman, I. and C. M.Werner (Eds.) *Home Environment* New York: Plenum Press. PP. 255-286.

Rau Z. (1991). *The Emergence of Civil Society in Eastern Europe and Soviet Union.* Boulder Co: Westview Press.

Regmi M. C. (1978a). *Land Tenure and Taxation in Nepal.* Kathmandu: Ratna Pustak Bhandar.

Regmi M. C. (1978b) *Thatched Huts and Stucco Palaces: Peasants and landlords in 19ᵗʰ Century Nepal.* Vranasi: Nath Publishing House.

Regmi M. C. (1976). *Land Ownership in Nepal.* Berkeley: University of California Press.

Regmi M.C. (1972) *A Study of Nepali Economic History 1768-1846.* Delhi: Adroit Publishers.

Regmi M. C. (1963). *Land Tenure and Taxation in Nepal. Vol. 1. The State as Landlord: Raikar Tenure.* Berkeley: University of California Press.

Rhoades E. R. (1997). *Pathways Towards a Sustainable Mountain Agriculture for the 21st Century: The Hindukush Himalayan Experience.* Kathmandu: ICIMOD.

Richards M. (1997). The Tragedy of the Commons for Community Based Forest Management in Latin America. *Natural Resource Perspective* No. 22. London: Overseas development institute.

Röling, N. 2000. *Gateway to the Global Garden: Beta/Gamma Science for*

Dealing with Ecological Rationality. Eighth Annual Hopper Lecture October 24, 200. University of Guelph, Canada.

Röling, N. and J. Jiggins (2001). Agents in Adaptive Collaborative Management: The Logic of Collective Cognition. In: Buck L., C. G. Geisler, W.J. Schelhas and E. Wollenberg (Eds.) *Biological Diversity: Balancing Interests through Adaptive Collaborative Management*. Boca Raton: (F1) CRC Press, (Life Science/ business Division).

Röling N. (1999). Modelling Soft Side of Land: The Potential of Multiagent System. In:. Leeuwis, C. (Ed.) *Integral Design: Innovation in Agriculture and Resource Management*. Mansholt Studies 15. Mansholt Institute, Wageningen University. Pp. 73-97.

Röling N and M. Maarleveld (1999). Facing Strategic Narratives: An Argument for Interactive Effectiveness. *Journal of Agriculture and Human Value*. 16: 295-308.

Röling N. and A. Wagemakers (Eds.) (1998). *Facilitating Sustainable Agriculture*. Cambridge: Cambridge University Press.

Röling N. and J. Jiggins (1998). The Ecological Knowledge System. Chapter 16 In: Röling, N. and A. Wagemakers (Eds.) *Facilitating Sustainable Agriculture: Participatory Learning and Adaptive Management in Times of Environmental Uncertainties*. Cambridge University Press. Pp. 283-307.

Röling N. (1997). The Soft Side of Land. *ITC Journal* 1997, No 3 and 4, Special Congress Issue. Pp. 248-262.

Röling N. (1996). Creating Human Platforms to Manage Natural Resources: First Results of Research Programme. In: Budelman, A.. (Ed.) *Agricultural R&D at the Crossroads. Managing Systems Research and Social Actor Approaches*. The Hague: Royal Tropical Institute.

Rubenstein R. E. (1993). Analysing and Resolving Class Conflict. In: Dennis J., D. Sandole and H. v. d. Merwe, (Eds.) *Conflict Resolution Theory and Practice: Integration and Application*. Manchester: Manchester University Press. Pp. 146 57.

Rubin J. Z., D. G. Pruitt, and S. H. Kim (Ed.) (1994). *Social Conflict: Escalation, Stalemate, and Settlement*. New York: McGraw-Hill, Inc.

Sanddelin R. (1997). *Interpersonal Relationships and Conflict Resolution. Community Resource Guide*. URL: http:// www.infoteam.community/nonprofit/nica/resolution.html

Sangraula Y. R. and S. K. Gurung, (undated). *Arbitration as an Effective Forum for Alternative Dispute Resolution: Problems and Prospects in Nepal*. (No publisher and date of publication available).

Saptahik Bimarha (Weekly), June 16, 2000. http:// www.nepalnews.com.np/contents/nepaliweekly/bimarsa/ 2000/june/juen16/index.htm

Schlager E. and E. Ostrom (1992). Property Right Regimes and Natural Resources. *Land Economics*. 68(8): 249-262.

Schwandt T. A. (1998). Constructivst, Interpretivist Approaches to Human Inquiry. In: Denzin K. and Y. S. Lincoln (Eds.) *The Landscape of Qualitative Research: Theories and Issues*. London: Sage Publications. Pp. 221-259.

Scimecca J.A. (1993). Theory and Alternative Dispute Resolution: A Contradiction in Terms? In: Sandole D. J. D and H. van der Merwe (Eds.) *Conflict Resolution: Theory and Practice: Integration and Application*. Manchester: Manchester University Press. Pp. 211-221.

Seale C. (1998). *Researching Society and Culture* (Ed.) London: Sage Publications.

Seddon D. (1987) *Nepal: A State of Poverty*. New Delhi: Vikash Publishing House.

Seddon D. (1984). Nepal-A State of Poverty: The Political Economy of Population Growth and Social Deprivation. *Monograph in Development Studies* No 11, School of Development Studies. University of East Anglia.

Shivakoti G., G. Varughese, E. Ostrom, A. Sukla, and G. Thapa. (Eds.) (1996). *People and Sustainable Development: Understanding the Dynamics of Natural Resources System*. IAAS/TU, Indiana University. Kathmandu: FAO Farmer-Centred Agricultural Resources Management Programme and Winrock Institute for Agricultural Development.

Shrestha K. B. (1996a). *Community Forestry in Nepal: An Overview of Conflict*. Discussion Paper Series No MNR 96/2. Kathmandu: ICIMOD.

Shrestha K. B. (1996b). Conflict in Community Forest. In: Khanal, R. (Compiled) *Report on Conflict Resolution Workshop, August 11-13 Dhulikhel*. Kathmandu: Nepal Madhysthata Samuha (Nepal Mediation Group).

Shrestha N. R. (1997). *In the Name of Development: A Reflection in Nepal*. Kathmandu: Educational Enterprise.

Shrestha T. N. (1999). *The Implementation of Decentralisation Scheme in Nepal: An Assessment and Lessons for the Future*. Kathmandu: Joshi Publications.

Sidaway R. (1996). *Outdoor Recreation and Nature Conservation: Conflicts and their Solution*. Unpublished PhD Dissertation. The University of Edinburgh.

Silverman D. (1993).*Interpreting Qualitative Data: Methods of Analysing Talk, Text and Interaction*. London: Sage Publications.

Smith P. (1997) Civil Society and Violence: Narrative Forms and the Regulation of Social Conflict. In: Turpin J. and L. R. Kurtz (Eds.) *The Web of Violence: From Interpersonal to Globa*. Illinois: University of Illinois Press.

SNV(Netherlands Development Co-operation) (1998). *SNV-Nepal 1985-1995 Evaluation Report*. The Hague: Netherlands Development Co-operation.

Spiertz H. L. J. (2000). Water Rights and Legal Pluralism: Some Basics of a legal Anthropological Approach. In: Burns B. R. and R. S. Meinzen-Dick (Eds.) *Negotiating Water Rights*. International Food Policy Research Institute. Intermediate Technology Publication Limited, London. Pp. 162-199.

Spradely J. (1979). *The Ethnographic Interview*. New York: Holt Rinehart, Winston.

Steins N. A. (1999). *All hands on Deck: An Interactive Perspective on Complex Common Pool Resource Management Based on Case Studies in the Coastal Waters of the Isle of Wight (UK), Connemara (Ireland) and the Dutch Wadden Sea*. Published PhD Dissertation. Wageningen: Wageningen University.

Stiller L. F. (1976). *The Silent Cry: The People of Nepal 1816-1839*. Kathmandu: Sahayogi Press.

Stiller L. F. and R. P. Yadav (1979). *Planning for People*. Kathmandu: Sahayogi Press.

Stiller L. F. J. (1993). *Nepal: Growth of Nation*. Kathmandu: Human Resource Development Research Centre.

Sukla A., N. Joshi, G. Shivakoti, R. Poudel and N. Shrestha. (1997). Dynamics in Water Rights, and Arbitration on Water Right Conflicts: Case of FMISs from Eastern Chitawan. In: Pradhan R., F. Benda-Beckmann, K. Benda-Beckmann, H. L. Spiertz, S. K.

Khadka, and H. Azharul v *Water Rights, Conflicts and Policy..* Proceeding of Workshop held in Kathmandu, Nepal. Jan. 22-24, 1996.

Susskind L. and J. Cruikshank (1989). *Breaking Impasse: Consensual Approaches to Resolving Public Disputes.* New York: Basic Books, Inc.

Tear Funds (1999). Looking After Our Land. *Footsteps* No 41, Dec. 1999. Teddington: Tear Fund.

Thapa G.B. and K.E. Weber (1994). Managing Mountain Watersheds in Nepal: Issues and Policies. *International Journal of Water Resources Development.* 10 (4): 475-495.

Thapa S. B. (2000). Obstacles for Effective Use of Foreign Aid. *Deshantar Weekly.* ULR: http://www.nepalmews.com.np/ unprotected/nepaliweekly/deshantar/2000/august/A../ view.ht

The Kathmandu Post National Daily, 12 July 2000. Kathmandu: The Kantipur Publication.

The Rising Nepal, 25 July 2000. ULR: http://www.nepalnews.com.np/contents/englishdaily/trn/ 2000/jul/jul25/index.htm#11

The Telegraph, 28 June, 2000. ULR: http:// www.nepalnews.com.np/telegraph.htm

Turrel H. (1995). Recent Trends in Irrigation Management-Changing Directions for the Public Sectors. *Natural resource Perspective* No. 5. London: Overseas development institute.

UNDP (United Nations Development Programme) (1998). *Human Development Report-Nepal.* Kathmandu: United Nations Development Programme.

Uphoff N. (1985). People's Participation in Water Management: Gal Oya, Sri Lanka. In: Garcia-Zamor J.C. (Ed.) *Public Participation in Development Planning.* Bolder: Westview press. Pp. 131-178.

Uphoff N. (1986). *Improving International Irrigation Management with Farmers Participation: Getting the Process Right.* Bolder: Westview Press.

Uphoff N. (2000). *Understanding Social Capital: Learning from the Analysis and Experience of Participation.* HLR: http:// www.sls.wau.nl/mi/Education/index.html (circulated for his group presentation on Wednesday 13 September 200 in Wageningen).

Upreti, B. R. (2001a) *Conflict Management in Natural Resources: A Study of Land, Water and Forest Conflict in Nepal.* Published PhD Dissertation. Wagenignen University.

Upreti, B. R (2001b). Contribution of Community Forestry in Rural Social Transformation: Some observations from Nepal. *Journal of Forestry and Livelihood* 1(1): 31-34.

Upreti B. R. (2000a). Beyond Rhetorical Success: Advancing the Potential for the Nepalese Community Forestry Programme to Address Equity Concerns. In: Wollenberg E., D. Edmunds, L. Buck, J. Fox and S. Brodt (Eds.) *Social Learning in Community Forest Management: Linking Concept and Practice.* A Joint Publication of CIFOR and the East-West Centre.

Upreti B. R. (2000b). Resource Use Negotiation as an Alternate Strategy for Sustainable Water Resource Management: Experience from Nepal. *The Journal of Agricultural Education and Extension, International Journal on Changes in Knowledge and Action Systems* 7(1) Pp. 11-20.

Upreti B.R. (2000c). *External Intervention and Conflict: Experience from Farmers-Managed Irrigation System in Nepal.* Paper presented in International Seminal on Challenges to Farmer-Managed Irrigation Systems, organised by FMIS Promotion Trust in Kathmandu from 28-29 March 2000 .

Upreti B.R. (2000d). Community Level Water Use Negotiation Practice: An Implication for Water Resource Management. In: Pradhan R., F. Benda-Beckmann and K. Benda-Beckmann (Eds.) *Water, Land and Law.* Kathmandu: FREEDEAL. Pp 249-269.

Upreti B. R. (2000e). The Effects of Changing Land use Systems in Agricultural Biodiversity: Experiences and Lessons from Nepal. In: Xu Jianchu (Ed.) *Links Between the Culture and Biodiversity.* Proceedings of the Culture and Biodiversity Congress 20-30 July, Cunming, Yunnan, China, 21-30 July 2000. Yunnan Science and Technology. Pp. 327-337.

Upreti B. R. (1999a) *A Study on SDC Approach of Management of Natural Resources and Bio-Diversity: Experiences and Lessons from Nepal. Assessment of the Impacts and the Validity of the Solutions Executed by Nepal Swiss Community Forestry Project on Equity, Poverty, Gender and Empowerment Aspects of target Population and Management of Natural Resources and Bio-diversity.* SDC-Nepal.

Upreti B. R. (1999b). Managing local Conflicts over Water

Resources: A Case Study from Nepal. *AgREN, ODI Network Paper* No 95, July 1999.London: Overseas Development Institute. .

Upreti B. R. (1998a). *Hill Irrigation Development Process in Nepal: Past Experiences and Future Options.* Proceedings of Workshop on 'the Acts of Man and Nature? Different Constructions of Natural and Social Resource Dynamics. Bergen, The Netherlands, 22-24 Oct. 1998. Research School for Resource Studies for Development.

Upreti B. R. (1998b). *Searching for an Alternate Approach for Community Level Natural Resource Management in Nepal.* MSc Thesis. Wageningen Agricultural University, The Netherlands.

Upreti B. R. (1995). *Women's' Participation in Development Activities: A Case Study of Mechi Hill Development Programme in Ilam District.* M. A. Thesis. Kathmandu: Department of Sociology/ Anthropology, Tribhuvan University.

Upreti B. R. (1988). *Impact of Land Reform on Small Farmers of Nepal.* Unpublished Term Paper. Rampur: Department of Extension and Rural Sociology. Institute of Agriculture and Animal Sciences.

Ury W., J. Brett and S. Goldberg (1989). *Getting Disputes Resolved.* San Francisco: Jossey-Bass Publishers.

Van den Ban A. W. (1997). Successful Extension Agencies are Learning Organisations. In: Samanta, R. K and S. K. Arora (Eds.) *Management of Agricultural Extension in Global Perspective.* Delhi: B. R. Publishing Corporation. Pp 47-77.

Van der Fliert (1993) *Integrated Pest management: Farmers Field Schools Generate Sustainable Practices. A Case Study in Central Java Evaluating IPM Training.* Published PhD Dissertation. Wageningen; Wageningen Agricultural University.

Vayrynen R. (Ed.) (1991). *New Directions in Conflict Theory.* London: Sage Publications.

Vidich A. J. and S. M. Lyman (1998). Qualitative Methods: Their History in Sociology and Anthropology. In: Denzin K. and Y. S. Lincoln (Eds.) *The Landscape of Qualitative Research: Theories and Issues.* London: Sage Publications. Pp. 47-110.

Vincent L. (1996). Irrigation as Technology, Irrigation as Resource: Hill Irrigation and Natural Resource Systems. In: Shivakoti G., G. Varughese, E. Ostrom, A. Sukla and G. Thapa (Eds.) *People and Participation in Sustainable Development. Understanding the*

Dynamics of Natural Resource Systems. Kathmandu: FAO Farmer-Centred Agricultural Resources Management Programme and Winrock Institute for Agricultural Development.

Wade R. (1982). The Study of Administrative and Political Corruption: Canal Irrigation in South India. *Journal of Development Studies.* 18(3): 287-328.

Walker G. B. and S. E. Daniels (1997). Foundations of Natural Resource Conflict: Conflict Theory and Public Policy. In: Solberg, B. and S. Miina (Eds.) *Conflict Management and Public Participation in Land Management,* S. EFT Proceeding No 14. European Forest Institute. Pp. 13-36.

Warner M. and P. Jones (1998). Assessing the Need to Manage Conflict in Community Based Natural Resource Project. *Natural Resource Perspective.* No 35. Aug., 1998. London: Overseas development institute.

Warner M. (2001). *Complex Problems-Negotiated Solutions: Strategies and Tools for Reducing Conflict as an Obstacle to Sustainable Rural Livelihoods.* London: Overseas Development Institute.

Warner M. (2000). Conflict Management in Community Based Natural Resource Projects: Experiences from Fiji and Papua New Guinea. *ODI Working Paper* 135. London: Overseas Development Institute.

Wilson K. and G. E. B. Morren (1990). *Systems Approaches for Improvement in Agriculture and Resource Management.* New York: Macmillan Publishing Company.

World Water Forum (2000). *A Vision of Water for Food and Rural Development.* The Hague: World Water Council.

Yin K.R. (1984). *Case Study Research: Design and Methods.* London and Beverly Hills: Sage Publications.

Yoder R. (1991). Assistance to Farmer-Managed Irrigation Systems: Experiences from WECS/IIMI/Ford Action Research Project in Indrawati watershed basin. In: DOI (Ed.) *Assistance to Farmer-Managed Irrigation Systems: Experience from Nepal.* Kathmandu: Department of Irrigation.

Yoder R. (1994). *Locally Managed Irrigation System: Essential Tasks and Implications for Assistance, Management Transfer and Turnover Programme.* Colombo: International Irrigation Management Institute.

Yordan C.L. (2000). Instituting Problem Solving Processes as a

Means of Constructive Social Change. *Online Journal of Peace and Conflict Resolution* 1.4. http://members.aol.com/_ht_a/peacejnl/1_4yordan.htm

Zaman M.A. (1973). *Evaluation of Land Reform in Nepal*. HMG/N, Kathmandu: Ministry of Land Reform.

Glossary

Actor: An individual or group of people who carry out human activities (Wilson and Morren, 1990).

Adaptive management: The release of human opportunities that requires flexible, diverse and redundant regulation and monitoring that leads to corrective action (Holing, 1978, Lee, 1993).

Collective action: Action taken by a group or a community in pursuit of their perceived shared interests (adapted from Stein, 1999).

Common Property: User rights to common pool resources attached to a specified user group/community (adapted from Stein, 1999).

Communication: Communication is the process of transmission and reception of ideas, facts, opinions, attitudes and feelings through one or more information media that produce a response (Hellriegel *et al.*, 1999)

Communicative rationality: The realisation of an individual goal when the action plan to achieve that goal is harmonised with other goal-oriented actors on the basis of a common understanding of a situation (adapted from Stein, 1999).

Conciliation in conflict: It is a process where a neutral third party communicates separately with conflicting parties to reduce tension and agree on a process to resolve the conflict (Pendzich, 1993).

Conflict: Antagonism caused by a clash of cultural, social, economic and/or political interests between individuals and groups (Furtze and Stafford, 1994).

Conflict management: Guiding conflict towards constructive rather than destructive outcomes.

Corruption: Behaviour which deviates from the formal duties of a public role because of private (personal, close family, private clique) pecuniary or status gains or which violates rules as a result of certain types of personal influence.

Culture: The shared products of a given society including its values, knowledge, norms and material goods (Furtze and Stafford, 1994:29).

Ethnography: Process of recording and interpreting another peoples' way of life, through intimate participation in a community and observation of modes of behaviour and organisation of social life.

Facilitation: Providing help and guidance through experiential learning, adaptive management and knowledge system management. It guides people through the process of learning to create common knowledge that can be used to improve problematic situation (adapted from Boer, 2000; Wilson and Morren, 1990).

Human Activity System: Conceptual construct that represents purposeful human action used in a debate about possible changes to improve the problematic situation through human action (adapted from Wilson and Morren, 1990; Boer, 2000). .

Learning: Process whereby individuals or organisations acquire and internalise experiences, language, social and institutional behaviour, responses, understanding, meaning, knowledge actions, plans, etc. (adapted from Boer, 2000).

Local knowledge: Knowledge possessed by local people about ecosystem processes, community organisation and structure.

Legal pluralism: This is a concept which focuses on the co-existence of multiple legal and normative arrangements such as state laws, religious and customary laws, unwritten local rules, etc.

Mediation: Mediation is the intervention in conflict situation, of an acceptable, impartial and neutral third party who has no final decision making authority but who will assist to negotiate an acceptable settlement of conflict.

Negotiation: Negotiation is a voluntary process that deals with the conflict situation between the negotiating parties where two or more people meet face to face and communicate with each other.

Platform: A group of social actors involved in a process of social learning, building new institutions and facilitating joint innovations, resources-use negotiation or any collective decision making and concerted action. (Röling, 1996; Boer, 2000)

Power: The ability of individuals or groups to further their own interests. This is the key concept in water resource management. Societies and communities are not homogenous entities. They are hierarchical, where individuals and groups have influence over others. This influence can be legitimate or illegitimate, traditional or a result of non-traditional forces. It definitely exists and may impact on the working of external intervention.

Property regime: A decision making arrangement that defines the condition of access to, allocation of and control over a range of benefits arising from a resources (adapted from Stein, 1999).

Property rights: Social institutions that have evolved as a means of enforcing claims to a flow of benefit (adapted from Stein, 1999).

Social institutions: These express the organisation of social, economic and political activity, which is followed by the majority of the members of a society. These usually include the family, the education system, a system of religion, a political and economic system and the more general patterns of community norms and values.

Soft system: This is formed when social actors become collectively engage to form a system through jointly agreed and negotiated goals and activities (Checklands and Scholes, 1990).

System thinking: It conceptualises the complexity and dynamics in terms of holism, means of measurement and control, emergent properties, structures, communication, etc. (adapted from Boer, 2000; Wilson and Morren, 1990).

Values: Ideas individuals have about what is good and bad, right and wrong, important and unimportant, harmful and safe, just and unjust, etc.